REPRODUCTIONS OF MURAL DECORATIONS
FROM THE LIBRARY OF CONGRESS, WASHINGTON

"LYRIC POETRY"

Photo-engraving in colors after the original painting by
H. O. WALKER

The original of this picture occupies a large tympanum and presents seven figures. For reasons of space only the central section containing the five principal figures is given here. The figure standing in the centre represents Lyric Poetry; while on each side are arrayed the sentiments called forth by her song. To her left are Pathos, looking upward as if calling upon Heaven to allay her grief; and Truth, a beautiful nude woman exhorting the singer to remain within the bounds of reason. On the other side of the panel are Passion, poised in eagerness and rapture; and Beauty, calm and contented.

COMMITTEE OF SELECTION

EDWARD EVERETT HALE, Author of "The Man Without a Country."

JOHN B. GORDON, Former United States Senator.

NATHAN HASKELL DOLE, Associate Editor "International Library of Famous Literature."

JAMES B. POND, Manager Lecture Bureau; Author of " Eccentricities of Genius.'

GEORGE MCLEAN HARPER, Professor of English Literature, Princeton University.

LORENZO SEARS, Professor of English Literature, Brown University.

EDWIN M. BACON, Former Editor "Boston Advertiser" and "Boston Post."

J. WALKER MCSPADDEN, Managing Editor "Édition Royale" of Balzac's Works.

F. CUNLIFFE OWEN, Member Editorial Staff "New York Tribune."

TRUMAN A. DEWEESE, Member Editorial Staff "Chicago Times-Herald."

CHAMP CLARK, Member of Congress from Missouri.

MARCUS BENJAMIN, Editor, National Museum, Washington, D. C.

CLARK HOWELL, Editor "Atlanta Constitution."

INTRODUCTIONS AND SPECIAL ARTICLES BY

THOMAS B. REED,   HAMILTON WRIGHT MABIE,
LORENZO SEARS,   JONATHAN P. DOLLIVER,
CHAMP CLARK,   EDWARD EVERETT HALE,
          ALBERT ELLERY BERGH.

NOTE.—A large number of the most distinguished speakers of this country and Great Britain have selected their own best speeches for this Library. These speakers include Whitelaw Reid, William Jennings Bryan, Henry van Dyke, Henry M. Stanley, Newell Dwight Hillis, Joseph Jefferson, Sir Henry Irving, Arthur T. Hadley, John D. Long, David Starr Jordan, and many others of equal note.

ORATORY PAST AND PRESENT

"An Oratour is he, that can or may speke or reason in euery question sufficetly, elegantly and to perswade properly, accordynge to the dygnitie of the thyng that is spoken of, the oppertunitye of tyme, and pleasure of them that be herers."—Sir Thomas Elyot, The Governor, book I, ch. XIII.

THE Republican party, and the protectionists generally, if, as they claim, they have reduced white paper to the low price which now prevails, have a heavy responsibility upon their consciences. Not only are books now within the reach of all, but miniature libraries are springing up on all hands, and very soon the wonder of carpets and handsome furniture in the homes of the men whose daily toil is their only resource, will give way to the new wonder of libraries in every household. Newspapers, also, are enlarging their fields of endeavor, and seem to be more than keeping pace with the movement of the time. So far have they gone, both in the greater and the smaller cities, that the venerable persons who come down to us from a former generation are in much doubt as to whether the great Sunday editions are a joy or an affliction.

One would naturally suppose that the manifest change which has taken place in methods of displaying and receiving ideas would have left the old methods stranded high up on the shores of time. The earliest method of spreading information and moulding opinions, however, has not passed away. Men still talk to each other face to face, and oratory still plays a great part in the instruc-

tion of modern times. It is true that the orator reaches
his largest audience by the aid of the newspaper, but the
newspaper nowadays depicts the applause and dissent of
the audience, and gives, so far as it can, the atmosphere
with which the orator is surrounded, and makes the
reader appreciate the full human nature involved in the
whole scene. The very postures, also, of the orator are
displayed.

But, however well any article may be written, and however well any speech may be reported, there is a charm in
the spoken word, in the utterance of the living man,
which no beauty of style can imitate, and no collocation of
words can equal. Probably Æschines never said : " You
should have heard the lion himself," when in exile he
praised his superior, but if he was made to say it—if the
story was invented—it was because the truth was deeper
than the fact.

What we call in America " Stump Oratory "—oratory
in its roughest and most familiar shape—still plays a
great part—a part which hardly seems to lessen in its
influence over the people at large. To be fully satisfied,
they must hear the man speak, and give themselves up to
the sound of his voice. Whenever a campaign comes on,
all the available vocal power is called into action, and
whoever watches the effect will see that the oratory of
the campaign is a very powerful and invigorating force.
In 1872 a large number of the leading men and newspapers had placed themselves in opposition to General
Grant, and there were weeks during which his election
seemed more than doubtful; but the campaign orator
had not been at work a fortnight before you could feel
the change. Not only were there words, but you had
looked into the face of the man who said them. When
you read what is written, the power of the written word
depends much upon your mood. When you hear a man
speak, his power depends much on his mood. You naturally lend your thoughts to him. Moreover, the rest of
your fellows in the audience do their part, and there comes
on that irresistible power of human sympathy which gives
you your share of the emotion of others and mingles your
thoughts with theirs.

Of course, oratory can never again have the relative

importance which it had in the early days when there
were fewer things to do and fewer things to think of. In
those old days you could meet and harangue the whole
deciding multitude; for Athens in its prime had but
twenty thousand free citizens; eight thousand was good
attendance; and the human voice could have reached
them all. In New York, Cooper Union holds less than
three thousand people, and Madison Square Garden
thirteen thousand! If the orator could convert them all,
he would hardly disturb the majority of either party.
What a difference between an audience in either place and
the audience Demosthenes addressed when, in the Oration on the Crown, he reached the summit of fame,
whereon he has stood for three and twenty centuries in
solitary and unapproached preëminence. Even Cicero
himself, his only rival in historic renown, concedes that
Demosthenes is the standard of perfection. His audience
was all the people, and not an inappreciable fraction.
His oration did not have to share place in Athenian minds
with absorbing business and with newspapers laden with
the doings of a world.

So, the preacher, in the early days had the advantage
of the influence of the next world, and a goodly portion
of this. Men are so busy now with the things of earth
that there is little room for thoughts of the hereafter.
Chrysostom, he whose mouth was of gold, the great
preacher of antiquity, would hardly be on the road to so
wide a fame in this age as he was in the age wherein he
lived. The advocate, also, is crowded into obscurity, and
Hortensius and Sulpicius in the modern world would
hardly preserve, in our age, what antiquity has given
them, the shadow of a name, and even Cicero as an
advocate would have to eke out his reputation at the bar
with his fame as a statesman.

Nevertheless, oratory survives and seems in as great
demand as ever, though the prizes have grown smaller,
or, perhaps, strictly speaking, the other prizes of human
endeavor have grown larger.

The lecture field is still open, and if oratory shares
public attention more fully with other attractions and
does not hold, as in the days of Beecher and Curtis and
Wendell Phillips, its old preëminence, the audiences

which listen to General Gordon and Henry Watterson have not lost their old interest and enjoyment.

Those who have reached the age which naturally praises the days gone by still look back on the old lecture platform as the golden time of oratory in the New World. The men who laid the foundations of American literature in those days shed their light from many eminences all over the land, and taught high thinking and clean living to eager listeners not yet wedded to the pursuit of wealth, and not yet yearning for unwilling empire. They spoke to audiences which longed for the ideal life of the saints and sages, and made possible the dream of that freedom for all which Jefferson put into words in the Declaration of Independence, and Lincoln put into the deeds which preceded and followed his second inaugural. But, in this crowded world, when the work is done the instrumentalities pass away, for the earth does not long allow itself to be encumbered by the ruins of even its loftiest temples or its most sumptuous palaces. When the worship has ceased and the King is dead, time, the devourer, does his work, and institutions perish as well as the men who made them. Only vitality itself, the living germ, can resist decay, and even that must pay the homage of a new incarnation into a life not always loftier or more noble.

The oratory of Congress has certainly increased in volume, and for aught we know, has increased in ability, but, like all things else in a republic grown from three to seventy-six millions, it has lost its old proportion, and now struggles in vain for an audience as wide as of yore. No metropolitan paper publishes even a synopsis of the debates, and a member acquainted with its business cannot tell what is going on after a three days' absence. Each paper gives room to the doings of its own legislature, and erases Congress to give place to what used to seem to be smaller things. Probably the Record, the official publication, is to blame for this, and the member, to insure his appearing at full length in one place, has surrendered his chance to appear in all places. Nevertheless, a speech suitable for a campaign, and delivered at the proper time, may still have wide circulation and a three months' immortality.

Commencements have not lost their liking for orations, and as the number and size of colleges and universities have greatly increased, with them has also increased the desire for the spoken word. Whoever has reputation enough of any kind to make people anxious to see him will not lack invitations to appear before fine audiences and enforce whatever ideas he may have of life and duty. Of course, from all this effort on the part of orators and all this endurance on the part of the people, there comes much diffusion of knowledge and a spread of thought and of new ideas which would wait long if only the printed word were at the service of the world. Parker and Phillips poured a great part of their noble work into these channels and were able to make men think as they did by the fact that the magic of their presence supported and sustained the magic of their words.

The funeral oration must have had, and did have, its origin in far antiquity. No time has ever been, and no time can ever be, when the closing of life will cease to be its great event. What it means to him who has passed away only revelation or fancy can depict. What, however, it is to him it will also be to all of us. We tread the path with no consciousness of companionship, and yet we know that all the countless generations of the myriad years of the past and of all the years of the future are our sure companions. To us, then, who survive, there comes a certain tenderness of heart which has never come before. The rival is a rival no longer. His hopes and ambitions have fallen by the wayside. In like manner ours will surely fall. If we have been foes our greatest longing in the first revulsion of feeling is to call oblivion down upon the fierce fights of the past; our first desire is to atone for the selfish greed of power or money or place which led to the long and bitter contentions and the cruel enmities now ended forever. Before an audience thus disposed it is not difficult to stir to its depths the human soul. Here we tell the truth with all its warmth and none of its coldness. Our sentences may be well rounded, for they need not be strictly just.

Where we are at liberty to limit no adjective and curtail no sentence there results a beauty of diction, a tenderness of phrase, a full recognition of the hopes of

an unknown world beyond, whose peace seems to be on
us with the benedictions of the eternal. When we think
of the foundation of the funeral oration, for the foundations of all moving speech must be in the audience, we
cease to wonder that the most beautiful phrases, the
loftiest sentiments and the richest recognitions of immortal life, were the productions of an age which to-day
the world, still wicked and still far from the glory of God,
looks down upon as an age of gilded sin fitly followed
by the butcheries of Parisian mobs and the swift-running
guillotine.

When you read the beautiful discourse of the "Eagle
of Eloquence," whose name rises at once to your lips as
you speak of the funeral oration, you know, if you know
history at all, that you must forget the real lives of those
whom Bossuet so lovingly praises in death if you are at
all to be moved by the hope of triumphant glory which
he depicts for those whose reverence for the Ten Com-
mandments could have begun only after their death. The
funeral oration, however, has not yet passed away, nor
will it ever pass away until the last man has taken his
place in the innumerable caravan. Families and friends
love to treasure up the words spoken of their dead companions and to hold for truth forever the outbursts of
kindly enthusiasm which death has ushered in.

In Congress the funeral oration still survives, and
much eloquence still pervades the halls when death
comes. Of course, there is much uttered which makes
the judicious smile, but there is also much that is
worthy of the themes, which, after all, are themes that
involve all of this world and all of its achievements with
all the possibilities of the land across the barriers of
which the dead man has been borne. Mankind, however,
has been trying to phrase these great conditions which
embrace all the past and all the future, ever since the
world began. In conflict, therefore, with all past history
the oration can have little hope of originality, and the
temptation to borrow has sometimes been found to be
irresistible. If we ever learn to treat the living with
the tenderness with which we instinctively treat the dead,
we shall then have a civilization well worth distributing.

The sermon may seem not to fully belong to the

domain of the oration, which, in its ordinary acceptation, means a discourse against adversaries and involves immediate conviction and persuasion. As we think of an oration we think of a discourse which seems to be the sudden and consecutive outpouring of a full mind at that moment aroused to action by the opponent who stands before the speaker. The sermon, however, may have all those characteristics, and then become a pulpit oration, subject to the same laws of criticism. Such certainly were the sermons of Martin Luther and of John Knox.

If it should be said that any sermon has to encounter the great adversary of the human race, or, if the preacher does not recognize the personality of Satan, that he at least has to encounter human nature, our greatest adversary, I presume I should have to admit that perhaps the difference is only one of degree, and that the sermon resembles all oratory, and that, in being more sober and using fewer arts, it in that very way accomplishes the work of persuasion.

Usually, however, the sermon is wholly or largely written out, and lends itself to the informing rather than the stirring of the audience. It can have little recourse to those enlivenments which come from wit and humor, though much has been permitted in these modern days which even so recently as Henry Ward Beecher's time shocked the religious mind. Dean Swift, himself a wit almost without an equal, cautions his young clergyman to avoid the endeavoring at wit, not only because the chances were little less than a million to one that he had none, but because he had better not use it in a sermon, even if he did have it. A sermon, the famous Dean seemed to think, was a means of permanent improvement of the human soul, and that, therefore, it was out of place in the pulpit to use what he calls the "pathetic" or temporarily moving expedients of oratory. The victories of righteousness should be the permanent results of pitched battles, and not the display of the banners of the army and the sound of its trumpets.

The after-dinner speech, the antipodes of the funeral oration, has, like that, equal date with Andes and with Ararat. Hardly had the family relation been well established before the guild began. So far back as we know

anything of the history of any people, we find them
associating in groups of a character more or less permanent as the cause of association was temporary or
persistent. With the association came the cement-
ing influence of the banquet, with food and flowing
bowl. To watch at any dinner now the gradual ex-
haustion of talk between neighbors, and the gradual extension of conversation to those farther off, is to understand in some measure the yearning for speeches which
takes possession of any large assembly. Either speeches
or dispersion the multitude must have, and so people with
the most honest intentions as to silence break forth into
sound. To-day associations to protect rights and insure
liberty are not so much needed, but the old habits prevail, and the after-dinner speech has, next to the banquet,
become the main object of the festival, if, indeed, the
interest in it does not exceed that of the main purpose,
the banquet itself. Societies, the demand of which for
comradeship arises from common nationality and common origin of any kind, have so multiplied in the land
that every great city and many small ones renew every
year the tribute of grateful memories to the land of birth
and to the associations of the old home. Here can be
easily seen great opportunities for the "pathetic" and
for "wit," occasions where Dean Swift's young clergyman might solace himself for the abstention which the
pulpit enjoins, where the statesman might, even in talking
of public affairs, relieve himself from too sober a presen-
tation of his cares, and where the lawyer might free
himself from his duties to his client and find an audience
who had not heard the facts which limit his eloquence at
the bar.

Here there is room for all, and more than room for all,
that are fit, for the demand for such oratory far exceeds
the supply.

The popular notion is that this display of wit and
eloquence is an easy task. But there is no audience more
critical than the one which greets the after-dinner
speaker. No party spirit helps him, and he has only
the sympathy he himself creates. It is true that he
cannot be too serious, but he may preach a serious discourse if he lights up the sombre background by the

light of eloquent diction or of quaint and humorous
phrase. Before this audience he wins the highest praise
who adds to the charm of his discourse the soundest
wisdom of any orator, the knowledge or instinct of where
to stop. The world owes many a worthy lesson to the
orator who uses the "Puritan," the "Land o' Cakes,"
and the names of St. George and St. David to point a
modern moral and to justify the doubtful present by
joining it on to a past which is secure. The records of
these societies show many examples of eloquence of the
highest order, some of which ought to be given to a
larger world than they reached when delivered.

It is a popular idea that those who are gifted with
oratorical power have few other gifts, that their influence
perishes with the moving of popular audiences and that
they have not in other spheres the power they show in
arousing the multitude. In many cases this is so, but
those who move public sentiment move it in different
degrees. Public sentiment also is of two different kinds:
the voice of the people, which is the hurried result of the
untrained and uninstructed emotions, and that voice of
the people, uttered after due thought and experience,
which is the solid and enduring basis of human action.
Gales, which are but air in motion, may toss the surface
of the seas into wild and ravening waves; but the great
strength of the ocean is underneath it all, and, aided by
the steadfast genius of man, transports to every shore
the products of every land.

Men who stir the surface of thought for the moment
may be inferior and command little permanent respect,
but the great orators have left too many landmarks behind them to be confounded with retoricians and men of
the moment. We have not one of his orations left by
which we might judge for ourselves, but if there be anything in the testimony of all the men of his time, Julius
Cæsar is entitled to rank among the greatest orators of
his age. Yet, however much we may mourn over the
passage of the Rubicon, we cannot deny to Cæsar the
highest rank of all those who have managed the affairs
of practical life. Daniel Webster, who was our greatest
orator, has never been denied the rank of a great man.
Henry Clay, whose oratory was of that sympathetic kind

which we most suspect, was the most powerful party leader who ever dictated his will to others.

While we must acknowledge the faults of Cicero, we can also demonstrate that his great superior, "The Orator" himself, has not only left behind him orations which are the models for the emulation of all the world, but also the memory of a life of patriotic devotion and wisdom which, if the Immortal Gods had so willed, might have saved to Athens its preëminence among the cities of Greece and preserved the liberties of the ancient world.

LECTURES AND LECTURERS

I T is said that more popular lectures have been delivered in the United States in the past year than in any period of its history. People talk of what they call the "lecture system." And, sometimes they even speak of it as a part of the national system of education. It is certainly true, as the reader shall see, that the earlier lectures of the Nineteenth century were prepared and delivered with a definite idea of education. It is also true, however, that with the changes of methods and resources, the lecture system is now to be classed as a part of the system of public entertainment. A good lecturer now may teach or not, but he must entertain.

Lecture courses, on plans which have some similarity to the methods of to-day, were delivered in New England early in the century. The history of American lectures, however, goes even further back. It is matter of amusement now to remember that when the first plays were acted in Boston, they were advertised as moral lectures. Thus Garrick's farce of "Lethe" was produced as a satirical lecture called "Lethe, or Æsop in the Shades," by Mr. Watts and Mr. and Mrs. Solomon. Otway's "Venice Preserved" was announced as a moral lecture in five parts, "in which the dreadful effects of conspiracy will be exemplified"; and "Romeo and Juliet," and "Hamlet," etc., were masked under the same catching and hypocritical phraseology. On October 5, 1785, was produced a moral lecture, in five parts, "wherein the pernicious tendency of libertinism will be exemplified in the tragical history of 'George Barnwell, or, the London Merchant,' delivered by Messrs. Harper, Morris, Watts, Murray.

Solomon, Redfield, Miss Smith, Mrs. Solomon, and Mrs. Gray."

The name "lecture" had been familiar to the New England Puritan and his descendants since 1630. It would hardly be an exaggeration to say that half of the people who crossed the Atlantic in that year came because they wanted to hear lectures. This was one desire among many which led them to emigrate. And there was, perhaps, no desire which expressed itself so often or so simply. After their arrival a regular week-day "lecture" in each settlement was just as much a matter of course as a regular Sunday service. In the contemporary narratives of the first ten years, as in such books as Winthrop's "Journal," there are more references to these week-day lectures than there are to public schools.

The reason for this is to be found in the English history of that time. It is easy to understand that the enthusiastic Puritan preachers did not care to confine themselves to the limited range of the book of Homilies. Nor did they care much for saints' days, and they would range far afield in their choice of subjects for Sunday preaching. But this was a matter where it was hard for Archbishop Laud or any high churchman to interfere. It was when John Cotton left his own pulpit and went up and down in England delivering week-day lectures that Laud and that set saw the danger of such voices crying aloud in their wilderness, and tried to silence them. Many a radical Puritan preacher won his public reputation outside of his parish church. And it is easy enough to see that any attempt on the part of the authorities to stop such week-day lectures, proved to be simply what our modern Philistinism calls a good advertisement. If John Cotton were turned out from Leicester and not permitted to lecture one Thursday, all the people of Leicester would be eager to hear John Wheelwright when it was announced that he would lecture the next Thursday.

Archbishop Laud, however, was not a person easily discouraged. As the phrase of the time went, he was "thorough": a word from which, I suppose, our word Tory was born. The more the Puritan preachers lectured on week-days, the more the Archbishop suppressed them. And this was a grievance which came home to everybody.

Other attacks on Puritan preaching fell upon the ministers. A man would not make the sign of the cross in baptism, and he would not wear a surplice when the Archbishop wanted him to. But such attacks did not concern the laity directly. When, however, the Archbishop said that they should not go to hear lectures, the personal right of an Englishman to use his time as he chose was wounded. And, of course, the more men were told that they must not go to week-day lectures, the more those men swore, that, as God lived, they would.

It is curious to me to see that for twenty references to these Puritan lectures which I could find in our New England records, I should find it hard to discover one in the local authorities in English literature. Even in so careful and complete a book as Masson's "Life of Milton," which covers wonderfully well the Puritan history of most of the Seventeenth century, I have not found one reference to this distinctly Puritan method of exciting and warning the people, of educating them to a larger social and political life. In John Bunyan's Memoirs, however, there is one distinguished exception to this silence. Here is more than one reference either to his speaking on week-days or listening at week-day addresses. I suppose that where the parson in a village looked with favor on the traveling lecturer, he would throw open the village church that the people might hear. Or, if the parson were not favorable, the lecturer had only to avail himself of the audience afforded by a country fair or a market-day, and to advertise his lecture by announcing freely that the parson had closed the doors of the church against him. Then a larger congregation would assemble than would have welcomed him within doors. I think, but am not certain, that for success every such traveling preacher needed ready power of extempore speech. I do not believe that the word lecture implied what its origin seems to require—that it should be read.

The origin of such lectures delivered in different places by speakers other than the resident clergy seems to go back as far as the reign of Edward VI. Dr. Brown writes me from England: "In my own native county of Lancashire, in the reign of Edward VI, seeing that the old Catholic feeling was still strong among many of the

people, four 'King's preachers' were appointed at a sti-
pend of £50 each whose duty it was not only to take
parochial services in their own churches, but also to itin-
erate in the neighborhood and preach the doctrines of
the Reformation. John Bradford, one of the martyrs in
Mary's time, was one of the first four appointed. In Elizabeth's time, one Richard Midgley, for some fourteen
years (circa 1580-1594) traveled over the county as
licensed preacher, or, as Mr. Raines, the antiquary, suggests, as "not improbably one of the four 'Queen's
preachers.'" This arrangement continued during the
Protectorate, the stipends of the preachers being augmented, but on the Restoration were again reduced to
the original estimate. It is very probable that something
of the kind obtained in Lincolnshire, and that John Cotton
was one of the 'King's preachers.'

"But I think we must draw a distinction between these
itinerants and the Puritan lecturers proper. These last
were an addition to the regular ministry of rectors and
vicars, were paid for out of a special fund raised by the
people, and were appointed by the people, not by the
patron of the living. While preaching at the churches at
a different time in the day, they were absolutely independent of the rector or vicar. In my native town,
Bolton-le-Moors, a place so strongly in favor of Puritanism as to be called 'the Geneva of Lancashire,' a will
bearing date 1622, left part of an estate to pay the sti-
pend of a 'Preacher distinct from the vicar of Bolton, to
preach in the parish church upon every Lord's Day and
Monday.' It is on record also that the lecturer not only
officiated in the church, but previous to the Act of Uniformity, he preached at the Market-Cross which stood
at the junction of four principal streets. While fulfilling
the duties of lecturer, one John Smith published a work
on the Patriarchal Sabbath, which probably was a summary of some of his lectures. In Manchester, ten miles
away in the same county, the Puritan lecture was held
on Thursdays, which were market-days, when there was
a great concourse of people.

"The itinerancy, then, I take it, was primarily a distinctly Protestant propaganda; and the Puritan lecture-
ship an independent provision made voluntarily by the

people themselves, of more distinctly Puritan sort than
that provided by the regular clergy, though they preached
on week-days at the Market-Cross, they were not, however, necessarily, itinerant, and if they published any of
their lectures, they are probably not different from the
ordinary Puritan prelections of the period."

Such lectures as these speakers delivered became especially distasteful to Archbishop Laud and his party.

So much reason has the loyal, devout wife who is going
to the "Wednesday evening lecture" in some American
country parish for reminding her husband, who wants
to stay at home, that all of their five hundred and twelve
ancestors who came over in the fleet with Winthrop and
Dudley would have cited as one of the principal reasons
for their coming their wish to hear week-day lecturers.
They would have expressed in the most bitter way their
indignation that King Charles and Archbishop Laud
tried to take away their right to hear them.

Once arrived here, they took measures to carry out
their wish and purpose. The Wednesday Evening Lecture of the Evangelical churches of New England, and
of many other parts of the nation, are survivals of regular lectures established by way of defying the King as
well as serving God. The Thursday Lecture still survives in Boston, in the First Church of that city, after
different adventures of decline and resurrection.

In theory, perhaps, such lectures took on a tone somewhat more secular than that of the Sunday sermon. I
have fancied that the week-day lecture was longer than
even the Sunday sermon. I have fancied that, on the
average, it was perhaps more entertaining. But it is
difficult to establish such fancies with certainty from the
rather dreary study of the sermons or the lectures.

Here are the titles of two of such lectures. But, though
the titles are attractive, I do not venture to reprint the
lectures themselves in a collection which means to be
interesting to intelligent readers in the Twentieth century:—

John Cotton, Sermon at the Boston Lecture After Repeated Shocks
of the Earthquake.

Cotton Mather—The Present State of New England—Discourse
on the Necessity and Advantages of a Public Spirit. Lecture on the
News of an Invasion.

Meanwhile, what were called lectures were almost, of course, kept up in the universities and in the College of Physicians and Surgeons. But I do not believe that in the English and American universities what were called lectures were generally discourses written out so that they could be read in the same form to other audiences. I think that when a man is said to have attended the lectures, say of Bentley or of Porson, he really went into the "lecture rooms" of those men and translated aloud this or that classical author, and listened to the criticisms of the teacher, perhaps took notes of them. On the Continent, I suppose the custom was different. Certainly, as far back as Abelard, he wrote down for his students what he knew, read it to them, and they took notes of what he said for their after study. Observe that printing was not yet introduced, and each man in practice made his own books. But if such had been the custom in England, we should have more books than we have belonging to the Seventeenth and Eighteenth centuries which have been made up from such courses of lectures. In English literature that class of books belongs mostly to the century which has just now closed.

The most remarkable step forward, as our own century came in, in this method of public address, was that taken by Coleridge and his friends in the year 1807. Coleridge had broken into life as a Unitarian preacher. It may be guessed that his Sunday preaching was ethical rather than devout, if we are to take the one sermon which is remembered as an illustration of all. For it is said that the subject was "The Tax on Hair Powder." In later life, Coleridge once asked Charles Lamb if he had ever heard him preach. Lamb said in reply that he never heard him do anything else. Coleridge and his friends conceived the idea of bringing into a focus the brilliant rays of his conversation, and in the year 1807 announced a series of lectures by him to be delivered in the daytime on "Poetry and Fine Arts."

These lectures were well attended by people of intelligence and of distinction, but they do not seem to have been followed by any other course on a similar plan. The popular science lectures in England were purely elementary and were delivered in the evening to working people supposed to know nothing, who had been engaged at their trades all day.

Mr. Emerson told me in 1849 that when in 1848 his friends arranged for his lectures in London, and for Carlyle's, no one thought of evening audiences. The constituency for which they were delivered were people who had more time in the daytime for such purposes than they had in the evening. And he said also that to find any precedents in London for such courses, they had to go back to the courses of Coleridge. Nothing of the sort had been attempted in the meantime

Novel readers will recollect that none of Miss Austen's heroines in London or in Bath ever go to a lecture, though they do go to concerts and the opera. The same thing is true of other novels of English life, at that time. As late as 1825 Frank and Mary go to a lecture but it is a scientific lecture (purely elementary)—on astronomy—with the illustration of an orrery.

In a community like that of New England already prepared with a considerable body of well-trained listeners, and a small body of public speakers, it was natural that courses of lectures on subjects aside from theological inquiry should find their way. In Boston, as early as the year 1825, Dr. Jacob Bigelow announced a course of lectures on botany. Dr. Bigelow was already known to the world of science, both in America and England, as a botanist who had given careful attention as well to the flora of New England as to the science of botany. His lectures were cordially received in the very well educated circles in which they were delivered. I think this is the first instance in Boston of public scientific lectures delivered to all comers.

The time of the "moral lectures," which were simply "A School for Scandal" and all similar plays such as have been named was forty years earlier.

In the year 1821-22 Edward Everett, who had returned from long travel in what was then distant Europe, delivered a course of lectures on "Greece and the Antiquities of Greece." It was just at the time when the Greek revolution was interesting every one in that country. Mr. Everett's lectures were accompanied by an exhibition of large pictures of the monuments still existing in Greece not then nearly so well known to the general public as now.

In 1830 Henry Ware, whose name is still remembered among the preachers and poets of the beginning of the century, delivered a very popular course of lectures on "Palestine, Its Geography and History."

Meanwhile, in England, the work of the Society for the Diffusion of Useful knowledge had begun. What was called the "march of intellect" by Lord Brougham, attracted attention on the right hand and on the left. There were, in fact, many people, not insane people, but of as much sense as Bentham and the men around him, who thought if people only knew their multiplication-table well enough and the facts that are connected, more or less distinctly, with the multiplication-table, the kingdom of heaven would come on earth, and people who had died would enter into a similar kingdom. That is to say, the folly was in the air of supposing if people only know " what is right they will practise what they know." This "march of intellect" was very cleverly satirized in a little play which went over England and America in which a boy named Burke appeared as professor of six different sciences, and made the people on the scenes think that they knew everything before the play was over. In following the English step in this matter, it was thought well, in New England, to organize societies which could arrange for courses of lectures with more success than individuals could.

The Boston Society for the Diffusion of Useful Knowledge was organized about the year 1828. It printed some books which would not have been printed by private publishers. Daniel Webster was the first President. He delivered an inaugural address at the beginning of the first course of its lectures. This society relied mostly upon the professors of Harvard University for its courses. True to the theory of its foundation, that from physical science all truth could be evolved, these lectures were on chemistry, the steam-engine, and other subjects of what was then called " Natural Philosophy."

The Boston Lyceum was organized on the same plan. The Mechanics' Association fell rapidly into the same line; the Historical Society came with its courses, so that for several winters it would have been possible on almost any evening for a man or woman to attend lectures which gave valuable information on the elements of physical science as then understood. Of course the different societies could not pretend to give any systematic order to these lectures, but all the same, the course sprinkled in a good deal of valuable information with regard to facts, and with regard to the supplementary theories into which these facts were combined.

Through the larger towns of New England a similar disposition showed itself. Some of the local lyceums founded in that day are still existing as working societies. I think the Concord Lyceum was founded as early as the year, 1830. These local lyceums had no neighboring universities to draw upon for lectures, but every decent minister of a parish considered it his duty to prepare at least one lecture which he could deliver not only to his own congregation, but to the neighboring towns. The more public-spirited teachers would do the same thing; and, gradually, educated gentlemen regarded it as quite as much a part of their public duty to have a "lecture" which could be delivered when it would do any good, as they considered it their duty to attend to elections or to the government of the town.

Generally speaking, if these lectures were outside of the city of Boston, or some of the other large towns, the attendance on them was without tickets. The whole business was nearly gratuitous. The cost of lighting and warming the church in which the lecture was delivered, possibly the cost of the traveling expenses of the lecturer —these were the only expenses which the lyceum committee was at first involved in. Gradually, however, and naturally, it proved that some people lectured much better than others, and it also proved if a man were lecturing three or four times in a week and going from place to place, he could not do much else. The law of supply and demand established itself. It was whispered with more or less surprise that Mr. So-and-so had been paid for his lecture. The compensation at first was of the very humblest character, and I think that gentlemen who found they were receiving five dollars or ten dollars were astonished. I remember an intimation of this sort as late as James Russell Lowell's time. In one of his letters he says that somebody had paid him five dollars for his lyceum lecture, rather to his astonishment.

To the disgust of a large part of the people who had promoted the "lecture system," came the same experience which had startled and confounded Archbishop Laud in England. For certain edicts and traditions prevented the discussion in most pulpits on Sunday of some subjects of very critical importance in national affairs. The anti-slavery question began to work its way to the front, and there were many people in New England congregations, perhaps the majority, who considered that "the North had no business with the South," and who would be very indignant were the subject of slavery introduced into the pulpit. Over the lyceum lecture, however, there was no such curtain of tradition. What it said, it said. Nobody was responsible for the lecture; and, in consequence, its utterances on matters of public interest were much more free than were the sermons of most of the churches. There came, therefore, upon the lecture platform a body of public speakers who had nothing to do with physical science and discussion of natural forces, but who discussed political principles, and that without hindrance. Such names as those of Wendell Phillips, Theodore Parker, and Mr. Garrison, and names of speakers on temperance and other lines of philanthropic reform, will readily suggest themselves to the American reader. These lyceums, if one may speak of the lecture system by that name, became an important factor in the political, philanthropic, and other sociological movements of the time. It was no longer to be considered as a simple agency for instruction in physical and natural sciences.

It is hardly necessary to pass any general judgment on what is called the lecture system of to-day. Indeed, it is hardly a system. The "general public" of America has learned how much entertainment may be offered by spirited and wide-awake speakers, and is quite ready to give them an opportunity for delivering such lectures as they may prepare, if only these be entertaining. With the abolition of slavery the exciting subjects which did so much to give popularity to lectures a generation ago have been removed. And I do not know any course, so-called, which cares to attempt a lecture on the subject of tariff reform.

Wendell Phillips used to tell an excellent story of his own success in obtaining an audience for a subject which was unpopular. When he arrived at the city where he was announced as lecturer for the evening, he asked the committee whether they wanted him to deliver an anti-slavery address or to read his famous lecture on "The Lost Arts." Unfortunately the committee had been divided exactly evenly, and could not determine which of the two the public should hear. Phillips, with his own facility, instantly said he would deliver both. He would deliver "The Lost Arts" first and have an intermission. He would follow it with the anti-slavery address. It need not be said that no one left the hall after he had heard the brilliant lecture on "The Lost Arts"; and Phillips, therefore, got exactly what he wanted—an audience of people friendly to himself whom he might convert or awaken.

I do not doubt that this system which provides so wide and innocent and general entertainment for the people of the nation, will extend itself and improve itself. I cannot but think that the volumes of which the reader holds the first in his hand, may do their part in such improvement and enlargement.

No view of the subject, however, would be perfect which does not allude to the signs which are evident, in various places, of the determination to return to courses of lectures more distinctly instructive and prepared more fully on system than the courses which have been described.

As early as 1832 Mr. John Lowell, Jr., left a very large sum of money for courses to be delivered in the city of Boston. Similar courses have been established since in the larger cities of America and have been made a necessity of public education. The Lowell courses, the Graham courses, the Peabody courses, and others which could be named, have brought forward some very careful students of the specific subjects chosen by the lecturers. In many instances these lectures have been published together, and have proved valuable contributions in the scientific, ethical, and political literature of the time.

Granting now that the original system is at an end, by which a local board of educators provided a course of

lectures for every winter, and setting aside what we have
called the present system, as not even pretending to
educate people, one is tempted to suggest an improvement in both. If the professional lecturer will regard himself as having a conscientious responsibility beyond the hour of an evening address, he will find he can do
a great deal. Really his position is that of an apostle,
with the walk of his apostleship, if you please, limited to
a range not much wider than the subject of his lectures.
But he ought to be willing to lead the community in
which he speaks forward in the line of his particular subject. It is just as a Christian minister going into a new
town, does not feel that his work is done when he con-
ducts a Sunday service. He even goes from house to
house, he uses the newspaper of the town as far as he
can. In whatever way, he tries to influence public opinion, so that there may be a Methodist church or a Baptist
church, or in general, a Christian church established
which the town has not.

One can conceive thus of a gentleman, who proposes
to lecture on American history, as going to a place where
no course of lectures has been arranged for the winter.
He would see the leaders of the town in their homes. He
would lay before them the programme of the subject
which he means to consider. He would bring the people
together to interest them in those subjects. In such a
way he would obtain their permission and coöperation in
"starting a course," as the phrase is. Now suppose that
course has been "started"; his business is not simply to
go into a hall and read his lecture and go away again.
His business is to be present for half an hour before the
lecture, and he ought to make an appointment, either for
the same evening or for the next day, in which he can
meet those who are interested and give them suggestions
as to their reading and their study. He ought to carry
with him and leave on the spot some of the most important books of reference. A young reader is very much
stimulated by merely dipping into a book. If you say,
"You should look at Wilkinson's 'Herodotus,'" that
means nothing to him, but if you show him Wilkinson's
"Herodotus" and he reads two pages of it, he will
probably resolve to read the whole.

If the subject were American history, the lecturer ought to be prepared to start his hearers on local pilgrimages, or to interest them in their local antiquities. If his subject were botany or geology, he ought to know how to interest them in the botany and geology of their own neighborhood. And so in other instances, he ought to show them that he is not a bird of passage, flying across, in the hope that he might find for himself a fish in their pond. He ought to understand that he has come in as one of themselves, that their interests are his interests, and that their progress is his success; and that he occupies the same place to them, in the matter of science or literature, as a religious guide would occupy in the matter of religion.

In the suggestion which I have thus made, I do not draw upon fancy for a possibility, Utopian or imaginary, or such as has never been put in practice. Such courses are limited to a particular subject, and treat that subject in a continuous series, reinforced and illustrated by the personal advice of the lecturer, and by books well chosen by him, and lent to his hearers for their use. Such courses are those provided by what is called the " University Extension System." This is a very poor name invented for a convenient and practicable plan which has attained considerable success in England and has been introduced in this country.

This plan supposes that a number of gentlemen competent to teach, and thoroughly in earnest in their wish to teach, unite themselves as the governing body, undertaking, not amateur work, but a series of lectures improving, entertaining, and instructive, which they are ready to deliver. When the plan is fully carried out, it contemplates at least one lecture a week for the autumn, winter, and early spring, perhaps thirty lectures in all. So long a course might be divided between four topics. You might say eight or nine lectures on History, as many biographical lectures, to be followed by as many on Government and Administration, and again by as many on some subject of Natural History, Botany, perhaps, or Geology.

Each of these sub-courses would be delivered by one competent man. And it is supposed that for the time, he makes it his whole occupation. He would then go from town to town, lecturing perhaps four times a week or even five.

When the system is well established, the central committee is ready, with a well-selected library of books, of illustration or reference, on each of the subjects on which lecturers are to speak. Supposing the order named above to have been chosen, the arrival of the first lecturer in any town is preceded by the arrival of the historical books, two or three hundred in number at the very least. These are arranged by the local committee, ready for prompt and easy consultation by the persons who take tickets for the lectures. If there is a town library the local committee does its best to strengthen that library on the different sides where the lectures will need illustration.

With such preliminaries, when the lecturer arrives on the field, the field is in a measure prepared for him. He finds, for instance, that the local press, a very important accessory, is helping him in his enterprise. After the lecture, perhaps before the lecture, he gives time for the group of persons who wish to talk with him about their difficulties or their expectations. The next morning, as life arranges itself with us, most of them will be engaged in other cares. But not all of them. He can manage to meet them, a little central club, which will include some of the persons who have arranged the lectures, and again he can answer inquiries and make suggestions. For such purposes as are outlined here, the University Extension Club of Philadelphia has lending libraries which number in all some thousands of books. And for precisely similar purposes, the State Library of New York distributes in every year many thousands of books with very little charge to the readers. Practically, the State imposes no condition but that, in each case where a special library is asked for, there shall be an organized class of readers who will profit by using it.

Edw. E. Hale

CONTENTS

VOLUME IV

xxix

ILLUSTRATIONS

VOLUME IV

LOUIS JEAN RODOLPHE AGASSIZ

MAN AND MONKEYS

[Lecture by Louis Agassiz, naturalist (born in Mortier, Canton Fribourg, Switzerland, May 28, 1807; died in Cambridge, Mass., December 14, 1873), delivered in Cooper Institute Hall, New York, February 26, 1867, the last in his series of six on the "Geological Formation of the Valley of the Amazon," given before the Association for the Advancement of Science and Art. In this series Professor Agassiz presented some of the results of his investigations during his expedition of the previous summer to Brazil, and the delivery of them attracted large and popular audiences, notwithstanding their technical character. This closing lecture of the course drew an especially distinguished auditory, since it expressed Professor Agassiz's attitude toward the Darwinian theory of evolution. Its formal title was, "The Monkey and the Native Inhabitants of South America." At the close of its delivery, the historian, George Bancroft, rose and with a few complimentary remarks proposed the following resolution, which was adopted with hearty applause: "*Resolved*, that the thanks of this great assembly of delighted hearers be given to the illustrious Professor Agassiz, for the fulness of his instruction, for the clearness of his method of illustration, for his exposition of the idea as antecedent to form; of the superiority of the undying, original, and eternal force over its transient manifestations; for happy hours which passed too rapidly away; for genial influences of which the memory will last forever." These lectures were in some respects the most notable ones delivered by the great Swiss naturalist since his first appearance in America with his course on "The Plan of Creation as Shown in the Animal Kingdom," given as a Boston Lowell Institute course in December, 1846, which resulted in his engagement to remain in America.]

LADIES AND GENTLEMEN:—In an unguarded moment I proposed for this evening's lecture the subject which has been announced upon the tickets. If I had considered the matter more maturely, I would probably have abstained from bringing into such public notice a subject so full of difficulties, respecting which, after all, so little is known,

and with reference to which there are such extreme views
entertained by the most competent investigators. As it
is, I have nothing left but candidly to express my convictions without reticence and, if I can, without prepossess-
sion. Of course, you do not expect that I shall tell you
anecdotes concerning the monkeys which I have seen
flying in the trees in the valley of the Amazon, nor to
contrast with them the habits of the native inhabitants,
but that I shall take a broader view of the subject, and
discuss before you the relations which exist between the
monkeys and mankind—a subject which for the last ten
years has engaged the direct attention of all naturalists,
with reference to which all the investigations made within
this period have been more or less directly connected; for
nowadays when a naturalist studies the anatomy of an animal, it is with reference to the possible explanation of the
manner in which the complicated structure was brought
into existence. If a naturalist nowadays investigates the
embryology of an animal, that is, its transformations, its
successive changes, it is with the view of ascertaining how
that law which regulates those changes was stamped upon
it as a living being. When naturalists now investigate the
geographical distribution of the animals upon the surface
of our earth, it is with the view of ascertaining, if it can
possibly be done, in what way the diversity which prevails all over the globe has been produced, what is the
primitive origin of this great diversity. When geologists
investigate the fossil remains which are embedded in the
strata of our earth, and when they trace the order in which
they have followed one another in the course of time, it
is at present with the view of ascertaining how this succession has been introduced, which were the first, which
have followed, and in what relations they stand to one another. And when men investigate all differences which
exist among their fellow-men, it is with the view of ascertaining whether men originated from one pair or whether
there is a multiple origin to humanity. You see that
wherever naturalists nowadays approach their subject it is
everywhere with one view—to ascertain, if it can be done,
in what way things originated and what is the primary
cause of the differences which we observe among them.

LOUIS JEAN RODOLPHE AGASSIZ

Photogravure after a photograph from life

And the subject is just opening. We have hardly any results to present to you. On the contrary, we have extreme views clashing with one another, as much as the views which divide men concerning matters of their salvation, which interest men with reference to their social organizations; for we have schools in natural history, as there have been schools in philosophy. We have, as it were, sects, as there are different denominations among Christians; and no one has a right to present his view of the subject as the only correct one. His obligation is to present his facts and to discuss his arguments in the hope of pressing his views, if he believes them, if he is chiefly convinced of their accuracy, upon his hearers, but not with the pretension that he has found the final solution of the problem. There is a great change in that respect. It is no longer possible for any man, or for any set of men, to assume that the truth is in them exclusively. Men have learned that there is only one common foundation for their beliefs, however they may differ from one another in their religious principles. Men have learned that there is only one source for their knowledge, which is Nature, however much they may differ in their interpretation of Nature's facts; and it is with that conviction that I present, this evening, my views upon the subject of the relation which exists between man and the monkey, urging them with the consciousness that there are other views entertained by others. [Applause.]

I wish, however, to begin my statement with a clean record, and therefore I want to consider accusations which have been made against me in scientific as well as other journals. It has been stated that in my public lectures I make loose statements which are not accurate in matters of fact; that I allow myself to be carried away by the impulse of the moment, and that my statements lack that precision which entitles them to respect and confidence; and examples of such loose statements are quoted. Now I will, that you may know within what limit my statements are considered, answer just a few of these charges. In some of the lectures I have stated that vertebrates have four limbs, and it is argued that everybody who is familiar with the last records of our science knows that whales, that porpoises, that manatuses, and dugongs have only two limbs. That I know is the statement of the text-books, but text-books are only compilations of our knowledge, and if these critics had looked at the original information upon this matter, if they had consulted the best authorities upon the subject, they would know that rudimentary posterior elements exist in all these animals, and that they are only concealed by the skin. I have dissected porpoises, and I have had the opportunity of dissecting the manatus on the Amazon, so that I know from personal observation that these assertions I have quoted are correct, that besides the fully developed pair of limbs upon the side of the crustacea they have a second pair concealed under the skin which are imperfectly developed. I therefore reiterate my statement that there is a natural tendency in all vertebrates to develop four limbs, and that here and there only two are developed, and in some a second pair is concealed under the skin. And even the snakes have been ascertained to sustain a pair of rudimentary limbs under the skin. So much for that one statement. [Applause.] The second is that I affirm that fishes have lived —and a long list of other errors are enumerated—that I affirm that fishes have existed from the beginning of creation, as early as other animals, while in reality they existed only from the time of the Devonian period. Now, how is it with dates? If, in the older strata, the remains were preserved as perfect, it might be as easy to distinguish a group of lobster from a group of fish; but in these older beds, the remains which we have, and which have been interpreted by some as fish and by others as crustacea, there are only fragmentary spines, such as we have in the fin of some fishes; for instance, in the common dogfish, the dorsal fin has in its anterior part a small, bony spine which projects in this way. On the other hand, the horse-shoe group has upon the sides of the second shield a series of spines which are somewhat alike in appearance to those spines. Now, spines of the kind resembling these are numerous in the oldest beds in which fossil remains have been found, and the question is whether they are the remains of crustacea or the remains of fishes. Some naturalists have affirmed that they are the remains of crustacea. I have affirmed that they are the remains of fishes, and I have based my assertion upon this: that the structure of the spines of the crustacea when examined microscopically have all the characteristics of the horny substance which forms the shield of crustacea, while the spines of fishes have the characteristic structure, microscopically, of bones, which is easily distinguished from every other structure. Now, those spines of the oldest deposits have the characteristic of bones; therefore, I say again, that these spines are the spines of fishes, and I am not wrong when I say that fishes existed as early as any other animals. [Applause.]

But this is no place for a controversy, and I will now turn to the subject of this evening's lecture, and consider with you the question of the relation which exists between the monkey and man. That question is a recent question. Ancient naturalists did not think of comparing man and monkeys any more specifically than they compared man with other animals. The works of Aristotle, in which we have the earliest comparisons of this kind, two thousand years ago, discussed the structure of man as compared with animals, but he did not find a special resemblance between monkeys and man any more than between man and the other warm-blooded vertebrates. And the reason is very obvious. In those days the only monkeys known were of three species. The bifacus, as Aristotle calls him, the common monkey of Northern Africa, which was frequently, no doubt, brought to Greece, as in our days it is frequently brought to the southern parts of Europe; the second was the cebus, or the red monkey of North Africa, which is quite common on the coast of Barbary, a long-tailed monkey of reddish color, with a pointed snout somewhat like the common monkeys that obtain over South America, but differing from them in many respects—in the peculiarities of face, teeth, and the like. The third species the baboon, of which representations are to be seen on ancient Egyptian monuments. Now, neither of these classes of monkeys has anything particularly human about it. The baboon has a head not unlike that of a bull-dog; and it was called by the ancients, kunocephalous, or dog-headed, on account of that peculiar constitution of its head. But after the passage to the East Indies around by the Cape of Good Hope had been discovered, naturalists became acquainted with several kinds of monkeys in the East Indies and on the West Coast of Africa which stand far above those known to the ancients; and among them are none more striking than the orangoutang of Borneo, Java, and Sumatra, and the chimpanzee of the Coast of Guinea. These two species excited the curiosity of anatomists to the utmost, and at once their comparison with man was called for in consequence of the higher form of the head and the peculiar development of the features of the face. From that time comparisons between monkeys and men have been introduced in all treatises on natural history. These comparisons have always had for their object, to establish the differences which exist between the two. Recently, a third kind of monkey, closely allied to the last mentioned, has been found—the baboons, which, encountered in the more southern parts of West Africa, have been described under the name of gorillas. It is now ascertained that these animals were already known to the Greeks, though very imperfectly; for in the writings of Anno there is an allusion to a small kind of hairy men, observed on the West Coast of Africa, which could not speak, and which were very savage and indomitable. Now that the gorilla is known, it cannot be doubted that the animal mentioned by Anno was this kind of monkey.

Now the question is, what are the structural relations which exist between these monkeys and other kinds of monkeys, and between all monkeys taken together and mankind? Before I proceed to compare them more closely, let me say a few general words concerning their distribution. All the monkeys known are to be found within the tropics; for it is only upon the borders of the tropics, in the parts adjoining the warm temperate zone, in the Old World, on the southern extremity of Spain, on the rocks of Gibraltar, that a few monkeys have been found; and a few also in the southernmost part of Japan. Otherwise the home of all monkeys is within the tropics, with the exception of Australia in which none exist at all. But monkeys are not the same in different parts of the world;

there is a wide difference among them. In the first place, as a natural group, distinct among the other mammalia, monkeys are characterized by an anatomical fact which is very striking. They have all four hands, while other animals have four feet, and man has two feet and two hands. The difference which characterizes the hands and the feet is very obvious. A limb terminated with fingers which are all on one level, and which all point in the same direction, is a foot. A limb which has a number of fingers bending in the same way, while one finger may be opposed to the others, and may be successively brought into contact with each of the other fingers, is a hand. The thumb, as a part of the hand, is flexible in any direction from the fingers, and it may be brought in juxtaposition successively with each of the fingers, while that is utterly impossible with the toes of the feet. They all point in the same direction, and the large toe cannot be brought in juxtaposition successively with the other toes. All animals which have feet at the extremity of their four limbs are quadrupeds, all animals which have four hands and no feet, are monkeys; for all monkeys have hands at the end of their hind limbs as well as their fore limbs. But man has a pair of feet and a pair of hands. This is perhaps the most prominent difference which may be noticed among these animals, and the characteristic features of the great order of monkeys. There are some slight modifications in this respect among the monkeys, inasmuch as there are some in which the thumb is so short that it cannot be as readily brought in juxtaposition with the other fingers as in the hand of man; and there are even monkeys in which the thumb is quite rudimentary, so that four fingers only are developed, the thumb being almost entirely wanting. Again, what constitutes a finger is the position of the nail upon the termination of the last joint of the finger. In the perfect hand the last joint of every finger has a flat nail, covering only the upper part of the joint, not extending forward, and not bending over the last joint. This is the case with all the nails of our hand, and it is the case also with the nails of our foot. But in all other animals which have an imperfect hand we find that perhaps the thumb, and one, or two, or three fingers, may have a perfect nail, and the others may have curved nails bending beyond the termination of the finger. That is the case even among some of the monkeys; and we have even monkeys in which the thumb alone and the first finger have a real flat nail, while the other fingers have a claw bending over the termination of the finger. Again, among the monkeys we have a great variety as to size. Some of them are not longer than our small striped squirrels, while others approach even the stature of man; and there are all possible intermediate dimensions existing between them.

Monkeys are scattered in Asia and Africa and in Central and South America; but in each of these parts of the world they present special characteristics. The monkeys of the Old World, that is, those inhabiting the tropical parts of Africa and Asia, are all remarkable for the greater height of the forehead and the greater angle of the face. Naturalists have been in the habit of measuring what is called the facial angle—that is, the angle which one line passing from the forehead over the upper jaw will make with another line passing along the base of the skull. In intellectual men this angle is nearly a right angle; and the ancients understood this so well, that in their statues, when they wanted to exhibit an intellectual man more prominently than usual, they exaggerated the inclination of that line; and in their Jupiter, who was the representation of creative power, they gave a prominence to the forehead which overstepped the right angle, so that the forehead is prominent over the face. This was well understood as the characteristic feature of the highest organization of the vertebrate type. In this respect the monkeys of the Old World approach man more nearly than any other monkeys, and the young chimpanzee and the young orangoutang approach the child much nearer than the adult monkey approaches the adult man. It is a curious fact that, in their earlier age, when the characteristic features are not yet stamped with all their rigidity upon animals closely related to one another, they resemble one another more than in their adult stage. And so we find a greater resemblance between the young of the higher monkeys and the children of men than between the adults themselves.

Another feature of the monkeys of the Old World consists in the constitution of the nose. The nose is one of the most prominent features of the face. But through all higher types of the animal world, in man and in monkeys, we find that the most characteristic differences between the different representatives of these two great groups are marked by striking differences in the form of the nose. The white man has a prominent aquiline nose, and he has nostrils which are open so that the point of the nose is the most prominent part of the face. Other races of men have, on the contrary, a flattened nose, and the nostrils opening sidewise, so that the width of the nostril is from within outward. Now similar differences are observed among the monkeys. The monkeys of the Old World have narrow nostrils, the nostrils opening as in the white man, from forward backward, with the partition which divides the nostrils very narrow. Then again, it is among the monkeys of the Old World that we find the largest number of those which are destitute of the tail. Neither the orang-outang, nor the chimpanzee, nor the gorilla, nor the macaqua of North Africa have any caudal appendage. Upon the Sunda Islands, and upon the peninsula of Malacca, there is a large tribe of monkeys with exceedingly long arms, and all destitute of tails. Among the large kinds of monkeys of Africa, as the baboon, we find short-tailed species. It is only among the slender kinds of the Old World that we find those which have as long a tail as the monkeys of Africa generally have. Then, if we pass from the Old World to the New World, we find that the monkeys here not only are generally smaller, and generally have a more prolonged snout, but that their facial angle is less than that of the monkeys of the Old World; and, what is curious, that their nostrils are broad —the partition between them remarkably broad, so that they open in a measure sidewise. And among them we find a large number of kinds which have remarkably long tails. Some of these have a tail which terminates with a naked surface underneath, which can be used as an additional limb, for these monkeys have so much dexterity in the use of the tail that they can seize small objects by clasping the end of the tail around them, with as much precision as they can seize objects with their hands. All monkeys with such a prehensile tail are peculiar to South America. Not one of the Old World has this peculiarity. And there are even those which have a prehensile tail covered all over with hair. Then there are a certain number of the monkeys of South America which have somewhat less tail; but there is not one on the whole continent of America which is entirely destitute of the caudal appendage. So we have here two well-marked groups—the monkeys of the Old World and the monkeys of the New World, the former of which, on account of the peculiarity of the form of the nose, have been distinguished as catarhine, or narrow-nosed, and the latter platyrhine, or broad-nosed.

Then there are two families of monkeys which have a special character: the little squirrel-monkeys which inhabit several tropical parts of South America, the valley of the Amazon, and the northern parts of Brazil, each differing from all other monkeys in having their grinding teeth provided with numerous prongs, and their hands small and imperfect, more resembling paws, unlike the hands of any other monkeys; and yet the possibility of opposing the thumb to the other fingers shows them to be monkeys also. Another difference which I have noticed between the monkeys of the Old World and those of the New World consists in the dentation. Man has five grinders above and below, right and left, making twenty grinding teeth, and so have all the monkeys of the Old World; but the monkeys of the New World have one tooth more on each side, above and below, the number of their grinders being twenty-four. These little squirrel-monkeys, again, have only twenty, five on each side. And now the fourth group of monkeys, known under the name of lemurs or makis; these inhabit Madagascar, and they are exclusively found on that island, the genuine maki. A few somewhat allied to the makis are found on the opposite shores of Africa. What distinguishes these monkeys from all others is the form of the head, which is protruded like a fox, and they are occasionally called "fox monkeys" on that account. They have a pointed snout, are more carnivorous than monkeys generally are, and their fingers are more numerously provided with claws than with flat nails.

Here we have four groups of monkeys which are characterized by peculiarities of structure, easily recognized and unmistakable—the monkeys resembling the squirrels, which inhabit tropical South America; the monkeys with broad nostrils, which inhabit South America generally within the tropics; and the monkeys of the Old World which are found in Africa, and in Asia within the tropics, but not in Madagascar nor in Australia. It is curious that here, a tropical region in which palm-trees, the principal abode of monkeys, abound—as Australia—should be destitute of monkeys, when on some of the adjoining islands monkeys are not only common, but even the highest kinds of monkeys are found. This shows, in my estimation, one thing—that all the differences which exist among animals cannot be ascribed to climatic influences, or, at all events, that similar climates do not necessarily produce animals which are akin; for there, in Australia, which exhibits all the peculiar climatic conditions of the tropics and the temperate zone, we have neither monkeys nor carnivorous animals, nor ruminants, nor pachyderms; there are neither deer, nor elks, nor antelopes, nor elephants, nor rhinoceroses, nor hippopotamuses, nor any of those large animals which everywhere else inhabit tropical climates; nor any giraffes, nor any camels; nor are there any of the carnivorous tribe, no bears, no weasels, no foxes, no dogs, no bulls, no cats, no tigers, no lions; nothing of that kind: but the whole of the continent is peopled by quadrupeds of a peculiar sort, the marsupials or kangaroo family, all of which are remarkable for the peculiarity of having, like our opossum (which is one of that family, and the only genus of that family found on this continent), under the abdomen a pouch, in which the young, that are born in a very immature condition, are transferred, and where they remain until they have reached a greater progress in their development. Now that group of marsupials, as they are called, is the peculiar group of quadrupeds of Australia, and in their various forms they ape all the other families which are so common in other parts of the world. There are some which recall the monkeys, though they have not the characteristics of the monkeys; there are others which recall the carnivorous animals, though they have not the characteristic features of the carnivorous; and others which recall in a measure the ruminants, though they are not ruminants, properly speaking.

It would lead me too far away from my subject were I to enter into a detailed description of all those animals. All I want now to impress upon your minds is the fact that every part of the world has its peculiar tribes of animals, and that these tribes do not possess such a close relation to the climatic condition that their peculiarities give us any kind of satisfactory evidence that they are to be ascribed to the climatic influences in which they live.

Now, among these monkeys there are innumerable varieties or species or genera, as you may call them, for the term is not of very great importance here. What I want to make clear is the nature of these differences. There are among them those, such as the orang-outang, the chimpanzee, and the gorilla, which have the hand made in the same manner, teeth of about the same proportions, and present in the structure of the details the same relation; they are therefore considered as one group. Those higher monkeys are designated by the name of anthropoid, or man-like. Then we have those in which the snout is very prominent and large, somewhat dog-like, the tail short, the limbs very stout, the bodies heavily built. They are the baboons. But among these baboons there are several kinds—that is, different species, differing in size, differing in color, differing in the length of hair over the head and on the neck, in the mane, and so on. Then we have another group: the long-tailed monkeys in the Old World, which are remarkable for their slender form, the great length of the tail, the more prominent snout, the more tuberculated grinding teeth, and the like. And so it is with the monkeys of the New World. In South America there is the genus cebus, or sapajou—monkeys with a prehensile tail, but in which the tail is more covered with hair than in the howling monkeys, in which the lower part of the tail is entirely destitute of hair. The latter have in the throat an enlargement of the larynx, by which they can produce a reverberation of the sounds they utter, which is very loud; hence the name by which they are designated, "howling" monkeys. Of them there are a variety of species, occupying different parts of South America. So again with the shorter tailed monkeys of South America, and so with the squirrel-monkeys—a great number of both species showing those peculiarities of structure which rest in the mode of execution of the details, the tail, hands, face, and the like, and presenting differences which rest in the color, in the absolute size of the animal, in the relative proportions of the limbs, in their length as compared with the body, and so forth.

Now, then, what do we find among men? Similar differences again. For men have not all the same complexion, nor do they all exhibit the same characteristic features. And here let me urge upon you this fact, for we cannot consider the relations of mankind to monkeys unless we are aware how widely men differ from one another. While they have all the characteristics of humanity, there are yet among them differences about as striking as the differences which distinguish some of these genera of monkeys from one another—as striking, unquestionably, as the differences of some of the species of monkeys from one another. And I am bound to say that unless we recognize the differences among men, and the identity of these differences with the differences which exist among animals, we are not true to our subject. Whatever be the origin of these differences they are of some account; and if it ever is proved that all men have a common origin, then it will be at the same time proved that all monkeys have a common origin, and it will by the same evidence be proved that men and monkeys cannot have a different origin. This is the appalling feature of the subject—that the characteristics which distinguish the different races of men are of the same nature as the characteristics which distinguish the different kinds of monkeys. And it was for that reason that early I maintained that the different races of men must have had an independent origin, because I saw the time coming when the question of the origin of man would be mixed up with the question of the origin of animals, and a community of origin might be affirmed for all.

Now, I hold that the idea of the community of the origin

of man and monkeys and the other quadrupeds is a fallacy,
the foundation of which I shall try to explain presently.
But if it is an error to consider men as derived from monkeys, we must admit that men are not derived from a
common stock, because the differences which exist among
men are of the same kind and quite as striking as the differences which exist between monkeys and between the
lower animals. [Sensation.] Let me say in what respects
all men agree, and in what all differ from monkeys. All
men agree in having four limbs, one pair of which terminates with feet and the other pair terminates with hands.
All men are endowed with the ability of standing erect,
and their constitution is such that the erect position is not
one resulting from education, is not the result of successive change, but is one of the constitutive peculiarities of
the human frame. The whole backbone is so organized
that man can carry with ease his heavy broad head only
in a vertical position. He has not, as animals have, a liga-
ment with which he may support the head in a horizontal
position with ease; but the head must be balanced on the
top of the vertical column in order that it may be moved
with facility in every direction. Then man has limbs on
the side of the chest so organized that he can move them
in every direction and touch every part of his body with
them. And that pair of limbs terminates with the most
perfect hand known in nature; and that hand is so constituted as rapidly to carry out the mandate of the mind.
It is brought into the service of the intellect, and is no
longer an organ of locomotion, as is the case with the
monkey.

All these peculiarities are characteristic of all men, and
between monkeys and men there is no structural transition
—there is no gradation. From the highest monkey to the
lowest race of men, all these attempts at bringing man
closer to the monkey by lower types of humanity overlook
these fundamental differences which make man, however
low and inferior, a man, and which separate him from the
monkey, however high as a monkey he may stand. [Ap-
plause.] But while we recognize certain structural at-
tributes as particularly human, let us not overlook the
great differences which exist among men both in structure

and attainments. In the first place color—these differences are obvious, but they are comparatively of slight importance. Next in hair—there is a marked difference; the flowing, straight hair of the white race is very different already from the stiff and wiry hair of the Indian; and when we come to compare that hair with that of the Australian, or with that of the Malay, or with that of the Fiji Islander, or, still more strikingly, with that of the negro, we find differences which are most marked. The hair of the white race is semicircular; the hair of the negro is flat, it is woolly, it is curly. And these peculiarities are not peculiarities brought about by climate, for white men have existed in close proximity with negroes ever since the two races have been known to exist side by side on earth, and the white man has not assumed the woolly hair of the negro, nor has the negro assumed the straight hair of the white race. [Applause.] Then there is a difference in the dentition, and a very marked one. All the white race have teeth vertical, the jaw short; and the manner in which the teeth fit one upon the other is perpendicularly, so that when we close the mouth we bring the lower teeth against the upper teeth in such a juxtaposition that the two sets stand vertical, one above the other. The races of men which have that kind of dentition are called orthognate, that is, straight-jawed races; while there are other races—and, among others, all the inhabitants of the South Sea Islands and all the inhabitants of Africa south of the Atlas—that have their front teeth inclined, so that the upper teeth and the lower teeth, when brought against one another, form an angle and the mouth is more prominent; these men are called prognate. And that difference is a constant one. All the races of men with prognate jaws have also thicker and more prominent lips. They have also flat noses, which I have already described, with broad partitions between the nostrils, and the nostrils opening sideways.

These differences have been known among them ever since men have been observed by man. On the ancient monuments of Egypt there are figures of negroes, there are figures of Egyptians, there are figures of Jews, there are figures of white men as characteristic in all these par-

ticulars as we see them now; so that for at least as long
a time as these monuments have been in existence these
features of humanity have remained what they were then,
and have retained their peculiarities. Now, then, the question is, how were these peculiarities brought about? Are
they innate?—that is, are they primal, or are they the result of change? If these differences are the result of
change, then why should not the differences which we
observe among monkeys be the result of change also?
And if changes as great can take place, why should not
changes a little greater occur? And, therefore, why should
not all the differences which exist among living beings be
the result of successive changes?

It is upon this line of reasoning that a scientific argument has been based, which is known as the transmutation
doctrine, and which has been discussed for centuries, but
which has been revived in a more recent form, and with
more recent argument, by Darwin, and is now the question prominently agitated among naturalists. Now, I propose to show you on what fallacies this view rests, and I
will repeat my statement in another form. The question
is whether we are the lineal descendants of monkeys, or
whether we are the children of a creative mind; whether
we are the result of a natural evolution, or whether we are
the expression of a specific act of creation. In establish-
ing the difference I do not mean to charge those who
entertain the idea of a transmutation with denying the
intervention of a creative power in the acts of the world.
I do not charge them with denying the interference of
God in nature, but I charge them with denying the immediate direct intervention in the production of these
differences. Whether they are right or wrong depends
upon the interpretation of the facts which we have before
us, and it is to the examination of these facts to which I
would call your attention. [Applause.] I must crave your
indulgence, for the hour is already over and I have hardly
begun my subject.

In the first place I would say that man is rated in the
animal kingdom in a manner which makes it impossible
to separate the conclusions which relate to his existence
from those which relate to the animal kingdom. When

we examine the order of succession of animals, through all geological times, we find from the beginning to the end a definite relation to something higher and higher, and we find that in the last geological epoch only has man been introduced. So that, in the order of succession of the living races which have at different times peopled the surface of our globe, we see man announced from the beginning; and we can say, as one of the scientific results of the comparison of all these races, that from the beginning man was meant to be at the head of creation, and that upon the plan upon which animals living upon our earth are constructed there is no possibility of a higher being than man himself. And this generalization can be sustained by an examination of the structure of the brain alone.

Without entering into an extensive argument, I will show you that such is the structure of the highest systems of organs in the whole series of animals that from the fish to man there is one gradual gradation, and that in the structure of man there is a consummation which shows that he is the highest possible form of the series which begins with the fish. [The Professor here used the blackboard to illustrate his subject.] Suppose this to be the brain of a fish. We have here, as in all brains, a front swelling from which arise the nerves which go to the nostrils; here a middle swelling from which arise the nerves which go to the eyes; and a third swelling from which arises the nerve which goes to the ear, and other nerves which go to different parts, about which I need not now trouble you. These three swellings are so constituted that the first formation is the smallest, the middle formation occupies the middle position, and the hindmost is the largest. In reptiles we find that these three swellings have about the same dimensions; that the front swelling begins to rise, so as to stand on a level with the middle swelling, which itself is about as large as the hind swelling, which is receding in dimensions from the others. In birds we find that the front part is so far developed as already to cover, in a measure, the middle swelling, the hind swelling being left uncovered. When from the bird we rise to the quadruped, we find that the front swelling covers

2

the middle swelling completely, though it does not cover the hind swelling at all. When we come to man, we find that not only is the middle swelling, but the hind swelling also, covered in such a manner that the position is so changed that, instead of extending on the same plane, or rising slowly, as is the case in the reptile, or slanting, as is the case in the bird and mammalia, in man the brain is brought to stand at right angles with the spinal marrow, which extends through the series of backbones along the vertebral column. Beyond this you see at once there is no progress possible. Here we have acquired the most complete development of the anterior part of the brain. It extends from the middle and posterior region of the middle and hind parts of the brain in a perfect harmonious manner, and the whole commands the whole system in a manner which, if attempted to be exceeded, would lead to a retrograde movement, and not to an onward progress. [Applause.] Take the different forms of brain which we have among men and you will find the variety a little more or less developed; pass from them to the monkeys and you will find this gradually receding, you will find the cerebellum will be uncovered very slowly, and then gradually more and more. In fact, you have a complete series, which shows that between man and monkeys, and monkeys and quadrupeds, and quadrupeds and birds, and birds and reptiles, and reptiles and fishes, there is an uninterrupted gradation of more or less complicated structures, but with this remarkable peculiarity: that the distances from one to the other are unequal, that there is not that even gradation or that even succession, that from one stage to the other the distance or the difference should be perfectly uniform. There is always more or less distance from one to the other, and not equal in measure, in steps from any lower to the next higher type.

And now, in the order of succession of animals, we find something similar. Suppose I represent here the lowest level on which any animal has existed upon the surface of our earth, and here mark the name of the geological formations as they have followed one another [illustrating on blackboard] from the azoic period, through the Silurian age, through the Devonian and carboniferous age, the

Permian, the Triassic, the Jurassic, the Cretaceous, the Eocene, the Miocene, the Pliocene, and the present period. And here I represent by this line the present surface of our earth, with all the varieties of animals living upon it. Here we have a compartment for the radiates, which, you may remember, constitute one of the great types of the animal kingdom, and are divided into three classes—the polyps and jellyfishes, the starfishes, sea-urchins and the like. Here we have another compartment for the mollusks, and among these mollusks we have also three classes—the bivalve shells, the univalve shells, and the chamber shells, for we have here another compartment for the articulates, and we divide them into three classes; also the worms, the crustacea, and the insects. And here we have the last compartment for the vertebrates, which also comprise three classes; the fishes and they are subdivided into several classes, which I need not notice now; the reptiles with their subdivisions, the birds, and mammalia.

Now we will inquire when were these animals called into existence. Mark that the transmutation doctrine assumes that animals are derived from one another, and that there is a primitive cell formed from which all animals may have been evolved. The doctrine is that all vertebrates are descended from one primitive vertebrate, that all articulates are descended from one primitive articulate, that all mollusks are derived from one primitive mollusk, that all radiates are derived from one primitive radiate, and that those four primitive types are derived themselves from the primitive cell formed by the combination of those fortuitous elements which are acting wherever light, moisture, and matter are brought into contact with one another. It is the doctrine professed by Moleschott, by Carl Vogt, by Buchner, by Czolbe, and by all those who have advocated the transmutation doctrine, on the ground that everything which exists has started spontaneously from the formation of a primitive cell under the influence of light acting upon matter. Moleschott's paper on the action of light upon matter in organizing beings is one of the most striking productions of that school. Darwin and the English defenders of the transmutation doctrine present it in a somewhat different light. They assume that the first impulse was given by an intellectual power, and that this impulse has resulted in an unfolding, in an evolution out of the first germs created of all that has followed. The doctrine which I support is that it is not only the few which were started in the beginning by a creative act, but the many, and that it was not at one time only that creation was limited, but that the creation has gone on through all ages, and that under the direct influences of creative power most all the differences which exist have been brought about. [Applause.] These are generalizations. Now let us see what the facts are, whether the German transmutation doctrine comes nearer to the fact, whether the English transmutation doctrine comes nearer, or whether the doctrine of special creation comes nearer to the fact; and if the latter is the case, then I shall have proved my statement that we are not the lineal descendants of monkeys, but we are children of God. [Applause.] We are the chosen productions of an intellect; we are made in His resemblance. [Applause.]

I say these are interpretations. Let us see to the facts once more, and ascertain how close they come to the translation I have presented. Polyps have existed from the beginning. They are found in the geological formations, they are found through all geological formations, and they exist now. Acalephs have been found in the oldest geological formations, through all geological formations, and they exist now; and echinoderms have been found in the oldest and through all geological formations, and they exist now. So we have three classes of radiates represented from the beginning. Lately a fossil has been discovered in Canada, and described, which purports to be the first animal living on earth. Whether it be an animal is not even fully ascertained; there are controversies upon that point, and within the last few months discussions have arisen in learned societies whether this Aozone Canadensis was or was not the remains of a living being. I say, let us, in such instances of observations which are so far out of the path of all information obtained before, reject them until they are so clearly sustained that there can be no doubt about the fact. So I say, leave the Aozone Canadensis out of consideration until it is known that it was a living being, and until its structure is so far disclosed that some theory can be predicated regarding its affinities. Among mollusks we have bivalve shells existing from the oldest time to the present day, and univalve shells and chambered shells existing from the oldest time to the present day. Among worms we have those with solid covering up to the present day; and among crustacea we have them from the oldest time. Among insects the first we find belong to the carboniferous period, and not before. Then among vertebrates we have, as I have shown you, fishes from the beginning, notwithstanding the objection to the statement I made before. Then we have reptiles from the carboniferous period. We have birds either from the Triassic or the Jurassic period—it is questionable which—and we have mammalia also from that period. You see, then, how many classes we had from the beginning, and how many of these were cotemporaneous with one another.

Can it be said that animals which were cotemporaneous were descendants of one another, or that animals which appeared together at the same time were derived one from the other? Certainly not. It is not so. We have at least so many beginnings as are representatives of these different classes in the earliest strata. But this is not all. The polyps have existed from the beginning through all ages; but the polyps of the earliest period are among the lowest, while we have polyps of a much higher grade living now. The acalephs of the oldest times are among the lowest, while we have acalephs of a much higher grade living now. The echinoderms existing then were of the lowest order, while we have echinoderms of a higher grade now. So it seems as if all these types had been improving; as if they had undergone changes, and as if those changes had led successively to something higher. So it seems, but it is not so; because while we have polyps now which are superior to those which formerly lived, we have by the side of them polyps which are as low as the earliest known. The functions and structure at the present time are the same as those existing at the earliest epochs. The Crinoids to-day are as low as the earliest known. Now I would ask, what started these simple forms into a desire and gave them a capacity to become something higher and to go on becoming higher, and at the same time what made them feel that they had done enough in the direction of something higher? What gave them the power at the same time to remain on the lower level? That is the character of the facts as we have them. We have certain lowest forms rising gradually higher and higher, and we have the lowest forms by the side of the higher at the same time. So that we should have, according to the transmutation doctrine, beings capable of changing themselves, and at the same time remaining as they were; at the same time, influences which would produce a change and which would prevent a change from going on. I say that is not logical, and that a doctrine which has facts against it so glaring is not a true interpretation of nature.

We have the same here with the mollusks. We have the lingula, the lowest bivalve shell known to this day, while we have the branchiopods, the clams, the fresh-water mussels of a higher type. What started the lingula to change to these other forms, and at the same time secured to it a condition in which it should not change? I do not know a physical force, and I do not know a natural agency which is capable of producing such results. But I know that mind can do it. I know that when an author sets out to record the processes of his mind he can do it at every stage of perfection; he can do it in such a manner that the records may be the evidence of his gradual progress; and in the end may be the evidence of his highest culture, while at the same time he may record, if only for memory's sake, the doings of his early days by the side of the productions of his maturer years. It is just that which we read in nature. We have the earlier manifestations of creative power, and we have the later and higher productions. And we have by the side of these later productions the reproductions, as it were, of what had been in the beginning. This is to be traced in the gasteropods, of which we find the lowest forms here at present. It is the case with cephalopods, of which the earliest forms are here now; and by their side are the nautili and all the variety of cephalopods belonging to our day. So it is with the worms. So it is with the crustacea. So, I may say, it is also with the insects, though that class begins only in the carboniferous period. The fact that the insects begin only in that age is another indication of the working of mind in this process. For during the earliest periods of the earth's history the whole of its surface was covered with water. There was no land, no terrestrial animals. But when vegetation began to be extensive, and especially terrestrial vegetation, we have the first indication of land animals in the production of insects.

Here let me call attention to another fact. Is it because nature has undergone successive changes that animals and plants have made their appearance? or is it the physical change which has called into existence these living beings? or have the physical changes, as they have taken place, been directed in such a manner as to prepare the home upon which living beings could be distributed in a manner suited to the conditions prevailing on the earth? The question is simply this: Has the physical world in all its changes been productive of the organic world, or has there been an intellectual power superintending the whole in such a manner that the physical condition should be brought about by which the living beings should find an appropriate home for their growth? [Applause.] In other words, has man sprung upon earth because our earth had become what it was, or has the earth been prepared for man, that he might develop in that way his capacities in the most appropriate manner upon its surface? If we look at the order of the succession of vertebrates we find an answer to that question. We find, first, that fishes have existed as long as the surface of this earth was in the condition during which all these aquatic animals could alone exist. Then reptiles have been called into existence, just at the time when the land above the sea had become extensive enough to put forth a proper abode for the large masses of reptiles at the earliest periods. We find afterward the introduction of birds at the time when our atmosphere had been deprived of its accumulation of carbon, before which birds could not breathe. The accumulation of coal in beds, in the carboniferous period, freed the atmosphere of this element which had existed in such a proportion at an earlier period that the existence of warm-blooded animals would have been impossible. Here is a physical fact which precedes the introduction of these living beings which required a purer atmosphere. Now the question is, has this freeing of the atmosphere of the carbon been the cause of the coming in of the birds and mammalia, or have the processes of nature been so conducted by a surprising intellect that at a certain time the atmosphere should be free of its impure matter, that higher forms of being might be called into existence? When we see that there is such a gradation, and when we find that there are no intermediate forms, it seems hardly possible that causes and influences which are ever acting in the same way should have produced this result.

I wish I had time to enter into an elaborate argument upon this point. I will only sum up my evidence in a few sentences. The physical causes are the same now as they were before. Chemical agencies, physical agencies, act now as they have acted from the beginning. We have the evidence of this in the identical character of the rocks of the older and more recent formations; we have evidence of it in the chemical identity of the materials of which celestial bodies are formed, of which the more recent investigations of physicists have given us satisfactory demonstrations. The physical world remains the same. The laws which govern it remain the same, and from the beginning until now they have acted in the same way. Are, then, the different animals which have existed at different times and which differ in the most varied manner the result of causes which do not vary, which act ever in the same manner? This is contrary to all argument, contrary to any evidence we have. We cannot ascribe diversified results to uniform causes. We cannot ascribe the cause of certain facts to agencies the action of which is known to us. Physicists and chemists know perfectly well what electricity, what light, what magnetism can produce. They know perfectly well what are the possible combinations between chemical elements; and they know perfectly well that these various combinations and these various causes are different from the causes whose effects we witness in the animal kingdom. Therefore I say that it is not logical to ascribe the diversity which exists among living beings to causes which exhibit uniformity of nature and uniformity of action. I can conceive only one possible cause, and that is the intervention of mind in such a way that it shall produce what we have seen. We know perfectly well how the human mind acts—how free it is; and how in its manifestation we recognize the stamp of Him who manifests Himself. In the works of the highest intellect we recognize the peculiar mode and manner in which His mind manifests itself. In the poet, in the painter, in the architect, in the sculptor at all times we see this manifestation. Now why should we not have something of the same kind in Nature? Mind is not a manifestation of matter. It is something independent of it. To the extent to which we know its freedom, to the extent to which we can maintain independence of certain influences, to that extent, and in a similar manner, do I conceive the intervention of kind in the production of living beings for all time upon a plan laid out and carried out from the beginning, with reference to an end; and that there is that reference to an end, and that the end is man, is seen in the relation which man bears to the lowest vertebrata, the fishes. That there is a reference to man is seen from the gradation which we observe through all times, from the beginning to the end. That this cannot be the result of merely physical conditions is further shown by the fact which is constantly recurring, of the transformations reproduced every day through the whole animal kingdom in the production of new individuals.

And here I come to the closing evidence I would submit. All living beings are born of eggs, and developed from eggs. All end their growth in changes which have begun with the egg. Every successive generation begins anew with this egg. Since there have been men or quadrupeds on earth, since animals have existed, they have reproduced in every generation all the changes in their growth and transformation which are characteristic of their race. Now see what this amounts to. There are several hundred thousand different kinds of animals living on this globe of the different types. Every one of them has its line of development. Every sparrow begins with the egg, and goes through all the changes which are characteristic of sparrow life, until it is capable of producing new eggs, which will go through the same change. Every butterfly comes from the egg, which produces the caterpillar, which becomes a chrysalis, and then a butterfly, laying eggs to go through the same changes. So with all animals, whether of higher or lower type. In fact, the animal kingdom as it is now, is undergoing greater changes every year than the whole animal kingdom has ever passed through from the beginning until now; and yet we never see one of these animals swerve from the plan pointed out, or produce anything else than that which is like itself. [Applause.] This is the great fact. Every being reproduces itself under conditions which are as varied as they have been from the beginning of the world until now; and yet they do not change. Why is that? Because by nature they are not changeable. That is what we must infer. And if those which live now are not changeable, and do not pass from one to another, though they represent all the changes which animals can pass through, is it logical to assume that those of early ages have become what we see now in consequence of changes in successive generations? Have the laws of nature changed in such a manner that what does not take place now has taken place in early times? I say, no. I say, just as the cycle which every animal passes through in its development from the egg to its perfect condition, returns to the plan impressed upon that animal by the Creator, just so have the various forms, the remains of which we find preserved in the rocks, been, from the beginning of the steps through which it has pleased the Creator to carry the animal kingdom up to man, that being made in His own image, who is endowed with a spirit akin to His, by virtue of which alone we can understand nature. Were we not made in the image of the Creator, did we not possess a spark of that divine spirit which is a godlike inheritance, why should we understand nature? Why is it that nature is not to us a sealed book? It is because we are akin to the world, not only the physical and the animal world, but to the Creator himself, that we can read the world and understand that it comes from God. [Applause.]

MATTHEW ARNOLD

NUMBERS; OR, THE MAJORITY AND THE REMNANT

[Lecture by Matthew Arnold, poet and critic (born in Laleham, England, December 24, 1822; died in Liverpool, April 15, 1888), delivered first in New York, Chickering Hall, October 30, 1883, opening his series of " Discourses in America " (the others being " Literature and Science " and " Emerson ") given during his visit to the United States in the autumn and winter of 1883–84. The lecturer was introduced to his New York audience, a large and representative gathering, by Parke Godwin, who took occasion to pay a tribute to him as a critic, philosopher, and poet, and also to his father, Dr. Thomas Arnold, " the schoolmaster of Rugby, who enlarged his classroom till it comprised the whole English-speaking race." When Mr. Arnold made his first appearance in Boston, with this lecture, in Horticultural Hall, November 7th, he was introduced by Dr. Oliver Wendell Holmes, as follows: " *Ladies and Gentlemen:* The position in which I find myself this evening reminds me of a story told me by a schoolmate, a nephew of the late Washington Allston, in reference to Mr. Edmund Dana. He was of short stature, and was walking the streets of London with a gentleman much taller than himself, when the latter was run against by one of those persons styled roughs, but more fittingly ruffians. The gentleman who experienced the collision promptly handed his coat to the little man, and struck an attitude of resistance. The conference was not a long one, and the tall man having got the better of it, one of the English crowd, who always like fair play, shouted, ' Hurrah for the gentleman!' Another voice supplemented the cry with, ' And hurrah for the little man that held his coat.' [Laughter.] The friend who was to have played the part of the ' little man ' of my story was Rev. Phillips Brooks, who is unfortunately prevented from coming this evening by indisposition. I have been asked to fill his place, which, in my point of view, is beyond my capacity. [Laughter.] Happily, little is required of one who is to introduce the distinguished speaker of this evening. Were it only that he is the son of Thomas Arnold his welcome would be as wide as the realm over which the English language is spoken. Were he of unknown parentage he would be welcomed as a poet,

27

the writer of noble verse, lofty and inspiring; as a critic, incisive, plain-spoken, honest, going to the heart of his subjects, the terror of Dagon and the Philistines; as a man, worthy of the grand name he bears. I have the pleasure of introducing Mr. Matthew Arnold." [Applause.] The audience, which then greeted Mr. Arnold with warm applause, was described as " characteristic of Boston—a grouping of men and women prominent in the leading professions and in society, whose presence insured the distinguished visitor a satisfying welcome and an intelligent reception of his ideas." The " Literature and Science," which was not new, having been originally given as the Rede Lecture at Cambridge, England, was read first in Brooklyn, in the Academy of Music, on November 19th, Dr. Richard S. Storrs introducing the lecturer. The " Emerson " was delivered first in Boston, in Chickering Hall, November 30th. These lectures were repeated in various parts of the country, " Numbers " perhaps the most frequently. The term " the remnant," as Mr. Arnold subsequently wrote home to one of his friends, went the rounds of the United States, and, he added, " I now understand what ' Dizzy ' * meant when he said that I performed a ' great achievement ' by ' launching phrases.' "]

LADIES AND GENTLEMEN:—There is a characteristic saying of Dr. Johnson: " Patriotism is the last refuge of a scoundrel." The saying is cynical, many will even call it brutal; yet it has in it something of plain, robust sense and truth. We do often see men passing themselves off as patriots, who are in truth scoundrels; we meet with talk and proceedings laying claim to patriotism, which are these gentlemen's last refuge. We may all of us agree in praying to be delivered from patriots and patriotism of this sort. Short of such, there is undoubtedly, sheltering itself under the fine name of patriotism, a good deal of self-flattery and self-delusion which is mischievous. " Things are what they are, and the consequences of them will be what they will be; why, then, should we desire to be deceived? " In that uncompromising sentence of Bishop Butler's is surely the right and salutary maxim for both individuals and nations.

Yet there is an honorable patriotism which we should satisfy if we can, and should seek to have on our side. At home I have said so much of the characters of our society and the prospects of our civilization, that I can hardly escape the like topic elsewhere. Speaking in America, I cannot well avoid saying something about the prospects

* Disraeli.

of society in the United States. It is a topic where one is apt to touch people's patriotic feelings. No one will accuse me of having flattered the patriotism of that great country of English people on the other side of the Atlantic, amongst whom I was born. Here, so many miles from home, I begin to reflect with tender contrition, that perhaps I have not—I will not say flattered the patriotism of my own countrymen enough, but regarded it enough. Perhaps that is one reason why I have produced so very little effect upon them. It was a fault of youth and inexperience. But it would be unpardonable to come in advanced life and repeat the same error here. You will not expect impossibilities of me. You will not expect me to say that things are not what, in my judgment, they are, and that the consequences of them will not be what they will be. I should make nothing of it; I should be a too palpable failure. But I confess that I should be glad if in what I say here I could engage American patriotism on my side, instead of rousing it against me. And it so happens that the paramount thoughts which your great country raises in my mind are really and truly of a kind to please, I think, any true American patriot, rather than to offend him.

The vast scale of things here, the extent of your country, your numbers, the rapidity of your increase, strike the imagination, and are a common topic for admiring remark. Our great orator, Mr. Bright, is never weary of telling us how many acres of land you have at your disposal, how many bushels of grain you produce, how many millions you are, how many more millions you will be presently, and what a capital thing this is for you. Now, though I do not always agree with Mr. Bright, I find myself agreeing with him here. I think your numbers afford a very real and important ground for satisfaction.

Not that your great numbers, or indeed great numbers of men anywhere, are likely to be all good, or even to have the majority good. " The majority are bad," said one of the wise men of Greece; but he was a pagan. Much to the same effect, however, is the famous sentence of the New Testament: " Many are called, few chosen." This appears a hard saying; frequent are the endeavors to elude

it, to attenuate its severity. But turn it how you will,
manipulate it as you will, the few, as Cardinal Newman
well says, can never mean the many.

Perhaps you will say that the majority is, sometimes,
good; that its impulses are good generally, and its action
is good occasionally. Yes, but it lacks principle, it lacks
persistence; if to-day its good impulses prevail, they suc-
cumb to-morrow; sometimes it goes right, but it is very
apt to go wrong. Even a popular orator, or a popular
journalist, will hardly say that the multitude may be trusted
to have its judgment generally just, and its actions generally virtuous. It may be better, it is better, that the
body of the people, with all its faults, should act for itself,
and control its own affairs, than that it should be set aside
as ignorant and incapable, and have its affairs managed
for it by a so-called superior class, possessing property and
intelligence. Property and intelligence cannot be trusted
to show a sound majority themselves; the exercise of
power by the people tends to educate the people. But
still, the world being what it is, we must surely expect the
aims and doings of the majority of men to be at present
very faulty, and this in a numerous community no less
than in a small one. So much we must certainly, I think,
concede to the sages and to the saints.

Sages and saints are apt to be severe, it is true; apt to
take a gloomy view of the society in which they live, and
to prognosticate evil to it. But then it must be added
that their prognostications are very apt to turn out right.
Plato's account of the most gifted and brilliant community
of the ancient world, of that Athens of his to which we all
owe so much, is despondent enough. " There is but a very
small remnant," he says, " of honest followers of wisdom,
and they who are of these few, and who have tasted how
sweet and blessed a possession is wisdom, and who can
fully see, moreover, the madness of the multitude, and that
there is no one, we may say, whose action in public matters is sound, and no ally for whosoever would help the
just, what," asks Plato, " are they to do? They may be
compared," says Plato, " to a man who has fallen among
wild beasts; he will not be one of them, but he is too un-
aided to make head against them; and before he can do

any good to society or his friends, he will be overwhelmed and perish uselessly. When he considers this, he will resolve to keep still, and to mind his own business; as it were standing aside under a wall in a storm of dust and hurricane of driving wind; and he will endure to behold the rest filled with iniquity, if only he himself may live his life clear of injustice and of impiety, and depart, when his time comes, in mild and gracious mood, with fair hope."

Plato's picture here of democratic Athens is certainly gloomy enough. We may be sure the mass of his contemporaries would have pronounced it to be monstrously overcharged. We ourselves, if we had been living then, should most of us have by no means seen things as Plato saw them. No, if we had seen Athens even nearer its end than when Plato wrote the strong words which I have been quoting, Athens in the very last days of Plato's life, we should most of us probably have considered that things were not going badly with Athens. There is a long sixteen years' administration—the administration of Eubulus —which fills the last years of Plato's life, and the middle years of the fourth century before Christ. A temperate German historian thus describes Athens during this ministry of Eubulus: "The grandeur and loftiness of Attic democracy had vanished, while all the pernicious germs contained in it were fully developed. A life of comfort and a craving for amusement were encouraged in every way, and the interest of the citizens was withdrawn from serious things. Conversation became more and more superficial and frivolous. Famous courtesans formed the chief topic of talk; the new inventions of Thearion, the leading pastry-cook in Athens, were hailed with loud applause; and the witty sayings which had been uttered in gay circles were repeated about town as matters of prime importance."

No doubt, if we had been living then to witness this, we should from time to time have shaken our heads gravely, and said how sad it all was. But most of us would not, I think, have been seriously disquieted by it. On the other hand, we should have found many things in the Athens of Eubulus to gratify us. "The democrats," says the same historian whom I have just quoted, "saw in Eubulus one

of their own set at the head of affairs;" and I suppose no
good democrat would see that without pleasure. Moreover,
Eubulus was of popular character. In one respect he
seems to have resembled your own "heathen Chinee";
he had "guileless ways," says our historian, "in which
the citizens took pleasure." He was also a good speaker,
a thorough man of business; and, above all, he was very
skilful in matters of finance. His administration was both
popular and prosperous. We should certainly have said,
most of us, if we had encountered somebody announcing
his resolve to stand aside under a wall during such an
administration, that he was a goose for his pains; and if
he had called it "a falling among wild beasts" to have
to live with his fellow-citizens who had confidence in
Eubulus, their country, and themselves, we should have
esteemed him very impertinent.

Yes;—and yet at the close of that administration of
Eubulus came the collapse, and the end of Athens as an
independent State. And it was to the fault of Athens herself that the collapse was owing. Plato was right after
all; the majority were bad, and the remnant were impotent.

So fared it with that famous Athenian State, with the
brilliant people of art and intellect. Now let us turn to
the people of religion. We have heard Plato speaking of
the very small remnant which honestly sought wisdom.
The remnant!—it is the word of the Hebrew prophets also,
and especially is it the word of the greatest of them all,
Isaiah. Not used with the despondency of Plato, used
with far other power informing it, and with a far other
future awaiting it, filled with fire, filled with hope, filled
with faith, filled with joy, this term itself, the remnant, is
yet Isaiah's term as well as Plato's. The texts are familiar
to all Christendom. "Though thy people Israel be as the
sand of the sea, only a remnant of them shall return."
Even this remnant, a tenth of the whole, if so it may be,
shall have to come back into the purging fire, and be again
cleared and further reduced there. But nevertheless, "as
a terebinth-tree, and as an oak, whose substance is in them,
though they be cut down, so the stock of that burned
tenth shall be a holy seed."

Yes, the small remnant should be a holy seed; but the

great majority, as in democratic Athens, so in the kingdom of the Hebrew nation, were unsound, and their State was doomed. This was Isaiah's point. The actual commonwealth of the "drunkards" and the "blind," as he calls them, in Israel and Judah, of the dissolute grandees and gross and foolish common people, of the great majority, must perish; its perishing was the necessary stage toward a happier future. And Isaiah was right, as Plato was right.

No doubt to most of us, if we had been there to see it, the kingdom of Ephraim or of Judah, the society of Samaria and Jerusalem, would have seemed to contain a great deal else besides dissolute grandees and foolish common people. No doubt we should have thought parts of their policy serious, and some of their alliances promising. No doubt, when we read the Hebrew prophets now, with the larger and more patient temper of a different race and an augmented experience, we often feel the blame and invective to be too absolute. Nevertheless, as to his grand point, Isaiah, I say, was right. The majority in the Jewish State, whatever they might think or say, whatever their guides and flatterers might think or say, the majority were unsound, and their unsoundness must be their ruin.

Isaiah, however, does not make his remnant confine itself, like Plato's, to standing aside under a wall during this life and then departing in mild temper and good hope when the time for departure comes; Isaiah's remnant saves the State. Undoubtedly he means to represent it as doing so. Undoubtedly he imagines his Prince of the house of David who is to be born within a year's time, his royal and victorious Immanuel, he imagines him witnessing as a child the chastisement of Ephraim and the extirpation of the bad majority there; then witnessing as a youth the chastisement of Judah and the extirpation of the bad majority there also; but finally, in mature life, reigning over a State renewed, preserved, and enlarged, a greater and happier kingdom of the chosen people.

Undoubtedly Isaiah conceives his remnant in this wise; undoubtedly he imagined for it a part which, in strict truth, it did not play, and could not play. So manifest was the non-fulfilment of his prophecy, taken strictly, that

3

ardent souls feeding upon his words had to wrest them from their natural meaning, and to say that Isaiah directly meant something which he did not directly mean. Isaiah, like Plato, with inspired insight foresaw that the world before his eyes, the world of actual life, the State and city of the unsound majority, could not stand. Unlike Plato, Isaiah announced with faith and joy a leader and a remnant certain to supersede them. But he put the leader's coming, and he put the success of the leader's and the remnant's work, far, far too soon; and his conception, in this respect, is fantastic.

Plato betook himself for the bringing in of righteousness to a visionary republic in the clouds; Isaiah—and it is the immortal glory of him and of his race to have done so—brought it in upon earth. But Immanuel and his reign, for the eighth century before Christ, were fantastic. For the kingdom of Judah they were fantastic. Immanuel and the remnant could not come to reign under the conditions there and then offered to them; the thing was impossible.

The reason of the impossibility is quite simple. The scale of things, in petty States like Judah and Athens, is too small; the numbers are too scanty. Admit that for the world, as we hitherto know it, what the philosophers and prophets say is true: that the majority are unsound. Even in communities with exceptional gifts, even in the Jewish State, the Athenian State, the majority are unsound. But there is " the remnant." Now the important thing, as regards States such as Judah and Athens, is not that the remnant bears but a small proportion to the majority; the remnant always bears a small proportion to the majority. The grave thing for States like Judah and Athens is, that the remnant must in positive bulk be so small, and therefore so powerless for reform. To be a voice outside the State, speaking to mankind or to the future, perhaps shaking the actual State to pieces in doing so, one man will suffice. But to reform the State in order to save it, to preserve it by changing it, a body of workers is needed as well as a leader;—a considerable body of workers, placed at many points, and operating in many directions.

This considerable body of workers for good is what is

wanting in petty States such as were Athens and Judah. It is said that the Athenian State had in all but 350,000 inhabitants. It is calculated that the population of the kingdom of Judah did not exceed a million and a quarter. The scale of things, I say, is here too small, the numbers are too scanty, to give us a remnant capable of saving and perpetuating the community. The remnant, in these cases, may influence the world and the future, may transcend the State and survive it; but it cannot possibly transform the State and perpetuate the State: for such a work it is numerically too feeble.

Plato saw the impossibility. Isaiah refused to accept it, but facts were too strong for him. The Jewish State could not be renewed and saved, and he was wrong in thinking that it could. And therefore I call his grand point this other, where he was altogether right: that the actual world of the unsound majority, though it fancied itself solid, and though most men might call it solid, could not stand. Let us read him again and again, until we fix in our minds this true conviction of his, to edify us whenever we see such a world existing: his indestructible conviction that such a world, with its prosperities, idolatries, oppression, luxury, pleasures, drunkards, careless women, governing classes, systems of policy, strong alliances, shall come to nought and pass away; that nothing can save it. Let us do homage, also, to his indestructible conviction that States are saved by their righteous remnant, however clearly we may at the same time recognize that his own building on this conviction was premature.

That, however, matters to us little. For how different is the scale of things in the modern States to which we belong, how far greater are the numbers! It is impossible to overrate the importance of the new element introduced into our calculations by increasing the size of the remnant. And in our great modern States, where the scale of things is so large, it does seem as if the remnant might be so increased as to become an actual power, even though the majority be unsound. Then the lover of wisdom may come out from under his wall, the lover of goodness will not be alone among the wild beasts. To enable the remnant to succeed, a large strengthening of its numbers is everything.

Here is good hope for us, not only, as for Plato's recluse, in departing this life, but while we live and work in it. Only, before we dwell too much on this hope, it is advisable to make sure that we have earned the right to entertain it. We have earned the right to entertain it only when we are at one with the philosophers and prophets in their conviction respecting the world which now is, the world of the unsound majority; when we feel what they mean, and when we go thoroughly along with them in it. Most of us, as I have said already, would by no means have been with them when they were here in life, and most of us are not really with them now. What is saving? Our institutions, says an American; the British Constitution, says an Englishman; the civilizing mission of France, says a Frenchman. But Plato and the sages, when they are asked what is saving, answer: "To love righteousness, and to be convinced of the unprofitableness of iniquity." And Isaiah and the prophets, when they are asked the same question, answer to just the same effect: that what is saving is to "order one's conversation right"; to "cease to do evil"; to "delight in the law of the Eternal"; and to "make one's study in it all day long."

The worst of it is, that this loving of righteousness and this delighting in the law of the Eternal sound rather vague to us. Not that they are vague really; indeed, they are less vague than American institutions, or the British Constitution, or the civilizing mission of France. But the phrases sound vague because of the quantity of matters they cover. The thing is to have a brief but adequate enumeration of these matters. The New Testament tells us how righteousness is composed. In England and America we have been brought up in familiarity with the New Testament. And so, before Mr. Bradlaugh on our side of the water, and the Congress of American Freethinkers on yours, banish it from our education and memory, let us take from the New Testament a text showing what it is that both Plato and the prophets mean when they tell us that we ought to love righteousness and to make our study in the law of the Eternal, but that the unsound majority do nothing of the kind. A score of texts offer themselves in a moment. Here is one which will serve very well: " Whatsoever things are true, whatsoever things are elevated, whatsoever things are just, whatsoever things are pure, whatsoever things are amiable, whatsoever things are of good report; if there be any virtue, and if there be any praise; have these in your mind, let your thoughts run upon these." [Philippians iv. 8.] That is what both Plato and the prophets mean by loving righteousness, and making one's study in the law of the Eternal.

Now the matters just enumerated do not come much into the heads of most of us, I suppose, when we are thinking of politics. But the philosophers and prophets maintain that these matters, and not those of which the heads of politicians are full, do really govern politics and save or destroy States. They save or destroy them by a silent, inexorable fatality; while the politicians are making believe, plausibly and noisily, with their American institutions, British Constitution, and civilizing mission of France. And because these matters are what do really govern politics and save or destroy States, Socrates maintained that in his time he and a few philosophers, who alone kept insisting on the good of righteousness and the unprofitableness of iniquity, were the only real politicians then living.

I say, if we are to derive comfort from the doctrine of the remnant (and there is great comfort to be derived from it), we must also hold fast to the austere but true doctrine as to what really governs politics, overrides with an inexorable fatality the combinations of the so-called politicians, and saves or destroys States. Having in mind things true, things elevated, things just, things pure, things amiable, things of good report; having these in mind, studying and loving these, is what saves States.

There is nothing like positive instances to illustrate general propositions of this kind, and to make them believed. I hesitate to take an instance from America. Possibly there are some people who think that already, on a former occasion, I have said enough about America without duly seeing and knowing it. So I will take my instances from England, and from England's neighbor and old co-mate in history, France.

The instance from England I will take first. I will take it from the grave topic of England's relations with Ireland. I am not going to reproach either England or Ireland. To reproach Ireland here would probably be indiscreet. As to England, anything I may have to say against my own countrymen I prefer to say at home; America is the last place where I should care to say it. However, I have no wish or intention now to reproach either the English or the Irish. But I want to show you from England's relations with Ireland how right the philosophers and prophets are. Every one knows that there has been conquest and confiscation in Ireland. So there has elsewhere. Every one knows that the conquest and the confiscation have been attended with cupidity, oppression, and ill-usage. So they have elsewhere. " Whatsoever things are just " are not exactly the study, so far as I know, of conquerors and confiscators anywhere; certainly they were not the study of the English conquerors of Ireland. A failure in justice is a source of danger to States. But it may be made up for and got over; it has been made up for and got over in many communities. England's confiscations in Ireland are a thing of the past; the penal laws against Catholics are a thing of the past; much has been done to make up for the old failure in justice; Englishmen generally think that it has been pretty well made up for, and that Irishmen ought to think so too. And politicians invent Land Acts for curing the last results of the old failure in justice, for insuring the contentment of the Irish with us, and for consolidating the Union: and are surprised and plaintive if it is not consolidated.

But now see how much more serious people are the philosophers and prophets than the politicians. Whatsoever things are amiable!—the failure in amiability, too, is a source of danger and insecurity to States, as well as the failure in justice. And we English are not amiable, or at any rate, what in this case comes to the same thing, do not appear so. The politicians never thought of that! Quite outside their combinations lies this hindrance, tending to make their most elaborate combinations ineffectual.

Thus the joint operation of two moral causes together—the sort of causes which politicians do not seriously regard—tells against the designs of the politicians with what seems to be an almost inexorable fatality. If there were not the failure in amiability, perhaps the original failure in justice might by this time have been got over; if there had not been the failure in justice, perhaps the failure in amiability might not have mattered much. The two failures together create a difficulty almost insurmountable. Public men in England keep saying that it will be got over. I hope that it will be got over, and that the union between England and Ireland may become as solid as that between England and Scotland. But it will not become solid by means of the contrivances of the mere politician, or without the intervention of moral causes of concord to heal the mischief wrought by moral causes of division. Everything, in this case, depends upon the " remnant," its numbers and its powers of action.

My second instance is even more important. It is so important, and its reach is so wide, that I must go into it with some little fulness. The instance is taken from France. To France I have always felt myself powerfully drawn. People in England often accuse me of liking France and things French far too well. At all events I have paid special regard to them, and am always glad to confess how much I owe to them. M. Sainte-Beuve wrote to me in the last years of his life: " You have passed through our life and literature by a deep inner line, which confers initiation, and which you will never lose." *Vous avez traversé notre vie et notre littérature par une ligne intérieure, profonde, qui fait les initiés, et que vous ne perdrez jamais.* I wish I could think that this friendly testimony of that accomplished and charming man, one of my chief benefactors, were fully deserved. But I have pride and pleasure in quoting it; and I quote it to bear me out in saying, that whatever opinion I may express about France, I have at least been a not inattentive observer of that great country, and anything but a hostile one.

The question was once asked by the town clerk of Ephesus: " What man is there that knoweth not how that the city of the Ephesians is a worshipper of the great god-

dess Diana?" Now really, when one looks at the popular
literature of the French at this moment—their popular
novels, popular stage-plays, popular newspapers—and at
the life of which this literature of theirs is the index, one
is tempted to make a goddess out of a word of their own,
and then, like the town clerk of Ephesus, to ask: "What
man is there that knoweth not how that the city of
the French is a worshipper of the great goddess Lubricity?" Or rather, as Greek is the classic and euphonious
language for names of gods and goddesses, let us take her
name from the Greek Testament, and call her the goddess
Aselgeia. That goddess has always been a sufficient power
amongst mankind, and her worship was generally supposed to need restraining rather than encouraging. But
here is now a whole popular literature, nay, and art too,
in France at her service! stimulations and suggestions by
her and to her meet one in it at every turn. She is becoming the great recognized power there; never was anything like it. M. Renan himself seems half inclined to
apologize for not having paid her more attention. "Nature cares nothing for chastity," says he; *Les frivoles ont
peut-être raison;* "The gay people are perhaps in the right."
Men even of this force salute her; but the allegiance now
paid to her, in France, by the popular novel, the popular
newspaper, the popular play, is, one may say, boundless.

I have no wish at all to preach to the French; no intention whatever, in what I now say, to upbraid or wound
them. I simply lay my finger on a fact in their present
condition; a fact insufficiently noticed, as it seems to me,
and yet extremely potent for mischief. It is well worth
while to trace the manner of its growth and action.

The French have always had a leaning to the goddess
of whom we speak, and have been willing enough to let
the world know of their leaning, to pride themselves on
their Gaulish salt, their gallantry, and so on. But things
have come to their present head gradually. Catholicism
was an obstacle; the serious element in the nation was
another obstacle. But now just see the course which things
have taken, and how they all, one may say, have worked
together for this goddess. First, there was the original
Gaul, the basis of the French nation; the Gaul, gay, so-

ciable, quick of sentiment, quick of perception; apt, however, very apt, to be presumptuous and puffed up. Then came the Roman conquest, and from this we get a new personage, the Gallo-Latin; with the Gaulish qualities for a basis, but with Latin order, reason, lucidity, added, and also Latin sensuality. Finally, we have the Frankish conquest and the Frenchman. The Frenchman proper is the Gallo-Latin, with Frankish or Germanic qualities added and infused. No mixture could be better. The Germans have plenty of faults, but in this combination they seem not to have taken hold; the Germans seem to have given of their seriousness and honesty to the conquered Gallo-Latin, and not of their brutality. And mediæval France, which exhibits the combination and balance, under the influence then exercised by Catholicism, of Gaulish quickness and gayety with Latin rationality and German seriousness, offers to our view the soundest and the most attractive stage, perhaps, in all French history.

But the balance could not be maintained; at any rate, it was not maintained. Mediæval Catholicism lost its virtue. The serious Germanic races made the Reformation, feeling that without it there was no safety and continuance for those moral ideas which they loved and which were the ground of their being. France did not go with the Reformation; the Germanic qualities in her were not strong enough to make her go with it. " France did not want a reformation which was a moral one," is Michelet's account of the matter: *La France ne voulait pas de réforme morale.* Let us put the case more favorably for her, and say that perhaps, with her quick perception, France caught sense, from the very outset, of that intellectual unsoundness and incompleteness in the Reformation, which is now so visible. But, at any rate, the Reformation did not carry France with it; and the Germanic side in the Frenchman, his Germanic qualities, thus received a check. They subsisted, however, in good force still; the new knowledge and new ideas, brought by the revival of letters, gave an animating stimulus; and in the seventeenth century the Gaulish gayety and quickness of France, the Latin rationality, and the still subsisting German seriousness, all combining under the puissant breath of the Renascence, produced a literature, the strongest, the most substantial and the most serious which the French have ever succeeded in producing, and which has, indeed, consummate and splendid excellences.

Still, the Germanic side in the Frenchman had received a check, and in the next century this side became quite attenuated. The Germanic steadiness and seriousness gave way more and more; the Gaulish salt, the Gaulish gayety, quickness, sentiment, and sociability, the Latin rationality, prevailed more and more, and had the field nearly to themselves. They produced a brilliant and most efficacious literature—the French literature of the eighteenth century. The goddess Aselgeia had her part in it; it was a literature to be praised with reserves; it was, above all, a revolutionary literature. But European institutions were then in such a superannuated condition, straightforward and just perception, free thought and rationality, were at such a discount, that the brilliant French literature in which these qualities predominated, and which by their predominance was made revolutionary, had in the eighteenth century a great mission to fulfil, and fulfilled it victoriously.

The mission is fulfilled, but meanwhile the Germanic quality in the Frenchman seems pretty nearly to have died out, and the Gallo-Latin in him has quite got the upper hand. Of course there are individuals and groups who are to be excepted; I will allow any number of exceptions you please; and in the mass of the French people, which works and is silent, there may be treasures of resource. But taking the Frenchman who is commonly in view—the usual type of speaking, doing, vocal, visible Frenchman—we may say, and he will probably be not at all displeased at our saying, that the German in him has nearly died out, and the Gallo-Latin has quite got the upper hand.

For us, however, this means that the chief source of seriousness and of moral ideas is failing and drying up in him, and that what remains are the sources of Gaulish salt, and quickness, and sentiment, and sociability, and sensuality, and rationality. And, of course, the play and working of these qualities is altered by their being no longer in combination with a dose of German seriousness, but left to work by themselves. Left to work by themselves, they give us what we call the *homme sensuel moyen*, the average sensual man. The highest art, the art which by its height, depth, and gravity possesses religiousness—such as the Greeks had, the art of Pindar and Phidias; such as the Italians had, the art of Dante and Michael Angelo—this art, with the training which it gives and the standard which it sets up, the French have never had. On the other hand, they had a dose of German seriousness, a Germanic bent for ideas of moral duty, which neither the Greeks had, nor the Italians. But if this dies out, what is left is the *homme sensuel moyen*.

This average sensual man has his very advantageous qualities. He has his gayety, quickness, sentiment, sociability, rationality. He has his horror of sour strictness, false restraint, hypocrisy, obscurantism, cretinism, and the rest of it. And this is very well; but on the serious, moral side he is almost ludicrously insufficient. Fine sentiments about his dignity and his honor and his heart, about the dignity and the honor and the heart of France, and his adoration of her, do duty for him here; grandiose phrases about the spectacle offered in France and in the French Republic of the ideal for our race, of the *épanouissement de l'élite de l'humanité*, " the coming into blow of the choice flower of humanity." In M. Victor Hugo we have (his worshippers must forgive me for saying so) the average sensual man impassioned and grandiloquent; in M. Zola we have the average sensual man going near the ground. " Happy the son," cries M. Victor Hugo, " of whom one can say, ' He has consoled his mother! ' Happy the poet of whom one can say, ' He has consoled his country! ' " The French themselves, even when they are severest, call this kind of thing by only the mild name of emphasis, " *emphase* "—other people call it fustian. And a surly Johnson will growl out in answer, at one time, that " Patriotism is the last refuge of a scoundrel "; at another time, that fine sentiments about *ma mère* are the last refuge of a scoundrel. But what they really are is the creed which in France the average sensual man rehearses, to do duty for serious moral ideas. And, as the result, we have a popular literature and a popular art serving, as has been already said, the goddess Aselgeia.

Such an art and literature easily make their way everywhere. In England and America the French literature of the seventeenth century is peculiarly fitted to do great good, and nothing but good; it can hardly be too much studied by us. And it is studied by us very little. The French literature of the eighteenth century, also, has qualities to do us much good, and we are not likely to take harm from its other qualities; we may study it to our great profit and advantage. And it is studied by us very little. The higher French literature of the present day has more knowledge and a wider range than its great predecessors, but less soundness and perfection, and it exerts much less influence than they did.

Action and influence are now with the lower literature of France, with the popular literature in the service of the goddess Aselgeia. And this popular modern French literature, and the art which corresponds to it, bid fair to make their way in England and America far better than their predecessors. They appeal to instincts so universal and accessible; they appeal, people are beginning boldly to say, to Nature herself. Few things have lately struck me more than M. Renan's dictum, which I have already quoted, about what used to be called the virtue of chastity. The dictum occurs in his very interesting autobiography, published but the other day. M. Renan, whose genius I unfeignedly admire, is, I need hardly say, a man of the most perfect propriety of life; he has told us so himself. He was brought up for a priest, and he thinks it would not have been in good taste for him to become a free liver. But this abstinence is a mere matter of personal delicacy, a display of good and correct taste on his own part in his own very special circumstances. "Nature," he cries, "cares nothing about chastity." What a slap in the face to the sticklers for "Whatsoever things are pure"!

I have had to take a long sweep to arrive at the point which I wished to reach. If we are to enjoy the benefit, I said, of the comfortable doctrine of the remnant, we must be capable of receiving also, and of holding fast, the hard doctrine of the unsoundness of the majority, and of the certainty that the unsoundness of the majority, if it is not withstood and remedied, must be their ruin. And therefore, even though a gifted man like M. Renan may be so carried away by the tide of opinion in France where he lives, as to say that Nature cares nothing about chastity, and to see with amused indulgence the worship of the great goddess Lubricity, let us stand fast, and say that her worship is against nature, human nature, and that it is ruin. For this is the test of its being against human nature, that for human societies it is ruin. And the test is one from which there is no escape, as from the old tests in such matters there may be. For if you allege that it is the will of God that we should be pure, the sceptical Gallo-Latins will tell you that they do not know any such person. And in like manner, if it is said that those who serve the goddess Aselgeia shall not inherit the kingdom of God, the Gallo-Latin may tell you that he does not believe in any such place. But that the sure tendency and upshot of things establishes that the service of the goddess Aselgeia is ruin, that her followers are marred and stunted by it and disqualified for the ideal society of the future, is an infallible test to employ.

The saints admonish us to let our thoughts run upon whatsoever things are pure, if we would inherit the kingdom of God; and the divine Plato tells us that we have within us a many-headed beast and a man, and that by dissoluteness we feed and strengthen the beast in us, and starve the man; and finally, following the divine Plato among the sages at a humble distance, comes the prosaic and unfashionable Paley, and says in his precise way that " this vice has a tendency, which other species of vice have not so directly, to unsettle and weaken the powers of the understanding; as well as, I think, in a greater degree than other vices, to render the heart thoroughly corrupt." True; and once admitted and fostered, it eats like a canker, and with difficulty can ever be brought to let go its hold again, but forever tightens it. Hardness and insolence come in its train; an insolence which grows until it ends by exasperating and alienating everybody; a hardness which grows until the man can at last scarcely take pleasure in anything, outside the service of his goddess, except cupidity and greed, and cannot be touched with emotion by any language except fustian. Such are the fruits of the worship of the great goddess Aselgeia.

So, instead of saying that Nature cares nothing about chastity, let us say that human nature, our nature, cares about it a great deal. Let us say that, by her present popular literature, France gives proof that she is suffering from a dangerous and perhaps fatal disease; and that it is not clericalism which is the real enemy to the French so much as their goddess; and if they can none of them see this themselves, it is only a sign of how far the disease has gone, and the case is so much the worse. The case is so much the worse; and for men in such case to be so vehemently busy about clerical and dynastic intrigues at home, and about alliances and colonial acquisitions and purifications of the flag abroad, might well make one borrow of the prophets and exclaim, " Surely ye are perverse "! perverse to neglect your really pressing matters for those secondary ones.

And when the ingenious and inexhaustible M. Blowitz, of our great London " Times," who sees everybody and knows everything, when he expounds the springs of politics and the causes of the fall and success of ministries, and the combinations which have not been tried but should be, and takes upon him the mystery of things in the way with which we are so familiar—to this wise man himself one is often tempted, again, to say with the prophets: " Yet the Eternal also is wise, and will not call back his words." M. Blowitz is not the only wise one; the Eternal has His wisdom also, and somehow or other it is always the Eternal's wisdom which at last carries the day. The Eternal has attached to certain moral causes the safety or the ruin of States, and the present popular literature of France is a sign that she has a most dangerous moral disease.

Now if the disease goes on and increases, then, whatever sagacious advice M. Blowitz may give, and whatever political combinations may be tried, and whether France gets colonies or not, and whether she allies herself with this nation or with that, things will only go from bad to worse with her; she will more and more lose her powers of soul and spirit, her intellectual productiveness, her skill in counsel, her might for war, her formidableness as a foe, her value as an ally, and the life of that famous State will be more and more impaired, until it perish. And this is that hard but true doctrine of the sages and prophets, of the inexorable fatality of operation, in moral failure of the unsound majority, to impair and destroy States.

But we will not talk or think of destruction for a State with such gifts and graces as France, and which has had such a place in history, and to which we, many of us, owe so much delight and so much good. And yet if France had no greater numbers than the Athens of Plato or the Judah of Isaiah, I do not see how she could well escape out of the throttling arms of her goddess and recover. She must recover through a powerful and profound renewal, a great inward change, brought about by " the remnant " amongst her people; and, for this, a remnant small in numbers would not suffice. But in a France of thirty-five millions, who shall set bounds to the numbers of the remnant, or to its effectualness and power of victory?

In these United States (for I come round to the United States at last) you are fifty millions and more. I suppose that, as in England, as in France, as everywhere, so likewise here, the majority of people doubt very much whether the majority is unsound; or, rather, they have no doubt at all about the matter, they are sure that it is not unsound. But let us consent to-night to remain to the end in the ideas of the sages and prophets whom we have been following all along; and let us suppose that in the present actual stage of the world, as in all the stages through which the world has passed hitherto, the majority is and must be in general unsound everywhere—even in the United States, even here in New York itself. Where is the failure?

I have already, in the past, speculated in the abstract about you, perhaps, too much. But I suppose that in a democratic community like this, with its newness, its magnitude, its strength, its life of business, its sheer freedom and equality, the danger is in the absence of the discipline of respect; in hardness and materialism, exaggeration and boastfulness; in a false smartness, a false audacity, a want of soul and delicacy. " Whatsoever things

are elevated "—whatsoever things are nobly serious, have
true elevation [″Οσα σεμνά]—that perhaps, in our catalogue
of maxims which are to possess the mind, is the maxim
which points to where the failure of the unsound majority,
in a great democracy like yours, will probably lie. At any
rate let us for the moment agree to suppose so. And the
philosophers and the prophets, whom I at any rate am
disposed to believe, and who say that moral causes govern
the standing and the falling of States, will tell us that the
failure to mind whatsoever things are elevated must impair with an inexorable fatality the life of a nation, just
as the failure to mind whatsoever things are just, or whatsoever things are amiable, or whatsoever things are pure,
will impair it; and that if the failure to mind whatsoever
things are elevated should be real in your American
democracy, and should grow into a disease, and take firm
hold on you, then the life of even these great United States
must inevitably suffer and be impaired more and more,
until it perish.

Then from this hard doctrine we will betake ourselves
to the more comfortable doctrine of the remnant. " The
remnant shall return; " shall " convert and be healed " itself first, and shall then recover the unsound majority.
And you are fifty millions and growing apace. What a
remnant yours may be, surely! A remnant of how great
numbers, how mighty strength, how irresistible efficacy!
Yet we must not go too fast, either, nor make too sure of
our efficacious remnant. Mere multitude will not give us
a saving remnant with certainty. The Assyrian Empire
had multitude, the Roman Empire had multitude; yet
neither the one nor the other could produce a sufficing
remnant any more than Athens or Judah could produce
it, and both Assyria and Rome perished like Athens and
Judah.

But you are something more than a people of fifty millions. You are fifty millions mainly sprung, as we in England are mainly sprung, from that German stock which
has faults indeed—faults which have diminished the extent
of its influence, diminished its power of attraction and the
interest of its history, and which seems moreover just now,
from all I can see and hear, to be passing through a not

very happy moment, morally, in Germany proper. Yet of
the German stock it is, I think, true, as my father said
more than fifty years ago, that it has been a stock " of the
most moral races of men that the world has yet seen, with
the soundest laws, the least violent passions, the fairest
domestic and civil virtues." You come, therefore, of
about the best parentage which a modern nation can have.
Then you have had, as we in England have also had, but
more entirely than we and more exclusively, the Puritan
discipline. Certainly I am not blind to the faults of that
discipline. Certainly I do not wish it to remain in possession of the field forever, or too long. But as a stage
and a discipline, and as means for enabling that poor inattentive and immoral creature, man, to love and appropriate and make part of his being divine ideas, on which
he could not otherwise have laid or kept hold, the discipline of Puritanism has been invaluable; and the more
I read history, the more I see of mankind, the more I
recognize its value.

Well, then, you are not merely a multitude of fifty millions; you are fifty millions sprung from this excellent
Germanic stock, having passed through this excellent
Puritan discipline, and set in this enviable and unbounded
country. Even supposing, therefore, that by the necessity
of things your majority must in the present stage of the
world probably be unsound, what a remnant, I say—what
an incomparable, all-transforming remnant — you may
fairly hope with your numbers, if things go happily, to
have!

HENRY WARD BEECHER

Photogravure after a photograph from life

HENRY WARD BEECHER

THE REIGN OF THE COMMON PEOPLE

[Lecture by Henry Ward Beecher (born in Litchfield, Conn., June 24, 1813; died in Brooklyn, N. Y., March 8, 1887), delivered first in Exeter Hall, London, August 19, 1886, when making his last tour of England, Scotland, and Ireland. The chairman on the occasion, Mr. Benjamin Scott, Lord Chamberlain of the City of London, was the same gentleman who presided when Mr. Beecher spoke in the same hall at the close of his previous visit to Great Britain in 1863, in the height of the American Civil War. Upon taking the chair Mr. Scott recalled the meeting in this place twenty-three years before, and remarked that he had never regretted the part he took in it; he was present to act in a similar capacity now, as then, in response to Mr. Beecher's request. The audience was distinguished by the presence of a number of eminent English clergymen.]

LADIES AND GENTLEMEN:—The noise [referring to the applause and cheers with which he was greeted, the audience standing during the demonstration] very vividly recalls twenty-three years ago, although it is of a very different kind to what it was then. Twenty-three years in a man's life corrects a great many hasty impressions, gives more solidity and more sagacity of judgment. When I look back upon all the things that happened at and before the time that I was here, I can scarcely reproach the English people for their misjudgment of the meaning of that great issue which God was trying by the arbitrament of the sword. It is not strange. At that time the thought, the feeling, the institutions, the tendency, the genius of the American people were very little known abroad; they are better understood now; and notwithstanding the temporary and not unnatural irritation which prevailed when England was neutral, to say the least, with the passing away of that cloud a better feeling prevails everywhere. The pride of heritage comes to every generous American bosom; we are a younger oak than you are, but you bore the acorns which were planted for us, and we are of your lineage and of your blood, and if you are not proud of us we will make you so before we have done.

It has been the effect of modern investigation to throw light without illumination upon the most interesting period of human history. When the old chronology prevailed, and it was thought that this world was built about six thousand years ago, men had of necessity one way of looking at things; but now it is agreed upon all hands that we cannot count the chronology of this world by thousands, more likely by millions, of years. Nor was the system of immediation in creation which prevailed at the time favorable to the discovery of truth. God who dwells in eternity has time enough to build worlds which require millions of years; and whatever may be the cause of the origin of the human race, and I have my own opinion on that subject—confidential, however—I think it may be said that the earliest appearance of man upon earth was in the savage condition. He began as low down as he could and be a man rather than an animal, and the question of profound interest is one that can probably never be answered except by guess—and guess is not philosophy altogether—How did man emerge from that savage condition? There were then no schools, no churches, no prophets, no priests, no books, presses—nothing. Wild tribes in the wild wilderness, how did they come toward civilization? You say that the first industries were those that supplied appetite—food, shelter, clothing. That is doubtless true, although we only infer it. But how did the brain, which is the organ of the man, begin to unfold— not the simple knowledge that lay close in the neighborhood of every man, but how did it come to build institutions, found communities, and develop them, till now the human race in civilized countries are as far removed from their ancestors as their ancestors were from the animals below them? It is on this broad field that light falls, but not illumination. But later down, supposing that industries were educators, supposing that men were educated by war itself, by combinations required by skill and leadership, by ten thousand forms of growing social life, by the love of property, the instinct that is fundamental to human nature—suppose that all this indirectly evolved the intelligence of the human family, how do we come at length to the period in which the unfolding of the hidden powers of the human soul became an object of direct instruction?

The earliest attempt to develop men, on purpose, was in Egypt, so far as we know. The Egyptian school has all the marks in it of antiquity and of primitive development, for it was limited in the numbers admitted and limited in the topics taught. Only the royal family could go to the schools of Egypt. That included, of course, the priesthood; and putting aside some slight mathematical teaching, it is probable that mysteries and superstitions were the whole subjects taught, and that mainly to teach men how to be hierarchs or rulers of some sort. When we cross over the sea to Greece, at a period much later, though how much we know not, we find that schools had developed, and that the idea of making more of men than natural law makes of them, or the casual influences of human society—the attempt directly to train intelligence and to produce knowledge—was farther advanced; for anybody could go to a Greek school that had the means to pay— anybody but slaves and women: they trained very near together in antiquity, and they are not quite far enough apart yet. And yet I am bound to correct myself when I say that women were not privileged; they were. It is probable that in no period of human history has more pains been taken with the education of women than was taken in Greece. In all their accomplishments, in learning, in music, in the dance, in poetry, in literature, in history, in philosophy, even in statesmanship, women were very highly educated, provided they were to live the lives of courtesans. The fact is simply astounding that in the age of Pericles intelligence and accomplishments were associated with impudicity, and were the signs of it, and that ignorance and modesty were associated ideas. If a woman would have the credit of purity and uprightness in social relations she must be the drudge of the household, and if any woman radiant in personal beauty and accomplished, fitted for conversation with statesmen and philosophers, appeared, it was taken for granted that she was accessible.

We have a side-light thrown on this subject in the New Testament, not well understood hitherto. That noble old Jewish book, the Bible, reveals a higher station to womanhood in the ancient Israelitish days than in any other Oriental land; and from the beginning of the Old Testament to the end of it there is no limitation of a woman's rights, her functions, and her position. She actually was public in the sense of honor and function; she went with unveiled face if she pleased; she partook of religious services and led them; she was a judge, she was even a leader of armies; and you shall not find, either in the Old Testament or in the New, one word that limits the position of a woman till you come to the Apostle's writings about Grecian women; for only in Corinthians and in the writings of Paul to Timothy, who was the bishop of the Greek Churches in Asia Minor, do you find any limitation made. Knowing full well what this public sentiment was, Paul said: "Suffer not a woman to teach in your assemblies, let your women keep silence." Why? Because, all, in that corrupt public sentiment, looking upon intelligent teachers in the Christian Church would have gone away and said: "It is all done of licentiousness, women are teaching;" and in a public sentiment that associated intelligence and immorality, it is not strange that, prudentially and temporarily, women were restrained. But that has all gone, woman has risen, not only in intelligence, but as the universal teacher; not alone in the household, but in the school; not alone in common schools, but in every grade, till she has attained professorships in universities and even presidency in women's colleges—at least in our land. She is the right hand of the charities of the church; she walks unblushing with an unveiled face where men do walk; and she is not only permitted in the great orthodox churches of New England to speak in meeting, but when they send her abroad, ordained to teach the Gospel to the heathen, there she is permitted to preach; and when they come home women may still teach in a hall, but not in a church, and dear old men there are yet so conservative that they are reading through golden spectacles their Bibles, and saying: "I suffer not a woman to preach."

We hardly can trace the unfolding of human intelligence after it plunged into that twilight or darkness of the Middle Ages. Then we begin to find intelligence developed through mechanical guilds, and in various ways of commerce; but schools, such as we now understand schools to be, are very imperfectly traced out in the Middle Ages. But when that new impulse came to the moral nature, and the civil nature, and the intellectual and philosophical nature, to art, to literature, to learning—when the Reformation came, whose scope was not ecclesiastical alone by any means—it was a resurrection of the human intelligence throughout its whole vast domain—schools began to appear to be, as John Milton says,

"Raked embers out of the ashes of the past,"

and they began to glow again. And from that time on, the progress of the efforts to develop, by actual teaching, human intelligence grows broader, brighter, and more effectual down to our present day; and to-day in the principal nations of Europe education is compulsory, the education not of favored classes, not of the children of the wealthy, not of those that have inherited genius, but the children of the common people. It is held that it is unsafe for a State to raise ignorant men. Ignorant men are like bombs, which are a great deal better to be shot into an enemy's camp than to be kept at home, for where an ignorant man goes off he scatters desolation; and it is not safe to have ignorant men, for an ignorant man is an animal, and the stronger his passions and the feebler his conscience and intellect, the more dangerous he is. Therefore, for the sake of the commonwealth, our legislators wisely, whether they be republican institutions or monarchical institutions or aristocratical institutions, have at last joined hands on one thing—that it is best to educate the people's children, from the highest to the lowest everywhere. [Applause.]

And what, in connection with various other general causes, has been the result of this unfolding of intelligence among the common people? It has not yet gone down to the bottom; there is a strata of undeveloped intelligence among the nations of Europe certainly; I am not speaking now of the residuum that falls down from the top like the slime of the ocean, but of those who are reasonable and honest and virtuous and useful. It may be said that, as the sun touches the tops of the mountains first and works its way downward through the valley later and later in the day, so there is very much to be done in Europe yet to bear knowledge and intelligence, which is better than knowledge, to the lowest classes of the common people. But even in this condition, what has been the result in Europe of the education of the common people? All those heavings, all those threatened revolutions, all those civil and commercial developments that are like the waves of the sea, are springing from the fact that God in His providence has thrown light and intelligence upon the great under-mass of society; and the under-parts of society, less fortunate in every respect than those that are advanced, are seeking room to develop themselves; they are seeking to go up, and no road has been found along which they can travel as yet. I do not believe in Nihilism in Russia. If I had been born and brought up there, and had felt the heel on my neck, I would have been a Nihilist. I am poor stuff to make an obedient slave out of! Nevertheless, they are like blind men trying to find their way into the open air, and if they stumble or go into wrong departments, are they to be derided and cursed? Because they are seeking to construct a government after they shall have destroyed government and made a wilderness, are they, because they are doing the best they know how— are they, therefore, to be cursed? or pitied, better directed, emancipated? When they come to America to teach us how to make commonwealths, we think they are out of place, decidedly. Well, that is our trait. We thank Europe for a great deal—for literature, ancient and modern; we thank Europe for teachers in art, in color, in form, in sound; we are grateful for all these things; but when the Socialists of Germany, and the Communists of France, and the Nihilists of Russia come to teach us how to reorganize human society, they have come to the wrong place. Their ignorance is not our enlightenment. [Applause.]

The main cause of all this, the cause of causes, lies in the swelling of the intelligence of the great, hitherto neglected, and ignorant masses of Europe. They are seeking elevation, they are seeking a larger life, and as men grow in intelligence life must grow too. When a man is an animal he does not want much except straw and fodder; but when a man begins to be a rational and intelligent creature, he wants a good deal more than the belly asks; for reason wants something, taste needs something, conscience needs something; every faculty brought into ascendancy and power is a new hunger, and must be supplied. No man is so cheap as the brutal, ignorant man; no man can rise up from the lower stations of life and not need more for his support from the fact that he is civilized and Christianized, and although he may not have it individually, the community must supply it for him. He must have resources of knowledge, he must have means of refinement, he must have limitations of taste or he feels himself slipping backward; and as I look upon the phenomena of society in Europe it is the phenomena of God calling to the great masses of a growingly enlightened people, " Come up," and they are saying, " Which way? By what road? How? " And they must needs pass through the experiment of ignorance, tentative ignorance, and failure in a thousand things. They must pass through these preliminary stages, for as it was necessary when they came out of the bondage of Egypt that the children of Israel should go through the wilderness for forty years, so all people have to go forty years and more through the wilderness of mistake, through the wilderness of trials and attempts that fail; and it may be said, indeed, that the pyramid of permanent society is built up on blocks of blunders, and it is mistakes that have pointed out the true way to mankind. Now what has taken place among the common people? Once they thought about their own cottage and their own little steading; they have gradually learned to think about the whole neighborhood. Once they were able to look after their own limited affairs; they recognize the community of men, and are beginning to think about the affairs of other men—as the Apostle said: " Look ye every man on his own things, but also every man on the things of others." They are having a society interest among themselves. Once they had limited thoughts and bits of knowledge; now they have the mother of knowledge—intelligence; they are competent to think, to choose discriminately; they are competent to organize themselves; they are learning that self-denial by which men can work in masses of men; they are beginning to have a light in light transcendentally higher than the old contentment of the bestial state of miserable labor in miserable Europe. [Applause.] Such are the results, briefly stated, to which God in His providence has brought the masses of the common people, and the promise of the future is brighter even than the fulfilment of the past. What the issues will be and what the final fruits will be God knows and man does not know!

Now, if you cross the sea to our own land, my own land, the land of my fathers, we shall find that there are influences tending to give power to the brain, alertness, quickness; to give to it also a wider scope and range than it has in the average of the laboring classes in Europe. Here and there are communities, which if transplanted on the other shore, will scarcely know that they were not born and brought up there; but this is not true of the great mass of the common people of all Europe. Our climate is stimulating. Ship-masters tell me that they cannot drink in New York as they do in Liverpool. Heaven help Liverpool! There is more oxygen in our air. It has some importance in this, that anything that gives acuteness, vivacity, spring, to the substance of the brain prepares it for education and larger intelligence. A dull, watery, sluggish brain may do for a conservative; but God never made them to be the fathers of progress. They are very useful as brakes on the wheel down hill; but they never would draw anything up hill in the world. And yet, in the fanatic influence that tends to give vitality and quickness, force and continuity to the human brain, lies the foundation for the higher style of manhood; and although it is not to be considered as a primary and chief cause of smartness, if you will allow that word, yet it is one among others. And then, when the child is born on the other side, he is born into an atmosphere of expectation. He is not out of the cradle before he learns that he has got to earn his own living; he is hereditarily inspired with the idea of money. Sometimes, when I see babies in the cradle apparently pawing the air, I think that they are making change in their own minds of future bargains. But this has great force as an educating element in early childhood: " You will be poor if you do not exert yourself; " and at every future stage it lies with each man what his condition in society is to be.

This becomes a very powerful developer of the cerebral mass, and from it comes intelligence and power of intellect. And then, up side of that, when he goes into life the whole style of society tends toward intense cerebral excitability. For instance, as to business, I find in London that you may go down at nine o'clock and there is nobody in his office; at ten o'clock the clerks are there, at eleven o'clock some persons do begin to appear. By that time the Yankees have got half through the day. And it is in excess; it is carried to a fault; for men there are ridden by two demons. They desire excessive property—I do not know that they are much distinguished from their ancestors—they desire more than enough for the uses of the family, and when a man wants more money than he can use he wants too much. But they have the ambition of property, which is accursed, or should be. Property may be used in large masses to develop property, and co-ordinated estates may do work that single estates cannot do; I am not, therefore, speaking of vast enterprises like railroads and factories. But the individual man thinks in the beginning, " If I could only make myself worth a hundred thousand dollars, I should be willing to retire from business." Not a bit of it. A hundred thousand dollars is only an index of five hundred thousand; and when he has come to five hundred thousand he is like Moses—and very unlike him—standing on the top of the mountain and looking over the promised land, and he says to himself, " A million! a million! " and a million draws another million, until at last he has more than he can use, more than is useful to him, and he won't give it away—not till after his death. That is cheap benevolence. [Applause.] Well, this is the first element of mistake among large classes of commercial life in America.

The second is, they want it suddenly. They are not willing to say, " For forty years I will lay gradually the foundations, and build the golden stones one above another." No; they want grass lands. They want to win by gambling, for that is gambling when a man wants money without having given a fair equivalent for it. And so they press nature to her utmost limits till the very diseases of our land are changing; men are dropping dead with heart disease; men are dropping dead—it is paralysis; men are dropping dead—it is Bright's disease. Ah! it is the violence done to the brain by excessive industry, through excessive hours, and through excessive ambition, which is but another name for excessive avarice.

But outside of that there is still another excitement, and that is politics. Now, you in this insular and cool climate are never excited in politics at all; but we are in our sunshiny land. Especially are we so once in four years, when the great quadrennial election comes off, and when the most useless thing on God's earth is built on God's earth—namely, a political platform, which men never use and never stand on after it is once built. Then the candidates are put forth, and every newspaper editor, and every public-spirited citizen and elector goes before the people and declares to them that the further existence of the Government depends on the election of both parties. [Laughter.] Now, nations have a wondrous way of continuing to live after they are doomed to death, and we contrive to get along from four years to four years. Nevertheless the excitement is prodigious. Men say these wild excitements are not wholesome, I say they are the best things that can happen to the community. I say the best speeches of the community scattered through the land, discussing finance, taxes, education, are the education of the common people, and they learn more in a year of universal debate than they would in twenty years of reading and thinking without such help.

Well, outside of that there is still another excitement, and that is in the Church, which is the hottest place of all.

I do not mean a torrid heat; I do not mean a fuliginous kind of heat; I mean simply this—honest—that, even under its poorest administration, religion brings to bear upon the human brain the most permanent and the most profound excitements that are known to humanity. Now, if you take denominations as they are now, you could not illustrate much by them, for they are mere incidents in the history of time, and they are no permanent, cohesive, systematic developments. You must shuffle the cards and have a new deal for an illustration, and I divide all Christian denominations into three sections: those that work by doctrines, those that work by emotion, and those that work by devotion. The men that work by doctrines are men that think they have found out the universe; they have not only got it, but they have formulated it; they know all about the Infinite, they have sailed round Eternity, they know all about the Eternal and the Everlasting God, and you will hear them discuss questions of theology: " Now, God could not, consistent with consistency, do so-and-so." They know all His difficulties; they know how He got round them. One might easily come to think that God was their next-door neighbor. Well, after all, whether it is true or false—their systematic views, their dogmas— the pedagogic views are very important to teach young and middle-aged and old to attempt, by philosophic reasoning, to reach into these unfathomable depths. They produce a power upon the brain of most transcendent importance; they in their way may not increase the sum of human knowledge, but they increase the capacity of the human brain for profound thought and investigation.

Then there are the joyous churches, that love hallelujahs, songs, hymns—revival churches, Moody and Sankey movements, Methodist movements of all kinds. I need not undertake to show you that this emotion tends to produce cerebral activity, and has an educating force in regard to the facility with which the brain acts.

Then there come those churches that run on devotion, formulated prayers, printed services. One would not think that stereotyped prayers read in the dim light of a painted window would produce great conflagration! Nor, indeed, do they. But when you come to the inner life [a Voice:

" We cannot hear! "]—that was a part I did not want you to hear [laughter]—when you come to look at the interior life of these churches, you shall find that their charities, their sense of responsibility to the weak and the poor and to the ignorant, are perpetually acting as an inward fire, and developing intelligence in ways not common to the other forms of religious worship.

Well, what has been the result of all these influences which have been superadded to those universal stimuli to which all the civilized world outside of our land has been subject? What has been the result on our side? We have 60,000,000 men, women, and children in America; we have common schools for every living soul that is born on that continent—except the Chinese. Now, in the States where, twenty-five years ago, it was a penitentiary offence to teach a slave how to read, we are sending out a thousand educated colored teachers to teach schools, to practice law and medicine through the colored population of the South; the Government is enlisted in their behalf, and the States are proud of their colored schools that a little time ago would have burnt a man who dared to advocate the education of the slave. We are the harbor to which all the sails of the world crowd with emigrants, and we bless God for it. Their letters go back thicker than leaves in autumn, to those that are left behind; and we have a vast population from Spain, from Portugal, from Italy, from Hungary, from Austria, from Germany, from Russia; we have a vast population from all the Scandinavian lands, from Scotland, from England, and occasionally from Ireland. Let them come; if you don't want them, we do. It takes a little time, you know, to get them used to things; but whenever the children of foreign emigrants, of whom we have 8,000,000 born and bred in our land; whenever these children have gone through our common-schools, they are just as good Americans as if they had not had foreign parents. The common-schools are the stomachs of the Republic, and when a man goes in there he comes out, after all, American.

Well, now, we are playing the experiment before the world on a tremendous scale, and the world does not quite believe in it. I do. They say: " With regard to your success in government of the people, by the people, for the people, in the language of the Liturgy, you are dependent upon extraneous conditions; it is not philosophically to be inferred from the principles of your government; you have got so much land, wait till the struggle for existence takes place, as in the denser populations of Europe, and then you will find that self-government will be but flimsy to hold men's passions in check, and then, by and by, you will go from anarchy to a centralized and strong government." I do not blame them for thinking so. If I had been brought up as they have been, perhaps I should think so; but they do not understand it; they do not understand the facts which actually are in existence, and are fundamental. For we are not attempting to build Society; we are by Society attempting to build the individual. We hold that the State is strong in the proportion in which every individual in that State is free, large, independent. You have a finer educated upper class than we; you have nobler and deeper scholars in greater numbers than we have; you have institutions, compared with which ours are puny; you are educating the top, we are educating society from the bottom to the top; we are not attempting to lift favored classes higher; we are not attempting to give to those that already have; we are attempting to put our hands under the foundations of human life, and lift everybody up. That is a slower work; but when it is done and its fruits are ripe you will never doubt again which is the wisest and best policy.

I do not suppose that if you were to go and look upon the experiment of self-government in America you would have a very high opinion of it. I have not either if I just look on the surface of things. Why, men will say: " It stands to reason that 60,000,000 ignorant of law, ignorant of constitutional history, ignorant of jurisprudence, of finance, and taxes and tariffs and forms of currency—60,000,000 people that never studied these things—are not fit to rule. Your diplomacy is as complicated as ours, and it is the most complicated on earth, for all things grow in complexity as they develop toward a higher condition. What fitness is there in these people? Well, it is not democracy merely; it is a representative democracy. Our people do not vote in mass for anything; they pick out captains of thought, they pick out the men that do know, and they send them to the Legislature to think for them, and then the people afterward ratify or disallow them.

But when you come to the Legislature I am bound to confess that the thing does not look very much more cheering on the outside. Do they really select the best men? Yes; in times of danger they do very generally, but in ordinary time "kissing goes by favor." What is that dandy in the Legislature for? His father was an eminent judge, and they thought it would be a compliment to the old gentleman to send his son up to the Legislature, not because he knows anything, but because his father does. It won't do to make too close an inquisition as to why people are in legislatures. What is that weasel-faced lawyer doing there? Well, there may be ten or twenty gentlemen who wanted legislation that would favor their particular property interest instead of the commonwealth, and they wanted somebody to wriggle a bill through the Legislature; and so he sits for the commonwealth. That great blustrous man squeezing on the front seats; what is he there for? He? He could shake hands with more mothers, kiss more pretty girls and more babies, and tell more funny stories in an hour than any other man in a month, and so they send him up to make laws. [Laughter.] When they get there it would do your heart good just to go and look at them. You know what the duty of a regular Republican-Democratic legislator is. It is to get back again next winter. His second duty is what? His second duty is to put himself under that extraordinary providence that takes care of legislators' salaries. The old miracle of the prophet and the meal and the oil is outdone immeasurably in our days, for they go there poor one year, and go home rich; in four years they become money-lenders, all by a trust in that gracious providence that takes care of legislators' salaries. Their next duty after that is to serve the party that sent them up, and then, if there is anything left of them, it belongs to the commonwealth. Some one has said very wisely, that if a man travelling wishes to relish his dinner he had better not go into the kitchen to see where it is cooked: if any man wishes to

respect and obey the law, he had better not go to the
Legislature to see where that is cooked. This, I presume,
is entirely an American point of view. [Applause.]

Well, there are a great many more faults in self-government, but time will not permit me to enumerate them all,
and yet I say that self-government is the best government
that ever existed on the face of the earth. How should
that be with all these damaging facts? "By their fruits
ye shall know them." What a government is, is to be
determined by the kind of people it raises, and I will defy
the whole world in time past, and in time present, to show
so vast a proportion of citizens so well off, so contented,
so remunerated by their toil. The average of happiness
under our self-government is greater than it ever has been,
or can be, found under any sky, or in any period of human
history. And the philosophical reason is not far to find;
it belongs to that category in which a worse thing is sometimes a great deal better than a better thing. William
has been to school for over a year, and his teacher says
to him one day: "Now, William, I am afraid your father
will think that I am not doing well by you; you must
write a composition—you must send your father a good
composition to show what you are doing." Well, William
never did write a composition, and he does not know how.
"Oh, write about something that you do know about—
write about your father's farm," and so, being goaded to
his task, William says: "A cow is a useful animal. A
cow has four legs and two horns. A cow gives good milk.
I love good milk.—William Bradshaw." The master looks
over his shoulder, and says: "Pooh! your father will
think you are a cow. Here, give me that composition,
I'll fix it." So he takes it home and fixes it. Here it
reads: "When the sun casts off the dusky garments of
the night, and appearing o'er the orient hills, sips the dew-
drops pendant from every leaf, the milkmaid goes afield
chanting her matin song," and so on, and so on. [Ap-
plause.] Now I say that, rhetorically, the master's composition was unspeakably better than William's; but as a
part of William's education, his poor scrawly lines are unspeakably better than the one that has been "fixed" for
him. No man ever yet learned by having somebody else

learn for him. A man learns arithmetic by blunder in and
blunder out, but at last he gets it. A man learns to write
through scrawling; a man learns to swim by going into
the water, and a man learns to vote by voting. Now we
are not attempting to make a government; we are attempting to teach 60,000,000 of men how to conduct a government by self-control, by knowledge, by intelligence, by
fair opportunity to practise. It is better that we should
have 60,000,000 of men learning through their own mistakes how to govern themselves, than it is to have an
arbitrary government with the whole of the rest of the
people ignorant.

Thus far I have spoken of the relation of the development of the common people—their relations to political
economy and to government and politics, but I have left
out the more important, the less traversed part. I affirm
that the intelligence of the great mass of the common people has a direct bearing upon Science, upon Art, upon
Morality, upon Religion itself. It would not seem as
though the men that were superior in education and
knowledge could receive anything from those below; perhaps not, perhaps yes, for that which education gives is
more nearly artificial than that which is inspired by the
dominant sense and lower condition of the human mind
that unites people in greater mass. Why, two hundred
years ago there was but one doctor in the village; nobody
but him knew anything of medicine. To-day, hygiene and
physiology are taught in our schools, are spread abroad
by newspapers or in lectures, or from the pulpit, and the
common people, at any rate in our land, have their divi-
dends of human knowledge. A woman that has brought
up six children knows more about medicine than the village
doctor two hundred years ago did. Two hundred years
ago nobody knew anything about law but the judge and
the counsellors. To-day everybody knows something
about law. We have broken open the arcana, we have distributed its treasures of knowledge, and the laborer knows
something about law, the farmer, the mechanic, the merchant—everybody has an elementary knowledge of law.
Has it destroyed the profession of the law? There never
were so many highly educated men as now in the pro-

fession of the law, never were they more trustworthy and honorable, never had larger interests put into their hands, never had larger fees, and never were more willing to have them than they are now. They do not suffer by the intelligence of the common people which comes from distribution of the elementary forms of professional knowledge.

Well, how is it with regard to the Church? Just the same; just the same. Three hundred years ago there was but one Bible in a parish in England, and that was chained to a column in the church; and there was but one man to read it—the priest. And the people did not understand it then, and it was a part of official duty to go from house to house on the theory that the average parent did not know enough to teach the children the first principles of morality and of religion. Go to-day over the same community, and on the Sabbath morning you shall see the girls and the young men with Bibles under their arms, themselves teachers, going down to mission schools, going down to instruct their inferiors. The profession has distributed its functions among the common people. Has it destroyed the profession? It never was stronger, never was as strong as it is to-day. Thank God as to mere professional nomination, say by ordination, say by some endowment from without, there never was a time when they had so little influence since the Advent as they have to-day: and it is growing less and less, and with the ages they will grow so pale that they cannot cast a shadow. There never was a time when the man of God, because he was a man moved by the Holy Spirit of God to unfold his own moral consciousness, living among men, tied to them by no other ties than the sympathies of love, there never was a time when he had so much influence as he has to-day. [Applause.] And let me say that with regard to the title "ministers of the Gospel" everywhere, who have great and proper influence, it is not the paraphernalia, but it is the man inside of all these things that is the power. An ennobled manhood is coming into a position of influence in this world that it never had in any other period, nor in any other nation. This great English stock is the root, as the Germanic from which it sprung, of the grandest manhood that ever has been; but the stature has yet to be greater, and the power and the character are yet to be greater. Now, has it changed the economy of the Church? has it destroyed it? The Church was never so strong as it is to-day. It is not the pastor's business any longer to go from house to house as if the people were ignorant. Fathers and mothers of children have now more knowledge than three hundred years ago the minister himself had, and the families are the bulwarks of the Church. It may be said that the Church has protected the family, but the Church itself has had its life from the family emancipated and made larger and nobler. Well, has it promoted morality? Yes! Of all the schools on earth where intelligence and piety dwell together, the father lip and the mother love have been the instructors of the children. There is more in these centres of real purity, and stanch honesty, and thorough integrity, than in any other institutions that are upon the earth.

Well, has it made any difference with theology? Yes, thank God, a great deal of difference. Theology in every age is the best account that men can give of the relations of the human family to God, and the types must be the types that society in those periods is best acquainted with; and when men thought that the King was divinely King, and that the channel of instruction to mankind came through the King, it was almost inevitable that the God should be nothing but a superhuman King, having no consideration for the individual, but only thinking about His law, and about the universe, and about the national life, not the individual life; and that theology underlays much of their Evangelicanism, and men are running round it or creeping over it, or running against it and knocking their brains out. Well, what has the education of the common people done in that regard? It has taught men the meaning of the first sentence of the Lord's Prayer: " Our Father." The old theology is from the forge, from law, from government among men; the New Testament theology takes its centre in the Fatherhood of God and in the Divine love. And how has that theology been changed? If there be one thing which the family can teach men it is the doctrine of love, and if there be one priestess that

can teach it above all others it is the mother. Hers are
the sufferings that precede the child's existence; through
the pangs of the mother it comes to life. She is the food
of the child, she watches it. If it is sick, she is the nurse;
if it suffers, she suffers yet more. She gives up all her
natural liberty, she accounts no assembly so full of pleasure, and nowhere else is her life so sweet to her as by the
side of the cradle or with the babe in her lap. For this
she suffered, for this she gives all her knowledge; and as
it grows up step by step she feeds it, and she becomes its
knowledge and its rightcousness, and its justice and its
sanctification; she stands for it, and out of her it lives.
And when the father even has lost out of his ear the
funeral bell when the child is gone, the mother hears it
toll to the end of her life. Or, when, misled and over-
tempted, a child in ascending years breaks away from
family influence and goes down step by step to disgrace
and misery, and at last is afar off, the dear child sends back
word: "Oh, mother, may I come home to die?" there
is no reproach, the one word that rings out like an angel's
trumpet is: "Oh, my child, come home," and the mother's
knee to the returning prodigal is the most sacred place in
the universe this side of the feet of Jesus Christ; and if
there be one single creature out of Heaven or on the earth
that is able to teach the theologian what is the love of
God, it is the mother. [Applause.] And that work has
but begun. And both the teacher, the preacher, and the
Church are to see balmier and better days in the time
to come, when at last we shall have a theology that
teaches the Fatherhood of God and the brotherhood
of man.

Men are alarmed, they want peace. Well, you can find
it in the graveyard, and that is the only place. [Laughter.]
Among living men you can find no peace. Growth means
disturbance; peace means death in any such sense as that
of ron-investigation, not changing, and if men say: "If
you give up the old landmark you do not know where
you will land." I know where you will land if you do not.
Do you believe in God? I do. Do you believe that He
has a providence over human affairs? I do. And I believe that that hand that has steered this vagrant world

through all the dark seas and storms of the past has hold of the helm yet, and through all seeming confusions He will steer the nations and the people to the golden harbor of the millennium safe.   Trust Him, love Him, and rejoice.   [Applause.]

AUGUSTINE BIRRELL

EDMUND BURKE

[Lecture by Augustine Birrell, Quain Professor of Law in University College, London, since 1896, Member of Parliament since 1889 (born in Wavertree, near Liverpool, England, January 19, 1850), delivered before the Edinburgh Philosophical Society.]

MR. JOHN MORLEY, who amongst other things has written two admirable books about Edmund Burke, is to be found in the Preface to the second of them apologizing for having introduced into the body of the work extracts from his former volume—conduct which he seeks to justify by quoting from the Greek (always a desirable thing to do when in a difficulty), to prove that, though you may say what you have to say well once, you cannot so say it twice. A difficulty somewhat of the same kind cannot fail to be felt by every one who takes upon himself to write on Burke; for however innocent a man's own past life may be of any public references to the subject, the very many good things other men have said about it must seriously interfere with true liberty of treatment.

Hardly any man, and certainly no politician, has been so bepraised as Burke, whose very name, suggesting, as it does, splendor of diction, has tempted those who would praise him to do so in a highly decorated style, and it would have been easy work to have brought together a sufficient number of animated passages from the works of well-known writers all dedicated to the greater glory of Edmund Burke, and then to have tagged on half a dozen specimens of his own resplendent rhetoric, and so to have come to an apparently natural and long-desired conclusion without exciting any more than the usual post-lectorial grumble.

71

This course, however, not recommending itself, some other method had to be discovered. Happily, it is out of the question within present limits to give any proper summary of Burke's public life. This great man was not, like some modern politicians, a specialist, confining his activities within the prospectus of an association; nor was he, like some others, a thing of shreds and patches, busily employed to-day picking up the facts with which he will overwhelm his opponents on the morrow; but was one ever ready to engage with all comers on all subjects from out the stores of his accumulated knowledge. Even were we to confine ourselves to those questions only which engaged Burke's most powerful attention, enlisted his most active sympathy, elicited his most bewitching rhetoric, we should still find ourselves called upon to grapple with problems as vast and varied as Economic Reform, the Status of our Colonies, our Empire in India, our relations with Ireland both in respect to her trade and her prevalent religion; and then, blurring the picture, as some may think—certainly rendering it Titanesque and gloomy—we have the spectacle of Burke in his old age, like another Laocoön, writhing and wrestling with the French Revolution; and it may serve to give us some dim notion of how great a man Burke was, of how affluent a mind, of how potent an imagination, of how resistless an energy, that even when his sole unassisted name is pitted against the outcome of centuries, and we say Burke and the French Revolution, we are not overwhelmed by any sense of obvious absurdity or incongruity.

What I propose to do is merely to consider a little Burke's life prior to his obtaining a seat in Parliament, and then to refer to any circumstances which may help us to account for the fact that this truly extraordinary man, whose intellectual resources beggar the imagination, and who devoted himself to politics with all the forces of his nature, never so much as attained to a seat in the Cabinet —a feat one has known to be accomplished by persons of no proved intellectual agility. Having done this, I shall then, bearing in mind the aphorism of Lord Beaconsfield, that it is always better to be impudent than servile, essay an analysis of the essential elements of Burke's character.

The first great fact to remember is, that the Edmund Burke we are all agreed in regarding as one of the proudest memories of the House of Commons was an Irishman. When we are in our next fit of political depression about that island, and are about piously to wish, as the poet Spenser tells us men were wishing even in his time, that it were not adjacent, let us do a little national stock-taking, and calculate profits as well as losses. Burke was not only an Irishman, but a typical one—of the very kind many Englishmen, and even possibly some Scotchmen, make a point of disliking. I do not say he was an aboriginal Irishman, but his ancestors are said to have settled in the county of Galway, under Strongbow, in King Henry II's time, when Ireland was first conquered and our troubles began. This, at all events, is a better Irish pedigree than Mr. Parnell's.

Skipping six centuries, we find Burke's father an attorney in Dublin—which somehow sounds a very Irish thing to be—who in 1725 married a Miss Nagle, and had fifteen children. The marriage of Burke's parents was of the kind called mixed—a term which doubtless admits of wide application, but when employed technically signifies that the religious faith of the spouses was different; one, the father, being a Protestant, and the lady an adherent to what used to be pleasantly called the " old religion." The severer spirit now dominating Catholic councils has condemned these marriages, on the score of their bad theology and their lax morality; but the practical politician, who is not usually much of a theologian—though Lord Melbourne and Mr. Gladstone are distinguished exceptions— and whose moral conscience is apt to be robust (and here I believe there are no exceptions), cannot but regret that so good an opportunity of lubricating religious differences with the sweet oil of the domestic affections should be lost to us in these days of bitterness and dissension. Burke was brought up in the Protestant faith of his father, and was never in any real danger of deviating from it; but I cannot doubt that his regard for his Catholic fellow-subjects, his fierce repudiation of the infamies of the Penal Code—whose horrors he did something to mitigate—his respect for antiquity, and his historic sense, were all quickened by the fact that a tenderly loved and loving mother belonged through life and in death to an ancient and an outraged faith.

The great majority of Burke's brothers and sisters, like those of Laurence Sterne, were "not made to live;" and out of the fifteen but three, besides himself, attained maturity. These were his eldest brother, Garrett, on whose death Edmund succeeded to the patrimonial Irish estate, which he sold; his younger brother, Richard, a highly speculative gentleman, who always lost; and his sister, Juliana, who married a Mr. French, and was, as became her mother's daughter, a rigid Roman Catholic—who, so we read, was accustomed every Christmas Day to invite to the Hall the maimed, the aged, and distressed of her vicinity to a plentiful repast, during which she waited upon them as a servant. A sister like this never did any man any serious harm.

Edmund Burke was born in 1729, in Dublin, and was taught his rudiments in the country—first by a Mr. O'Halloran, and afterward by a Mr. FitzGerald, village pedagogues both, who at all events succeeded in giving their charge a brogue which death alone could silence. Burke passed from their hands to an academy at Ballitore, kept by a Quaker, from whence he proceeded to Trinity College, Dublin. He was thus not only Irish born, but Irish bred. His intellectual habit of mind exhibited itself early. He belonged to the happy family of omnivorous readers, and, in the language of his latest schoolmaster, he went to college with a larger miscellaneous stock of reading than was usual with one of his years; which, being interpreted out of pedagogic into plain English, means that "our good Edmund" was an enormous devourer of poetry and novels, and so he remained to the end of his days. That he always preferred Fielding to Richardson is satisfactory, since it pairs him off nicely with Dr. Johnson, whose preference was the other way, and so helps to keep an interesting question wide open. His passion for the poetry of Virgil is significant. His early devotion to Edward Young, the grandiose author of the "Night Thoughts," is not to be wondered at; though the inspiration of the youthful Burke, either as poet or critic, may be questioned, when we find him rapturously scribbling in the margin of his copy:—

"Jove claimed the verse old Homer sung,
But God Himself inspired Dr. Young."

But a boy's enthusiasm for a favorite poet is a thing to rejoice over. The years that bring the philosophic mind will not bring—they must find—enthusiasm.

In 1750, Burke (being then twenty-one) came for the first time to London, to do what so many of his lively young countrymen are still doing—though they are beginning to make a grievance even of that—eat his dinners at the Middle Temple, and so qualify himself for the Bar. Certainly that student was in luck who found himself in the same mess with Burke; and yet so stupid are men— so prone to rest with their full weight on the immaterial and slide over the essential—that had that good fortune been ours we should probably have been more taken up with Burke's brogue than with his brains. Burke came to London with a cultivated curiosity, and in no spirit of desperate determination to make his fortune. That the study of the law interested him cannot be doubted, for everything interested him, particularly the stage. Like the sensible Irishman he was, he lost his heart to Peg Woffington on the first opportunity. He was fond of roaming about the country, during, it is to be hoped, vacation-time only, and is to be found writing the most cheerful letters to his friends in Ireland (all of whom are persuaded that he is going some day to be somebody, though sorely puzzled to surmise what thing or when, so pleasantly does he take life), from all sorts of out-of-the-way country places, where he lodges with quaint old landladies who wonder maternally why he never gets drunk, and generally mistake him for an author until he pays his bill. When in town he frequented debating societies in Fleet Street and Covent Garden, and made his first speeches; for which purpose he would, unlike some debaters, devote studious hours to getting up the subjects to be discussed. There is good reason to believe that it was in this manner his attention was first directed to India.

He was at all times a great talker, and, Dr. Johnson's
dictum notwithstanding, a good listener. He was end-
lessly interested in everything—in the state of the crops,
in the last play, in the details of all trades, the rhythm of
all poems, the plots of all novels, and indeed in the course
of every manufacture. And so for six years he went up
and down, to and fro, gathering information, imparting
knowledge, and preparing himself, though he knew not
for what.

The attorney in Dublin grew anxious, and searched for
precedents of a son behaving like his, and rising to emi-
nence. Had his son got the legal mind?—which, according to a keen observer, chiefly displays itself by illustrating
the obvious, explaining the evident, and expatiating on the
commonplace. Edmund's powers of illustration, explanation, and expatiation could not indeed be questioned; but
then the subjects selected for the exhibition of those powers
were very far indeed from being obvious, evident, or commonplace; and the attorney's heart grew heavy within
him. The paternal displeasure was signified in the usual
manner—the supplies were cut off. Edmund Burke, however, was no ordinary prodigal, and his reply to his father's
expostulations took the unexpected and unprecedented
shape of a copy of a second and enlarged edition of his
treatise on the "Sublime and Beautiful," which he had
published in 1756 at the price of three shillings. Burke's
father promptly sent the author a bank-bill for £100—
conduct on his part which, considering he had sent his son
to London and maintained him there for six years to study
law, was, in my judgment, both sublime and beautiful.
In the same year Burke published another pamphlet—a
one-and-sixpenny affair—written ironically, in the style of
Lord Bolingbroke, and called "A Vindication of Natural
Society; or, a View of the Miseries and Evils arising to
Mankind from Every Species of Civil Society." Irony is
a dangerous weapon for a public man to have ever employed, and in after-life Burke had frequently to explain
that he was not serious. On these two pamphlets' airy
pinions Burke floated into the harbor of literary fame. No
less a man than the great David Hume referred to him, in
a letter to the hardly less great Adam Smith, as an Irish

gentleman who had written a " very pretty treatise on the Sublime."

After these efforts, Burke, as became an established wit, went to Bath to recruit, and there, fitly enough, fell in love. The lady was Miss Jane Mary Nugent, the daughter of a celebrated Bath physician; and it is pleasant to be able to say of the marriage that was shortly solemnized between the young couple, that it was a happy one, and then to go on our way, leaving them—where man and wife ought to be left—alone. Oddly enough, Burke's wife was also the offspring of a " mixed marriage "—only in her case it was the father who was the Catholic; consequently both Mr. and Mrs. Edmund Burke were of the same way of thinking, but each had a parent of the other way. Although getting married is no part of the curriculum of a law student, Burke's father seems to have come to the conclusion that after all it was a greater distinction for an attorney in Dublin to have a son living amongst the wits in London, and discoursing familiarly on the " Sublime and Beautiful," than one prosecuting some poor countryman, with a brogue as rich as his own, for stealing a pair of breeches; for we find him generously allowing the young couple £200 a year, which no doubt went some way toward maintaining them. Burke, who was now in his twenty-eighth year, seems to have given up all notion of the law. In 1758 he wrote for Dodsley the first volume of the " Annual Register," a melancholy series which continues to this day. For doing this he got £100. Burke was by this time a well-known figure in London literary society, and was busy making for himself a huge private reputation. The Christmas Day of 1758 witnessed a singular scene at the dinner-table of David Garrick. Dr. Johnson, then in the full vigor of his mind, and with the all-dreaded weapons of his dialectics kept burnished by daily use, was flatly contradicted by a fellow-guest some twenty years his junior, and, what is more, submitted to it without a murmur. One of the diners, Arthur Murphy, was so struck by this occurrence, unique in his long experience of the Doctor, that on returning home he recorded the fact in his journal, but ventured no explanation of it. It can only be accounted for—so at least I venture

to think—by the combined effect of four wholly independent circumstances: First, the day was Christmas
Day, a day of peace and good-will, and our beloved Doctor
was amongst the sincerest, though most argumentative of
Christians, and a great observer of days. Second, the
house was David Garrick's, and consequently we may be
certain that the dinner had been a superlatively good one;
and has not Boswell placed on record Johnson's opinion
of the man who professed to be indifferent about his dinner? Third, the subject under discussion was India, about
which Johnson knew he knew next to nothing. And
fourth, the offender was Edmund Burke, whom Johnson
loved from the first day he set eyes upon him to their last
sad parting by the waters of death.

In 1761 that shrewd old gossip, Horace Walpole, met
Burke for the first time at dinner, and remarks of him in
a letter to George Montague: "I dined at Hamilton's
yesterday; there were Garrick, and young Mr. Burke, who
wrote a book in the style of Lord Bolingbroke, that was
much admired. He is a sensible man, but has not worn
off his authorism yet, and thinks there is nothing so charming as writers, and to be one. He will know better one of
these days."

But great as were Burke's literary powers, and passionate
as was his fondness for letters and for literary society, he
never seems to have felt that the main burden of his life
lay in that direction. He looked to the public service,
and this though he always believed that the pen of a great
writer was a more powerful and glorious weapon than any
to be found in the armory of politics. This faith of his
comes out sometimes queerly enough. For example, when
Dr. Robertson in 1777 sent Burke his cheerful "History
of America" in quarto volumes, Burke, in the most perfect good faith, closes a long letter of thanks thus: "You
will smile when I send you a trifling temporary production
made for the occasion of the day, and to perish with it, in
return for your immortal work."

I have no desire, least of all in Edinburgh, to say anything disrespectful of Principal Robertson; but still, when
we remember that the temporary production he got in
exchange for his "History of America" was Burke's im-

mortal letter to the Sheriffs of Bristol on the American War, we must, I think, be forced to admit that, as so often happens when a Scotchman and an Irishman do business together, the former got the better of the bargain.

Burke's first public employment was of a humble character, and might well have been passed over in a sentence, had it not terminated in a most delightful quarrel, in which Burke conducted himself like an Irishman of genius. Some time in 1759 he became acquainted with William Gerard Hamilton, commonly called " Single-speech Hamilton," on account of the celebrity he gained from his first speech in Parliament, and the steady way in which his oratorical reputation went on waning ever after. In 1761 this gentleman went over to Ireland as Chief Secretary, and Burke accompanied him as Secretary's secretary, or, in the unlicensed speech of Dublin, as Hamilton's jackal. This arrangement was eminently satisfactory to Hamilton, who found, as generations of men have found after him, Burke's brains very useful, and he determined to borrow them for the period of their joint lives. Animated by this desire, in itself praiseworthy, he busied himself in procuring for Burke a pension of £300 a year on the Irish establishment, and then the simple " Single-speech " thought the transaction closed. He had bought his poor man of genius, and paid for him on the nail with other people's money. Nothing remained but for Burke to draw his pension and devote the rest of his life to maintaining Hamilton's reputation. There is nothing at all unusual in this, and I have no doubt Burke would have stuck to his bargain, had not Hamilton conceived the fatal idea that Burke's brains were exclusively his (Hamilton's). Then the situation became one of risk and apparent danger.

Burke's imagination began playing round the subject: he saw himself a slave, blotted out of existence—mere fuel for Hamilton's flame. In a week he was in a towering passion. Few men can afford to be angry. It is a run upon their intellectual resources they cannot meet. But Burke's treasury could well afford the luxury; and his letters to Hamilton make delightful reading to those who, like myself, dearly love a dispute when conducted according to the rules of the game by men of great intellectual wealth. Hamilton demolished and reduced to stony silence, Burke sat down again and wrote long letters to all his friends, telling them the whole story from beginning to end. I must be allowed a quotation from one of these letters, for this really is not so frivolous a matter as I am afraid I have made it appear—a quotation of which this much may be said, that nothing more delightfully Burkean is to be found anywhere:—

" My dear Mason :—I am hardly able to tell you how much satisfaction I had in your letter. Your approbation of my conduct makes me believe much the better of you and myself; and I assure you that that approbation came to me very seasonably. Such proofs of a warm, sincere, and disinterested friendship were not wholly unnecessary to my support at a time when I experienced such bitter effects of the perfidy and ingratitude of much longer and much closer connections. The way in which you take up my affairs binds me to you in a manner I cannot express; for to tell you the truth, I never can (knowing as I do the principles upon which I always endeavor to act) submit to any sort of compromise of my character; and I shall never, therefore, look upon those who, after hearing the whole story, do not think me perfectly in the right, and do not consider Hamilton an infamous scoundrel, to be in the smallest degree my friends, or even to be persons for whom I am bound to have the slightest esteem, as fair and just estimators of the characters and conduct of men. Situated as I am, and feeling as I do, I should be just as well pleased that they totally condemned me, as that they should say there were faults on both sides, or that it was a disputable case, as I hear is (I cannot forbear saying) the affected language of some persons. . . . You cannot avoid remarking, my dear Mason, and I hope not without some indignation, the unparalleled singularity of my situation. Was ever a man before me expected to enter into formal, direct, and undisguised slavery? Did ever man before him confess an attempt to decoy a man into such an alleged contract, not to say anything of the impudence of regularly pleading it? If such an attempt be wicked and unlawful (and I am sure no one ever doubted it), I have only to confess his charge, and to admit myself his dupe, to make him pass, on his own showing, for the most consummate villain that ever lived. The only difference between us is, not whether he is not a rogue—for he not only admits but pleads the facts that demonstrate him to be so; but only whether I was such a fool as to sell myself absolutely for a consideration which, so far from being adequate, if any such could be adequate, is not even so much as certain. Not to value myself as a gentleman, a free man, a man of education, and one pretending to literature; is there any situation in life so low, or even so criminal, that can subject a man to the possibility of such an engagement? Would you dare attempt to bind your footman to such terms? Will the law suffer a felon sent to the plantations to bind himself for his life, and to renounce all possibility either of elevation or quiet? And am I to defend myself for not doing what no man is suffered to do, and what it would be criminal in any man to submit to? You will excuse me for this heat."

I not only excuse Burke for his heat, but love him for letting me warm my hands at it after a lapse of a hundred and twenty years.

Burke was more fortunate in his second master, for in 1765, being then thirty-six years of age, he became private secretary to the new Prime Minister, the Marquis of Rockingham; was by the interest of Lord Verney returned to Parliament for Wendover, in Bucks; and on January 27, 1766, his voice was first heard in the House of Commons.

The Rockingham Ministry deserves well of the historian, and on the whole has received its deserts. Lord Rockingham, the Duke of Richmond, Lord John Cavendish, Mr. Dowdeswell, and the rest of them, were good men and true, judged by an ordinary standard; and when contrasted with most of their political competitors, they almost approach the ranks of saints and angels. However, after a year and twenty days, his Majesty King George III managed to get rid of them, and to keep them at bay for fifteen years. But their first term of office, though short, lasted long enough to establish a friendship of no ordinary powers of endurance between the chief members of the party and the Prime Minister's private secretary, who was at first, so ran the report, supposed to be a wild Irishman,

6

whose real name was O'Bourke, and whose brogue seemed
to require the allegation that its owner was a popish emis-
sary. It is satisfactory to notice how from the very first
Burke's intellectual pre-eminence, character, and aims were
clearly admitted and most cheerfully recognized by his
political and social superiors; and in the long correspondence in which he engaged with most of them, there is not
a trace to be found, on one side or the other, of anything
approaching to either patronage or servility. Burke ad-
vises them, exhorts them, expostulates with them, condemns their aristocratic languor, fans their feeble flames,
drafts their motions, dictates their protests, visits their
houses, and generally supplies them with facts, figures,
poetry, and romance. To all this they submit with much
humility. The Duke of Richmond once indeed ventured
to hint to Burke, with exceeding delicacy, that he (the
Duke) had a small private estate to attend to as well as
public affairs; but the validity of the excuse was not admitted. The part Burke played for the next fifteen years
with relation to the Rockingham party reminds me of the
functions I have observed performed in lazy families by
a soberly clad and eminently respectable person who pays
them domiciliary visits, and, having admission everywhere,
goes about mysteriously from room to room, winding up
all the clocks. This is what Burke did for the Rockingham party—he kept it going.

But, fortunately for us, Burke was not content with
private adjuration, or even public speech. His literary instincts, his dominating desire to persuade everybody that
he, Edmund Burke, was absolutely in the right, and every
one of his opponents hopelessly wrong, made him turn to
the pamphlet as a propaganda, and in his hands

> " The thing became a trumpet, whence he blew
> Soul-animating strains."

So accustomed are we to regard Burke's pamphlets as
specimens of our noblest literature, and to see them printed
in comfortable volumes, that we are apt to forget that in
their origin they were but the children of the pavement,
the publications of the hour. If, however, you visit any

old public library, and grope about a little, you are likely
enough to find a shelf holding some twenty-five or thirty
musty, ugly little books, usually lettered " Burke," and on
opening any of them you will come across one of Burke's
pamphlets as originally issued, bound up with the replies
and counter-pamphlets it occasioned. I have frequently
tried, but always in vain, to read these replies, which are
pretentious enough—usually the works of deans, members
of Parliament, and other dignitaries of the class Carlyle
used compendiously to describe as " shovel-hatted "—and
each of whom was as much entitled to publish pamphlets
as Burke himself. There are some things it is very easy
to do, and to write a pamphlet is one of them; but to
write such a pamphlet as future generations will read with
delight is perhaps the most difficult feat in literature. Milton, Swift, Burke, and Sydney Smith are, I think, our only
great pamphleteers.

I have now rather more than kept my word so far as
Burke's pre-Parliamentary life is concerned, and will proceed to mention some of the circumstances that may serve
to account for the fact, that when the Rockingham party
came into power for the second time in 1782, Burke, who
was their life and soul, was only rewarded with a minor
office. First, then, it must be recorded sorrowfully of
Burke that he was always desperately in debt, and in this
country no politician under the rank of a baronet can ever
safely be in debt. Burke's finances are, and always have
been, marvels and mysteries; but one thing must be said
of them—that the malignity of his enemies, both Tory
enemies and Radical enemies, has never succeeded in
formulating any charge of dishonesty against him that has
not been at once completely pulverized, and shown on the
facts to be impossible.* Burke's purchase of the estate
at Beaconsfield in 1768, only two years after he entered

*All the difficulties connected with this subject will be found col-
lected, and somewhat unkindly considered, in Mr. Dilke's " Papers of
a Critic," vol. ii. The equity draftsman will be indisposed to attach
importance to statements made in a Bill of Complaint filed in Chan-
cery by Lord Verney against Burke fourteen years after the trans-
action to which it had reference, in a suit which was abandoned after
answer was put in. Yet Mr. Dilke thought it worth while to reprint
this ancient Bill.

Parliament, consisting as it did of a good house and 1,600 acres of land, has puzzled a great many good men—much more than it ever did Edmund Burke. But how did he get the money? After an Irish fashion—by not getting it at all. Two-thirds of the purchase-money remained on mortgage, and the balance he borrowed; or, as he puts it, " With all I could collect of my own, and by the aid of my friends, I have established a root in the country." That is how Burke bought Beaconsfield, where he lived till his end came; whither he always hastened when his sensitive mind was tortured by the thought of how badly men governed the world; where he entertained all sorts and conditions of men—Quakers, Brahmins (for whose ancient rites he provided suitable accommodation in a greenhouse), nobles and abbés flying from revolutionary France, poets, painters, and peers; no one of whom ever long remained a stranger to his charm.

Burke flung himself into farming with all the enthusiasm of his nature. His letters to Arthur Young on the subject of carrots still tremble with emotion.

You all know Burke's " Thoughts on the Present Discontents." You remember—it is hard to forget—his speech on Conciliation with America, particularly the magnificent passage beginning, " Magnanimity in politics is not seldom the truest wisdom, and a great empire and little minds go ill together." You have echoed back the words in which, in his letter to the Sheriffs of Bristol on the hateful American War, he protests that it was not instantly he could be brought to rejoice when he heard of the slaughter and captivity of long lists of those whose names had been familiar in his ears from his infancy, and you would all join with me in subscribing to a fund which should have for its object the printing and hanging up over every editor's desk in town and country a subsequent passage from the same letter: " A conscientious man would be cautious how he dealt in blood. He would feel some apprehension at being called to a tremendous account for engaging in so deep a play without any knowledge of the game. It is no excuse for presumptuous ignorance that it is directed by insolent passion. The poorest being that crawls on earth, contending to save itself from injustice and oppression, is an object respectable in the eyes of God and man. But I cannot conceive any existence under heaven (which in the depths of its wisdom tolerates all sorts of things) that is more truly odious and disgusting than an impotent, helpless creature, without civil wisdom or military skill, bloated with pride and arrogance, calling for battles which he is not to fight, and contending for a violent dominion which he can never exercise. . . . If you and I find our talents not of the great and ruling kind, our conduct at least is conformable to our faculties. No man's life pays the forfeit of our rashness. No desolate widow weeps tears of blood over our ignorance. Scrupulous and sober in a well-grounded distrust of ourselves, we would keep in the port of peace and security; and perhaps in recommending to others something of the same diffidence, we should show ourselves more charitable to their welfare than injurious to their abilities."

You have laughed over Burke's account of how all Lord Talbot's schemes for the reform of the king's household were dashed to pieces, because the turnspit of the king's kitchen was a member of Parliament. You have often pondered over that miraculous passage in his speech on the Nabob of Arcot's debts, describing the devastation of the Carnatic by Hyder Ali—a passage which Mr. John Morley says fills the young orator with the same emotions of enthusiasm, emulation, and despair that (according to the same authority) invariably torment the artist who first gazes on " The Madonna " at Dresden, or the figures of " Night " and " Dawn " at Florence.

All these things you know, else are you mighty self-denying of your pleasures. But it is just possible you may have forgotten the following extract from one of Burke's farming letters to Arthur Young :—

" One of the grand points in controversy (a controversy indeed chiefly carried on between practice and speculation) is that of deep ploughing. In your last volume you seem, on the whole, rather against that practice, and have given several reasons for your judgment which deserve to be very well considered. In order to know how we ought to plough, we ought to know what end it is we propose to ourselves in that operation. The first and instrumental end is to divide the soil; the last and ultimate end, so far as regards the plants, is to facilitate the pushing of the blade upward, and the shooting of the roots in all the inferior directions. There is further proposed a more ready admission of external influences—the rain, the sun, the air, charged with all those heterogeneous contents, some, possibly all, of which are necessary for the nourishment of the plants. By ploughing deep you answer these ends in a greater mass of the soil. This would seem in favor of deep ploughing as nothing else than accomplishing, in a more perfect manner, those very ends for which you are induced to plough at all. But doubts here arise, only to be solved by experiment. First, is it quite certain that it is good for the ear and grain of farinaceous plants that their roots should spread and descend into the ground to the greatest possible distances and depths? Is there not some limit in this? We know that in timber, what makes one part flourish does not equally conduce to the benefit of all; and that which may be beneficial to the wood, does not equally contribute to the quantity and goodness of the fruit; and, *vice versâ*, that what increases the fruit largely is often far from serviceable to the tree. Secondly, is that looseness to great depths, supposing it is useful to one of the species of plants, equally useful to all? Thirdly, though the external influences—the rain, the sun, the air—act undoubtedly a part, and a large part, in vegetation, does it follow that they are equally salutary in any quantities, at any depths? Or that, though it may be useful to diffuse one of these agents as extensively as may be in the earth, that therefore it will be equally useful to render the earth in the same degree pervious to all? It is a dangerous way of reasoning in physics, as well as morals, to conclude, because a given proportion of anything is advantageous, that the double will be quite as good, or that it will be good at all. Neither in the one nor the other is it always true that two and two make four."

This is magnificent, but it is not farming, and you will easily believe that Burke's attempts to till the soil were more costly than productive. Farming, if it is to pay, is a pursuit of small economies; and Burke was far too Asiatic, tropical, and splendid to have anything to do with small economies. His expenditure, like his rhetoric, was in the "grand style." He belongs to Charles Lamb's great race, "the men who borrow." But indeed it was not so much that Burke borrowed as that men lent. Right-feeling men did not wait to be asked. Dr. Brocklesby, that good physician, whose name breathes like a benediction through the pages of the biographies of the best men of his time, who soothed Dr. Johnson's last melancholy hours, and for whose supposed heterodoxy the dying man displayed so tender a solicitude, wrote to Burke, in the strain of a timid suitor proposing for the hand of a proud heiress, to know whether Burke would be so good as to accept £1,000 at once, instead of waiting for the writer's death. Burke felt no hesitation in obliging so old a friend. Garrick, who, though fond of money, was as generous-hearted a fellow as ever brought down a house, lent Burke £1,000. Sir Joshua Reynolds, who has been reckoned stingy, by his will left Burke £2,000, and forgave him another £2,000 which he had lent him. The Marquis of Rockingham by his will directed all Burke's bonds held by him to be cancelled. They amounted to £30,000. Burke's patrimonial estate was sold by him for £4,000; and I have seen it stated that he had received altogether from family sources as much as £20,000. And yet he was always poor, and was glad at the last to accept pensions from the Crown in order that he might not leave his wife a beggar. This good lady survived her illustrious husband twelve years, and seemed as his widow to have some success in paying his bills, for at her death all remaining demands were found to be discharged. For receiving this pension Burke was assailed by the Duke of Bedford, a most pleasing act of ducal fatuity, since it enabled the pensioner, not bankrupt of his wit, to write a pamphlet, now of course a cherished classic, and introduce into it a few paragraphs about the House of Russell and the cognate subject of grants from the Crown.

But enough of Burke's debts and difficulties, which I only mention because all through his life they were cast up against him. Had Burke been a moralist of the calibre of Charles James Fox, he might have amassed a fortune large enough to keep up half a dozen Beaconfields, by simply doing what all his predecessors in the office he held, including Fox's own father, the truly infamous first Lord Holland, had done—namely, by retaining for his own use the interest on all balances of the public money from time to time in his hands as Paymaster of the Forces. But Burke carried his passion for good government into actual practice, and, cutting down the emoluments of his office to a salary (a high one, no doubt), effected a saving to the country of some £25,000 a year, every farthing of which might have gone without remark into his own pocket.

Burke had no vices, save of style and temper; nor was any of his expenditure a profligate squandering of money. It all went in giving employment or disseminating kindness. He sent the painter Barry to study art in Italy. He saved the poet Crabbe from starvation and despair, and thus secured to the country one who owns the unrivalled distinction of having been the favorite poet of the three greatest intellectual factors of the age (scientific men excepted)—Lord Byron, Sir Walter Scott, and Cardinal Newman. Yet so distorted are men's views that the odious and anti-social excesses of Fox at the gambling-table are visited with a blame usually wreathed in smiles, whilst the financial irregularities of a noble and pure-minded man are thought fit matter for the fiercest censure or the most lordly contempt.

Next to Burke's debts, some of his companions and intimates did him harm and injured his consequence. His brother Richard, whose brogue we are given to understand was simply appalling, was a good-for-nothing, with a dilapidated reputation. Then there was another Mr. Burke, who was no relation, but none the less was always about, and to whom it was not safe to lend money. Burke's son, too, whose death he mourned so pathetically, seems to have been a failure, and is described by a candid friend as a nauseating person. To have a decent following is important in politics.

A third reason must be given: Burke's judgment of men and things was often both wrong and violent. The story of Powell and Bembridge, two knaves in Burke's own office, whose cause he espoused, and whom he insisted on reinstating in the public service after they had been dismissed, and maintaining them there, in spite of all protests, till the one had the grace to cut his throat and the other was sentenced by the Queen's Bench to a term of imprisonment and a heavy fine, is too long to be told, though it makes interesting reading in the twenty-second volume of Howell's "State Trials," where at the end of the report is to be found the following note: "The proceedings against Messrs. Powell and Bembridge occasioned much animated discussion in the House of Commons, in which Mr. Burke warmly supported the accused. The compassion which on these and all other occasions was manifested by Mr. Burke for the sufferings of those public delinquents, the zeal with which he advocated their cause, and the eagerness with which he endeavored to extenuate their criminality, have received severe reprehension, and in particular when contrasted with his subsequent conduct in the prosecution of Mr. Hastings."

The real reason for Burke's belief in Bembridge is, I think, to be found in the evidence Burke gave on his behalf at the trial before Lord Mansfield. Bembridge had rendered Burke invaluable assistance in carrying out his reforms at the Paymaster's Office, and Burke was constitutionally unable to believe that a rogue could be on his side; but, indeed, Burke was too apt to defend bad causes with a scream of passion, and a politician who screams is never likely to occupy a commanding place in the House of Commons. A last reason for Burke's exclusion from high office is to be found in his aversion to any measure of Parliamentary Reform. An ardent reformer like the Duke of Richmond—the then Duke of Richmond—who was in favor of annual parliaments, universal suffrage, and payment of members, was not likely to wish to associate himself too closely with a politician who wept with emotion at the bare thought of depriving Old Sarum of parliamentary representation.

These reasons account for Burke's exclusion, and jealous as we naturally and properly are of genius being snubbed by mediocrity, my reading at all events does not justify me in blaming anyone but the Fates for the circumstance that Burke was never a Secretary of State. And after all, does it matter much what he was? Burke no doubt occasionally felt his exclusion a little hard; but he is the victor who remains in possession of the field; and Burke is now, for us and for all coming after us, in such possession.

It now only remains for me, drawing upon my stock of assurance, to essay the analysis of the essential elements of Burke's mental character, and I therefore at once proceed to say that it was Burke's peculiarity and his glory to apply the imagination of a poet of the first order to the facts and the business of life. Arnold says of Sophocles—

"He saw life steadily, and saw it whole."

Substitute for the word " life " the words " organized society," and you get a peep into Burke's mind. There was a catholicity about his gaze. He knew how the whole world lived. Everything contributed to this: his vast desultory reading; his education, neither wholly academical nor entirely professional; his long years of apprenticeship in the service of knowledge; his wanderings up and down the country; his vast conversational powers; his enormous correspondence with all sorts of people; his unfailing interest in all pursuits, trades, manufactures,—all helped to keep before him, like motes dancing in a sunbeam, the huge organism of modern society, which requires for its existence and for its development the maintenance of credit and of order. Burke's imagination led him to look out over the whole land: the legislator devising new laws, the judge expounding and enforcing old ones, the merchant despatching his goods and extending his credit, the banker advancing the money of his customers upon the credit of the merchant, the frugal man slowly accumulating the store which is to support him in old age, the ancient institutions of Church and University with their seemly provisions for sound learning and true religion, the parson in his pulpit, the poet pondering his rhymes, the farmer eying his crops, the painter covering his canvases, the player educating the feelings. Burke saw all this with the fancy of a poet, and dwelt on it with the eye of a lover.

But love is the parent of fear, and none knew better than Burke how thin is the lava layer between the costly fabric

of society and the volcanic heats and destroying flames of
anarchy. He trembled for the fair frame of all established
things, and to his horror saw men, instead of covering the
thin surface with the concrete, digging in it for abstractions, and asking fundamental questions about the origin
of society, and why one man should be born rich and another poor. Burke was no prating optimist: it was his
very knowledge how much could be said against society
that quickened his fears for it. There is no shallower criticism than that which accuses Burke in his later years of
apostasy from so-called Liberal opinions. Burke was all his
life through a passionate maintainer of the established order
of things, and a ferocious hater of abstractions and metaphysical politics. The same ideas that explode like bombs
through his diatribes against the French Revolution are to
be found shining with a mild effulgence in the comparative
calm of his earlier writings. I have often been struck with
a resemblance, which I hope is not wholly fanciful, between
the attitude of Burke's mind toward government and that
of Cardinal Newman toward religion. Both these great
men belong, by virtue of their imaginations, to the poetic
order, and they both are to be found dwelling with amazing eloquence, detail, and wealth of illustration on the
varied elements of society. Both seem as they write to
have one hand on the pulse of the world, and to be forever
alive to the throb of its action; and Burke, as he regarded
humanity swarming like bees into and out of their hives
of industry, is ever asking himself, How are these men
to be saved from anarchy? while Newman puts to himself
the question, How are these men to be saved from atheism? Both saw the perils of free inquiry divorced from
practical affairs.

" Civil freedom," says Burke, " is not, as many have endeavored to persuade you, a thing that lies hid in the depth
of abstruse science. It is a blessing and a benefit, not an
abstract speculation; and all the just reasoning that can
be upon it is of so coarse a texture as perfectly to suit
the ordinary capacities of those who are to enjoy and of
those who are to defend it."

" Tell men," says Cardinal Newman, " to gain notions
of a Creator from His works, and if they were to set about

it (which nobody does), they would be jaded and wearied by the labyrinth they were tracing; their minds would be gorged and surfeited by the logical operation. To most men argument makes the point in hand more doubtful and considerably less impressive. After all, man is not a reasoning animal, he is a seeing, feeling, contemplating, acting animal."

Burke is fond of telling us that he is no lawyer, no antiquarian, but a plain, practical man; and the Cardinal, in like manner, is ever insisting that he is no theologian— he leaves everything of that sort to the Schools, whatever they may be, and simply deals with religion on its practical side as a benefit to mankind.

If either of these great men has been guilty of intellectual excesses, those of Burke may be attributed to his dread of anarchy, those of Newman to his dread of atheism. Neither of them was prepared to rest content with a scientific frontier, an imaginary line. So much did they dread their enemy, so alive were they to the terrible strength of some of his positions, that they could not agree to dispense with the protection afforded by the huge mountains of prejudice and the ancient rivers of custom. The sincerity of either man can only be doubted by the bigot and the fool.

But Burke, apart from his fears, had a constitutional love for old things, simply because they were old. Anything mankind had ever worshipped, or venerated, or obeyed, was dear to him. I have already referred to his providing his Brahmins with a greenhouse for the purpose of their rites, which he watched from outside with great interest. One cannot fancy Cardinal Newman peeping through a window to see men worshipping false though ancient gods. Warren Hastings's high-handed dealings with the temples and time-honored if scandalous customs of the Hindoos filled Burke with horror. So, too, he respected Quakers, Presbyterians, Independents, Baptists, and all those whom he called Constitutional Dissenters. He has a fine passage somewhere about Rust, for with all his passion for good government he dearly loved a little rust. In this phase of character he reminds one not a little of another great writer—whose death literature has still reason to

deplore—George Eliot; who, in her love for old hedge-
rows and barns and crumbling moss-grown walls, was a
writer after Burke's own heart, whose novels he would
have sat up all night to devour; for did he not deny with
warmth Gibbon's statement that he had read all five volumes of " Evelina " in a day? " The thing is impossible,"
cried Burke; " they took me three days, doing nothing
else." Now, " Evelina " is a good novel, but " Silas
Marner " is a better.

Wordsworth has been called the High Priest of Nature.
Burke may be called the High Priest of Order—a lover
of settled ways, of justice, peace, and security. His writings are a storehouse of wisdom, not the cheap shrewdness
of the mere man of the world, but the noble, animating
wisdom of one who has the poet's heart as well as the
statesman's brain. Nobody is fit to govern this country
who has not drunk deep at the springs of Burke. " Have
you read your Burke? " is at least as sensible a question
to put to a parliamentary candidate as to ask him whether
he is a total abstainer or a desperate drunkard. Something
there may be about Burke to regret, and more to dispute;
but that he loved justice and hated iniquity is certain, as
also it is that for the most part he dwelt in the paths of
purity, humanity, and good sense. May we be found ad-
hering to them!

EDWARD WILLIAM BOK

THE KEYS TO SUCCESS

[Lecture by Edward Bok, editor of the " Ladies' Home Journal,"
Philadelphia, since 1888 (born in Helder, Holland, October 9, 1863;
——), delivered in various places during the lecture seasons of 1898-
1900.]

LADIES AND GENTLEMEN:—At a large dinner party in
Washington, a lady sitting next to William M. Evarts, then
Secretary of State, said to him: " Mr. Evarts, don't you
think that a woman is the best judge of other women? "
" Ah, madam," said the great lawyer, " she is not only the
best judge, but the best executioner."

Perhaps Mr. Evarts might have said the same thing had
he been asked if a young man is the best judge of other
young men.

Of one thing I am certain; I do not ask for that remarkable confidence which the young English laborer
showed in his family physician. He went to the register's
office, you know, to record his father's death, and when
the register asked the date of death, said: " Well, father
ain't dead yet. But he will be dead before morning, and
I thought it would save me another trip if you would put
it down now." " Oh, that won't do at all," said the register. " Why, your father may be well before morning."
" Ah, no, he won't," said the young laborer. " Our doctor says he won't, and he knows what he's given father."

Now, my friends, it is a position just between these two
that I would like to take this evening. As a young man
in the thick of the battle for success, who leaves the battle-
field just for a few moments to talk with his comrades.

To strike that same key-note which Chauncey M. Depew struck the other day when a young man asked him: "Mr. Depew, what is the secret to success?" And Mr. Depew answered: "My boy, there is no secret to it. It is just dig, dig, dig."

And that is exactly the key-note which every young man must learn who is striving to succeed. He must put success in its rightful, simple place. For there is nothing simpler; so long as we do not give it a wrong meaning.

Take ten young men, for example, and ask them what success means, and nine of them will associate it with something for only those who are exceptionally clever. That is the popular impression: that success means the possession of some commanding talent. We look at a man of exceptional capacity, who has done something unusual in the world, and we say: "He is a successful man." Of course he is, but his is the success of the leader, and very few of us are born to be leaders. But success does not stop at such heights. The men, for example, who sailed with Lieutenant Hobson on that short but perilous voyage into the mouth of Santiago harbor, accomplished just as much in their positions as did their lieutenant in his. Each had to accomplish; each had to do what and all that he could do. It was as important that the man in the hold with his hand on the engine which propelled that ship should make a success of his position and keep the ship moving, as it was for Hobson to order her to stop at the right point in the channel, drop the anchors, and sink the big collier. Both had to carry to a successful termination what they started out to do; and that is what success really is and means. What a man does well, he succeeds in.

Now, a young man, before he starts out to succeed, must get that truth well fixed in his head. He must fix success in its rightful place; then it becomes possible to him. Let him fix it too high and it becomes an impossibility; a discouragement instead of a stimulus.

The correct definition of success is accomplishment; the favorable termination of anything attempted—anything, remember—a result, in other words, which answers the particular purpose intended.

Nor must a young man compare himself with others or

measure his success by theirs. It makes no difference how other men succeed. Their success is theirs; not yours. It matters nothing to me that Edison can invent the electric light and I can't; that Kipling can write a " Recessional " and I can't; that you can plead the law and I can't. You can do one thing; I try to do another. But success is for both of us just so far as we do well what we can do. Every man is himself, and it is in proportion as he gets out of himself the power there is within him that he succeeds—succeeds in doing the thing he is best fitted to do.

We must not get ourselves into the frame of mind of the two little English girls, one the daughter of a curate and the other of an English bishop, who were quarrelling over the comparative success of their fathers in the ministry. " My father can preach better than your father, because he is a bishop," said one. That was too weighty a reason for the curate's little girl. But she quickly recovered and said: " Well, anyhow, we've got a hen in our yard which lays an egg every day." " That's nothing," retorted the bishop's daughter; " my father lays a corner-stone every week."

Nor must young men get the idea that if a man is known he is a success. Reputation is not success. Many a man has achieved reputation without having achieved success. Every good business man will tell you that the success most highly regarded in the business world of to-day is that which is won on conservative lines. The meteors in the commercial heavens, so admired by the average young man, are viewed only with suspicion by experienced business men. That was clearly enough demonstrated last spring when a young Chicago speculator set out to control the wheat of the world. In a few months he found his level, and at the same time a shortage in his bank account of ten millions of dollars. The man who goes up like a rocket always comes down like a stick. True success is earned slowly, and by doing everything we do the very best we can.

That is success. And that is all there is to it. It has no secret, as Mr. Depew said. There is nothing mysterious about it. All it has is a price. Any young man in this house can make a success in proportion to his capacities, as he is willing to pay the price: first, hard work; and, second, personal sacrifices. Edison, you know, when recently asked his definition of genius, answered: "Two per cent. is genius, and ninety-eight per cent. is hard work." And when the great inventor was asked upon another occasion: "Mr. Edison, don't you believe that genius is inspiration?" he replied: "No! Genius is *per*-spiration."

Now, when I speak of hard work, I do not mean work which a man accomplishes simply as an incident of his life. I mean an unflagging industry—an absolute love for one's work. There is no better test of a man's fitness for his work than his love for it. And that is the answer and the only one which can be made to the question so often asked by young men: "How can I tell for which particular trade or profession I am fitted?" If a man loves his work, no matter what it may be, that is the work he is best fitted for.

And I would like to say one word just here to the parents in this audience. Be careful, my friends, how you try to dissuade your son from the kind of work for which he hungers or shows decided taste. It may not be agreeable to you that he wishes to be a physician. You would rather see him a lawyer, as his father is. But, remember, it does not necessarily follow that he can be one. If your son's tastes tend toward medicine, be careful how you try to turn them toward the law. There are enough bad lawyers now who might have been great doctors had they been left to choose their own careers. A prominent New York man identified with the two leading law and medical schools of that city told me not long ago that each year these schools were turning out scores of young men who drifted at once into car conductors, station agents, and commercial clerks. And this is simply because of the mistakes of parents in attempting to force round pegs into square holes. It cannot be done. No sight is so sad as that of a son forced by his parents into a trade or profession which is uncongenial and distasteful to him. A young man cannot honestly make a success in any business unless he loves his work, any more than a married man can be happy in his home unless he loves his wife.

Now, really hard work is understood by very few young men. The average young man is either afraid of it or he has no taste for it. I am afraid that there was a good deai of truth in the answer made to the editor of a Western newspaper who sent to all the successful men in his city this question: "Why is it that not more of our young men succeed?" And one answer came in this laconic phrase: "Because too many of them are looking for white-shirt jobs." It was a homely way of putting it, but there is much truth in it. Young men want success, but they are unwilling to work for it.

But hard work must become a habit before any degree of success whatever is attained. And it must be an absolute devotion to one purpose. Not several, for this is an age of specialties. If there ever was a time when it was demanded of a man that he should do one thing supremely well, it is now. I know we hear it said sometimes of a man, disparagingly, that he knows nothing outside of his one line of work. But it must not be forgotten that competition is so keen to-day that a man who would be supreme in his own line has not much time to know more than one thing well.

The man of to-day who has to do with the employment of men, witnesses no sadder sight than the procession of unemployed men who are exemplary in life, have some general intelligence, are respectable, honest, and frequently of good social position, and yet who can get only menial, routine places. The reason of this is that they have no definite knowledge; no special experience. "They can do almost anything," they say, which really means that they can do nothing. The successful man of to-day is the man who in business knows the one thing which he is doing better than any other man does. To do one thing supremely well takes a great man.

Now, I know there seem to many young men to be instances of exception to success won by hard work. But they are all in the seeming. Things in this world never just happen. There is always a reason for everything if you will only look for it. So with success. It is not a thing of chance. It comes to men only because they work intelligently for it and along legitimate lines. No man in this world ever made a lasting success except by hard work. Study the lives of successful men, and the story will be found in each case exactly the same. The methods vary, as they must, but the actual basis of every successful life is the persistent, hard, hard work of years, and many a personal sacrifice. This is not always apparent, simply because we are all too apt to look at a man when he has achieved his success. But there was a digging period.

In a business transaction with Henry Ward Beecher I had occasion one time to give him a check for $250. "Well," said the great preacher, looking at the check, "I know the time when I would have done ten times as much work for two hundred and fifty cents. Time makes a difference." "Is it only time?" I asked. "Well, with thirty-eight years of hard work packed in," was the reply. And there was hard work packed in there. Three hundred dollars a year was Mr. Beecher's first salary, and so small were the quarters in which they lived that Mrs. Beecher had to go out on the porch and make up the bed through the window.

I might go on indefinitely with such stories. I could tell you of the small boy in Philadelphia who for $2 a week ran errands in a store and swept the sidewalk each morning. But that boy ran those errands so well and swept that sidewalk so thoroughly that when he died the whole country knew of George W. Childs and his wealth.

Or of that boy who came to New York penniless and a beggar, and who in three years earned just $300. But he kept at it. He worked day and night, and always beside a tank, foul with the smell of oil. Yet he made that oil so well that now scarcely one of us in this entire country can burn a drop of oil that is not bought of his vast Standard Oil Company.

We are apt to say of these men that they rose from nothing; and that is generally true. But upon that nothing they built a lot of tremendous hard work.

Years ago, in one of our Western towns, a young man sat in a dingy office digging away at the law. He had no teacher; no one to help him. But he kept digging away until he made himself the ablest constitutional lawyer in

America, and the people made Benjamin Harrison President of the United States. But he worked hard, and he loved his work.

Some few years ago two men sat in a small insurance office in New York and found that the loss of their company for the previous month was just $400. At the end of the next month their loss was $900. Month after month went by and the losses increased. But they kept at it. All comforts and pleasures were put aside. "Many a time," said one of these men to me, "we went to the office on Monday morning and never left it until Tuesday midnight." Finally, at the end of fourteen months of constant losses, a balance of $6 was shown as the first profit the company had ever seen. The tide had turned. To-day the company, of which one of these men is president, has the largest number of policy-holders on its books of any single company in America, and it puts aside each year $2,000,000 as invested profits.

It is one thing to work hard when things are all going your way. But when everything seems to be going the other way, when there is so much to discourage and so little to encourage—then hard work becomes doubly hard. The only thing then that can save a man is his enthusiasm for his work—his love for it. That is the power which impels men onward. He must have confidence in his work: more confidence than did the little boy who had been put to bed during a violent thunder-storm; the poor little chap was scared half to death, but his mother told him that he need not be afraid: that God was with him and would take care of him. "Yes, I know," said the little boy, "but why can't I go down-stairs and stay with papa, and you stay up here with God?" Now, that boy lacked confidence.

Now, someone may ask: "Is success worth this price? Is it worth while?" That, my friend, you must decide for yourself. I believe it is. I think it is a magnificent thing for a young man to rise to the very best that is within him; to make the most of what he is. This hard work does for him. It brings out what he has in him.

See what hard work will do for a nation. Into the soil of no other nation on this earth has there been put more hard work than the American man has put into this American continent. What is the result? We cannot begin to eat what we grow; we cannot begin to use what we produce. We have become the stewards of the world. Now, some people have an idea that hard work hurts and sometimes even kills a man. It doesn't. Hard work never yet killed a man, nor hurt him. Worry kills, but not work. What is called overwork is nothing but over-worry. The healthiest men are the men who work the hardest. A man feels well after he has worked hard. He goes to bed at night with a healthy fatigue. There is nothing so satisfying to a man as a healthy, busy day—a day which at its close makes him feel glad that he was part of it. Hard work is not irksome; it is a healthy price which any man pays for success. Spasmodic work tires, but constant, persistent work becomes a pleasure. It is the man that sticks, who keeps everlastingly at it, that makes a success.

When a young man goes into business he must have two keys to success: a principle, and a method. When you say to a young man that the only principle he can follow in business is honesty, it sounds very trite to him. But let me explain why there can be no other. Just stop and think what business really is and means. Business is simply a system of trade, of exchange between men: a system by which one man transfers to another certain goods in trade or performs certain services in a profession. A fixed amount of money is paid as an equivalent for the goods or the services. That is the visible part of the trans-action. But what is the real basis? The confidence of man in man that certain goods or services rendered are what they are represented to be. Now, that is all that business is; it rests upon the trust of one man in the word of another. Consider, for instance, the striking fact that only five per cent. of the world's entire business is con-ducted on a cash basis; ninety-five per cent. on credit, or, in other words, on confidence in the integrity of man. Now, let a man destroy that confidence, and what is there left? Absolutely nothing. Therefore, the question of whether a man can or cannot, whether he should or should not be honest in business, answers itself by the very condition of business itself. It is not a case of can, or should, but one of must.

If one-tenth of what we constantly hear about dishonesty in business were actually true, business would cease. But it does go on, because there are far more honest than dishonest men in business.

I know it is sometimes very hard for young men to believe this. They see some dishonest man prosper. But watch him, and sooner or later you will see the turn in the road. It is bound to come. There is no escaping it. He may go on for years, perhaps, but the longer he lasts the greater will be his drop when the fall does come. We cannot get away from it, my friends: a young man must be honest in business. And he must be steadfast and unbending in this. Without absolute honesty success is impossible; it is simply out of the question.

Now, with honesty as a principle, we must adopt a method. And the best one is that given by H. B. Claflin, the great New York merchant, to a young man, who asked him: " Mr. Claflin, can you, in one word, give me the key to successful business? " and the millionaire merchant said: " Yes: thoroughness." And never was there given to young men a better word to remember in business—thoroughness. It is the surest key to success in business: thoroughness in everything a man does; thoroughness, especially in little things. An absolute regard for the small things is necessary in every undertaking. It is the little courtesies of every-day life which make life worth the living; so details are the bone and sinew of any success. The most important results sometimes hang on small things. For instance, in a lawsuit in New York not long ago, the entire proceedings turned upon one sentence in a letter. The stenographer to whom the letter was dictated had destroyed her notes. The letter itself was lost. There was nothing left but the impression of it in the firm's copying-book. But the office-boy had hastily copied it; the impression was so faint that although every ingredient known to chemistry was tried it could not be made clear. This was simply a lack of thoroughness on the part of the office-boy. The mere copying of that letter was too small

a thing to him to be considered of importance. And yet
the absence of that letter was the sole basis for a judgment
for $350,000. An important will-suit, only last year, was
lost because of the failure to date a letter. A thing half
or three-quarters done, my friends, is far worse than not
done at all.

One of the largest and most prosperous business houses
I know of never allows abbreviations of any sort in its
correspondence. Everything about its letters has a finished look; evidence of thoroughness. If a letter is addressed to a correspondent in Baltimore the word Mary-
land is written out in full, the same as the city. But isn't
that going pretty far? someone may ask. Not at all; the
character of a business house is unmistakably shown in
its correspondence, and where the practice is most fruitful
is in the lesson of thoroughness in small things which it
teaches to its employees. When a young man in business
overlooks the small things, or thinks they are not important enough to do them well and thoroughly, he leaves
out of his calculations one of the most important elements
in success.

There is everything in that one word—thoroughness;
personal interest; concentration; patience; forgetfulness
of self; close application; honest work. It completely
does away with those two unfortunate Americanisms,
" That will do " and " That is good enough." A thorough
workman never says, " There, that will do," but " There,
that is *it*." And this is what every young man in business
should learn: that absolutely nothing is good enough if
it can be made better, and better is never good enough
if it can be made best.

The real peril of the American young man of to-day is
that he is too content to be of the average, rather than of
the best. It is getting to be the exception to find in business a young man who is something more than a mere
automatic machine. He comes to his office at nine o'clock
in the morning; is faithful in the duties he performs. He
goes to lunch at twelve. He comes back at one. If by
some chance he happens to return five minutes before one,
he stands outside the door until the clock strikes, fearful
lest he should give one single extra moment to his work or

his employer. He takes up whatever he is told to do until five, and at the stroke of the clock closes his desk and goes home. His work for the day is done. One day is exactly the same to him as another. He has a certain routine of duties to do, and he does them day in and day out. He is the same yesterday and to-day. No special fault can be found with his work. He does it just as a machine would. He works with no definite point or plan in view. He is a mere drop-a-nickel-in-the-slot machine. You pay him so much; you get so much. If he detracts nothing from his employer's business, he certainly adds nothing to it. "But," he says, "I do everything I am told to do. What more can I do?" And that is just where so many young men fail, just at that "more" point. What more can they do?

It is the extra service rendered in business that tells with the employer; not giving him exactly what he bargained for, but a little more; a great deal more, if necessary; doing his business thoroughly no matter how long it takes.

It is no special art and it reflects very little credit on a young man simply to fill a position. That is expected of him; he is engaged to do that. The art lies in doing more than was bargained for; in proving greater than was expected; in making more of a position than was ever made before. The difference between a successful clerk and an unsuccessful clerk is that the one makes his position greater than he found it; the other keeps it where he found it, and it keeps him there.

Now, I would not be understood as belittling the value of faithfulness in an employé. But, after all, faithfulness is nothing more or less than a negative quality. It is not enough that a young man be faithful; he must be something more. Faithfulness must exist; but only as a foundation on which to build other qualities.

Now, young men sometimes say: "There is no advancement where I am. My employer is unappreciative. He is unjust." There are such instances, of course. There are mean men in business, no doubt. In a case where a circumstance cripples a young man, he must change the circumstance. But, as a rule, the fault lies more often with the young man than with his employer. Very few employers will prevent the cream of their establishments from rising to the surface. It wouldn't be good business to do so. The advance of an employé always means the advance of the employer's interest. If it didn't the employer wouldn't advance the employé. Men are in business for business; not for sentiment.

There are, of course, exceptions, as there are to every rule, but as a general thing a man gets paid in business about what he is worth, or not very far from it. The man who most loudly complains of being underpaid is generally very apt to be already overpaid.

The cause of discontent in business is generally found in inability of some sort. Business houses are not underpaying the right sort of young men who are valuable to them. They can't afford to. Young men of that kind are too scarce.

A. T. Stewart used to say that he always had plenty of vacancies in his store which he could not fill, although he wanted to, for $10,000 employees. And this is just as true of merchants of to-day. Let an important position open and every employer knows how hard it is to fill it: impossible, in fact, sometimes. It is not that the positions are not there: it is that the men are not there. If a young man has qualities in him that are worth $10,000 a year to an employer, the position will present itself to him fast enough. He doesn't need to be told where such a chance exists. He doesn't wait for others to show him the way. He finds the way himself.

A good deal of discontent in business comes from young men in what we call the smaller cities. They feel that if they could only get into one of our larger cities they could succeed. But, all the same, a man's success never depends on the place in which he lives: it depends on the man.

It is the man, not the place that counts. The magnet of worth is the drawing power in business. It is what you are, not where you are. If a young man has the right stuff in him, he need not fear where he lives or does his business. Many a large man has expanded a small place. The idea that a small place retards a man's progress is pure nonsense. If the community does not offer facilities for a growing business, they can be brought to it. Proper force can do anything. All that is needed is right direction. The vast majority of people are like sheep: they follow a leader. Success is the most contagious thing on earth: people love to be identified with it. And in a small community a young man has some chance to lead. A man can often throw a stronger light upon a metropolis when he is a little away from it than he could if he were in it and of it.

The higher salaries of the larger cities are, perhaps, what attract young men more potently than any other factor. But these salaries are not so high as they are often said to be, nor will the city income buy as much in the metropolis as is frequently believed. It is a common mistake of young men to base the higher salary of the larger city on the smaller expenses of the smaller city. This is always an attractive calculation; but, unfortunately, it won't work out. A salary of $2,000 a year in the big city will not bring a young man by far the comfortable living which $1,000 a year means to him in the smaller community. A rising young clerk, manager, or business man in the small city lives like a king in comparison to the man of equal position in the large centre. He need only earn a thousand a year to have his own little home, by lease or purchase, with God's pure sunshine on four sides of it; not a few filtered rays of light through an air-shaft. To the wife of such a man her neighbors mean her friends. She has time for her children, her home, her social duties, her reading, and her church. Her children have their own grass-plot for their play-ground. The fields and woods are within view or walk. The husband's friends live all around him. He knows the man who lives next door. The man in the large city doesn't. His neighbors' children are his children's playmates. His social life has a meaning to it. He has time to read, something which the man in the larger city, whom he envies, has not. His church is to him like a family gathering every Sunday morning. The blood of health rushes through the veins of his children as they sleep and play in an unpolluted atmosphere. Every step of progress which he makes in business is known to his friends. Life means something to such a man; it means happiness, and the wise man is he who stays where he is happy.

No young man need ever feel that, by reason of his residence in a smaller city, he is not a part of the life of the country. That very fact makes him an essential part of it. He is the producer. His city makes possible the greater centre. The sensible young man stays in the smaller city these days. Suppose the measure of success is smaller: the measure of happiness is greater. Happiness does not depend upon success any more than success means happiness. Emerson, in that magnificent essay on "The Young American," well says: "Money is of no value: it cannot spend itself. All depends upon the skill of the spender." Great successes do not by any means bring corresponding happiness. It is what a man gets out of his life that makes him happy.

I tell you, my friends, the really fortunate young man to-day, although he may not know it, is he who has good health, honest principles, a determination to succeed, lives in a small city and is content to stay there. He will find plenty of opportunities there for any talents he may possess, for any measure of success he can achieve. No town is too small for any success, any more than nothing is too small to be thoroughly done. A small thing is a pin, for example. But yet it takes seven men to make a perfect pin.

Thoroughness is the earning power of success, and success must always be earned. You cannot hurry it. It is like respect; you must earn it. It comes only to a man when, with honest principles and thoroughness of method, he has prepared himself for it, and when he is ready for it.

The best man is the man who does his best. When we make the most of what we do, we make the most of what we are.

I said a little way back that success called for certain sacrifices, and this especially applies to a young man's social life. Now, some young men have a dangerous belief that employers have no jurisdiction over their evening hours. But the fact is that an employer has some rights in this respect. He has a perfect right to expect that his employé shall not only carry himself respectably in his social life, but that he shall temper his social habits to business demands. No employer can afford to intrust responsibilities in the hands of a man in the daytime who endangers them by his social habits after nightfall.

The average young man is very apt to go to extremes in this. On the one hand there are those who so immerse themselves in business that they shut out every social pleasure. They get so weighted down with the serious problems of life that they become impatient with the lighter side of living as being frothy and silly. A young man who allows himself to get so thoroughly wedded to business that he can see no good in social life is his own worst enemy. He becomes unprofitable to himself, and uninteresting to other people. He stagnates. Business is like water and fire, my friends, an excellent servant, but dangerous if you allow it to become your master. Nothing in the world can make a man more thoroughly selfish and so forgetful of the rights and comforts of those in his home as too close an application to business. Business is for the office; very little of it for the home.

Every young man must have a certain amount of social life. It is good for him. His nature demands it. We must play in order to work better. The mind needs a change of thought just as the body needs a change of raiment. A wholesome social life broadens a young man: it rounds him out. But, on the other hand, there are young men who go to excess in their social life, and this is just as deadly as the other is stagnating. Social pleasures are like everything else in this world; their danger lies not in their use, but in their abuse. No mind can be fresh in the morning that has been kept at a tension the night before by late hours. A young man at twenty-five needs more sleep than does a man at fifty. It is his building time. Any young man who, except upon rare occasions, grants himself less than eight hours' sleep robs himself of just so much vitality. That should be every young man's positive rule. The midnight hours of eleven and twelve o'clock should always be passed in sleep. Asleep by eleven and up by seven is the course which hundreds of successful men have laid out for themselves. The

loss of vitality brought by less than eight hours' sleep may
not be felt or noticed at first. But sleeping is only Nature's banking system of principal and interest. A man to
be a factor in the business world must have a fresh mind
and a clear brain, and that is only possible where he gives
them proper rest. Social excesses make this impossible.
I care not how strong or robust a young fellow may be,
social dissipation will sooner or later influence his work.

Now, I am not a crank; I do not advocate total abstinence of any habits to which human nature is prone.
There are many good people who say to young men that
they mustn't smoke, they mustn't dance, they mustn't play
cards, they mustn't go to the theatre, they mustn't do this
and they mustn't do that. I know I am treading on thin
ice here, and I do not propose to advise any young man
which of these things he may do and which he may not
do. Every young man knows in his own heart what is
good for him and what is not good. But one thing I do
say, and it is this: I think a young man should have all
the good time he can during those years when he enjoys
a good time most.

Of course one's ideas of good times differ, like the two
little girls who had been in the country all day, and when
asked by their mother if they had enjoyed themselves, replied, with fervor: " Oh, yes, we had a bee-autiful time.
We saw two pigs killed, a house burn down, and a man
buried." Young men will have their pleasures and their
fun, and so long as those pleasures are wholesome no
rigid rule of unbending principles should be forced upon
them.

Taking a young man to task for questionable pleasures
always brings up the story of the young English curate
who was censured by his bishop for going fox-hunting.
It seemed to the bishop to be too worldly. The young
minister replied that his fox-hunting didn't seem to him
any more worldly than did the fact of the bishop's presence at a large masquerade ball a few evenings ago. The
bishop explained that while it was true he had been visiting the house where the ball had taken place, he had not
been within three rooms of the dancing any time during
the evening. " Oh, well, if it comes to that," said the

young minister, "I never get within three fields of the hounds."

There is no sense in saying to an active, healthy young fellow that he must sit home five nights in a week and read a book, and the other secular night go out and take a nice little walk. He won't do it, and I don't blame him. It's unnatural. Little Lord Fauntleroys are all very agreeable to read about, but I don't think we want them in actual life.

Now, young men often ask what are these social pleasures and indulgences which seriously affect a young man's success? A specific answer cannot be given. No one set of rules can be applied to all. An exhilarating pleasure to one is often a positive injury to another. The only rule by which a young man can live in his social life is this: any social pleasure which affects a young man's health, which clouds his mind, from which he rises the next morning tired rather than refreshed, is bad for him and affects his success. Good health is the foundation of all possible success in life; affect the one and you affect the other. If a pleasure refreshes and elevates your mind and body, if you feel better for it next morning, that is a pleasure good for you. No other rule can be given. Only one point of self-indulgence do I wish this evening to dwell upon in a specific manner, and that is an indulgence in alcoholic liquors. When I speak of this question I take it entirely away from any religious or moral stand-point. To me it is not a question whether it is right or wrong for a young man to indulge in spirituous liquors. It is rather can he do it than should he do it. Is it wise rather than is it wrong? And I say to him, plainly and directly, he cannot do it. I say this to every young fellow in this audience honestly from my own observation and experience as a mere boy who, when he started out, did not know exactly what position to take in this matter.

Some years ago there was in Brooklyn a boy about sixteen years old who began attending public dinners as a reporter. Wines were then more freely used at dinners than now. The first public dinner he was sent to report was a New England Society banquet. He was extremely anxious to succeed, because it would mean other assignments. He had been brought up in his father's home with wine on the table, because in his native country, Holland, light wine is the common beverage and not an intoxicant. The decision which the young reporter had to make in Brooklyn that night was, therefore, not approached with prejudice. His common-sense simply argued it out for him that if he drank liquors his mind might not be so clear to report the speeches he was sent there to take. And so he shielded his wine glasses—a practice which he has followed ever since.

Now, that young reporter simply argued to himself what was the wisest thing for him to do, and he did it. And that is the way I want every young man to decide this question. Never mind going into the question of whether it is right or wrong. That might lead to controversy or doubt. Simply take the hard common-sense view of it. The temporary exhilaration which is supposed to come from alcohol, either in diffused or concentrated form, is unnecessary to a young man in good health. Therefore, it can do him absolutely no good. He does not need it, and not an ounce of better health will come to him by reason of it. But it may do him harm. The chances are that it will. And no young man can afford to take a single risk or chance in the morning of a business career. He needs the unhampered use of all his powers; all his health, all his intellect, and all his manners.

I do not ask him to accept this on any ground but that of expediency. He will see for himself that for every young man in business who does drink, no matter how moderately, there is some young man of the abstaining kind waiting around the corner for his place and who will do his work all the better because he does abstain. And employers prefer the abstaining sort. The presidents of the two largest railroads in this country have each told me personally within the past year that they will no longer employ any man for any position on their roads who drinks even moderately. And this is growing to be a common custom in all branches of business. Alcohol is becoming more and more each day to be regarded in the business world as a positive detriment to a man's greatest usefulness.

I cannot, as a return for sobriety, promise to any young

man the remarkable reward of that little boy in Denver, who, with his class in school, was requested by his teacher to write a story. Each boy was to choose his own subject, and the story was to be read without revision by the teacher. So this particular boy chose as his subject: " Virtue Has Its Own Reward," and this was his story: " A poor young man fell in love with the daughter of a rich lady who kept a candy-shop. The poor young man could not marry the rich candy lady's daughter because he had not money enough to buy furniture. A wicked man offered to give the young man twenty-five dollars if he would become a drunkard. The young man wanted the money very much so he could marry the rich candy lady's daughter, but when he got to the saloon he turned to the wicked man and said: ' I will not become a drunkard even for great riches. Get thee behind me, Satan.' And as he turned around to go home he saw lying on the sidewalk a pocketbook containing a million dollars in gold. Then the young lady consented to marry him. They had a beautiful wedding and the next day they had twins. Thus you see that ' virtue has its own reward.' "

Now I cannot promise you a reward quite as speedy nor as rich as this. I can tell you, however, of a more likely one, a more possible one at least—the somewhat curious reward which unexpectedly came to the young reporter at that Brooklyn dinner, of whom I spoke before. One of the speeches he was to report at the banquet was that of the President of the United States, and, not being very expert in his stenography, he failed to get a large part of the speech. So, after the dinner was over, he sought the President, explained his plight, and asked the Chief Magistrate if he could give him a printed copy of the speech. The reporter found the eyes of the President curiously fixed upon him, and heard him say: " My boy, can you wait a few minutes? I want to speak to you." Of course, it was very easy for the boy to wait for the President of the United States and he did so. After fifteen minutes the President beckoned the boy reporter to him and said, abruptly: " Tell me, why did you refuse wine at the dinner this evening? "

Naturally the reporter was surprised. But he explained

the resolution he had made for the first time that evening; whereupon the President, reaching for one of the plate cards on the table, said: " I wish you would write your name and address on this card, please." Well, my friends, to make a long story short, that young reporter's paper the next day had the only verbatim report of the President's speech, whereas he himself received this note:

My dear young friend:—
I have been telling Mrs. Hayes this morning of what you told me at the dinner last evening and she was very much interested. She would like to see you, and asks if you will call at where we are stopping in Brooklyn, this evening at 8:30.
Very faithfully yours,
RUTHERFORD B. HAYES.

It was a valuable friendship which that young reporter made that evening, my friends. Other friendships were constantly made possible to him through it. And it is easy for that young reporter, speaking to you to-night, to look back and trace his starting point of acquaintance and opportunities to that unexpected friendship with the President of the United States and continued by a constant interchange of letters and advice until only a few days before his passing away.

I have told this story chiefly to impress upon young men the fallacy of the idea that a strict adherence to a principle, whether it relates to spirituous liquors or anything else, makes a young man appear rather " babyish," that he is tied to his mother's apron-strings as it is sometimes called, and in consequence is sometimes a barrier to his social popularity. In all the nineteen years in which that Brooklyn reporter has since refused to drink liquor at dinners, public or private, he has never found that he lost a single friend by his refusal. A young man who starts out in life with a fixed principle, whether it be that he will not drink, nor smoke, nor indulge in anything which in his heart he feels is not good for him, or in which he does not conscientiously believe, and adheres to that principle at all times, holds in his hand one of the most powerful elements of success in the world to-day. There is a great deal of good common-sense abroad in this world of ours, and a young man with a good principle is always safe to depend upon it. Aside from the specific habit I have touched upon, the key to success for a young man in his social life is that of moderation—of temperance. In the English language there is not a more beautiful word than that of temperance —not as we so commonly understand it as applying only to one indulgence and that in a prohibitive sense; I mean its true meaning—moderation. His social indulgences must be tempered with reason or common-sense. A young man whose thoughts during business hours recur to a pleasure of the evening before, or are constantly fixed upon a sport of the morrow, soon finds himself outdistanced in the race for success by those who keep such things in their proper places. When a young fellow knows the standing of the base-ball clubs in the various leagues, or the minute records of the crack bicyclists better than he knows the prices of the goods he is paid to sell, or the discounts which his house gives to its customers, his interest in sports is directed against his own good. What are called " base-ball cranks," or " bicycle fiends," or " foot-ball enthusiasts " are never good business men, and their standing in the community is always on a par with their overwrought interest.

In other words, a young man must remember that his days are for work—not for pleasure or thoughts of pleasure. If he feels that success allows him no leisure, he must remember that leisure is not for young men. That is something for which a man works. It comes when it is earned, and it generally comes at the right time in a man's life; when he has years enough and sense enough to know what to do with it. Young manhood is the time for work.

See how men are becoming more moderate; more temperate in every phase of life. Self-control is to-day the ruling tendency with men. In every direction we see a striving for self-poise. The finest type of man who exists to-day is he who takes no extreme position on any point, but who is calm in his demeanor, temperate in his judgment, judicial in his bearing, a man who has himself well in hand.

Prudence is teaching men that they cannot afford to have habits which put their health and self-control in peril.

One sees this moderation in all things. See how swearing is going out of vogue. The man whose speech is punctured with the oaths which characterized the conversation of gentlemen in former days, is to-day stamped as vulgar, as coarse. A drunkard to-day is declared a nuisance in the same society which only a few years back shielded his weakness. Coarse indulgences of all kinds have fallen under reproach. They are to-day offensive to good taste. So to say to a young man to study self-control, self-poise, temperance, moderation, is not alone to tell him what is best for him, but it is to place him exactly in line with the tendencies of other men.

The confusing assertion is sometimes made by young men that men are not so religious as they were. But the facts are that true, honest, practical religion actually holds a more secure place in the hearts of strong men than ever before. And this is the point I want to impress upon young men so far as their religious life is concerned; that religion does not imply a sickly sentimentality, as some young men believe. It is not a mark of intelligence to scoff at sacred things. A true belief in God is one of the manliest qualities which a young man can possess. Without a respect for sacred things no man can earn respect for himself. Religion is too much a matter of one's innermost feelings to be governed by rule. But in these days, when many of the truths which our forefathers held sacred are being discussed in so-called " new lights," and when the beliefs of many are in a sense disturbed by reason of these " new doctrines," it is well that young men should have it said to them to bear in mind one or two fundamental truths.

No matter what present revelations or subsequent discoveries may prove or seek to disprove as to religious teachings, one great essential can never be altered: that is, the necessity of a firm faith, an absolute belief that a wise God rules over this universe and over the destiny of each man, woman, or child. Whatever constitutes that God is not for us to solve. Enough is it for us to know that there is a God, that there is a Supreme Being, a Creator, a Ruler. No one should doubt that one great and essential fact, and the young man who hesitates or refuses to believe in the existence of that God makes the greatest and most momentous mistake of his life. Without that faith, without that absolute conviction, he will be hindered and crippled in whatever he undertakes. On that point he cannot afford to err; to doubt it, even in the light of the most advanced knowledge that can ever be presented, he cannot for one single moment allow himself. This much is absolute. Another point is that every person can go to that Creator and Dispenser of all good and receive, through supplication, guidance in all affairs. He must have, because he can have, an earnest, a heartfelt, an honest belief in prayer. Whatsoever arguments may be brought to bear upon this question, one thing remains undisputed: that an honest and earnest prayer sent forth from the human heart to its Heavenly Father, for guidance or for help, is sure, and absolutely sure, to bring strength to the soul and enlightenment to the mind. Nothing can ever refute this. Too many millions of people have experienced the truth of this in their lives. Argument on this point is fruitless. A young man might as well argue that he loved his mother. Conscious experience does more than theoretical argument, and that conscious experience has taught the happiest men and the best women that there is a direct communication between God and the humblest person on His footstool. A prayer for guidance sent from the heart of man to that God is never lost.

Have, then, an absolute faith in God and in prayer, and only one thing more is needed to complete the fundamental basis of all religions: an honest effort to live according to our conscience, to the best and truest that is within ourselves, and to do for others what we might wish they would do for us. For the greatest and final test of a Christian life is that, the love of one for another. Here is a simple code of religion for any young man. If his heart craves it and his mind can compass it, he can go deeper and believe more. But less he cannot accept. Nor, if he is wise, will he wish to accept less. It asks for no great mental capacity; it is beyond the mental power of none. It will stand the severest test. It is simple and yet ample.

I do not say that a young man should stop with this simple code. But, nevertheless, the great fact must not be forgotten that one reason why young men do not accept the principles of religion more than they do, is because those principles are, as a rule, made too complex for them: they are carried beyond their understanding. The simpler this whole question of religion is made, the better: the more attractive it is, the more appealing it becomes. For the true greatness of religion lies in its simplicity. Take a young man into the realm of creed and doctrine and you confuse him. I believe it is better to leave those questions, complex at their best as they are, and open to individual construction, until the judgment of maturity comes to the young man to help him to handle them intelligently.

I tell you, my young friend, you who sometimes are inclined to doubt the necessity or the efficacy of such a belief, there come times in the life of every man when absolutely nothing satisfies him short of a heart belief in a God and a faith that he can go to that God and pour out to Him the fulness of his heart. What I want young men to do is not to think of God as One unseen and unreachable, but as a Father, a Friend, a personal God, One to whom they can go at any time and talk as they would to an earthly father. Such a faith partakes of no gloom, but sheds light upon a man's every action. It means no depression of spirits, as so many young men interpret religion. On the contrary, it means an uplifting—an elevation of one's nature with which nothing that he can bring into his life can compare. For the only help, my friends, that, after all, really helps a man is when he looks up.

And now just a word on a subject always fresh and always interesting, that is—marriage, and then I am through.

When a young man deliberately lays out for himself a single life, based upon some wrong fancy, some idle notion, or pure selfishness, I believe he makes the mistake of his lifetime. " But," say young men, " the girls are so gay; so frivolous. They are too expensive." But I am inclined to think that the gayety and the frivolity which

is sometimes attributed to girls as their characteristics
might be found to be nothing more than superficialities
if our young men took the trouble to find out. Girls are
pretty much as men appeal to them. They show their best
side when that side is appealed to. And if a young man
can't find it, it doesn't prove that it isn't there, by any
means. What is worth having is worth taking some
trouble to find. As to the girls being expensive, well,
good things are expensive, and a good wife is a pretty
good thing. If she costs a bit, she's worth it. And the
better she is, the more she's worth. But young men must
remember one thing: a good wife never impoverishes a
man. She always makes him richer. A good wife always
brings more to a man than she takes from him. Nor are
our girls quite so expensive as they look. The fact is,
that girls are not given credit enough for a willingness to
do without. But a good deal depends upon who asks
them to do without. If it is the father, and he has a comfortable plenty, and the girl knows she can have pretty
things just as well as not—well, she loves her father, of
course; but she doesn't like to do without. Suppose,
however, someone else asks her to do without; someone
who asks her something else first and then asks her to do
without. And she happens to think that that somebody
is the only person in the world whom she wanted to ask
her the something else first? Then will she refuse or even
pout if he asks her to do without? I don't think so; not
the girl you ought to marry, at any rate.

" Well, all the same, I'm in doubt about them," still
says the young man. But that is only because he hasn't
met the right one. When he does, he won't be in doubt.
A man is never in doubt about the girl he loves, and he
never stops to argue whether she is frivolous, or gay, or
expensive. That isn't the way love works. It doesn't
stop to analyze. If it does, it isn't the kind of love on
which it is safe to marry. True love doesn't stop to consider how a girl appears; whether she is talented; whether
she is graceful, or pretty; whether she is educated or trav-
elled; whether she can dress well or entertain well. When
a man loves a girl he loves her for what she is. He doesn't
marry a dictionary for his library, or an ornament for his

home: he marries her because he feels that no home could be a home without her. A woman's charm lies not in what she knows, but in what she is. That is an old-fashioned idea, my friends, very old-fashioned in these days when we hear so much of the higher education of women. But we still have to prove that all things new are better than some of those old-fashioned ideas.

To marry a girl because of some particular trait; because a young man likes her better, perhaps, than he does some other girls; because, maybe, he respects, fancies, or admires her; because there happens to be some bond of sympathy in her nature and his: that is not the right basis for a happy marriage. They are things which appeal to us in any dear friend, man or woman. The girl that a young man should marry is she who fills all his life, his every thought, who guides him in his every act, whose face comes before him in everything that he does—the girl, in short, who is necessary to him; without whom he feels life would be a blank; without whom he could not live; who is the whole world to him; all that there is in life and all that there is in death. If you ask what love is, that is what it is. It is all or nothing. And when a young man feels that way for a girl, that is the girl he loves and the girl he ought to marry. It will make little difference to him whether she be rich or poor, pretty or homely, talented or not. Enough is it for him, as it should be, that she is affectionate in her nature, sympathetic with his aims in life, responsive to his thoughts, appreciative of his qualities. These are the traits in a woman which last the longest and remain with a man throughout his life.

The feeling upon which marriage should be based is the feeling upon which rested that exquisite tribute which that sweet spirit of American literature, Nathaniel Hawthorne, always paid to his wife by never opening a letter from her until he first washed his hands. Or, that graceful and most beautiful of all tributes I know of ever spoken by man of his wife, said by Joseph H. Choate, the great New York lawyer, who when someone asked him: " Mr. Choate, if you could not be yourself, whom would you rather be? " replied, " Mrs. Choate's second husband." When a man feels that way about a woman, that is the woman God intended for that man's wife. That is love.

And now, my friends, I have tried to give, not a new interpretation of success and the keys which are factors in it, for that is hardly possible for any man to do. Anything said on this subject is, of necessity, old; all that one can hope for is to say old things in a different way. Some of you may perhaps think that what I have said lacks idealization; that I have made success too material. But that has been my purpose; to aim only at material success, because I believe that that must come first to a young man. He must understand first what he must do for himself before he can do for others. He must put himself right first; then he can set others right. Understanding success himself, it will be made clear to him that a success which is of self alone is no success at all. He will find out for himself what success enables its possessor to do for others; that success is only satisfying to its possessor as it is made the instrument of helping others. Experience alone can teach him that higher meaning of success. Power simply for power is failure. The greatness of power is the good we do with it.

But all that comes afterward, as I say. The best way to help others, the community at large, as well as those of one's own immediate environment, is to do one's simple duty in one's proper sphere. If there is anyone who doubts this, let him test the proposition by reflecting how the unsuccessful man clogs his immediate surroundings; how costly he is to a community, and of how little aid he is in these contingencies which call for help for others. Nothing hinders others so much as our own failures; nothing, on the other hand, can make the success of so many possible as our own success. We cannot rise in this world without helping others to rise. But it all comes back to ourselves first. We must achieve success for ourselves before we can apply success to others and in its very best sense. We ourselves must learn before we can teach others. Peter Cooper, George Peabody, Stephen Girard, George W. Childs—all those whose lives meant something for others, had to make their own way first.

And as they made their own way they did what all should do and must do to get the only pleasure and reward there is in any success—they practised that highest altruism which made their names immortal and their memories sweet.

And so I leave these words with you. It is only a young man's message to young men. The message is simple enough. There's nothing impossible about it to any young man, so long as he bears in mind the salient points: First.—What success means; the successful doing, the doing well of whatever he does in whatever position he is. Second.—The price of success; hard work, patience, and a few sacrifices.

Then for his keys.—In his religious life: A firm, unwavering belief in God and in prayer, and a life consistent with that belief for himself and for others. In his social life: Moderation. In his marriage: Love. And in business: Thoroughness. Not thoroughness alone in large things or what is apparent to the eye; but thoroughness in all things; not slighting the small things.

CHARLES F. BROWNE

Photogravure after a photograph from life

CHARLES FARRAR BROWNE

("ARTEMUS WARD")

THE MORMONS

[Lecture by Charles F. Browne—"Artemus Ward"—humorist (born in Waterford, Maine, April 26, 1834; died in Southampton, England, March 6, 1867), delivered upon his first appearance before an English audience, in Egyptian Hall, Piccadilly, London, November 13, 1866. This was the most elaborate of all of his lectures, and included passages from both "The Babes in the Woods," and "Sixty Minutes in Africa," the delivery of which in various cities from the Atlantic to the Pacific coast, before he went abroad, had established his reputation as an American humorist. It was received by his English hearers with flattering comment. His jokes, one newspaper-writer remarked, "always came just in the place one least expected to find them. Half the enjoyment of the evening lay, to some of those present, in listening to the cachinnation of the people who only found them out some two or three minutes after they were made, and who then laughed apparently at some grave statement of fact. Reduced to paper, the showman's jokes are certainly not brilliant; almost their whole effect lies in their seemingly impromptu character. They are carefully led up to, of course, but they are uttered as if they were mere afterthoughts of which the speaker is hardly sure." Another critic has observed, "However much he caused his audience to laugh, no smile appeared upon his own face. It was grave even to solemnity while he was giving utterance to the most delicious absurdities." The inimitable drawl—impossible of suggestion or reproduction in type—which characterized his speech also added to its humor; while the droll mixture of fact and fancy, serious statement with extravagant flight, gave piquancy to the performance. The lecture was illustrated by a panorama, and the printed programme, reproduced in fac-simile on the following pages. gave a whimsical synopsis of the production, with a special note announcing that "Mr. Artemus Ward will call on the citizens of London, at their residences, and explain any jokes in his narrative which they may not understand."]

From "Complete Works f Artemus Ward," edited by "Eli Perkins" and published by the G. W. Dillingham Co., New York. Copyrighted.

123

EGYPTIAN HALL,
PICCADILLY.

Every Night (except Saturday) at 8,

SATURDAY AFTERNOON AT 3.

𝕬RTEMUS 𝕸ARD
AMONG THE MORMONS.

During the Vacation the Hall has been carefully Swept out, and a new Door-Knob has been added to the Door.

MR. ARTEMUS WARD *will call on the Citizens of London, at their residences, and explain any jokes in his narrative which they may not understand.*

A person of long-established integrity will take excellent care of Bonnets, Cloaks, etc., during the entertainment; the Audience better leave their money, however, with MR. WARD; he will return it to them in a day or two, or invest it for them in America, as they may think best.

☞ Nobody must say that he likes the Lecture unless he wishes to be thought eccentric; and nobody must say that he doesn't like it unless he really *is* eccentric. (This requires thinking over, but it will amply repay perusal.)

The Panorama used to Illustrate Mr. Ward's Narrative is rather worse than Panoramas usually are.

MR. WARD will not be responsible for any debts of his own contracting.

PROGRAMME.

———o———

I.

APPEARANCE OF ARTEMUS WARD,

Who will be greeted with applause. ☞ The Stall-keeper is particularly requested to attend to this. ✍ When quiet has been restored, the Lecturer will present a rather frisky prologue, of about ten minutes in length, and of nearly the same width. It perhaps isn't necessary to speak of the depth.

II.

THE PICTURES COMMENCE HERE, the first one being a view of the California Steamship. Large crowd of citizens on the wharf, who appear to be entirely willing that ARTEMUS WARD shall go. "Bless you, Sir!" they say. "Don't hurry about coming back. Stay away for years, if you want to!" It was very touching. Disgraceful treatment of the passengers, who are obliged to go forward to smoke pipes, while the steamer herself is allowed 2 Smoke Pipes amidships. At Panama. A glance at Mexico.

III.

THE LAND OF GOLD.

Montgomery Street, San Francisco. The Gold Bricks. Street Scenes. "The Orphan Cabman, or the Mule-Driver's Step-Father." The Chinese Theatre. Sixteen square yards of a Chinese Comic Song.

IV.

THE LAND OF SILVER.

Virginia City, the wild young metropolis of the new Silver State. Fortunes are made there in a day. There are instances on record of young men going to this place without a shilling—poor and friendless —yet by energy, intelligence, and a careful disregard to business, they have been enabled to leave there, owing hundreds of pounds.

V.

THE GREAT DESERT AT NIGHT.

A dreary waste of Sand. The Sand isn't worth saving, however. Indians occupy yonder mountains. Little Injuns seen in the distance trundling their war-hoops.

VI.

A BIRD'S-EYE VIEW OF GREAT SALT LAKE CITY.

With some entirely descriptive talk.

VII.

MAIN STREET, EAST SIDE.

The Salt Lake Hotel, which is conducted on Temperance principles. The landlord sells nothing stronger than salt butter.

VIII.

THE MORMON THEATRE.

The Lady of Lyons was produced here a short time since, but failed to satisfy a Mormon audience, on account of there being only one Pauline in it. The play was revised at once. It was presented the next night, with fifteen Paulines in the cast, and was a perfect success. ☞ All these statements may be regarded as strictly true. Mr. WARD would not deceive an infant.

IX.

MAIN STREET, WEST SIDE.

This being a view of Main Street, West side, it is naturally a view of the West side of Main Street.

X.

BRIGHAM YOUNG'S HAREM.

Mr. Young is an indulgent father, and a numerous husband. For further particulars call on Mr. WARD, at Egyptian Hall, any Evening this Week. This paragraph is intended to blend business with amusement.

XI.

HEBER C. KIMBALL'S HAREM.

We have only to repeat here the pleasant remarks above in regard to Brigham.

INTERMISSION OF FIVE MINUTES.

XII.

THE TABERNACLE.

XIII.

THE TEMPLE AS IT IS.

XIV.

THE TEMPLE AS IT IS TO BE.

XV.

THE GREAT SALT LAKE.

XVI.

THE ENDOWMENT HOUSE.

The Mormon is initiated into the mysteries of his faith here. The Mormon's religion is singular and his wives are plural.

XVII.

ECHO CAÑON.

XVIII.

THE DESERT, AGAIN.

A more cheerful view. The Plains of Colorado. The Colorado Mountains "might have been seen" in the distance, if the Artist had painted 'em. But he is prejudiced against mountains, because his uncle once got lost on one.

XIX.

BRIGHAM YOUNG AND HIS WIVES.

The pretty girls of Utah mostly marry Young.

XX.

THE ROCKY MOUNTAINS.

XXI.

THE PLAINS OF NEBRASKA.

XXII.

THE PRAIRIE ON FIRE.

RECOMMENDATIONS.

TOTNESS, *Oct. 20th*, 1866.

MR. ARTEMUS WARD: My dear sir—My wife was dangerously unwell for over sixteen years. She was so weak that she could not lift a teaspoon to her mouth. But in a fortunate moment she commenced reading one of your lectures. She got better at once. She gained strength so rapidly that she lifted the cottage piano quite a distance from the floor, and then tipped it over on to her mother-in-law, with whom she had had some little trouble. We like your lectures very much. Please send me a barrel of them. If you should require any more recommendations, you can get any number of them in this place, at two shillings each, the price I charge for this one, and I trust you may be ever happy.

I am, Sir,

Yours truly, and so is my wife, R. SPRINGERS.

An American correspondent of a distinguished journal in Yorkshire thus speaks of Mr. WARD's power as an orator:

It was a grand scene, Mr. ARTEMUS WARD standing on the platform, talking; many of the audience sleeping tranquilly in their seats; others leaving the room and not returning; others crying like a child at some of the jokes—all, all formed a most impressive scene, and showed the powers of this remarkable orator. And when he announced that he should never lecture in that town again, the applause was absolutely deafening.

Doors open at Half-past Seven, commence at Eight.

Conclude at Half-past Nine.

EVERY EVENING EXCEPT SATURDAY.

SATURDAY AFTERNOONS AT 3 P.M.

LADIES AND GENTLEMEN:—You are entirely welcome to my little picture-shop. [Alluding to his panorama.]

I couldn't give you a very clear idea of the Mormons—and Utah—and the Plains—and the Rocky Mountains—without opening a picture-shop——and therefore I open one.

I don't expect to do great things here—but I have thought that if I could make money enough to buy me a passage to New Zealand I should feel that I had not lived in vain.

I don't want to live in vain. I'd rather live in Margate —or here. But I wish when the Egyptians built this hall they had given it a little more ventilation.

If you should be dissatisfied with anything here to-night —I will admit you all free in New Zealand—if you will come to me there for the orders. Any respectable cannibal will tell you where I live. This shows that I have a for-giving spirit.

I really don't care for money. I only travel round to see the world and to exhibit my clothes. These clothes I have on were a great success in America. [He wore a fashion-ably cut dress suit.]

How often do large fortunes ruin young men! I should like to be ruined, but I can get on very well as I am.

I am not an Artist. I don't paint myself——though per-haps if I were a middle-aged single lady I should——yet I have a passion for pictures.—I have had a great many pictures—photographs—taken of myself. Some of them are very pretty—rather sweet to look at for a short time —and as I said before, I like them. I've always loved pictures. I could draw on wood at a very tender age. When a mere child I once drew a small cart-load of raw turnips over a wooden bridge.——The people of the village noticed me. I drew their attention. They said I had a future before me. Up to that time I had an idea it was behind me.

Time passed on. It always does, by the way. You may possibly have noticed that Time passes on.—It is a kind of way Time has.

I became a man. I haven't distinguished myself at all as an artist—but I have always been more or less mixed up

THE MORMONS 129

with art. I have an uncle who takes photographs—and I have a servant who —— takes anything he can get his hands on.

When I was in Rome——Rome in New York State, I mean——a distinguished sculpist wanted to sculp me. But I said "No." I saw through the designing man. My model once in his hands—he would have flooded the market with my busts——and I couldn't stand it to see everybody going round with a bust of me. Everybody would want one of course—and wherever I should go I should meet the educated classes with my bust, taking it home to their families. This would be more than my modesty could stand——and I should have to return to America—— where my creditors are.

I like art. I admire dramatic art—although I failed as an actor.

It was in my school-boy days that I failed as an actor.—— The play was "The Ruins of Pompeii."——I played the ruins. It was not a very successful performance—but it was better than the "Burning Mountain." He was not good. He was a bad Vesuvius.

The remembrance often makes me ask—"Where are the boys of my youth?" I assure you this is not a conundrum. Some are amongst you here——some in America——some are in jail.

Hence arises a most touching question—"Where are the girls of my youth?" Some are married——some would like to be.

Oh my Maria! Alas! she married another. They frequently do. I hope she is happy—because I am.—Some people are not happy. I have noticed that.

A gentleman friend of mine came to me one day with tears in his eyes. I said, "Why these weeps?" He said he had a mortgage on his farm——and wanted to borrow £200. I lent him the money——and he went away. Some time afterward he returned with more tears. He said he must leave me forever. I ventured to remind him of the £200 he borrowed. He was much cut up. I thought I would not be hard upon him — so told him I would throw off £100. He brightened—shook my hand —and said—"Old friend—I won't allow you to outdo me in liberality——I'll throw off the other hundred."

As a manager I was always rather more successful than as an actor.

Some years ago I engaged a celebrated Living American Skeleton for a tour through Australia. He was the thinnest man I ever saw. He was a splendid skeleton. He didn't weigh anything scarcely——and I said to myself—the people of Australia will flock to see this tremendous curiosity. It is a long voyage—as you know—from New York to Melbourne—and to my utter surprise the skeleton had no sooner got out to sea than he commenced eating in the most horrible manner. He had never been on the ocean before—and he said it agreed with him——I thought so! ——I never saw a man eat so much in my life. Beef, mutton, pork——he swallowed them all like a shark——and between meals he was often discovered behind barrels eating hard-boiled eggs. The result was that, when we reached Melbourne, this infamous skeleton weighed sixty-four pounds more than I did!

I thought I was ruined——but I wasn't. I took him on to California——another very long sea voyage——and when I got him to San Francisco I exhibited him as a fat man.

This story hasn't anything to do with my entertainment, I know——but one of the principal features of my entertainment is that it contains so many things that don't have anything to do with it.

My orchestra is small——but I am sure it is very good —so far as it goes. I give my pianist £10 a night—and his washing.

I like Music.—I can't sing. As a singist I am not a success. I am saddest when I sing. So are those who hear me. They are sadder even than I am.

The other night some silver-voiced young men came under my window and sang—" Come where my love lies dreaming."——I didn't go. I didn't think it would be correct.

I found music very soothing when I lay ill with fever in Utah——and I was very ill——I was fearfully wasted. My face was hewn down to nothing—and my nose was so sharp I didn't dare to stick it into other people's business—for fear it would stay there—and I should never get

it again. And on those dismal days a Mormon lady——
she was married—tho' not so much so as her husband—
he had fifteen other wives——she used to sing a ballad
commencing " Sweet bird—do not fly away! "——and I
told her I wouldn't. She played the accordion divinely—
accordingly I praised her.

I met a man in Oregon who hadn't any teeth—not a
tooth in his head——yet that man could play on the bass
drum better than any man I ever met. He kept a hotel.
They have queer hotels in Oregon. I remember one where
they gave me a bag of oats for a pillow——I had night
mares of course. In the morning the landlord said—
How do you feel—old hoss—hay?——I told him I felt
my oats.

Permit me now to quietly state that although I am here
with my cap and bells, I am also here with some serious
descriptions of the Mormons—their manners—their customs——and while the pictures I shall present to your
notice are by no means works of art—they are painted from
photographs actually taken on the spot—and I am sure I
need not inform any person present who was ever in the
Territory of Utah that they are as faithful as they could
possibly be.

I went to Great Salt Lake City by way of California.

I went to California on the steamer " Ariel."—This is the
steamer Ariel. [Pointing to the panorama.]

Oblige me by calmly gazing on the steamer " Ariel "——
and when you go to California be sure and go on some
other steamer——because the " Ariel " isn't a very good
one.

When I reached the " Ariel "—at pier No. 4—New York
—I found the passengers in a state of great confusion about
their things—which were being thrown around by the
ship's porters in a manner at once damaging and idiotic.
So great was the excitement—my fragile form was smashed
this way—and jammed that way—till finally I was shoved
into a state-room which was occupied by two middle-aged
females—who said, " Base man—leave us—O, leave us! "
——I left them——Oh—I left them!

We reached Acapulco, on the coast of Mexico, in due

time. Nothing of special interest occurred at Acapulco ——only some of the Mexican ladies are very beautiful. They all have brilliant black hair——hair " black as starless night "——if I may quote from the " Family Herald." It don't curl.——A Mexican lady's hair never curls—— it is straight as an Indian's. Some people's hair won't curl under any circumstances.——My hair won't curl under two shillings.

[Pointing to the panorama—] The Great thoroughfare of the imperial city of the Pacific Coast.

The Chinese form a large element in the population of San Francisco—and I went to the Chinese Theatre.

A Chinese play often lasts two months. Commencing at the hero's birth, it is cheerfully conducted from week to week till he is either killed or married.

The night I was there a Chinese comic vocalist sang a Chinese comic song. It took him six weeks to finish it— but, as my time was limited, I went away at the expiration of two hundred and fifteen verses. There were 11,000 verses to this song—the chorus being " Tural lural dural, ri fol day "——which was repeated twice at the end of each verse——making—as you will at once see—the appalling number of 22,000 " tural lural dural, ri fol days "——and the man still lives.

[Pointing to panorama—] Virginia City—in the bright new State of Nevada.

A wonderful little city—right in the heart of the famous Washoe silver regions——the mines of which annually produce over twenty-five millions of solid silver. This silver is melted into solid bricks—of about the size of ordinary house-bricks—and carted off to San Francisco with mules. The roads often swarm with these silver wagons.

One hundred and seventy-five miles to the east of this place are the Reese River silver mines—which are supposed to be the richest in the world.

[Pointing to panorama—] The great American Desert in winter-time——the desert which is so frightfully gloomy always. No trees——no houses——no people—save the miserable beings who live in wretched huts and have charge of the horses and mules of the Overland Mail Company.

This picture is a great work of art.——It is an oil paint-ing—done in petroleum. It is by the old masters. It was the last thing they did before dying. They did this and then they expired.

The most celebrated artists of London are so delighted with this picture that they come to the hall every day to gaze at it. I wish you were nearer to it—so you could see it better. I wish I could take it to your residences and let you see it by daylight. Some of the greatest artists in Lon-don come here every morning before daylight with lan-terns to look at it. They say they never saw anything like it before——and they hope they never shall again.

When I first showed this picture in New York, the audi-ences were so enthusiastic in their admiration of this picture that they called for the artist——and when he appeared they threw brick-bats at him. [It was the lecturer's first intention to have the pictures well painted, but he after-ward decided to burlesque the entire panorama and give additional material for his jests.]

[Pointing to panorama—] A bird's-eye view of Great Salt Lake City——the strange city in the desert about which so much has been heard——the city of the people who call themselves Saints.

I know there is much interest taken in these remarkable people—ladies and gentlemen——and I have thought it better to make the purely descriptive part of my enter-tainment entirely serious.——I will not—then—for the next ten minutes—confine myself to my subject.

Some seventeen years ago, a small band of Mormons—headed by Brigham Young—commenced in the present thrifty metropolis of Utah. The population of the Terri-tory of Utah is over 100,000—chiefly Mormons——and they are increasing at the rate of from five to ten thousand annually. The converts to Mormonism now are almost ex-clusively confined to English and Germans.—Wales and Cornwall have contributed largely to the population of Utah during the last few years. The population of Great Salt Lake City is 20,000. The streets are eight rods wide —and are neither flagged nor paved. A stream of pure mountain spring water courses through each street—and is conducted into the gardens of the Mormons. The houses are mostly of adobe—or sun-dried brick—and present a neat and comfortable appearance.—They are usually a story and a half high. Now and then you see a fine modern house in Salt Lake City—but no house that is dirty, shabby, and dilapidated—because there are no absolutely poor people in Utah. Every Mormon has a nice garden—and every Mormon has a tidy dooryard.—Neatness is a great characteristic of the Mormons.

The Mormons profess to believe that they are the chosen people of God———they call themselves Latter-day Saints———and they call us people of the outer world Gentiles. They say that Mr. Brigham Young is a prophet—the legitimate successor of Joseph Smith, who founded the Mormon religion. They also say they are authorized—by special revelation from heaven—to marry as many wives as they can comfortably support.

This wife-system they call plurality.—The world calls it polygamy. That, at its best, it is an accursed thing, I need not of course inform you———but you will bear in mind that I am here as a rather cheerful reporter of what I saw in Utah———and I fancy it isn't at all necessary for me to grow virtuously indignant over something we all know is hideously wrong.

You will be surprised to hear—I was amazed to see—that among the Mormon women there are some few persons of education—of positive cultivation. As a class, the Mormons are not an educated people—but they are by no means the community of ignoramuses so many writers have told us they were.

The valley in which they live is splendidly favored. They raise immense crops. They have mills of all kinds. They have coal, lead, and silver mines. All they eat, all they drink, all they wear, they can produce themselves, and still have a great abundance to sell to the gold regions of Idaho on the one hand and the silver regions of Nevada on the other.

The president of this remarkable community———the head of the Mormon church———is Brigham Young. He is called President Young—and Brother Brigham. He is about fifty-four years old—although he doesn't look to be over forty-five. He has sandy hair and whiskers—is of

THE MORMONS

medium height—and is a little inclined to corpulency. He was born in the State of Vermont. His power is more absolute than that of any living sovereign.—Yet he uses it with such consummate discretion that his people are almost madly devoted to him—and that they would cheerfully die for him if they thought the sacrifice were demanded, I cannot doubt.

He is a man of enormous wealth. One-tenth of everything sold in the Territory of Utah goes to the church——and Mr. Brigham Young is the church. It is supposed that he speculates with these funds——at all events, he is one of the wealthiest men now living——worth several millions, without doubt. He is a bold, bad man——but that he is also a man of extraordinary administrative ability no one can doubt who has watched his astounding career for the past ten years. It is only fair for me to add that he treated me with marked kindness during my sojourn in Utah.

[Pointing to the panorama—] The West Side of Main Street—Salt Lake City—including a view of the Salt Lake Hotel. It is a temperance hotel. I prefer temperance hotels—although they sell worse liquor than other kind of hotels. But the Salt Lake Hotel sells none——nor is there a bar in all Salt Lake City——but I found when I was thirsty—and I generally am—that I could get some very good brandy of one of the elders—on the sly—and I never on any account allow my business to interfere with my drinking.

[Pointing to panorama—] There is the Overland Mail Coach——that is, the den on wheels in which we have been crammed for the past ten days—and ten nights.——Those of you who have been in Newgate—— —— —— —— —— —— ——and stayed there any length of time ——as visitors——can realize how I felt.

The American Overland Mail Route commences at Sacramento, California, and ends at Atchison, Kansas. The distance is 2,200 miles——but you go part of the way by rail. The Pacific Railway is now completed from Sacramento, California, to Folsom, California,——which only leaves 2,211 miles to go by coach. This breaks the monotony——it came very near breaking my back.

[Pointing to panorama—]   The Mormon Theatre.—
This edifice is the exclusive property of Brigham Young.
It will comfortably hold 3,000 persons—and I beg you will
believe me when I inform you that its interior is quite as
brilliant as that of any theatre in London.

The actors are all Mormon amateurs, who charge nothing for their services.

You must know that very little money is taken at the
doors of this theatre. The Mormons mostly pay in grain
—and all sorts of articles.

The night I gave my little lecture there, among my re-
ceipts were corn, flour, pork, cheese, chickens——on foot
and in the shell.

One family went in on a live pig——and a man attempted to pass a " yaller dog " at the box-office—but my
agent repulsed him. One offered me a doll for admission
——another infant's clothing. I refused to take that——
as a general rule I do refuse.

In the middle of the parquet—in a rocking-chair—with
his hat on—sits Brigham Young. When the play drags
—he either goes out or falls into a tranquil sleep.

A portion of the dress-circle is set apart for the wives
of Brigham Young. From ten to twenty of them are usually present. His children fill the entire gallery—and more
too.

[Pointing to panorama—]   The East Side of Main
Street—Salt Lake City—with a view of the Council Building. The Legislature of Utah meets there. It is like all
legislative bodies. They meet this winter to repeal the laws
which they met and made last winter——and they will
meet next winter to repeal the laws which they met and
made this winter.

I dislike to speak about it——but it was in Utah that I
made the great speech of my life. I wish you could have
heard it. I have a fine education. You may have noticed
it. I speak six different languages——London—Chatham
—and Dover——Margate—Brighton—and Hastings.
My parents sold a cow and sent me to college when I was
quite young. During the vacation I used to teach a school
of whales—and there's where I learned to spout.——I don't
expect applause for a little thing like that. I wish you

could have heard that speech, however. If Cicero———
he's dead now———he has gone from us———but if old
Ciss could have heard that effort it would have given him
the rinderpest. I'll tell you how it was. There are stationed in Utah two regiments of United States troops———
the 21st from California, and the 37th from Nevada. The
20-onesters asked me to present a stand of colors to the
37-sters—and I did it in a speech so abounding in eloquence of a bold and brilliant character———and also some
sweet talk———real pretty shop-keeping talk———that I
worked the enthusiasm of those soldiers up to such a pitch
—that they came very near shooting me on the spot.

[Pointing to panorama—] Brigham Young's Harem.
—These are the houses of Brigham Young. The first one
on the right is the Lion House—so called because a crouch-
ing stone lion adorns the central front window. The adjoining small building is Brigham Young's office—and
where he receives his visitors.—The large house in the centre of the picture—which displays a huge bee-hive—is
called the Bee House. The bee-hive is supposed to be symbolical of the industry of the Mormons. Mrs. Brigham
Young the first—now quite an old lady—lives here with
her children. None of the other wives of the Prophet live
here. In the rear are the school-houses where Brigham
Young's children are educated.

Brigham Young has two hundred wives. Just think of
that! Oblige me by thinking of that. That is—he has
eighty actual wives, and he is spiritually married to one
hundred and twenty more. These spiritual marriages
———as the Mormons call them———are contracted with
aged widows—who think it a great honor to be sealed———
the Mormons call it being sealed———to the Prophet.

So we may say he has two hundred wives. He loves not
wisely—but two hundred well. He is dreadfully married.
He's the most married man I ever saw in my life.

I saw his mother-in-law while I was there. I can't exactly tell you how many there is of her—but it's a good
deal. It strikes me that one mother-in-law is about enough
to have in a family—unless you're very fond of excitement.

A few days before my arrival in Utah, Brigham was married again—to a young and really pretty girl———but he

says he shall stop now. He told me confidentially that he shouldn't get married any more. He says that all he wants now is to live in peace for the remainder of his days—and have his dying pillow soothed by the loving hands of his family. Well—that's all right——that's all right—I suppose——but if all his family soothe his dying pillow—he'll have to go out-doors to die.

By the way—Shakespeare indorses polygamy. He speaks of the Merry Wives of Windsor. How many wives did Mr. Windsor have?——But we will let this pass.

Some of these Mormons have terrific families. I lectured one night by invitation in the Mormon village of Provost ——but during the day I rashly gave a leading Mormon an order admitting himself and family. It was before I knew that he was much married——and they filled the room to overflowing. It was a great success——but I didn't get any money.

[Pointing to panorama—] Heber C. Kimball's Harem. Mr. C. Kimball is the First Vice-President of the Mormon Church, and would, consequently, succeed to the full Presidency on Brigham Young's death.

Brother Kimball is a gay and festive cuss, of some seventy summers——or som'ers thereabout. He has 1,000 head of cattle and a hundred head of wives. He says they are awful eaters.

Mr. Kimball had a son——a lovely young man——who was married to ten interesting wives. But one day—while he was absent from home——these ten wives went out walking with a handsome young man—which so enraged Mr. Kimball's son—which made Mr. Kimball's son so jealous—that he shot himself with a horse pistuel. The doctor who attended him——a very scientific man——informed me that the bullet entered the inner parallelogram of his diaphragmatic thorax, superinducing membraneous hemorrhage in the outer cuticle of his basiliconthamaturgist. It killed him. I should have thought it would. [Soft music.]

I hope his sad ending will be a warning to all young wives who go out walking with handsome young men. Mr. Kimball's son is now no more. He sleeps beneath the cypress, the myrtle, and the willow. This music is a dirge by the eminent pianist for Mr. Kimball's son. He died by request.

I regret to say that efforts were made to make a Mormon of me while I was in Utah.

It was leap-year when I was there—and seventeen young widows——the wives of a deceased Mormon——offered me their hearts and hands. I called on them one day—and, taking their soft white hands in mine—which made eighteen hands altogether——I found them in tears.

And I said——" Why is this thus? What is the reason of this thusness? "

They hove a sigh——seventeen sighs of different size. They said:

" Oh—soon thou wilt be gonested away! "

I told them that when I got ready to leave a place I wentested.

They said, " Doth not like us? "

I said, " I doth—I doth! "

I also said—" I hope your intentions are honorable—as I am a lone child——my parents being far, far away."

They then said—" Wilt not marry us? "

I said—" Oh—no——it cannot was."

Again they asked me to marry them—and again I declined. When they cried—

" Oh—cruel man! This is too much——oh! too much! "

I told them that it was on account of the muchness that I declined.

[Pointing to panorama—] This is the Mormon Temple. It is built of adobe, and will hold 5,000 persons quite comfortably. A full brass and string band often assists the choir of this church——and the choir, I may add, is a remarkably good one.

Brigham Young seldom preaches now. The younger elders—unless on some special occasion—conduct the services. I only heard Mr. Young once. He is not an educated man, but speaks with considerable force and clearness. The day I was there there was nothing coarse in his remarks.

[Pointing to panorama—] These are the Foundations of the Magnificent Temple the Mormons are building. It is to be built of hewn stone—and will cover several acres of ground. They say it shall eclipse in splendor all other temples in the world. They also say it shall be paved with solid gold.

It is perhaps worthy of remark that the architect of this contemplated gorgeous affair repudiated Mormonism—and is now living in London.

[Pointing to panorama—] The Temple as it is to be. This pretty little picture is from the architect's design—and cannot—therefore—I suppose, be called a fancy sketch.

Should the Mormons continue unmolested—I think they will complete this rather remarkable edifice.

[Pointing to panorama—] Great Salt Lake.————The great salt dead sea of the desert.

I know of no greater curiosity than this inland sea of thick brine. It is eighty miles wide and one hundred and thirty miles long. Solid masses of salt are daily washed ashore in immense heaps—and the Mormon in want of salt has only to go to the shore of this lake and fill his cart. Only—the salt for table use has to be subjected to a boiling process.

These are facts—susceptible of the clearest possible proof. They tell one story about this lake, however, that I have my doubts about. They say a Mormon farmer drove forty head of cattle in there once, and they came out first-rate pickled beef.————

.   .   .   .

I sincerely hope you will excuse my absence————I am a man short—and have to work the moon myself. I shall be most happy to pay a good salary to any respectable boy of good parentage and education who is a good moonist. [The lecturer here left the platform for a few moments, and pretended to be engaged behind the curtain. The picture was intended to show the moon rising over the lake and rippling on the waters. This effect was produced in the usual dioramic way, by making the track of the moon transparent, and throwing it on from the bull's-eye of a lantern. After the lecturer went behind, the moon became nervous and flickering, dancing up and down in a highly inartistic manner.]

[Pointing to panorama—] The Endowment House.—
In this building the Mormon is initiated into the mysteries
of the faith.

Strange stories are told of the proceedings which are
held in this building——but I have no possible means of
knowing how true they may be.

[Pointing to panorama—] Echo Cañon.—Salt Lake
City is fifty-five miles behind us—and this is Echo Cañon,
in reaching which we are supposed to have crossed the summit of the Wahsatch mountains. These ochre-colored
bluffs——formed of conglomerate sandstone—and full of
fossils——signal the entrance to the cañon. At its base
lies Weber Station.

Echo Cañon is about twenty-five miles long. It is really
the sublimest thing between the Missouri and the Sierra
Nevada. The red wall to the left develops farther up the
cañon into pyramids, buttresses, and castles——honey-
combed and fretted in nature's own massive magnificence
of architecture.

In 1856 Echo Cañon was the place selected by Brigham
Young for the Mormon General Wells to fortify and make
impregnable against the advance of the American army, led
by General Albert Sidney Johnston. It was to have
been the Thermopylæ of Mormondom——but it wasn't.
General Wells was to have done Leonidas——but he
didn't.

[Pointing to panorama—] A More Cheerful View of the
Desert.—The wild snow-storms have left us—and we have
thrown our wolf-skin overcoats aside. Certain tribes of far-
western Indians bury their distinguished dead by placing
them high in air and covering them with valuable furs
——that is a very fair representation of these mid-air
tombs. Those animals are horses——I know they are—
because my artist says so. I had the picture two years before I discovered the fact. The artist came to me about
six months ago, and said: "It is useless to disguise it
from you any longer——they are horses."

It was while crossing this desert that I was surrounded
by a band of Ute Indians. They were splendidly mounted.
They were dressed in beaver-skins, and they were armed
with rifles, knives, and pistols.

What could I do?——What could a poor, old orphan do? I'm a brave man. The day before the battle of Bull's Run I stood in the highway while the bullets——those dreadful messengers of death——were passing all around me thickly ——in wagons——on their way to the battle-field. But there were too many of these Injuns. There were forty of them—and only one of me——and so I said:—

"Great Chief, I surrender." His name was Wocky-bocky.

He dismounted—and approached me. I saw his toma-hawk glisten in the morning sunlight. Fire was in his eye. Wocky-bocky [pointing to panorama] came very close to me and seized me by the hair of my head. He mingled his swarthy fingers with my golden tresses—and he rubbed his dreadful Thomashawk across my lily-white face. He said:

"Torsha arrah darrah mishky bookshean!"

I told him he was right.

Wocky-bocky again rubbed his tomahawk across my face, and said: "Wink-ho—loo-boo!"

Says I: "Mr. Wocky-bocky," says I — "Wocky — I have thought so for years—and so's all our family."

He told me I must go to the tent of the Strong-Heart—and eat raw dog. It don't agree with me. I prefer simple food. I prefer pork-pie—because then I know what I'm eating. But as raw dog was all they proposed to give to me, I had to eat it or starve. So at the expiration of two days I seized a tin plate and went to the chief's daughter, and I said to her in a silvery voice——in a kind of German-silvery voice——I said:—

"Sweet child of the forest, the pale-face wants his dog."

There was nothing but his paws! I had paused too long! Which reminds me that time passes. A way which Time has.

I was told in my youth to seize opportunity. I once tried to seize one. He was rich. He had diamonds on. As I seized him—he knocked me down. Since then I have learned that he who seizes opportunity sees the peniten-tiary.

[Pointing to panorama—] The Rocky Mountains.—I take it for granted you have heard of these popular mountains. In America they are regarded as a great success, and we all love dearly to talk about them. It is a kind of weakness with us. I never knew but one American who hadn't something—some time—to say about the Rocky Mountains, and he was a deaf and dumb man who couldn't say anything about nothing.

But these mountains, whose summits are snow-covered and icy all the year round, are too grand to make fun of. I crossed them in the winter of '64—in a rough sleigh drawn by four mules.

This sparkling waterfall is the Laughing-Water alluded to by Mr. Longfellow in his Indian poem—" Higher-Water." The water is higher up there.

[Pointing to panorama—] The Plains of Colorado.— These are the dreary plains over which we rode for so many weary days. An affecting incident occurred on these plains some time since, and I am sure you will pardon me for introducing it here.

On a beautiful June morning—some sixteen years ago ——[Music, very loud, till the scene is off.]

. . . .

————and she fainted on Reginald's breast!

[Pointing to panorama—] The Prairie on Fire.—A prairie on fire is one of the wildest and grandest sights that can possibly be imagined.

These fires occur—of course—in the summer—when the grass is dry as tinder————and the flames rush and roar over the prairie in a manner frightful to behold. They usually burn better than mine is burning to-night. I try to make my prairie burn regularly—and not disappoint the public————but it is not as high-principled as I am.

[Pointing to panorama—] Brigham Young at Home. The last picture I have to show you represents Mr. Brigham Young in the bosom of his family. His family is large —and the olive branches around his table are in a very tangled condition. He is more a father than any man I know. When at home————as you here see him————he ought to be very happy with sixty wives to minister to his comforts —and twice sixty children to soothe his distracted mind. Ah! my friends————what is home without a family?

What will become of Mormonism? We all know and admit it to be a hideous wrong——a great immoral stain upon the 'scutcheon of the United States. My belief is that its existence is dependent upon the life of Brigham Young. His administrative ability holds the system together—— his power of will maintains it as the faith of a community. When he dies, Mormonism will die too. The men who are around him have neither his talent nor his energy. By means of his strength, it is held together. When he falls— Mormonism will also fall to pieces.

That lion—you perceive—has a tail. It is a long one already. Like mine—it is to be continued in our next.

ROBERT JONES BURDETTE

THE RISE AND FALL OF THE MUSTACHE

[Lecture by Robert J. Burdette, "The Hawkeye Man," humorist (born in Greensborough, Penn., July 30, 1844; ——), delivered originally in Western cities. This is called the best exposition of Mr. Burdette's humor as displayed in the several lectures of his series given since he first took the platform in 1876. At that time Mr. Burdette was managing editor of the "Burlington Hawkeye," through which he won his reputation as a humorist, his humorous paragraphs and sketches, often tinged with gentle satire, first appearing in its columns some years before. Subsequently, Mr. Burdette became a licensed minister of the Baptist Church, but he continued on the lecture platform.]

LADIES AND GENTLEMEN:—Adam raised Cain, but he did not raise a mustache. He was born a man, a full-grown man, and with a mustache already raised.

If Adam wore a mustache, he never raised it. It raised itself. It evolved itself out of its own inner consciousness, like a primordial germ. It grew, like the weeds on his farm, in spite of him, and to torment him. For Adam had hardly got his farm reduced to a kind of turbulent, weed-producing, granger fighting, regular order of things—had scarcely settled down to the quiet, happy, care-free, independent life of a jocund farmer, with nothing under the canopy to molest or make him afraid, with everything on the plantation going on smoothly and lovely, with a little rust in the oats; army-worm in the corn; Colorado beetles swarming up and down the potato patch; cutworms laying waste the cucumbers; curculio in the plums and borers in the apple-trees; a new kind of bug that he didn't know the name of desolating the wheat fields; dry weather burning up the wheat; wet weather blighting the corn; too cold for the melons, too dreadfully hot for the strawberries; chickens dying with the pip; hogs being gathered to their fathers with the cholera; sheep fading away with a complication of things that no man could remember; horses getting along as well as could be expected, with a little spavin, ring-bone, wolf-teeth, distemper, heaves, blind staggers, collar chafes, saddle galls, colic now and then, founder occasionally, epizootic when there was nothing else; cattle going wild with the horn ail; moth in the bee-hives; snakes in the milk-house; moles in the kitchen garden—Adam had just about got through breaking wild land with a crooked stick, and settled down comfortably, when the sound of the boy was heard in the land.

Did it ever occur to you that Adam was probably the most troubled and worried man that ever lived?

We have always pictured Adam as a careworn-looking man; a puzzled-looking granger who would sigh fifty times a day, and sit down on a log and run his irresolute fingers through his hair while he wondered what under the canopy he was going to do with those boys, and whatever was going to become of them. We have thought, too, that as often as our esteemed parent asked himself this conundrum, he gave it up. They must have been a source of constant trouble and mystification to him. For you see they were the first boys that humanity ever had any experience with. And there was no one else in the neighborhood who had any boy, with whom Adam, in his moments of perplexity, could consult. There wasn't a boy in the country with whom Adam's boys were on speaking terms, and with whom they could play and fight.

Adam, you see, labored under the most distressing disadvantages that ever opposed a married man, and the father of a family. He had never been a boy himself, and what could he know about boy nature or boy troubles and pleasure. His perplexity began at an early date.

Cain, when he made his appearance, was the first and only boy in the fair young world. And all his education depended on his inexperienced parents, who had never in their lives seen a boy until they saw Cain. And there wasn't an educational help in the market. There wasn't an alphabet-block in the county; not even a Centennial illustrated handkerchief. There were no other boys in the republic, to teach young Cain to lie, and swear, and smoke, and drink, fight, and steal, and thus develop the boy's dormant statesmanship, and prepare him for the sterner political duties of his maturer years. There wasn't a pocket-knife in the universe that he could borrow—and lose, and when he wanted to cut his finger, as all boys must do, now and then, he had to cut it with a clam-shell. There were no country relations upon whom little Cain could be inflicted for two or three weeks at a time, when his wearied parents wanted a little rest. There was nothing for him to play with. Adam couldn't show him how to make a kite. He had a much better idea of angels' wings than he had of a kite. And if little Cain had even asked for such a simple bit of mechanism as a shinny-club, Adam would have gone out into the depths of the primeval forest and wept in sheer mortification and helpless, confessed ignorance.

I don't wonder that Cain turned out bad. I always said he would. For his entire education depended upon a most ignorant man, a man in the very palmiest days of his ignorance, who couldn't have known less if he had tried all his life on a high salary and had a man to help him. And the boy's education had to be conducted entirely upon the catechetical system; only, in this instance, the boy pupil asked the questions, and his parent teachers, heaven help them, tried to answer them. And they had to answer at them. For they could not take refuge from the steady stream of questions that poured in upon them day after day, by interpolating a fairy story, as you do when your boy asks you questions about something of which you never heard. For how could Adam begin, " Once upon a time," when with one quick, incisive question, Cain could pin him right back against the dead-wall of creation, and make him either specify exactly what time, or acknowledge the fraud? How could Eve tell him about " Jack and the bean-stalk," when Cain, fairly crazy for someone to play with, knew perfectly well there was not, and never had been, another boy on the plantation? And as day by day Cain brought home things in his hands about which to ask questions that no mortal could answer, how grateful his bewildered parents must have been that he had no pockets in which to transport his collections. For many generations came into the fair young world, got into no end of trouble, and died out of it, before a boy's pocket solved the problem how to make the thing contained seven times greater than the container.

The only thing that saved Adam and Eve from interrogational insanity was the paucity of language. If little Cain had possessed the verbal abundance of the language in which men are to-day talked to death, his father's bald-head would have gone down in shining flight to the end of the earth to escape him, leaving Eve to look after the stock, save the crop, and raise her boy as best she could. Which would have been 6,000 years ago, as to-day, just like a man.

Because, it was no off-hand, absent-minded work answering questions about things in those spacious old days, when there was crowds of room, and everything grew by the acre. When a placid but exceedingly unanimous looking animal went rolling by, producing the general effect of an eclipse, and Cain would shout:

" Oh, lookee, lookee Pa! what's that? "

Then the patient Adam, trying to saw enough kitchen-wood to last over Sunday, with a piece of flint, would have to pause and gather up words enough to say:

" That, my son? That is only a mastodon giganteus; he has a bad look, but a Christian temper."

And then presently:

" Oh, pa! pa! What's that over yon? "

" Oh, bother," Adam would reply; " it's only a paleotherium, mammalia pachydermata." [Laughter.]

" Oh, yes; theliocomeafterus. Oh! lookee, lookee at this 'un! "

" Where, Cainny? Oh, that in the mud? That's only an acephala lamelli branchiata. It won't bite you, but you mustn't eat it. It's poison as politics."

" Whee! See there! see, see, see! What's him? "

" Oh, that? Looks like a plesiosaurus; keep out of his way; he has a jaw like your mother."

" Oh, yes; a plenosserus. And what's that fellow, poppy? "

" That's a silurus malaptorus. Don't you go near him, for he has the disposition of a Georgia mule."

" Oh, yes; a slapterus. And what's this little one? "

" Oh, it's nothing but an aristolochioid. Where did you

get it?   There, now, quit throwing stones at that acanthop-
terygian; do you want to be kicked?   And keep away from
the nothodenatrichomanoides.   My stars, Eve! where did
he get that anonaceo-hydrocharideo-nymphæoid?   Do you
never look after him at all?   Here, you Cain, get right away
down from there, and chase that megalosaurius out of the
melon patch, or I'll set the monopleuro branchian on you."
[Laughter.]

Just think of it, Christian man with a family to support,
with last year's stock on your shelves, and a draft as long
as a clothes-line to pay to-morrow!   Think of it, woman
with all a woman's love and constancy, and a mother's sympathetic nature, with three meals a day 365 times a year to
think of, and the flies to chase out of the sitting-room; think,
if your cherub boy was the only boy in the wide, wide world,
and all his questions which now radiate in a thousand directions among other boys, who tell him lies and help him to
cut his eye-teeth, were focused upon you!   Adam had only
one consolation that has been denied his more remote descendants.   His boy never belonged to a baseball club,
never smoked cigarettes, and never teased his father from
the first of November till the last of March for a pair of
roller-skates.

Well, you have no time to pity Adam.   You have your
own boy to look after.   Or, your neighbor has a boy, whom
you can look after much more closely than his mother does,
and much more to your own satisfaction than to the boy's
comfort.

Your boy is, as Adam's boy was, an animal that asks questions.   If there were any truth in the old theory of the transmigration of souls, when a boy died he would pass into an
interrogation point.   And he'd stay there.   He'd never get
out of it; for he never gets through asking questions.   The
older he grows the more he asks, and the more perplexing
his questions are, and the more unreasonable he is about
wanting them answered to suit himself.   Why, the oldest
boy I ever knew—he was fifty-seven years old, and I went
to school to him—could and did ask the longest, hardest,
crookedest questions [laughter], that no fellow, who used
to trade off all his books for a pair of skates and a knife

with a corkscrew in it, could answer. And when his questions were not answered to suit him, it was his custom—a custom more honored in the breeches, we used to think, than in the observance—to take up a long, slender, but exceedingly tenacious rod, which lay ever near the big dictionary, and smite with it the boy whose naturally derived Adamic ignorance was made manifest.

Ah, me! if the boy could only do as he is done by, and ferule the man or woman who fails to reply to his inquiries, as he is himself corrected for similar shortcomings, what a valley of tears, what a literally howling wilderness he could and would make of this world. [Laughter.]

Your boy, asking to-day pretty much the same questions, with heaven knows how many additional ones, that Adam's boy did, is told, every time he asks one that you don't know anything about, just as Adam told Cain fifty times a day, that he will know all about it when he is a man. And so from the days of Cain down to the present wickeder generation of boys, the boy ever looks forward to the time when he will be a man and know everything.

And now, not entirely ceasing to ask questions, your boy begins to answer them, until you stand amazed at the breadth and depth of his knowledge. He asks questions and gets answers of teachers that you and the school board know not of. Day by day, great unprinted books, upon the broad pages of which the hand of nature has traced characters that only a boy can read, are spread out before him. He knows now where the first snow-drop lifts its tiny head, a pearl on the bosom of the barren earth, in the spring; he knows where the last Indian pink lingers, a flame in the brown and rustling woods, in the autumn days. His pockets are cabinets, from which he drags curious fossils that he does not know the names of; monstrous and hideous beetles and bugs and things that you never saw before, and for which he has appropriate names of his own. He knows where there are three orioles' nests, and so far back as you can remember, you never saw an oriole's nest in your life. He can tell you how to distinguish the good mushrooms from the poisonous ones, and poison grapes from good ones, and how he ever found out, except by eating both kinds, is a mystery to his mother. Every root, bud, leaf, berry, or bark, that will make any bitter, horrible, semi-poisonous tea, reputed to have marvellous medicinal virtues, he knows where to find, and in the season he does find, and brings home, and all but sends the entire family to the cemetery by making practical tests of his teas.

And as his knowledge broadens, his human superstition develops itself. He has a formula, repeating which nine times a day, while pointing his finger fixedly toward the sun, will cause warts to disappear from the hand, or, to use his own expression, will " knock warts." [Laughter.] If the eight-day clock at home tells him it is two o'clock, and the flying leaves of the dandelion declare it is half-past five, he will stand or fall with the dandelion.

He has a formula, by which anything that has been lost may be found. He has, above all things, a natural, infallible instinct for the woods, and can no more be lost in them than a squirrel. If the cow does not come home—and if she is a town cow, like a town man, she does not come home, three nights in the week—you lose half a day of valuable time looking for her. Then you pay a man $3 to look for her two days longer, or so long as the appropriation holds out. Finally, a quarter sends a boy to the woods; he comes back at milking time, whistling the tune that no man ever imitated, and the cow ambles contentedly along before him.

He has one particular marble which he regards with about the same superstitious reverence that a pagan does his idol, and his Sunday-school teacher can't drive it out of him, either. Carnelian, crystal, bull's-eye, china, pottery, boly, blood-alley, or commie, whatever he may call it, there is " luck in it." When he loses this marble, he sees panic and bankruptcy ahead of him, and retires from business prudently, before the crash comes, failing, in true centennial style, with both pockets and a cigar-box full of winnings, and a creditor's meeting in the back room.

A boy's world is open to no one but a boy. You never really revisit the glimpses of your boyhood, much as you may dream of it. After you get into a tail coat, and tight boots, you never again set foot in boy world. You lose this marvellous instinct for the woods, you can't tell a pig-nut-tree from a pecan; you can't make friends with strange dogs; you can't make the terrific noises with your mouth, you can't invent the inimitable signals or the characteristic catchwords of boyhood.

He is getting on, is your boy. He reaches the dime-novel age. He wants to be a missionary. Or a pirate. So far as he expresses any preference, he would rather be a pirate, an occupation in which there are more chances for making money, and fewer opportunities for being devoured. He develops a yearning love for school and study about this time, also, and every time he dreams of being a pirate he dreams of hanging his dear teacher at the yard-arm in the presence of the delighted scholars. His voice develops, even more rapidly and thoroughly than his morals. In the yard, on the house-top, down the street, around the corner; wherever there is a patch of ice big enough for him to break his neck on, or a pond of water deep enough to drown in, the voice of your boy is heard. He whispers in a shout, and converses, in ordinary, confidential moments, in a shriek. He exchanges bits of back-fence gossip about his father's domestic matters, with the boy living in the adjacent township, to which interesting revelations of home life the intermediate neighborhood listens with intense satisfaction, and the two home circles in helpless dismay. He has an unconquerable hatred for company, and an aversion for walking downstairs. For a year or two his feet never touch the stairway in his descent, and his habit of polishing the stair-rail by using it as a passenger tramway, soon breaks the other members of the family of the careless habit of setting the hall-lamp or the water-pitcher on the baluster-post. He wears the same size boot as his father; and on the dryest, dustiest days in the year, always manages to convey some mud on the carpets. He carefully steps over the door-mat, and until he is about seventeen years old, he actually never knew there was a scraper at the front porch.

About this time, bold but inartistic pencil-sketches break out mysteriously on the alluring background of the wall-paper. He asks, with great regularity, alarming frequency, and growing diffidence, for a new hat. You might as well buy him a new disposition. He wears his hat in the air and on the ground far more than he does on his head, and he never hangs it up that he doesn't pull the hook through the crown; unless the hook breaks off or the hat-rack pulls over.

He is a perfect Robinson Crusoe in inventive genius. He can make a kite that will fly higher and pull harder than a balloon. He can, and, on occasion, will, take out a couple of the pantry shelves and make a sled that is amazement itself. The mouse-trap he builds out of the water-pitcher and the family Bible is a marvel of mechanical ingenuity. So is the excuse he gives for such a selection of raw material. When suddenly, some Monday morning, the clothes-line, without any just or apparent cause or provocation, shrinks sixteen feet, philosophy cannot make you believe that Professor Tice did it with his little barometer. Because, far down the dusty street, you can see Tom in the dim distance, driving a prancing team, six-in-hand, with the missing link.

You send your boy on an errand. There are three ladies in the parlor. You have waited as long as you can, in all courtesy, for them to go. They have developed alarming symptoms of staying to tea. And you know there aren't half enough strawberries to go round. It is only a three minutes' walk to the grocery, however, and Tom sets off like a rocket, and you are so pleased with his celerity and ready good-nature that you want to run after him and kiss him. He is gone a long time, however. Ten minutes become fifteen, fifteen grow into twenty; the twenty swell into the half-hour, and your guests exchange very significant glances as the half becomes three-quarters. Your boy returns at last. Apprehension in his downcast eyes, humility in his laggard step, penitence in the appealing slouch of his battered hat, and a pound and a half of shingle-nails in his hands.

" Mother," he says, " what else was it you told me to get besides the nails? " [Laughter.] And while you are counting your scanty store of berries to make them go round without a fraction, you hear Tom out in the back-yard whistling and hammering away, building a dog-house with the nails you never told him to get.

Poor Tom, he loves at this age quite as ardently as he makes mistakes and mischief. And he is repulsed quite as ardently as he makes love. If he hugs his sister, he musses her ruffle, and gets cuffed for it. Two hours later, another boy, not more than twenty-two or twenty-three years older than Tom, some neighbor's Tom, will come in, and will just make the most hopeless, terrible, chaotic wreck of that ruffle that lace or footing can be distorted into. And the only reproof he gets is the reproachful murmur, " Must he go so soon? " [laughter], when he doesn't make a movement to go until he hears the alarm clock go off upstairs and the old gentleman in the adjoining room banging around building the morning fires, and loudly wondering if young Mr. Bostwick is going to stay to breakfast?

Tom is at this age set in deadly enmity against company, which he soon learns to regard as his mortal foe. He regards company as a mysterious and eminently respectable delegation that always stays to dinner, invariably crowds him to the second table, never leaves him any of the pie, and generally makes him late for school. Naturally, he learns to love refined society, but in a conservative, non-committal sort of a way, dissembling his love so effectually that even his parents never dream of its existence until it is gone.

Poor Tom, his life is not all comedy at this period. Go up to your boy's room some night, and his sleeping face will preach you a sermon on the griefs and troubles that sometimes weigh his little heart down almost to breaking, more eloquently than the lips of a Spurgeon could picture them. The curtain has fallen on one day's act in the drama of his active little life. The restless feet that all day long have pattered so far—down dusty streets, over scorching pavements, through long stretches of quiet wooded lanes, along the winding cattle-paths in the deep, silent woods; that have dabbled in the cool brook where it wrangles and scolds over the shining pebbles, that have filled your house with noise and dust and racket, are still. The stained hand outside the sheet is soiled and rough, and the cut finger with the rude bandage of the boy's own surgery, pleads with a mute, effective pathos of its own, for the mischievous hand that is never idle. On the brown cheek the trace of a tear marks the piteous close of the day's troubles, the closing scene in a troubled little drama; troubled at school with books that were too many for him; troubled with temptations to have unlawful fun that were too strong for him, as they are frequently too strong for his father; trouble in the street with boys that were too big for him; and at last, in his home, in his castle, his refuge, trouble has pursued him, until, feeling utterly friendless and in everybody's way, he has crawled off to the dismantled den, dignified usually by the title of " the boy's room," and his overcharged heart has welled up into his eyes, and his last waking breath has broken into a sob, and just as he begins to think that after all, life is only one broad sea of troubles, whose restless billows, in neverending succession, break and beat and double and dash upon the short shore line of a boy's life, he has drifted away into the wonderland of a boy's sleep, where fairy fingers picture his dreams.   [Applause.]

How soundly, deeply, peacefully he sleeps.   No mother, who has never dragged a sleepy boy off the lounge at nine o'clock, and hauled him off upstairs to bed, can know with what a herculean grip a square sleep takes hold of a boy's senses, nor how fearfully and wonderfully limp and nerveless it makes him; nor how, in direct antagonism to all established laws of anatomy, it develops joints that work both ways, all the way up and down that boy.

And what pen can portray the wonderful enchantments of a boy's dreamland! No marvellous visions wrought by the weird, strange power of hasheesh, no dreams that come to the sleep of jaded woman or tired man, no ghastly spectres that dance attendance upon cold mince pie, but shrink into tiresome, stale, and trifling commonplaces compared with the marvellous, the grotesque, the wonderful, the terrible, the beautiful and the enchanting scenes and people of a boy's dreamland. This may be owing, in a great measure, to the fact that the boy never relates his dream until all the other members of the family have related theirs; and then he comes in, like a back county, with the necessary majority; like the directory of a western city, following the census of a rival town.

Tom is a miniature Ishmaelite at this period of his career. His hand is against every man, and about every man's hand, and nearly every woman's hand, is against him, off and on. Often, and then the iron enters his soul, the hand that is against him holds the slipper. He wears his mother's slipper on his jacket quite as often as she wears it on her foot. And this is all wrong, unchristian and impolitic. It spreads the slipper and discourages the boy. When he reads in his Sunday-school lesson that the wicked stand in slippery places, he takes it as a direct personal reference, and he is affronted, and maybe the seeds of atheism are implanted in his breast. Moreover, this repeated application of the slipper not only sours his temper, and gives a bias to his moral ideas, but it sharpens his wits. How many a Christian mother, her soft eyes swimming in tears of real pain that plashed up from the depths of a loving heart, as she bent over her wayward boy until his heart-rending wails and piteous shrieks drowned her own choking, sympathetic sobs, has been wasting her strength, and wearing out a good slipper, and pouring out all that priceless flood of mother love and duty and pity and tender sympathy upon a concealed atlas-back, or a Saginaw shingle. [Laughter.]

It is a historical fact that no boy is ever whipped twice for precisely the same offence. He varies and improves a little on every repetition of the prank, until at last he reaches a point where detection is almost impossible. He is a big boy then, and glides almost imperceptibly from the discipline of his father, under the surveillance of the police.

By easy stages he passes into the uncomfortable period of boyhood. His jacket develops into a tail-coat. The boy of to-day, who is slipped into a hollow, abbreviated mockery of a tail-coat, when he is taken out of long dresses, has no idea—not the faintest conception of the grandeur, the momentous importance of the epoch in a boy's life, that was marked by the transition from the old-fashioned cadet roundabout to the tail-coat. It is an experience that heaven, ever chary of its choicest blessings, and mindful of the decadence of the race of boys, has not vouchsafed to the untoward, forsaken boys of this wicked generation. When the roundabout went out of fashion, the heroic race of boys passed away from earth, and weeping nature sobbed and broke the moulds. The fashion that started a boy of six years on his pilgrimage of life in a miniature edition of his father's coat, marked a period of retrogression in the affairs of men, and stamped a decaying and degenerate race. There are no boys now, or very few, at least, such as peopled the grand old earth when the men of our age were boys. And that it is so, society is to be congratulated. The step from the roundabout to the tail-coat was a leap in life. It was the boy Iulus, doffing the *prætexta* and flinging upon his shoulders the *toga virilis* of Julius; Patroclus, donning the armor of Achilles, in which to go forth and be Hectored to death.

Tom is slow to realize the grandeur of that tail-coat, however, on its trial trip. How differently it feels from his good, snug-fitting, comfortable old jacket. It fits him too much in every direction, he knows. Every now and then he stops with a gasp of terror, feeling positive, from the awful sensation of nothingness about the neck, that the entire collar has fallen off in the street. The tails are prairies, the pockets are caverns, and the back is one vast, illimitable, stretching waste. How Tom sidles along as close to the fence as he can scrape, and what a wary eye he keeps in every direction for other boys. When he forgets the school, he is half tempted to feel proud of his toga; but when he thinks of the boys, and the reception that awaits him, his heart sinks, and he is tempted to go back home, sneak upstairs, and rescue his worn old jacket from the rag-bag. He glances in terror at his distorted shadow on the fence, and, confident that it is a faithful outline of his figure, he knows that he has worn his father's coat off by mistake.

As he reaches the last friendly corner that shields him from the pitiless gaze of the boys he can hear howling and shrieking not fifty yards away; he pauses to give the final adjustment to the manly and unmanageable raiment. It is bigger and looser, flappier and wrinklier than ever. New and startling folds, and unexpected wrinkles, and uncontemplated bulges develop themselves, like masked batteries, just when and where the effect will be most demoralizing. And a new horror discloses itself at this trying and awful juncture. He wants to lie down on the sidewalk and try to die. For the first time he notices the color of his coat. Hideous!

Oh, madness! The color is no color. It is all colors. It is a brindle—a veritable, undeniable brindle. There must have been a fabulous amount of brindle cloth made up into boys' first coats, sixteen or eighteen or nineteen years ago, because out of 894—I like to be exact in the use of figures, because nothing else in the world lends such an air of profound truthfulness to a discourse—out of 894 boys I knew in the first tail-coat period, 893 came to school in brindle coats. And the other one—the 894th boy—made his wretched début in a bottle-green toga, with dreadful, glaring brass buttons. He left school very suddenly, and we always believed that the angels saw him in that coat, and ran away with him. But Tom, shivering with apprehension, and faint with mortification over the discovery of this new horror, gives one last despairing scrooch of his shoulders, to make the coat look shorter, and, with a final frantic tug at the tails, to make it appear longer, steps out from the protecting ægis of the corner, is stunned with a vocal hurricane of——

" Oh, what a coat! " and his cup of misery is as full as a rag-bag in three minutes.

Passing into the tail-coat period, Tom awakens to a knowledge of the broad physical truth, that he has hands. He is not very positive in his own mind how many. At times he is ready to swear to an even two, one pair of good hands. Again, when cruel fate and the non-appearance of someone else's brother has compelled him to accompany his sister to a church sociable, he can see eleven; and as he sits bolt upright in the grimmest of straight-back chairs, plastered right up against the wall, as the " sociable " custom is, or used to be, trying to find enough unoccupied pockets in which to sequester all his hands, he is dimly conscious that hands should come in pairs, and vaguely wonders, if he has only five pairs of regularly ordained hands, where this odd hand came from. And hitherto, Tom has been content to encase his feet in anything that would stay on them. Now, however, he has an eye for a glove-fitting boot, and learns to wreathe his face in smiles, hollow, heartless, deceitful smiles, while his boots are as full of agony as a broken heart, and his tortured feet cry out for vengeance upon the shoemaker, and make Tom feel that life is a hollow mockery, and there is nothing real but soft corns and bunions.

And—his mother never cuts his hair again. Never. When Tom assumes the manly gown, she has looked her last upon his head, with trimming ideas. His hair will be trimmed and clipped, barberously it may be, but she will not be accessory before the fact. She may sometimes long to have her boy kneel down before her, while she gnaws around his terrified locks with a pair of scissors that were sharpened when they were made; and have since then cut acres of calico, and miles and miles of paper, and great stretches of cloth, and snarls and coils of string, and furlongs of lamp-wick; and have snuffed candles; and dug refractory corks out of the family ink-bottle; and punched holes in skate-straps; and trimmed the family nails; and have even done their level best, at the annual struggle, to cut stove-pipe lengths in two; and have successfully opened oyster and fruit-cans; and pried up carpet-tacks; and have many a time and oft gone snarlingly and toilsomely around Tom's head, and made him an object of terror to the children in the street, and made him look so much like a yearling colt with the run of a burr pasture, that people have been afraid to approach him too suddenly, lest he should jump through his collar and run away. [Applause.]

He feels, too, the dawning consciousness of another grand truth in the human economy. It dawns upon his deepening intelligence with the inherent strength and the unquestioned truth of a new revelation, that man's upper lip was designed by nature for a mustache pasture. How tenderly reserved he is when he is brooding over his momentous discovery. With what exquisite caution and delicacy are his primal investigations conducted. In his microscopical researches it appears to him that the down on his upper lip is certainly more determined down, more positive, more pronounced, more individual fuzz than that which vegetates in neglected tenderness upon his cheeks. He makes cautious explorations along the land of promise with the tip of his tenderest finger, delicately backing up the grade the wrong way, going always against the grain, that he may the more readily detect the slightest symptom of an uprising by the first feeling of velvety resistance. And day by day he is more and more firmly convinced that there is in his lip the primordial germs, the protoplasm of a glory that will, in its full development, eclipse even the majesty and grandeur of his first tail-coat.

And in the first dawning consciousness that the mustache is there, like the vote, and only needs to be brought out, how often Tom walks down to the barber-shop, gazes long-

ingly in at the window, and walks past. And how often,
when he musters up sufficient courage to go in, and climbs
into the chair, and is just on the point of huskily whispering
to the barber that he would like a shave, the entrance of a
man with a beard like Frederick Barbarossa, frightens away
his resolution, and he has his hair cut again. The third
time that week, and it is so short that the barber has to
hold it with his teeth while he files it off, and parts it with
a straight-edge and a scratch-awl. Naturally, driven from
the barber-chair, Tom casts longing eyes upon the ancestral shaving machinery at home. And who shall say by
what means he at length obtains possession of the paternal
razor? No one. Nobody knows. Nobody ever did know.
Even the searching investigation that always follows the
paternal demand for the immediate extradition of whoever
opened a fruit-can with that razor, which always follows
Tom's first shave, is always, and ever will be, barren of results.

All that we know about it is, that Tom holds the razor
in his hand about a minute, wondering what to do with it,
before the blade falls across his fingers and cuts every one
of them. First blood claimed and allowed, for the razor.
Then he strops the razor furiously. Or, rather, he razors
the strop. He slashes and cuts that passive instrument in
as many directions as he can make motions with the razor.
He would cut it oftener if the strop lasted longer. Then he
nicks the razor against the side of the mug. Then he drops
it on the floor and steps on it and nicks it again. They are
small nicks, not so large by half as a saw-tooth, and he flatters himself his father will never see them. Then he soaks
the razor in hot water, as he has seen his father do. Then
he takes it out, at a temperature anywhere under 980°
Fahrenheit, and lays it against his cheek, and raises a blister
there the size of the razor, as he never saw his father do, but
as his father most assuredly did, many, many years before
Tom met him. Then he makes a variety of indescribable
grimaces and labial contortions in a frenzied effort to get
his upper lip into approachable shape, and, at last, the first
offer he makes at his embryo mustache he slashes his nose
with a vicious upper-cut. He gashes the corners of his
mouth; wherever those nicks touch his cheek they leave a

scratch apiece, and he learns what a good nick in a razor is for, and at last when he lays the blood-stained weapon down, his gory lip looks as though it had just come out of a long, stubborn, exciting contest with a straw-cutter.

But he learns to shave, after a while—just before he cuts his lip clear off. He has to take quite a course of instruction, however, in that great school of experience about which the old philosopher had a remark to make. It is a grand old school; the only school at which men will study and learn, each for himself. One man's experience never does another man any good; never did and never will teach another man anything. If the philosopher had said that it was a hard school, but that some men would learn at no other than this grand old school of experience, we might have inferred that all women, and most boys, and a few men were exempt from its hard teachings. But he used the more comprehensive term, if you remember what that is, and took us all in. We have all been there. There is no other school, in fact. Poor little Cain; dear, lonesome, wicked little Cain— I know it isn't fashionable to pet him; I know it is popular to speak harshly and savagely about our eldest brother, when the fact is we resemble him more closely in disposition than any other member of the family—poor little Cain never knew the difference between his father's sun-burned nose and a glowing coal, until he had pulled the one and picked up the other. And Abel had to find out the difference in the same way, although he was told five hundred times, by his brother's experience, that the coal would burn him and the nose wouldn't. And Cain's boy wouldn't believe that fire was any hotter than an icicle, until he had made a digital experiment, and understood why they called it fire. And so Enoch and Methusaleh, and Moses, and Daniel, and Solomon, and Cæsar, and Napoleon, and Washington, and the President, and the Governor, and the Mayor, and you and I have all of us, at one time or another, in one way or another, burned our fingers at the same old fires that have scorched human fingers in the same monotonous old ways, at the same reliable old stands, for the past 6,000 years, and all the verbal instruction between here and the silent grave couldn't teach us so much, or teach it so thoroughly, as one well-directed singe. And a million of years

11

from now—if this weary old world may endure so long—
when human knowledge shall fall a little short of the infinite, and all the lore and erudition of this wonderful age
will be but the primer of that day of light—the baby that is
born into that world of knowledge and wisdom and progress, rich with all the years of human experience, will cry
for the lamp, and, the very first time that opportunity fa-
vors it, will try to pull the flame up by the roots, and will
know just as much as ignorant, untaught, stupid little Cain
knew on the same subject. [Laughter.] Year after year,
century after unfolding century, how true it is that the lion
on the fence is always bigger, fiercer, and more given to majestic attitudes and dramatic situations than the lion in the
tent. And yet it costs us, often as the circus comes around,
fifty cents to find that out.

But while we have been moralizing, Tom's mustache has
taken a start. It has attained the physical density, though
not the color, by any means, of the Egyptian darkness—it
can be felt; and it is felt; very soft felt. [Laughter.] The
world begins to take notice of the new-comer; and Tom, as
generations of Toms before him have done, patiently en-
dures dark hints from other members of the family about
his face being dirty. He loftily ignores his experienced
father's suggestions that he should perform his tonsorial
toilet with a spoonful of cream and the family cat. When
his sisters, in meekly dissembled ignorance, inquire, " Tom,
what have you on your lip? " he is austere, as becomes a
man annoyed by the frivolous small-talk of women. And
when his younger brother takes advantage of the presence
of a numerous company in the house, to shriek over the
baluster upstairs, apparently to any boy anywhere this
side of China, " Tom's a-raisin' mustachers! " [laughter]
Tom smiles, a wan, neglected-orphan smile; a smile that
looks as though it had come up on his face to weep over
the barrenness of the land; a perfect ghost of a smile, as
compared with the rugged, 7x9 smiles that play like animated crescents over the countenances of the company.
But the mustache grows. It comes on apace; very short
in the middle, very long at the ends, and very blond all
round. Whenever you see such a mustache, do not laugh
at it; do not point at it the slow, unmoving finger of

scorn. Encourage it; speak kindly of it; affect admiration
for it; coax it along. Pray for it—for it is a first. They
always come that way. And when, in the fulness of time, it
has developed so far that it can be pulled, there is all the
agony of making it take color. It is worse, and more obstinate, and more deliberate than a meerschaum. The sun,
that tans Tom's cheeks and blisters his nose, only bleaches
his mustache. Nothing ever hastens its color; nothing does
it any permanent good; nothing but patience, and faith, and
persistent pulling. [Laughter.]

With all the comedy there is about it, however, this is
the grand period of a boy's life. You look at them, with
their careless, easy, natural manners and movements in the
streets and on the base-ball ground, and their marvellous,
systematic, indescribable, inimitable and complex awk-
wardness in your parlors, and do you never dream, looking
at these young fellows, of the overshadowing destinies awaiting them, the mighty struggles mapped out in the earnest
future of their lives, the thrilling conquests in the world of
arms, the grander triumphs in the realm of philosophy, the
fadeless laurels in the empire of letters, and the imperishable
crowns that He who giveth them the victory binds about
their brows, that wait for the courage and ambition of these
boys? [Applause.]

Why, the world is at a boy's feet; and power and conquest and leadership slumber in his rugged arms and care-
free heart. A boy sets his ambition at whatever mark he
will—lofty or grovelling, as he may elect—and the boy who
resolutely sets his heart on fame, on wealth, on power, on
what he will; who consecrates himself to a life of noble endeavor, and lofty effort; who concentrates every faculty of
his mind and body on the attainment of his one darling
point; who brings to support his ambition, courage and industry and patience, can trample on genius; for these are
better and grander than genius; and he will begin to rise
above his fellows as steadily and as surely as the sun climbs
above the mountains. [Applause.]

You don't know how soon these happy-go-lucky young
fellows, making summer hideous with base-ball slang, or
gliding around a skating-rink on their back, may hold the
State and its destinies in their grasp; you don't know how

soon these boys may make and write the history of the hour; how soon, they alone, may shape events and guide the current of public action; how soon one of them may run away with your daughter or borrow money of you. [Laughter.]

Certain it is, there is one thing Tom will do, just about this period of his existence. He will fall in love with somebody before his mustache is long enough to wax. Perhaps one of the earliest indications of this event, for it does not always break out in the same manner, is a sudden and alarming increase in the number and variety of Tom's neckties. In his boxes and on his dressing-case, his mother is constantly startled by the changing and increasing assortment of the display. Monday he encircles his tender throat with a lilac knot, fearfully and wonderfully tied; a lavender tie succeeds, the following day; Wednesday is graced with a sweet little tangle of pale, pale blue, that fades at a breath; Thursday is ushered in with a scarf of delicate pea-green, of wonderful convolutions and sufficiently expansive, by the aid of a clean collar, to conceal any little irregularity in Tom's wash-day; Friday smiles on a sailor's-knot of dark blue, with a tangle of dainty forget-me-nots embroidered over it; Saturday tones itself down to a quiet, unobtrusive, neutral tint or shade, scarlet or yellow, and Sunday is deeply darkly, piously black. It is difficult to tell whether Tom is trying to express the state of his distracted feelings by his neckties, or trying to find a color that will harmonize with his mustache, or match Laura's dress.

And during the variegated necktie period of man's existence how tenderly that mustache is coaxed and petted and caressed. How it is brushed to make it lie down and waxed to make it stand out, and how he notes its slow growth, and weeps and mourns and prays and swears over it day after weary day.

The eye he has for immaculate linen and faultless collars. How it amazes his mother and sisters to learn that there isn't a shirt in the house fit for a pig to wear, and that he wouldn't wear the best collar in his room to be hanged in.

And the boots he crowds his feet into! A Sunday-school room, the Sunday before the picnic or the Christmas-tree, with its sudden influx of new scholars, with irreproachable morals and ambitious appetites, doesn't compare with the

overcrowded condition of those boots. Too tight in the in-
step; too narrow at the toes; too short at both ends; the
only things about those boots that don't hurt him, that don't
fill his very soul with agony, are the straps. When Tom
is pulling them on, he feels that if somebody would kindly
run over him three or four times with a freight train, the
sensation would be pleasant and reassuring and tranquil-
lizing. The air turns black before his starting eyes, there
is a roaring like the rush of many waters in his ears; he tugs
at the straps that are cutting his fingers in two and pulling
his arms out by the roots, and just before his bloodshot
eyes shoot clear out of his head, the boot comes on—or the
straps pull off. [Laughter.] Then when he stands up, the
earth rocks beneath his feet, and he thinks he can faintly
hear the angels calling him home. And when he walks
across the floor the first time, his standing in the church
and the Christian community is ruined forever. Or would
be if anyone could hear what he says. He never, never,
never gets to be so old that he cannot remember those boots,
and if it is seventy years afterward, his feet curl up in agony
at the recollection. The first time he wears them, he is
vaguely aware, as he leaves his room, that there is a kind
of " fixy " look about him, and his sisters' tittering is not
needed to confirm this impression.

He has a certain half-defined impression that everything
he has on is a size too small for any other man of his size.
Tom doesn't know all this: he has only a general, vague
impression that it may be so. And he doesn't know that his
sisters know every line of it. For he has lived many years
longer, and got in ever so much more trouble, before he
learns that one bright, good, sensible girl—and I believe
they are all that—will see and notice more in a glance, remember it more accurately, and talk more about it, than
twenty men can see in a week. Tom does not know, for his
crying feet will not let him, how he gets from his room to
the earthly paradise where Laura lives. Nor does he know,
after he gets there, that Laura sees him trying to rest one
foot by setting it up on the heel. And she sees him sneak it
back under his chair, and tilt it up on the toe, for a change.
She sees him ease the other foot a little by tugging the heel
of the boot at the leg of the chair—a hazardous, reckless,

presumptuous experiment. Tom tries it so far one night, and slides his heel so far up the leg of his boot, that his foot actually feels comfortable, and he thinks the angels must be rubbing it. He walks out of the parlor sideways that night, trying to hide the cause of the sudden elonga- tion of one leg, and he hobbles all the way home in the same disjointed condition. [Laughter.] But Laura sees that too. She sees all the little knobs and lumps on his foot, and sees him fidget and fuss, she sees the look of anguish flitting across his face under the heartless, deceitful veneering of smiles, and she makes the mental remark that Master Tom would feel much happier, and much more comfortable, and more like staying longer, if he had worn his father's boots.

But on his way to the house, despite the distraction of his crying feet, how many pleasant, really beautiful, romantic things Tom thinks up and recollects and compiles and com- poses to say to Laura, to impress her with his originality and wisdom and genius and bright, exuberant fancy and gen- eral superiority over all the rest of Tom-kind. Real earnest things, you know; no hollow, conventional compliments, or nonsense, but such things, Tom flatters himself, as none of the other fellows can or will say. And he has them all in beautiful order when he gets at the foot of the hill. The remark about the weather, to begin with; not the stereo- typed old phrase, but a quaint, droll, humorous conceit that no one in the world but Tom could think of. Then, after the opening overture about the weather, something about music and Beethoven's sonata in B flat, and Haydn's sym- phonies, and of course something about Beethoven's grand old Fifth symphony, somebody else's mass, in heaven knows how many flats; and then something about art, and a pro- found thought or two on science and philosophy, and so on to poetry, and from poetry to " business."

But alas, when Tom reaches the gate, all these well-or- dered ideas display evident symptoms of breaking up; as he crosses the yard, he is dismayed to know that they are in the convulsions of a panic, and when he touches the bell-knob, every, each, all and several of the ideas, original and com- piled, that he has had on any subject during the past ten years, forsake him and return no more that evening. [Laughter.]

When Laura opened the door, he had intended to say something real splendid about the imprisoned sunlight of something beaming out a welcome upon the what-you-may-call-it of the night, or something. Instead of which he says, or rather gasps:

" Oh, yes, to be sure; to be sure; ho."

And then, conscious that he has not said anything particularly brilliant or original, or that most any of the other fellows could not say with a little practice, he makes one more effort to redeem himself before he steps into the hall, and adds:

" Oh, good-morning; good-morning."

Feeling that even this is only a partial success, he collects .iis scattered faculties for one united effort, and inquires:

" How is your mother? "

And then it strikes him that he has about exhausted the subject and he goes into the parlor, and sits down, and just as soon as he has placed his reproachful feet in the least agonizing position, he proceeds to wholly, completely, and successfully forget everything he ever knew in his life. He returns to consciousness to find himself, to his own amazement and equally to Laura's bewilderment, conducting a conversation about the crops, and a new method of funding the national debt: subjects upon which he is about as well informed as the town clock. He rallies, and makes a successful effort to turn the conversation into literary channels by asking her if she has read " Daniel Deronda," and wasn't it odd that George Washington Eliot should name her heroine " Grenadine," after a dress-pattern? [Laughter.] And in a burst of confidence he assures her that he would not be amazed if it should rain before morning (and he. hopes it will, and that it may be a flood, and that he may get caught in it, without an ark nearer than Cape Horn).

And so, at last, the first evening passes away, and, after mature deliberation and many unsuccessful efforts, he rises to go. But he does not go. He wants to; but he doesn't know how. He says " good-evening." Then he repeats it in a marginal reference. Then he puts it in a foot-note. Then he adds the remarks in an appendix and shakes hands. By this time he gets as far as the parlor-door, and catches hold of the knob and holds on to it as tightly as though someone on the other side were trying to pull it through the door and run away with it. And he stands there a fidgety statue of the door-holder. He mentions, for not more than the twentieth time that evening, that he is passionately fond of music, but he can't sing. Which is a lie; he can. Did she go to the Centennial? " No." " Such a pity—" he begins, but stops in terror, lest she may consider his condolence a reflection upon her financial standing. Did he go? Oh, yes; yes; he says, absently, he went. Or, that is to say, no, not exactly. He did not exactly go to the Centennial; he stayed at home. In fact, he had not been out of town this summer. Then he looks at the tender little face; he looks at the brown eyes, sparkling with suppressed merriment; he looks at the white hands, dimpled and soft, twin daughters of the snow; and the fairy picture grows more lovely as he looks at it, until his heart outruns his fears; he must speak, he must say something impressive and ripe with meaning, for how can he go away with this suspense in his breast? His heart trembles as does his hand; his quivering lips part, and—Laura deftly hides a vagrant yawn behind her fan. Good-night, and Tom is gone.

There is a dejected droop to the mustache that night, when in the solitude of his own room Tom releases his hands from the despotic gloves, and tenderly soothes two of the reddest, puffiest feet that ever crept out of boots not half their own size, and swore in mute but eloquent anatomical profanity at the whole race of boot-makers. And his heart is nearly as full of sorrow and bitterness as his boots. It appears to him that he showed off to the worst possible advantage; he is dimly conscious that he acted very like a donkey, and he has the not entirely unnatural impression that she will never want to see him again. And so he philosophically and manfully makes up his mind never, never, never, to think of her again. And then he immediately proceeds, in the manliest and most natural way in the world, to think of nothing and nobody else under the sun for the next ten hours. How the tender little face does haunt him. He pitches himself into bed with an aimless recklessness that tumbles pillows, bolster, and sheets into one shapeless, wild, chaotic mass, and he goes through the motions of going to sleep, like a man who would go to sleep by steam. He stands his pillow up on one end, and pounds it into a wad, and he props his head upon it as though it were the guillotine block. He lays it down and smooths it out level, and pats all the wrinkles out of it, and there is more sleeplessness in it to the square inch than there is in the hungriest mosquito that ever sampled a martyr's blood. He gets up and smokes like a patent stove, although not three hours ago he told Laura that he de-test-ed tobacco.

This is the only time Tom will ever go through this, in exactly this way. It is the one rare, golden experience, the one bright, rosy dream of his life. He may live to be as old as an army overcoat, and he may marry as many wives as Brigham Young, singly, or in a cluster, but this will come to him but once. Let him enjoy all the delightful misery, all the ecstatic wretchedness, all the heavenly forlornness of it as best he can. And he does take good, solid, edifying misery out of it. How he does torture himself and hate Smith, the empty-headed donkey, who can talk faster than poor Tom can think, and whose mustache is black as Tom's boots, and so long that he can pull one end of it with both hands. And how he does detest that idiot Brown, who plays and sings, and goes up there every time Tom does, and claws over a few old, forgotten five-finger exercises and calls it music; who comes up there, some night when Tom thinks he has the evening and Laura all to himself, and brings up an old, tuneless, voiceless, cracked guitar, and goes crawling around in the wet grass under the windows, and makes night perfectly hideous with what he calls a serenade. And he speaks French, too, the beast. Poor Tom; when Brown's lingual accomplishments in the language of Charlemagne are confined to—" aw—aw—er ah—vooly voo? " and, on state occasions, to the additional grandeur of "avy voo mong shapo?" But poor Tom, who once covered himself with confusion by telling Laura that his favorite in " Robert le Diable " was the beautiful aria, " Robert toy que jam," considers Brown a very prodigal in linguistic attainments; another Cardinal Mezzofanti; and hates him for it accordingly. And he hates Daubs, the artist, too, who was up there one evening and made an off-hand crayon sketch of her in an album. The picture looked much more like Daubs' mother, and Tom knew it, but

Laura said it was oh, just delightfully, perfectly splendid, and Tom has hated Daubs most cordially ever since. In fact, Tom hates every man who has the temerity to speak to her, or whom she may treat with lady-like courtesy. [Laughter.]

Until there comes one night when the boots of the inquisition pattern sit more lightly on their suffering victims; when Providence has been on Tom's side and has kept Smith and Daubs and Brown away, and has frightened Tom nearly to death by showing him no one in the little parlor with its old-fashioned furniture but himself and Laura and the furniture; when, almost without knowing how or why, they talk about life and its realities instead of the last concert or the next lecture; when they talk of their plans, and their day-dreams and aspirations, and their ideals of real men and women; when they talk about the heroes and heroines of days long gone by, gray and dim in the ages that are ever made young and new by the lives of noble men and noble women who lived, and never died in those grand old days, but lived and live on, as imperishable and fadeless in their glory as the glittering stars that sang at creation's dawn; when the room seems strangely silent, when their voices hush; when the flush of earnestness upon her face gives it a tinge of sadness that makes it more beautiful than ever; when the dream and picture of a home Eden, and home life, and home love, grows every moment more lovely, more entrancing to him, until at last poor, blundering, stupid Tom speaks without knowing what he is going to say, speaks without preparation or rehearsal, speaks, and his honest, natural, manly heart touches his faltering lips with eloquence and tenderness and earnestness, that all the rhetoric in the world never did and never will inspire; and——. That is all we know about it. [Applause.] Nobody knows what is said or how it is done. Nobody. Only the silent stars or the whispering leaves, or the cat, or maybe Laura's younger brother, or the hired girl, who generally bulges in just as Tom reaches the climax. [Laughter.] All the rest of us know about it is, that Tom doesn't come away so early that night, and that when he reaches the door he holds a pair of dimpled hands instead of the insensate door-knob. He never clings to that door-knob again; never.

Unless ma, dear ma, has been so kind as to bring in her sewing and spend the evening with them. And Tom doesn't hate anybody, nor want to kill anybody in the wide, wide world, and he feels just as good as though he had just come out of a six months' revival; and is happy enough to borrow money of his worst enemy.

But, there is no rose without a thorn. Although, I suppose on an inside computation, there is, in this weary old world as much as, say a peck, or a peck and a half possibly, of thorns without their attendant roses. Just the raw, bare thorns. In the highest heaven of his newly found bliss, Tom is suddenly recalled to earth and its miseries by a question from Laura which falls like a plummet into the unrippled sea of the young man's happiness, and fathoms its depths in the shallowest place. " Has her own Tom "—as distinguished from countless other Toms, nobody's Toms, unclaimed Toms, to all intents and purposes swamp lands on the public matrimonial domain—" Has her own Tom said anything to pa? " [Laughter.]

" Oh, yes! pa, " Tom says. " To be sure; yes."

Grim, heavy-browed, austere pa. The living embodiment of business. Wiry, shrewd, the life and mainspring of the house of Tare & Tret. " 'M, Well. N' no," Tom had not exactly, as you might say, poured out his heart to pa. Somehow or other he had a rose-colored idea that the thing was going to go right along in this way forever. Tom had an idea that the programme was all arranged, printed and distributed, rose-colored, gilt-edged, and perfumed. He was going to sit and hold Laura's hands, pa was to stay down at the office, and ma was to make her visits to the parlor as much like angels', for their rarity and brevity, as possible. But he sees, now that the matter has been referred to, that it is a grim necessity. And Laura doesn't like to see such a spasm of terror pass over Tom's face; and her coral lips quiver a little as she hides her flushed face out of sight on Tom's shoulder, and tells him how kind and tender pa has always been with her, until Tom feels positively jealous of pa. And she tells him that he must not dread going to see him, for pa will be, oh, so glad to know how happy, happy, happy he can make his little girl. And as she talks of him, the hard-working, old-fashioned, tender-

hearted old man, who loves his girls as though he were yet
only a big boy, her heart grows tenderer, and she speaks so
earnestly and eloquently that Tom, at first savagely jealous
of him, is persuaded to fall in love with the old gentleman—
he calls him " pa," too, now—himself.

But by the following afternoon this feeling is very faint.
And when he enters the counting-room of Tare & Tret, and
stands before pa— Oh, land of love, how could Laura ever
talk so about such a man! Stubbly little pa; with a fringe
of the most obstinate and wiry gray hair standing all around
his bald, bald head; the wiriest, grizzliest mustache bristling
under his nose; a tuft of tangled beard under the sharp chin,
and a raspy undergrowth of a week's run on the thin jaws;
business, business, business, in every line of the hard,
seamed face, and profit and loss, barter and trade, dicker
and bargain, in every movement of the nervous hands. Pa;
old business! He puts down the newspaper a little way, and
looks over the top of it as Tom announces himself, glancing at the young man with a pair of blue eyes that peer
through old-fashioned iron-bowed spectacles, that look as
though they had known these eyes and done business with
them ever since they wept over their A B C's or peeked
into the tall stone jar Sunday afternoon to look for the
doughnuts.

Tom, who had felt all along there could be no inspiration
on his part in this scene, has come prepared. At least he
had his last true statement at his tongue's end when he entered the counting-room. But now, it seems to him that if
he had been brought up in a circus, and cradled inside of a
sawdust ring, and all his life trained to twirl his hat, he
couldn't do it better, nor faster, nor be more utterly incapable of doing anything else. At last he swallowed a lump
in his throat as big as a ballot-box, and faintly gasps:

" Good-morning."

Mr. Tret hastens to recognize him. " Eh? oh; yes; yes;
yes; I see; young Bostwick, from Dope & Middlerib's.
Oh, yes. Well——? "

" I have come, sir," gasps Tom, thinking all around the
world from Cook's explorations to " Captain Riley's Narrative," for the first line of that speech that Tare & Tret
have just scared out of him so completely that he doesn't

believe he ever knew a word of it. " I have come—" and he thinks if his lips didn't get so dry and hot that they make his teeth ache, that he could get along with it: " I have sir—come, Mr. Tret; Mr. Tret, sir—I have come—I am come——"

" Yes, ye-es," says Mr. Tret, in the wildest bewilderment, but in no very encouraging tones, thinking the young man probably wants to borrow money. " Ye-es; I see you've come. Well; that's all right; glad to see you. [Laughter.] Yes, you've come? "

Tom's hat is now making about nine hundred and eighty revolutions per minute, and apparently not running up to half its full capacity.

" Sir; Mr. Tret," he resumes, " I have come, sir; Mr. Tret—I am here to—to sue—to sue, Mr. Tret—I am here to sue——"

" Sue, eh? " the old man echoes sharply, with a belligerent rustle of the newspaper; " sue Tare & Tret, eh? · Well, that's right, young man; that's right. Sue, and get damages. We'll give you all the law you want."

Tom's head is so hot, and his heart is so cold, that he thinks they must be about a thousand miles apart.

" Sir," he explains, " that isn't it. It isn't that. I only want to ask—I have long known—sir," he adds, as the opening lines of his speech come to him like a message from heaven, " Sir, you have a flower, a tender, lovely blossom; chaste as the snow that crowns the mountain's brow; fresh as the breath of morn; lovelier than the rosy-fingered hours that fly before Aurora's car; pure as a lily kissed by dew. This precious blossom, watched by your paternal eyes, the object of your tender care and solicitude, I ask of you. I would wear it in my heart, and guard and cherish it—and in the——"

" Oh-h, ye-es, yes, yes," the old man says, soothingly, beginning to see that Tom is only drunk. " Oh, yes, yes; I don't know much about them myself; my wife and the girls generally keep half the windows in the house littered up with them, winter and summer, every window so full of house-plants the sun can't shine in. Come up to the house, they'll give you all you can carry away, give you a hatful of 'em."

" No, no, no; you don't understand," says poor Tom, and old Mr. Tret now observes that Tom is very drunk indeed. " It isn't that, sir. Sir, that isn't it. I—I—I want to marry your daughter! "

And there it is at last, as bluntly as though Tom had wadded it into a gun and shot it at the old man. Mr. Tret does not say anything for twenty seconds. Tom tells Laura that evening that it was two hours and a half before her father opened his head. Then he says, " Oh, yes, yes, yes, yes; to be sure; to—be—sure." And then the long pause is dreadful. " Yes, yes. Well, I don't know. I don't know about that, young man. Said anything to Jennie about it? "

" It isn't Jennie," Tom gasps, seeing a new Rubicon to cross; " it's——"

" Oh, Julie, eh? well, I don't——"

" No, sir," interjects the despairing Tom, " it isn't Julie, it's——"

" Sophie, eh? Oh, well, Sophie——"

" Sir," says Tom, " if you please, sir, it isn't Sophie, it's——"

" Not Minnie, surely? Why Minnie is hardly—well, I don't know. Young folks get along faster than——"

" Dear Mr. Tret," breaks in the distracted lover, " it's Laura."

As they sit and stand there, looking at each other, the dingy old counting-room, with the heavy shadows lurking in every corner, with its time-worn, heavy brown furnishings, with the scanty dash of sunlight breaking in through the dusty window, looks like an old Rubens painting; the beginning and finishing of a race: the old man, nearly ready to lay his armor off, glad to be so nearly and so safely through with the race and the fight that Tom, in all his inexperience and with all the rash enthusiasm and conceit of a young man, is just getting ready to run and fight, or fight and run, you never can tell which until he is through with it. And the old man, looking at Tom, and through him, and past him, feels his old heart throb almost as quickly as does that of the young man before him. For looking down a long vista of happy, eventful years bordered with roseate hopes and bright dreams and anticipations, he sees a tender face, radiant with smiles and kindled with blushes; he feels a soft hand drop into his own with its timid pressure; he sees the vision open, under the glittering summer stars, down mossy hill-sides, where the restless breezes, sighing through the rustling leaves, whispered their tender secret to the noisy katydids; strolling along the winding paths, deep in the bending wild grass, down in the starlit aisles of the dim old woods; loitering where the meadow-brook sparkles over the white pebbles or murmurs around the great flat stepping-stones; lingering on the rustic foot-bridge, while he gazes into eyes eloquent and tender in their silent love-light; up through the long pathway of years, flecked and checkered with sunshine and cloud, with storm and calm, through years of struggle, trial, sorrow, disappointment, out at last into the grand, glorious, crowning beauty and benison of hard-won and well-deserved success, until he sees now this second Laura, re-imaging her mother as she was in the dear old days. And he rouses from his dream with a start, and he tells Tom he'll " talk it over with Mrs. Tret and see him again in the morning." [Applause.]

And so they are duly and formally engaged; and the very first thing they do, they make the very sensible, though very uncommon, resolution to so conduct themselves that no one will ever suspect it. And they succeed admirably. No one ever does suspect it. They come into church in time to hear the benediction—every time they come together. They shun all other people when church is dismissed, and are seen to go home alone the longest way. At picnics they are missed not more than fifty times a day, and are discovered sitting under a tree, holding each other's hands, gazing into each other's eyes and saying—nothing. When he throws her shawl over her shoulders, he never looks at what he is doing, but looks straight into her starry eyes, throws the shawl right over her natural curls, and drags them out by the hair-pins. If, at sociable or festival, they are left alone in a dressing-room a second and a half, Laura emerges with her ruffle standing around like a railroad accident; and Tom has enough complexion on his shoulder to go around a young ladies' seminary. [Laughter.] When they drive out, they sit in a buggy with a seat eighteen inches wide, and there is two feet of unoccupied room at either end of it. Long years afterward, when they drive, a street-car isn't too wide for them; and when they walk, you could drive four loads of hay between them.

And yet, as carefully as they guard their precious little secret, and as cautious and circumspect as they are in their walk and behavior, it gets talked around that they are engaged. People are so prying and suspicious.

And so the months of their engagement run on; never before or since, time flies so swiftly—unless, it may be, some time when Tom has an acceptance in bank to meet in two days, that he can't lift one end of. [Laughter.] And the wedding day dawns, fades, and the wedding is over. Over, with its little circle of delighted friends, with its ripples of pleasure and excitement, with its touches of home love and home life, that leave their lasting impress upon Laura's heart, although Tom, with man-like blindness, never sees one of them. Over, with ma, with the thousand and one anxieties attendant on the grand event in her daughter's life hidden away under her dear old smiling face, down, away down under the tender, glistening eyes, deep in the loving heart; ma, hurrying here and fluttering there, in the intense excitement of something strangely made up of happiness and grief, of apprehension and hope; ma, with her sudden disappearances and flushed reappearances, indicating struggles and triumphs in the turbulent world downstairs; ma, with the new-fangled belt with the dinner-plate buckles, fastened on wrong side foremost, and the flowers dangling down the wrong side of her head, to Sophie's intense horror and pantomimic telegraphy; ma, flying here and there, seeing that everything is going right from kitchen to dressing-rooms; looking after everything and everybody, with her hands and heart just as full as they will hold, and more voices calling " ma," from every room in the house, than you would think one hundred mas could answer.

But she answers them all, and she sees after everything, and just in the nick of time prevents Mr. Tret from going downstairs and attending the ceremony in a loud-figured dressing-gown and green slippers; ma, who, with the quivering lip and glistening eyes, has to be cheerful, and lively, and smiling; because, if, as she thinks of the dearest and

best of her flock going away from her fold, to put her life
and her happiness into another's keeping, she gives way
for one moment, a dozen reproachful voices cry out, " Oh-h
ma!" How it all comes back to Laura, like the tender
shadows of a dream, long years after the dear, dear face,
furrowed with marks of patient suffering and loving care,
rests under the snow and the daisies; when the mother love
that glistened in the tender eyes has closed in darkness on
the dear old home; and the nerveless hands, crossed in
dreamless sleep upon the pulseless breast, can never again
touch the children's heads with caressing gesture; how the
sweet vision comes to Laura, as it shone on her wedding
morn, rising in tenderer beauty through the blinding tears
her own excess of happiness calls up, as the rainbow spans
the cloud only through the mingling of the golden sunshine
and the falling rain. [Applause.]

And pa, dear, old, shabby pa, whose clothes will not fit
him as they fit other men; who always dresses just a year
and a half behind the style; pa, wandering up and down
through the house, as though he were lost in his own home,
pacing through the hall like a sentinel, blundering aimlessly
and listlessly into rooms where he has no business, and being repelled therefrom by a chorus of piercing shrieks and
hysterical giggling; pa, getting off his well-worn jokes with
an assumption of merriment that seems positively real; pa,
who creeps away by himself once in a while, and leans his
face against the window, and sighs, in direct violation of
all strict household regulations, right against the glass, as
he thinks of his little girl going away to-day from the home
whose love and tenderness and patience she has known so
well. Only yesterday, it seems to him, the little baby girl,
bringing the first music of baby prattle into his home; then
a little girl in short dresses, with school-girl troubles and
school-girl pleasures; then an older little girl, out of school
and into society, but a little girl to pa still. And then——.
But somehow, this is as far as pa can get; for he sees, in
the flight of this, the first, the following flight of the other
fledglings; and he thinks how silent and desolate the old
nest will be when they have all mated and flown away. He
thinks, when their flight shall have made other homes
bright, and cheery, and sparkling with music and prattle

and laughter, how it will leave the old home hushed, and quiet, and still. And dreaming thus, when pa for a moment finds his little girl alone—his little girl who is going away out of the home whose love she knows, into a home whose tenderness and patience are all untried—he holds her in his arms and whispers the most fervent blessing that ever throbbed from a father's heart; and Laura's wedding day would be incomplete and unfeeling without her tears. So is the pattern of our life made up of smiles and tears, shadow and sunshine. Tom sees none of these background pictures of the wedding day. He sees none of its real, heartfelt earnestness. He sees only the bright, sunny tints and happy figures that the tearful, shaded background throws out in golden relief; but never stops to think that, without the shadows, the clouds, and the sombre tints of the background, the picture would be flat, pale, and lustreless.

And then, the presents. The assortment of brackets, serviceable, ornamental and—cheap. The French clock, that never went, that does not go, that never will go. And the nine potato-mashers. The eight mustard-spoons. The three cigar-stands. Eleven match-safes; assorted patterns. A dozen tidies, charity-fair styles, blue dog on a yellow background, barking at a green boy climbing over a red fence, after seal-brown apples. The two churns, old pattern, straight handle and dasher, and they have as much thought of keeping a cow as they have of keeping a section of artillery. Five things they didn't know the names of, and never could find anybody who could tell what they were for. And a nickel-plated pocket corkscrew, that Tom, in a fine burst of indignation, throws out of the window, which Laura says is just like her own impulsive Tom. And not long after, her own impulsive Tom catches his death of cold and ruins the knees of his best trousers crawling around in the wet grass hunting for that same corkscrew. Which is also just like her own impulsive Tom.

And then, the young people go to work and buy e-v-e-r-y-thing they need, the day they go to housekeeping. Everything. Just as well, Tom says, to get everything at once and have it delivered right up at the house, as to spend five or six or ten or twenty years in stocking up a house, as his father did. And Laura thinks so, too, and she wonders that

Tom should know so much more than his father. This worries Tom himself, when he thinks of it, and he never rightly understands how it is, until he is forty-five or fifty years old, and has a Tom of his own to direct and advise him. So they make out a list, and revise it, and rewrite it, until they have everything down, complete, and it isn't until supper is ready, the first day, that they discover there isn't a knife, a fork, or a plate or a spoon in the new house. And the first day the washerwoman comes, and the water is hot, and the clothes are all ready, it is discovered that there isn't a wash-tub nearer than the grocery. And further along in the day the discovery is made that while Tom has bought a clothes-line that will reach to the North Pole and back, and then has to be coiled up a mile or two in the back yard, there isn't a clothes-pin in the settlement. And, in the course of a week or two, Tom slowly awakens to the realization of the fact that he has only begun to get. So long as he lives, Tom goes on bringing home things that they need—absolute, simple necessities, that were never so much as hinted at in that exhaustive list.

And old Time comes along, and knowing that the man in that new house will never get through bringing things up to it, helps him out, and comes around and brings things, too. Brings a gray hair now and then, to stick in Tom's mustache, which has grown too big to be ornamental, and too wayward and unmanageable to be comfortable. He brings little cares and little troubles, and little trials and little butcher bills, and little grocery bills, and little tailor bills, and nice, large millinery bills, that pluck at Tom's mustache and stroke it the wrong way and make it look more and more as pa's did the first time Tom saw it. He brings, by and by, the prints of baby fingers, and pats them around on the dainty wall-paper. Brings, sometimes, a voiceless messenger that lays its icy fingers on the baby lips, and hushes their dainty prattle, and in the baptism of its first sorrow, the darkened little home has its dearest and tenderest tie to the upper fold. Brings, by and by, the tracks of a boy's muddy boots, and scatters them all up and down the clean porch. Brings a messenger, one day, to take the younger Tom away to college. And the quiet the boy leaves behind him, is so much harder to endure than

his racket, that old Tom is tempted to keep a brass band
in the house until the boy comes back. But old Time brings
him home at last, and it does make life seem terribly real
and earnest to Tom, and how the old laugh rings out and
ripples all over Laura's face, when they see old Tom's first
mustache, budding and struggling into second life, on
young Tom's face.

And still old Time comes round, bringing each year
whiter frosts to scatter on the whitening mustache, and
brighter gleams of silver to glint the brown of Laura's hair.
Bringing the blessings of peaceful old age and a lovelocked
home to crown these noble, earnest, real, human lives bristling with human faults, marred with human mistakes,
scarred and seamed and rifted with human troubles, and
crowned with the compassion that only perfection can send
upon imperfection. Comes, with happy memories of the
past, and quiet confidence for the future. Comes, with the
changing scenes of day and night; with winter's storm and
summer's calm; comes, with the sunny peace and the backward dreams of age; comes, until one day, the eye of the relentless old reaper rests upon old Tom, standing right in
the swath, amid the golden corn. The sweep of the noise-
less scythe, that never turns its edge, Time passes on, old
Tom steps out of young Tom's way, and the cycle of a life
is complete. [Applause.]

THOMAS CARLYLE

Photogravure after a photograph from life

THOMAS CARLYLE

MAHOMET

[Lecture by Thomas Carlyle (born in Dumfries, Scotland, December 4, 1795; died in Chelsea, London, February 4, 1881), delivered in London, May 8, 1840, second in his course of six lectures on the general theme of "Heroes, Hero Worship and the Heroic in History," given during May of that year, its subject being " The Hero as Prophet—Mahomet: Islam." This course was the last of Carlyle's series of public lectures read between 1836 and 1840 (the first being the course of twelve on "The History of Literature" given in April-July, 1838). For them, "in their form, at least of oral dissertations," as Henry D. Traill has written, "the world is indebted to poverty and Harriet Martineau." At the close of the series, the delivery of which had been most irksome to Carlyle, he spoke his farewell to his audience in these words: ". . . Here finally these wide roamings of ours through so many times and places in search and study of Heroes, are to terminate. I am sorry for it: there was pleasure for me in this business, if also much pain. It is a great subject, and a most wide and grave one, this which, not to be too grave about it, I have named Hero Worship. It enters deeply, as I think, into the secret of Mankind's ways and vitalest interests of this world, and is well worth explaining at present. With six months, instead of six days, we might have done better. I promised to break ground on it; I know not whether I have even managed to do that. I have had to tear it up in the rudest manner in order to get into it at all. Often enough with these abrupt utterances thrown out isolated, unexplained, has your tolerance been put to the trial. Tolerance, patient candor, all-hoping favor and kindness, which I will not speak of at present. The accomplished and distinguished, the beautiful, the wise, something of what is best in England, have listened patiently to my rude words. With many feelings I heartily thank you all, and say, God be with you all! "]

From the first rude times of Paganism among the Scandinavians in the North, we advance to a very different epoch of religion, among a very different people : Mahometanism among the Arabs. A great change; what a change and progress is indicated here, in the universal condition and thoughts of men!

The Hero is not now regarded as a God among his fellowmen; but as one God-inspired, as a Prophet. It is the second phasis of Hero-worship: the first or oldest, we may say, has passed away without return; in the history of the world there will not again be any man, never so great, whom his fellowmen will take for a god. Nay, we might rationally ask, Did any set of human beings ever really think the man they saw there standing beside them a god, the maker of this world? Perhaps not: it was usually some man they remembered, or had seen. But neither can this any more be. The Great Man is not recognized as a god any more.

It was a rude gross error, that of counting the Great Man a god. Yet let us say that it is at all times difficult to know what he is, or how to account of him and receive him! The most significant feature in the history of an epoch is the manner it has of welcoming a Great Man. Ever, to the true instincts of men, there is something godlike in him. Whether they shall take him to be a god, to be a prophet, or what they shall take him to be? that is ever a grand question; by their way of answering that, we shall see, as through a little window, into the very heart of these men's spiritual condition. For at bottom the Great Man, as he comes from the hand of Nature, is ever the same kind of thing: Odin, Luther, Johnson, Burns; I hope to make it appear that these are all originally of one stuff; that only by the world's reception of them, and the shapes they assume, are they so immeasurably diverse. The worship of Odin astonishes us—to fall prostrate before the Great Man, into *deliquium* of love and wonder over him, and feel in their hearts that he was a denizen of the skies a god! This was imperfect enough: but to welcome, for example, a Burns as we did, was that what we can call perfect? The most precious gift that Heaven can give to the Earth; a man of " genius " as we call it; the Soul of a Man actually sent down from the skies with a God's-message to us—this we waste away as an idle artificial firework, sent to amuse us a little, and sink it into ashes, wreck, and ineffectuality: such reception of a Great Man I do not call very perfect either! Looking into the heart of the thing, one may perhaps call that of Burns a still uglier phenomenon, betokening still sadder imperfections in mankind's ways, than the Scandinavian method itself! To fall into mere unreasoning *deliquium* of love and admiration, was not good; but such unreasoning, nay irrational supercilious no-love at all is perhaps still worse!—It is a thing forever changing, this of Hero-worship: different in each age, difficult to do well in any age. Indeed, the heart of the whole business of the age, one may say, is to do it well.

We have chosen Mahomet not as the most eminent Prophet; but as the one we are freest to speak of. He is by no means the truest of Prophets; but I do esteem him a true one. Further, as there is no danger of our becoming, any of us, Mahometans, I mean to say all the good of him I justly can. It is the way to get at his secret: let us try to understand what he meant with the world; what the world meant and means with him, will then be a more answerable question. Our current hypothesis about Mahomet, that he was a scheming Impostor, a Falsehood incarnate, that his religion is a mere mass of quackery and fatuity, begins really to be now untenable to any one. The lies, which well-meaning zeal has heaped round this man, are disgraceful to ourselves only. When Pocoke inquired of Grotius, Where the proof was of that story of the pigeon, trained to pick peas from Mahomet's ear, and pass for an angel dictating to him? Grotius answered that there was no proof! It is really time to dismiss all that. The word this man spoke has been the life-guidance now of a hundred and eighty millions of men these twelve hundred years. These hundred and eighty millions were made by God as well as we. A greater number of God's creatures believe in Mahomet's word at this hour than in any other word whatever. Are we to suppose that it was a miserable piece of spiritual legerdemain, this which so many creatures of the Almighty have lived by and died by? I, for my part, cannot form any such supposition. I will believe most things sooner than that. One would be entirely at a loss what to think of this world at all, if quackery so grew and were sanctioned here.

Alas, such theories are very lamentable. If we would

attain to knowledge of anything in God's true Creation, let us disbelieve them wholly! They are the product of an Age of Scepticism; they indicate the saddest spiritual paralysis, and mere death-life of the souls of men: more godless theory, I think, was never promulgated in this Earth. A false man found a religion? Why, a false man cannot build a brick house! If he do not know and follow truly the properties of mortar, burnt clay and what else he works in, it is no house that he makes, but a rubbish heap. It will not stand for twelve centuries, to lodge a hundred and eighty millions; it will fall straightway. A man must conform himself to Nature's laws, be verily in communion with Nature and the truth of things, or Nature will answer him, No, not at all! Speciosities are specious—ah me!—a Cagliostro, many Cagliostros, prominent world-leaders, do prosper by their quackery, for a day. It is like a forged bank-note; they get it passed out of their worthless hands: others, not they, have to smart for it. Nature bursts up in fire-flames, French Revolutions and suchlike, proclaiming with terrible veracity that forged notes are forged.

But of a Great Man especially, of him I will venture to assert that it is incredible he should have been other than true. It seems to me the primary foundation of him, and of all that can lie in him, this. No Mirabeau, Napoleon, Burns, Cromwell, no man adequate to do anything, but is first of all in right earnest about it; what I call a sincere man. I should say sincerity, a deep, great, genuine sincerity, is the first characteristic of all men in any way heroic. Not the sincerity that calls itself sincere: ah no, that is a very poor matter indeed;—a shallow braggart conscious sincerity; oftenest self-conceit mainly. The Great Man's sincerity is of the kind he cannot speak of, is not conscious of; nay, I suppose he's conscious rather of insincerity; for what man can walk accurately by the law of truth for one day? No, the Great Man does not boast himself sincere, far from that; perhaps does not ask himself if he is so: I would say rather, his sincerity does not depend on himself; he cannot help being sincere! The great Fact of Existence is great to him. Fly as he will, he cannot get out of the awful presence of this Reality. His mind is so made; he is great by that, first of all. Fearful and wonderful, real as Life, real as Death, is this Universe to him. Though all men should forget its truth, and walk in a vain show, he cannot. At all moments the Flame-image glares in upon him; undeniable, there, there!—I wish you to take this as my primary definition of a Great Man. A little man may have this, it is competent to all men that God has made: but a Great Man cannot be without it.

Such a man is what we call an original man; he comes to us at first-hand. A messenger he, sent from the Infinite Unknown with tidings to us. We may call him Poet, Prophet, God;—in one way or other, we all feel that the words he utters are as no other man's words. Direct from the Inner Fact of things;—he lives, and has to live, in daily communion with that. Hearsays cannot hide it from him; he is blind, homeless, miserable, following hearsays; it glares in upon him. Really his utterances, are they not a kind of "revelation";—what we must call such for want of other name? It is from the heart of the world that he comes; he is portion of the primal reality of things. God has made many revelations: but this man too, has not God made him, the latest and newest of all? The "inspiration of the Almighty giveth him understanding": we must listen before all to him.

This Mahomet, then, we will in no wise consider as an Inanity and Theatricality, a poor conscious ambitious schemer; we cannot conceive him so. The rude message he delivered was a real one withal; an earnest confused voice from the unknown deep. The man's words were not false, nor his workings here below; no Inanity and Simulacrum; a fiery mass of Life cast up from the great bosom of Nature herself. To kindle the world; the world's Maker had ordered it so. Neither can the faults, imperfections, insincerities even, of Mahomet, if such were never so well proved against him, shake this primary fact about him.

On the whole, we make too much of faults; the details of the business hide the real centre of it. Faults? The greatest of faults, I should say, is to be conscious of none. Readers of the Bible above all, one would think, might know better. Who is called there "the man according to God's own heart"? David, the Hebrew King, had fallen into sins enough; blackest crimes; there was no want of sins. And thereupon the unbelievers sneer and ask, Is this your man according to God's heart? The sneer, I must say, seems to me but a shallow one. What are faults, what are the outward details of a life; if the inner secret of it, the remorse, temptations, true, often-baffled, never-ended struggle of it, be forgotten? "It is not in man that walketh to direct his steps." Of all acts, is not, for a man, repentance the most divine? The deadliest sin, I say, were that same supercilious consciousness of no sin;—that is death; the heart so conscious is divorced from sincerity, humility, and fact; is dead: it is "pure" as dead dry sand is pure. David's life and history, as written for us in those Psalms of his, I consider to be the truest emblem ever given of a man's moral progress and warfare here below. All earnest souls will ever discern in it the faithful struggle of an earnest human soul towards what is good and best. Struggle often baffled, sore baffled, down as into entire wreck; yet a struggle never ended; ever, with tears, repentance, true unconquerable purpose, begun anew. Poor human nature! Is not a man's walking, in truth, always that: "a succession of falls"? Man can do no other. In this wild element of a Life, he has to struggle onward, now fallen, deep-abased; and ever, with tears, repentance, with bleeding heart, he has to rise again, struggle again still onwards. That his struggle be a faithful unconquerable one: that is the question of questions. We will put up with many sad details, if the soul of it were true. Details by themselves will never teach us what it is. I believe we misestimate Mahomet's faults even as faults: but the secret of him will never be got by dwelling there. We will leave all this behind us; and assuring ourselves that he did mean some true thing, ask candidly what it was or might be.

These Arabs Mahomet was born among are certainly a notable people. Their country itself is notable; the fit habitation for such a race. Savage inaccessible rock-mountains, great grim deserts, alternating with beautiful strips of verdure; wherever water is, there is greenness, beauty; odoriferous balm-shrubs, date-trees, frankincense-trees. Consider that wide waste horizon of sand, empty, silent, like a sand-sea, dividing habitable place from habitable. You are all alone there, left alone with the Universe; by day a fierce sun blazing down on it with intolerable radiance; by night the great deep Heaven with its stars. Such a country is fit for a swift-handed, deep-hearted race of men. There is something most agile, active, and yet most meditative, enthusiastic in the Arab character. The Persians are called the French of the East; we will call the Arabs Oriental Italians. A gifted noble people; a people of wild strong feelings, and of iron restraint over these: the characteristic of nobleminded-ness, of genius. The wild Bedouin welcomes the stranger to his tent, as one having right to all that is there; were it his worst enemy, he will slay his foal to treat him, will serve him with sacred hospitality for three days, will set him fairly on his way;—and then, by another law as sacred, kill him if he can. In words too, as in action. They are not a loquacious people, taciturn rather; but eloquent, gifted when they do speak. An earnest, truthful kind of men. They are, as we know, of Jewish kindred: but with that deadly terrible earnestness of the Jews they seem to combine something graceful, brilliant, which is not Jewish. They had "Poetic contests" among them before the time of Mahomet. Sale says, at Ocadh, in the South of Arabia, there were yearly fairs, and there, when the merchandising was done, Poets sang for prizes:—the wild people gathered to hear that.

One Jewish quality these Arabs manifest; the outcome of many or of all high qualities: what we may call religiosity. From of old they had been zealous worshippers, according to their light. They worshipped the stars, as Sabeans; worshipped many natural objects,—recognized them as symbols, immediate manifestations, of the Maker of Nature. It was wrong; and yet not wholly wrong. All God's works are still in a sense symbols of God. Do we not, as I urged, still account it a merit to recognize a certain inexhaustible significance, "poetic beauty" as we name it, in all natural objects whatsoever? A man is a poet, and honored, for doing that, and speaking or singing it,—a kind of diluted worship. They had many Prophets, these Arabs; Teachers each to his tribe, each according to

the light he had. But indeed, have we not from of old
the noblest of proofs, still palpable to every one of us, of
what devoutness and noble-mindedness had dwelt in these
rustic thoughtful peoples?   Biblical critics seem agreed
that our own Book of Job was written in that region of
the world. I call that, apart from all theories about it,
one of the grandest things ever written with pen. One
feels, indeed, as if it were not Hebrew; such a noble uni-
versality, different from noble patriotism or sectarianism,
reigns in it.   A noble Book; all men's Book!   It is our
first, oldest statement of the never-ending Problem,—
man's destiny, and God's ways with him here in this earth.
And all in such free flowing outlines; grand in its sincerity, in its simplicity; in its epic melody, and repose of re-
concilement.   There is the seeing eye, the mildly understanding heart.   So true everyway; true eyesight and
vision for all things; material things no less than spiritual:
the Horse,—" hast thou clothed his neck with thunder"?
—he "laughs at the shaking of the spear!"   Such living
likenesses were never since drawn.   Sublime sorrow, sublime reconciliation; oldest choral melody as of the heart
of mankind;—so soft, and great; as the summer midnight, as the world with its seas and stars!   There is
nothing written, I think, in the Bible or out of it, of
equal literary merit.

To the idolatrous Arabs one of the most ancient universal objects of worship was that Black Stone, still kept in
the building called Caabah at Mecca.   Diodorus Siculus
mentions this Caabah in a way not to be mistaken, as the
oldest, most honored temple in his time; that is, some half
century before our Era.   Silvestre de Sacy says there is
some likelihood that the Black Stone is an aerolite.   In
that case, some man might see it fall out of Heaven!   It
stands now beside the Well Zemzem; the Caabah is built
over both.   A Well is in all places a beautiful affecting
object, gushing out like life from the hard earth;—still
more so in those hot dry countries, where it is the first
condition of being.   The Well Zemzem has its name from
the bubbling sound of the waters, *zem-zem;* they think it
is the Well which Hagar found with her little Ishmael in
the wilderness: the aerolite and it have been sacred now,
and had a Caabah over them, for thousands of years.   A

curious object, that Caabah! There it stands at this hour, in the black cloth coverings the Sultan sends it yearly; "twenty-seven cubits high"; with circuit, with double circuit of pillars, with festoon rows of lamps and quaint ornaments: the lamps will be lighted again this night,—to glitter again under the stars. An authentic fragment of the oldest Past. It is the *Keblah* of all Moslem: from Delhi all onwards to Morocco, the eyes of innumerable praying men are turned towards it, five times, this day and all days: one of the notablest centres in the Habitation of Men.

It had been from the sacredness attached to this Caabah Stone and Hagar's Well, from the pilgrimings of all tribes of Arabs hither, that Mecca took its rise as a Town. A great town once, though much decayed now. It has no natural advantage for a town; stands in a sandy hollow amid bare barren hills, at a distance from the sea; its provisions, its very bread, have to be imported. But so many pilgrims needed lodgings: and then all places of pilgrimage do, from the first, become places of trade. The first day pilgrims meet, merchants have also met: where men see themselves assembled for one object, they find that they can accomplish other objects which depend on meeting together. Mecca became the Fair of all Arabia. And thereby indeed the chief staple and warehouse of whatever commerce there was between the Indian and the Western countries, Syria, Egypt, even Italy. It had at one time a population of 100,000; buyers, forwarders of those Eastern and Western products; importers for their own behoof of provisions and corn. The government was a kind of irregular aristocratic republic, not without a touch of theocracy. Ten Men of a chief tribe, chosen in some rough way, were Governors of Mecca, and Keepers of the Caabah. The Koreish were the chief tribe in Mahomet's time; his own family was of that tribe. The rest of the Nation, fractioned and cut asunder by deserts, lived under similar rude patriarchal governments by one or several: herdsmen, carriers, traders, generally robbers too; being oftenest at war one with another, or with all: held together by no open bond, if it were not this meeting at the Caabah, where all forms of Arab idolatry assembled in common adoration;—held mainly by the inward indissoluble bond of a common blood and language. In this way had the Arabs lived for long ages, unnoticed by the world; a people of great qualities, unconsciously waiting for the day when they should become notable to all the world. Their idolatries appear to have been in a tottering state; much was getting into confusion and fermentation among them. Obscure tidings of the most important Event ever transacted in this world, the Life and Death of the Divine Man in Judea, at once the symptom and cause of immeasurable change to all people in the world, had in the course of centuries reached into Arabia too; and could not but, of itself, have produced fermentation there.

It was among this Arab people, so circumstanced, in the year 570 of our Era, that the man Mahomet was born. He was of the family of Hashem, of the Koreish tribe as we said; though poor, connected with the chief persons of his country. Almost at his birth he lost his father; at the age of six years his mother too, a woman noted for her beauty, her worth and sense: he fell to the charge of his grandfather, an old man, a hundred years old. A good old man: Mahomet's father, Abdallah, had been his youngest favorite son. He saw in Mahomet, with his old life-worn eyes, a century old, the lost Abdallah come back again, all that was left of Abdallah. He loved the little orphan boy greatly; used to say, They must take care of that beautiful little boy, nothing in their kindred was more precious than he. At his death, while the boy was still but two years old, he left him in charge to Abu Thaleb the eldest of the uncles, as to him that now was head of the house. By this uncle, a just and rational man as everything betokens, Mahomet was brought up in the best Arab way.

Mahomet, as he grew up, accompanied his uncle on trading journeys and suchlike; in his eighteenth year one finds him a fighter following his uncle in war. But perhaps the most significant of all his journeys is one we find noted as of some years' earlier date: a journey to the Fairs of Syria. The young man here first came in contact with a quite foreign world,—with one foreign element of endless moment to him: the Christian Religion. I know not what to make of that "Sergius, the Nestorian Monk," whom Abu Thaleb and he are said to have lodged with; or how much any monk could have taught one still so young. Probably enough it is greatly exaggerated, this of the Nestorian Monk. Mahomet was only fourteen; had no language but his own: much in Syria must have been a strange unintelligible whirlpool to him. But the eyes of the lad were open; glimpses of many things would doubtless be taken in, and lie very enigmatic as yet, which were to ripen in a strange way into views, into beliefs and insights one day. These journeys to Syria were probably the beginning of much to Mahomet.

One other circumstance we must not forget: that he had no school learning; of the thing we call school learning none at all. The art of writing was but just introduced into Arabia; it seems to be the true opinion that Mahomet never could write! Life in the Desert, with its experiences, was all his education. What of this infinite Universe he, from his dim place, with his own eyes and thoughts, could take in, so much and no more of it was he to know. Curious, if we will reflect on it, this of having no books. Except by what he could see for himself, or hear of by uncertain rumor of speech in the obscure Arabian Desert, he could know nothing. The wisdom that had been before him or at a distance from him in the world was in a manner as good as not there for him. Of the great brother souls, flame-beacons through so many lands and times, no one directly communicates with this great soul. He is alone there, deep down in the bosom of the Wilderness; has to grow up so,—alone with Nature and his own Thoughts.

But, from an early age, he had been remarked as a thoughtful man. His companions named him "*Al Amin*, The Faithful." A man of truth and fidelity; true in what he did, in what he spake and thought. They noted that he always meant something. A man rather taciturn in speech; silent when there was nothing to be said; but pertinent, wise, sincere, when he did speak; always throwing light on the matter. This is the only sort of speech worth speaking! Through life we find him to have been regarded as an altogether solid, brotherly, genuine man. A serious, sincere character; yet amiable, cordial, companionable, jocose even;—a good laugh in him withal: there are men whose laugh is as untrue as anything about them; who cannot laugh. One hears of Mahomet's beauty: his fine sagacious honest face, brown florid complexion, beaming black eyes;—I somehow like too that vein on the brow, which swelled up black when he was in anger: like the "horse-shoe vein" in Scott's "Redgauntlet." It was a kind of feature in the Hashem family, this black swelling vein in the brow; Mahomet had it prominent, as would appear. A spontaneous, passionate, yet just, true-meaning man! Full of wild faculty, fire and light; of wild worth, all uncultured; working out his life-task in the depths of the Desert there.

How he was placed with Kadijah, a rich widow, as her Steward, and traveled in her business, again to the Fairs of Syria; how he managed all, as one can well understand, with fidelity, adroitness; how her gratitude, her regard for him grew: the story of their marriage is altogether a graceful intelligible one, as told us by the Arab authors. He was twenty-five; she forty, though still beautiful. He seems to have lived in a most affectionate, peaceable, wholesome way with this wedded benefactress; loving her truly, and her alone. It goes greatly against the impostor theory, the fact that he lived in this entirely unexceptionable, entirely quiet and commonplace way, till the heat of his years was done. He was forty before he talked of any mission from Heaven. All his irregularities, real and supposed, date from after his fiftieth year, when the good Kadijah died. All his "ambition," seemingly, had been, hitherto, to live an honest life; his "fame," the mere good opinion of neighbors that knew him, had been sufficient hitherto. Not till he was already getting old, the prurient heat of his life all burnt out, and peace growing to be the chief thing this world could give him, did he start on the "career of ambition"; and, belying all his past character and existence, set up as a wretched empty charlatan to acquire what he could now no longer enjoy! For my share, I have no faith whatever in that.

Ah, no: this deep-hearted Son of the Wilderness, with his beaming black eyes and open social deep soul, had other thoughts in him than ambition. A silent great soul; he was one of those who cannot but be in earnest; whom

Nature herself has appointed to be sincere. While others walk in formulas and hearsays, contented enough to dwell there, this man could not screen himself in formulas; he was alone with his own soul and the reality of things. The Great Mystery of Existence, as I said, glared in upon him, with its terrors, with its splendors; no hearsays could hide that unspeakable fact, " Here am I!" Such sincerity, as we named it, has in very truth something of divine. The word of such a man is a Voice direct from Nature's own Heart. Men do and must listen to that as to nothing else;—all else is wind in comparison. From old, a thousand thoughts, in his pilgrimings and wanderings, had been in this man: What am I? What is this unfathomable Thing I live in, which men name Universe? What is Life; what is Death? What am I to believe? What am I to do? The grim rocks of Mount Hara, of Mount Sinai, the stern sandy solitudes answered not. The great Heaven rolling silent overhead, with its blue-glancing stars, answered not. There was no answer. The man's own soul, and what of God's inspiration dwelt there, had to answer!

It is the thing which all men have to ask themeslves; which we too have to ask, and answer. This wild man felt it to be of infinite moment; all other things of no moment whatever in comparison. The jargon of argumentative Greek Sects, vague traditions of Jews, the stupid routine of Arab Idolatry: there was no answer in these. A Hero, as I repeat, has this first distinction, which indeed we may call first and last, the Alpha and Omega of his whole Heroism, That he looks through the shows of things into things. Use and wont, respectable hearsay, respectable formula: all these are good, or are not good. There is something behind and beyond all these, which all these must correspond with, be the image of, or they are—Idolatries; "bits of black wood pretending to be God"; to the earnest soul a mockery and abomination. Idolatries never so gilded waited on by heads of the Koreish, will do nothing for this man. Though all men walk by them, what good is it? The great Reality stands glaring there upon him. He there has to answer it, or perish miserably. Now, even now, or else through all Eternity never! Answer it; thou must find an answer. Ambition? What could all Arabia do for this man; with the crown of Greek Heraclius, of Persian Chosroes, and all crowns in the Earth;—what could they all do for him? It was not of the Earth he wanted to hear tell; it was of the Heaven above and of the Hell beneath. All crowns and sovereignties whatsoever, where would they in a few brief years be? To be Sheik of Mecca or Arabia, and have a bit of gilt wood put into your hand, —will that be one's salvation? I decidedly think, not. We will leave it altogether, this impostor hypothesis, as not credible; not very tolerable even, worthy chiefly of dismissal by us.

Mahomet had been wont to retire yearly, during the month Ramadhan, into solitude and silence; as indeed was the Arab custom; a praiseworthy custom, which such a man, above all, would find natural and useful. Communing with his own heart, in the silence of the mountains; himself silent; open to the "small still voices"; it was a right natural custom! Mahomet was in his fortieth year, when having withdrawn to a cavern in Mount Hara, near Mecca, during this Ramadhan, to pass the month in prayer, and meditation on those great questions, he one day told his wife Kadijah, who with his household was with him, or near him this year, That by the unspeakable special favor of Heaven he had now found it all out; was in doubt and darkness no longer, but saw it all. That all these Idols and Formulas were nothing, miserable bits of wood; that there was One God in and over all; and we must leave all Idols, and look to Him. That God is great; and that there is nothing else great! He is the Reality. Wooden Idols are not real; He is real. He made us at first, sustains us yet; we and all things are but the shadow of Him; a transitory garment veiling the Eternal Splendor. "*Allah akbar*, God is great";—and then also "*Islam*," That we must submit to God. That our whole strength lies in resigned submission to Him, whatsoever He do to us. For this world, and for the other! The thing He sends to us, were it death and worse than death, shall be good, shall be best; we resign ourselves to God. "If this be *Islam*," says Goethe, "do we not all live in *Islam*?" Yes, all of us that have any moral life; we all live so. It has ever been held the highest wisdom for a man not merely to submit to Necessity,—Necessity will make him submit,—but to know and believe well that the stern thing which Necessity had ordered was the wisest, the best, the thing wanted there. To cease his frantic pretension of scanning this great God's-World in his small fraction of a brain; to know that it had verily, though deep beyond his soundings, a Just Law, that the soul of it was Good;—that his part in it was to conform to the Law of the Whole, and in devout silence follow that; not questioning it, obeying it as unquestionable.

I say, this is yet the only true morality known. A man is right and invincible, virtuous and on the road towards sure conquest, precisely while he joins himself to the great deep Law of the World, in spite of all superficial laws, temporary appearances, profit-and-loss calculations; he is victorious while he co-operates with that great central Law, not victorious otherwise—and surely his first chance of co-operating with it, or getting into the course of it, is to know with his whole soul that it is; that it is good, and alone good! This is the soul of Islam; it is properly the soul of Christianity;—for Islam is definable as a confused form of Christianity; had Christianity not been, neither had it been. Christianity also commands us, before all, to be resigned to God. We are to take no counsel with flesh and blood; give ear to no vain cavils, vain sorrows and wishes: to know that we know nothing; that the worst and cruelest to our eyes is not what it seems; that we have to receive whatsoever befalls us as sent from God above, and say, It is good and wise, God is great! "Though He slay me, yet will I trust in Him." Islam means in its way Denial of Self, Annihilation of Self. This is yet the highest Wisdom that Heaven has revealed to our Earth.

Such light had come, as it could, to illuminate the darkness of this wild Arab soul. A confused dazzling splendor as of life and Heaven, in the great darkness which threatened to be death: he called it revelation and the angel Gabriel;—who of us yet can know what to call it? It is the "inspiration of the Almighty that giveth us understanding." To know; to get into the truth of anything, is ever a mystic act,—of which the best Logics can but babble on the surface. "Is not Belief the true god-announcing Miracle?" says Novalis. That Mahomet's whole soul, set in flame with this grand Truth vouchsafed him, should feel as if it were important and the only important thing, was very natural. That Providence had unspeakably honored him by revealing it, saving him from death and darkness; that he therefore was bound to make known the same to all creatures: this is what was meant by "Mahomet is the Prophet of God"; this too is not without its true meaning.

The good Kadijah, we can fancy, listened to him with wonder, with doubt: at length she answered: Yes, it was true this that he said. One can fancy too the boundless gratitude of Mahomet; and how of all the kindnesses she had done him, this of believing the earnest struggling word he now spoke was the greatest. "It is certain," says Novalis, "my Conviction gains infinitely, the moment another soul will believe in it." It is a boundless favor. He never forgot this good Kadijah. Long afterwards, Ayesha his young favorite wife, a woman who indeed distinguished herself among the Moslem, by all manner of qualities, through her whole long life; this young brilliant Ayesha was, one day, questioning him: "Now am not I better than Kadijah? She was a widow; old, and had lost her looks: you love me better than you did her?" "No, by Allah!" answered Mahomet: "No, by Allah! She believed in me when none else would believe. In the whole world I had but one friend, and she was that!" Seid, his Slave, also believed in him; these with his young Cousin Ali, Abu Thaleb's son, were his first converts.

He spoke of his Doctrine to this man and that; but the most treated it with ridicule, with indifference; in three years, I think, he had gained but thirteen followers. His progress was slow enough. His encouragement to go on was altogether the usual encouragement that such a man in such a case meets. After some three years of small success, he invited forty of his chief kindred to an entertainment; and there stood up and told them what his pretension was: that he had this thing to promulgate abroad to all men; that it was the highest thing, the one thing: which of them would second him in that? Amid the doubt and silence of all, young Ali, as yet a lad of sixteen, impatient of the silence, started up, and exclaimed in passion-

ate fierce language, That he would! The assembly,
among whom was Abu Thaleb, Ali's father, could not be
unfriendly to Mahomet; yet the sight there, of one unlettered elderly man, with a lad of sixteen, deciding on such
an enterprise against all mankind, appeared ridiculous to
them; the assembly broke up in laughter. Nevertheless
it proved not a laughable thing; it was a very serious
thing! As for this young Ali, one cannot but like him. A
noble-minded creature, as he shows himself, now and always afterwards; full of affection, of fiery daring. Something chivalrous in him; brave as a lion; yet with a grace,
a truth and affection worthy of Christian knighthood. He
died by assassination in the Mosque at Bagdad; a death
occasioned by his own generous fairness, confidence in
the fairness of others: he said, If the wound proved not
unto death, they must pardon the Assassin; but if it did,
then they must slay him straightway, that so they two in
the same hour might appear before God, and see which
side of that quarrel was the just one!

Mahomet naturally gave offense to the Koerish, Keepers of the Caabah, superintendents of the Idols. One or
two men of influence had joined him: the thing spread
slowly, but it was spreading. Naturally he gave offense
to everybody: Who is this that pretends to be wiser than
we all; that rebukes us all, as mere fools and worshippers
of wood! Abu Thaleb the good uncle spoke with him:
Could he not be silent about all that; believe it all for
himself, and not trouble others, anger the chief men,
endanger himself and them all, talking of it? Mahomet
answered: If the Sun stood on his right hand and the
Moon on his left, ordering him to hold his peace, he could
not obey! No: there was something in this Truth he had
got which was of Nature herself; equal in rank to Sun,
or Moon, or whatsoever thing Nature had made. It
would speak itself there, so long as the Almighty allowed
it, in spite of Sun and Moon, and all Koreish and all men
and things. It must do that, and could do no other. Mahomet answered so; and, they say, "burst into tears."
Burst into tears: he felt that Abu Thaleb was good to
him; that the task he had got was no soft, but a stern and
great one.

He went on speaking to who would listen to him; pub-

lishing his Doctrine among the pilgrims as they came to
Mecca; gaining adherents in this place and that. Continual contradiction, hatred, open or secret danger attended him. His powerful relations protected Mahomet
himself; but by and by, on his own advice, all his adherents
had to quit Mecca, and seek refuge in Abyssinia over the
sea. The Koreish grew ever angrier; laid plots, and
swore oaths among them, to put Mahomet to death with
their own hands. Abu Thaleb was dead, the good Kadijah was dead. Mahomet is not solicitous of sympathy
from us; but his outlook at this time was one of the dis-
malest. He had to hide in caverns, escape in disguise;
fly hither and thither; homeless, in continual peril of his
life. More than once it seemed all over with him; more
than once it turned on a straw, some rider's horse taking
fright or the like, whether Mahomet and his Doctrine
had not ended there, and not been heard of at all. But it
was not to end so.

In the thirteenth year of his mission, finding his enemies
all banded against him, forty sworn men, one out of
every tribe, waiting to take his life, and no continuance
possible at Mecca for him any longer, Mahomet fled to
the place then called Yathreb, where he had gained some
adherents; the place they now call Medina, or "*Medinat al
Nabi*, the City of the Prophet," from that circumstance.
It lay some 200 miles off, through rocks and deserts; not
without great difficulty, in such mood as we may fancy,
he escaped thither, and found welcome. The whole East
dates its era from this Flight, *Hegira*, as they name it:
the Year 1 of this Hegira is 622 of our Era, the fifty-third
of Mahomet's life. He was now becoming an old man;
his friends sinking around him one by one; his path desolate, encompassed with danger: unless he could find hope
in his own heart, the outward face of things was but hopeless for him. It is so with all men in the like case.
Hitherto Mahomet had professed to publish his Religion
by the way of preaching and persuasion alone. But now,
driven foully out of his native country, since unjust men
had not only given no ear to his earnest Heaven's message, the deep cry of his heart, but would not even let him
live if he kept speaking it,—the wild Son of the Desert resolved to defend himself, like a man and Arab. If the

Koreish will have it so, they shall have it. Tidings, felt
to be of infinite moment to them and all men, they would
not listen to these; would trample them down by sheer
violence, steel and murder: well, let steel try it then! Ten
years more this Mahomet had; all of fighting, of breathless impetuous toil and struggle; with what result we
know.

Much has been said of Mahomet's propagating his Religion by the sword. It is no doubt far nobler what we
have to boast of the Christian Religion, that it propagated
itself peaceably in the way of preaching and conviction.
Yet withal, if we take this for an argument of the truth
or falsehood of a religion, there is a radical mistake in it.
The sword indeed: but where will you get your sword!
Every new opinion, at its starting, is precisely in a minor-
ity of one. In one man's head alone, there it dwells as
yet. One man alone of the whole world believes it; there
is one man against all men. That he take a sword, and
try to propagate with that, will do little for him. You
must first get your sword! On the whole, a thing will
propagate itself as it can. We do not find, of the Christian Religion either, that it always disdained the sword,
when once it had got one. Charlemagne's conversion of
the Saxons was not by preaching. I care little about the
sword: I will allow a thing to struggle for itself in this
world, with any sword or tongue or implement it has, or
can lay hold of. We will let it preach, and pamphleteer,
and fight, and to the uttermost bestir itself, and do, beak
and claws, whatsoever is in it; very sure that it will, in the
long run, conquer nothing which does not deserve to be
conquered. What is better than itself, it cannot put away,
but only what is worse. In this great Duel, Nature herself is umpire, and can do no wrong: the thing which is
deepest-rooted in Nature, what we call truest, that thing
and not the other will be found growing at last.

Here however, in reference to much that there is in
Mahomet and his success, we are to remember what an
umpire Nature is; what a greatness, composure of depth
and tolerance there is in her. You take wheat to cast into
the Earth's bosom: your wheat may be mixed with chaff,
chopped straw, barn sweepings, dust and all imaginable
rubbish; no matter: you cast it into the kind just Earth;

she grows the wheat,—the whole rubbish she silently ab-
sorbs, shrouds it in, says nothing of the rubbish. The
yellow wheat is growing there; the good Earth is silent
about all the rest,—has silently turned all the rest to some
benefit too, and makes no complaint about it! So everywhere in Nature! She is true and not a lie; and yet so
great, and just, and motherly in her truth. She requires
of a thing only that it be genuine of heart; she will protect it if so; will not, if not so. There is a soul of truth in
all the things she ever gave harbor to. Alas, is not this
the history of all highest Truth that comes or ever came
into the world? The body of them all is imperfection, an
element of light in darkness: to us they have to come embodied in mere Logic, in some merely scientific Theorem
of the Universe; which cannot be complete; which cannot
but be found, one day, incomplete, erroneous, and so die
and disappear. The body of all Truth dies; and yet in all,
I say, there is a soul which never dies; which in new and
ever-nobler embodiment lives immortal as man himself!
It is the way with Nature. The genuine essence of Truth
never dies. That it be genuine, a voice from the great
Deep of Nature, there is the point at Nature's judgment-
seat. What we call pure or impure, is not with her the
final question. Not how much chaff is in you; but whether
you have any wheat. Pure? I might say to many a man:
Yes, you are pure; pure enough; but you are chaff,—insincere hypothesis, hearsay, formality; you never were in
contact with the great heart of the Universe at all; you
are properly neither pure nor impure: you are nothing,
Nature has no business with you.

Mahomet's Creed we called a kind of Christianity; and
really, if we look at the wild rapt earnestness with which
it was believed and laid to heart, I should say a better
kind than that of those miserable Syrian Sects, with their
vain janglings about *Homoiousion* and *Homoousion*, the
head full of worthless noise, the heart empty and dead!
The truth of it is imbedded in portentous error and falsehood; but the truth of it makes it be believed, not the
falsehood: it succeeded by its truth. A bastard kind of
Christianity, but a living kind; with a heart-life in it; not
dead, chopping, barren logic merely! Out of all that rubbish of Arab idolatries, argumentative theologies, tradi-

tions, subtleties, rumors and hypotheses of Greeks and
Jews, with their idle wiredrawings, this wild man of the
Desert, with his wild sincere heart, earnest as death and
life, with his great flashing natural eyesight, had seen into
the kernel of the matter. Idolatry is nothing: these
Wooden Idols of yours, "ye rub them with oil and wax,
and the flies stick on them"—these are wood, I tell you!
They can do nothing for you; they are an impotent blasphemous pretence; a horror and abomination, if ye knew
them. God alone is; God alone has power; He made us,
He can kill us and keep us alive: "*Allah akbar*, God is
great." Understand that His will is the best for you; that
howsoever sore to flesh and blood, you will find it the
wisest, best: you are bound to take it so; in this world
and in the next, you have no other thing that you can do!

And now if the wild idolatrous men did believe this, and
with their fiery hearts lay hold of it to do it, in what form
soever it came to them, I say it was well worthy of being
believed. In one form or the other, I say it is still the one
thing worthy of being believed by all men. Man does
hereby become the high priest of this Temple of a World.
He is in harmony with the Decrees of the Author of this
World; coöperating with them, not vainly withstanding
them: I know, to this day, no better definition of Duty
than that same. All that is right includes itself in this of
coöperating with the real Tendency of the World: you
succeed by this (the World's Tendency will succeed), you
are good, and in the right course there. *Homoiousion*,
Homoousion, vain logical jangle, then or before or at any
time, may jangle itself out, and go whither and how it
likes: this is the thing it all struggles to mean, if it would
mean anything. If it do not succeed in meaning this, it
means nothing. Not that Abstractions, logical Propositions, be correctly worded or incorrectly; but that living
concrete Sons of Adam do lay this to heart: that is the
important point. Islam devoured all these vain jangling
Sects; and I think had right to do so. It was a Reality,
direct from the great Heart of Nature once more. Arab
idolatries, Syrian formulas, whatsoever was not equally
real, had to go up in flame,—mere dead fuel, in various
senses, for this which was fire.

It was during these wild warfarings and strugglings,

especially after the Flight to Mecca, that Mahomet dictated at intervals his Sacred Book, which they name *Koran*, or *Reading*, "Thing to be read." This is the Work he and his disciples made so much of, asking all the world, Is not that a miracle? The Mahometans regard their Koran with a reverence which few Christians pay even to their Bible. It is admitted everywhere as the standard of all law and all practice; the thing to be gone upon in speculation and life: the message sent direct out of Heaven, which this Earth has to conform to, and walk by; the thing to be read. Their Judges decide by it; all Moslems are bound to study it, seek in it for the light of their life. They have mosques where it is all read daily; thirty relays of priests take it up in succession,—get through the whole each day. There, for twelve hundred years, has the voice of this Book, at all moments, kept sounding through the ears and the hearts of so many men. We hear of Mahometan Doctors that had read it seventy thousand times!

Very curious: if one sought for "discrepancies of national taste," here surely were the most eminent instance of that! We also can read the Koran; our Translation of it, by Sale, is known to be a very fair one. I must say, it is as toilsome reading as I ever undertook. A wearisome confused jumble, crude, incondite; endless iterations, long-windedness, entanglement; most crude, incondite;—insupportable stupidity, in short! Nothing but a sense of duty could carry any European through the Koran. We read in it, as we might in the State Paper Office, unreadable masses of lumber, that perhaps we may get some glimpses of a remarkable man. It is true we have it under disadvantages: the Arabs see more method in it than we. Mahomet's followers found the Koran lying all in fractions, as it had been written down at first promulgation; much of it, they say, on shoulder blades of mutton flung pell-mell into a chest; and they published it, without any discoverable order as to time or otherwise;—merely trying, as would seem, and this not very strictly, to put the longest chapters first. The real beginning of it, in that way, lies almost at the end: for the earliest portions were the shortest. Read in its historical sequence it perhaps would not be so bad. Much of it, too, they say, is rhythmic; a kind of wild chanting song, in the original. This may be a great point; much perhaps has been lost in the Translation here. Yet with every allowance, one feels it difficult to see how any mortal ever could consider this Koran as a Book written in Heaven, too good for the Earth; as a well-written book, or indeed as a book at all; and not a bewildered rhapsody; written, so far as writing goes, as badly as almost any book ever was! So much for national discrepancies, and the standard of taste.

Yet I should say, it was not unintelligible how the Arabs might so love it. When once you get this confused coil of a Koran fairly off your hands, and have it behind you at a distance, the essential type of it begins to disclose itself; and in this there is a merit quite other than the literary one. If a book come from the heart, it will contrive to reach other hearts; all art and authorcraft are of small amount to that. One would say the primary character of the Koran is this of the genuineness, of its being a *bona fide* book. Prideaux, I know, and others, have represented it as a mere bundle of juggleries; chapter after chapter got up to excuse and varnish the author's successive sins, forward his ambitions and quackeries: but really it is time to dismiss all that. I do not assert Mahomet's continual sincerity: who is continually sincere? But I confess I can make nothing of the critic, in these times, who would accuse him of deceit *prepense*; of conscious deceit generally, or perhaps at all;—still more, of living in a mere element of conscious deceit, and writing this Koran as a forger and juggler would have done! Every candid eye, I think, will read the Koran far otherwise than so. It is the confused ferment of a great rude human soul; rude, untutored, that cannot even read; but fervent, earnest, struggling vehemently to utter itself in words. With a kind of breathless intensity he strives to utter himself; the thoughts crowd on him pell mell: for very multitude of things to say, he can get nothing said. The meaning that is in him shapes itself into no form of composition, is stated in no sequence, method, or coherence;—they are not shaped at all, these thoughts of his; flung out unshaped, as they struggle and tumble there, in their chaotic inarticulate state. We said " stupid ": yet natural stupidity is by no means the character of Mahomet's Book;

it is natural uncultivation rather. The man has not studied speaking; in haste and pressure of continual fighting, has not time to mature himself into fit speech. The panting, breathless haste and vehemence of a man struggling in the thick of battle for life and salvation; this is the mood he is in! A headlong haste; for very magnitude of meaning, he cannot get himself articulated into words. The successive utterances of a soul in that mood, colored by the various vicissitudes of three and twenty years; now well uttered, now worse: this is the Koran.

For we are to consider Mahomet, through these three and twenty years, as the centre of a world wholly in conflict. Battles with the Koreish and Heathen, quarrels among his own people, backslidings of his own wild heart; all this kept him in a perpetual whirl, his soul knowing rest no more. In wakeful nights, as one may fancy, the wild soul of the man, tossing amid these vortices, would hail any light of a decision for them as a veritable light from Heaven; any making-up of his mind, so blessed, indispensable for him there, would seem the inspiration of a Gabriel. Forger and juggler? No, no! This great fiery heart, seething, simmering like a great furnace of thoughts, was not a juggler's. His life was a Fact to him; this God's Universe an awful Fact and Reality. He has faults enough. The man was an uncultured semi-barbarous Son of Nature, much of the Bedouin still clinging to him; we must take him for that. But for a wretched Simulacrum, a hungry Impostor without eyes or heart, practicing for a mess of pottage such blasphemous swindlery, forgery of celestial documents, continual high treason against his Maker and Self, we will not and cannot take him.

Sincerity, in all senses, seems to me the merit of the Koran; what had rendered it precious to the wild Arab men. It is, after all, the first and last merit in a book; gives rise to merits of all kinds—nay, at bottom, it alone can give rise to merit of any kind. Curiously, through these incondite masses of tradition, vituperation, complaint, ejaculation in the Koran, a vein of true direct insight, of what we might almost call poetry, is found straggling. The body of the Book is made up of mere tradition, and as it were vehement enthusiastic extempore

preaching. He returns forever to the old stories of the
Prophets as they went current in the Arab memory: how
Prophet after Prophet, the Prophet Abraham, the
Prophet Hud, the Prophet Moses, Christian and other
real and fabulous Prophets, had come to this Tribe and to
that, warning men of their sin; and been received by them
even as he Mahomet was—which is a great solace to him.
These things he repeats ten, perhaps twenty times; again
and ever again, with wearisome iteration; has never done
repeating them. A brave Samuel Johnson, in his forlorn
garret, might con over the Biographies of Authors in
that way! This is the great staple of the Koran. But
curiously, through all this, comes ever and anon some
glance as of the real thinker and seer. He has actually an
eye for the world, this Mahomet: with a certain directness
and rugged vigor, he brings home still, to our heart, the
thing his own heart has been opened to. I make but little
of his praises of Allah, which many praise; they are borrowed, I suppose, mainly from the Hebrew, at least they
are far surpassed there. But the eye that flashes direct
into the heart of things, and sees the truth of them; this is
to me a highly interesting object. Great Nature's own
gift; which she bestows on all; but which only one in the
thousand does not cast sorrowfully away: it is what I
call sincerity of vision; the test of a sincere heart.

Mahomet can work no miracles; he often answers im-
patiently: I can work no miracles. I? "I am a Public
Preacher"; appointed to preach this doctrine to all creatures. Yet the world, as we can see, had really from of
old been all one great miracle to him. Look over the
world, says he; is it not wonderful, the work of Allah;
wholly "a sign to you," if your eyes were open! This
Earth, God made it for you, "appointed paths in it"; you
can live on it, go to and fro on it. The clouds in the dry
country of Arabia, to Mahomet they are very wonderful;
Great clouds, he says, born in the deep bosom of the
Upper Immensity, where do they come from! They hang
there, the great black monsters; pour down their rain de-
luges "to revive a dead earth," and grass springs, and
"tall, leafy palm-trees with their date clusters hanging
round. Is not that a sign?" Your cattle, too—Allah
made them; serviceable dumb creatures; they change the

grass into milk; you have your clothing from them, very strange creatures; they come ranking home at evening time, "and," adds he, "and are a credit to you!" Ships also—he talks often about ships: Huge moving mountains, they spread out their cloth wings, go bounding through the water there, Heaven's wind driving them; anon they lie motionless, God has withdrawn the wind, they lie dead, and cannot stir! Miracles? cries he; What miracle would you have? Are not you yourselves there? God made you, "shaped you out of a little clay." Ye were small once; a few years ago ye were not at all. Ye have beauty, strength, thoughts, "ye have compassion on one another." Old age comes on you, and gray hairs; your strength fades into feebleness; ye sink down, and again are not. "Ye have compassion on one another": this struck me much: Allah might have made you having no compassion on one another—how had it been then! This is a great direct thought, a glance at first-hand into the very fact of things. Rude vestiges of poetic genius, of whatsoever is best and truest, are visible in this man. A strong, untutored intellect; eyesight, heart: a strong, wild man—might have shaped himself into Poet, King, Priest, any kind of Hero.

To his eyes it is forever clear that this world wholly is miraculous. He sees what, as we said once before, all great thinkers, the rude Scandinavians themselves, in one way or other, have contrived to see: That this so solid-looking material world is, at bottom, in very deed, Nothing; is a visual and tactual Manifestation of God's power and presence—a shadow hung out by Him on the bosom of the void Infinite; nothing more. The mountains, he says, these great rock-mountains, they shall dissipate themselves "like clouds"; melt into the Blue as clouds do, and not be! He figures the Earth, in the Arab fashion. Sale tells us, as an immense Plain or flat Plate of ground, the mountains are set on that to steady it. At the Last Day they shall disappear "like clouds"; the whole Earth shall go spinning, whirl itself off into wreck, and as dust and vapor vanish in the Inane. Allah withdraws his hand from it, and it ceases to be. The universal empire of Allah, presence everywhere of an unspeakable Power, a Splendor, and a Terror not to be named, as the true force, essence and reality, in all things, in all things whatsoever, was continually clear to this man. What a modern talks-of by the name, Forces of Nature, Laws of Nature; and does not figure as a divine thing; not even as one thing at all, but as a set of things, undivine enough—salable, curious, good for propelling steamships! With our Sciences and Cyclopædias, we are apt to forget the divineness, in those laboratories of ours. We ought not to forget it! That once well forgotten, I know not what else were worth remembering. Most sciences, I think, were then a very dead thing; withered, contentious, empty;—a thistle in late autumn. The best science, without this, is but as the dead timber; it is not the growing tree and forest—which gives ever new timber, among other things! Man cannot know either, unless he can worship in some way. His knowledge is a pedantry, and dead thistle, otherwise.

Much has been said and written about the sensuality of Mahomet's Religion; more than was just. The indulgences, criminal to us, which he permitted, were not of his appointment; he found them practiced, unquestioned from immemorial time in Arabia; what he did was to curtail them, restrict them, not on one but on many sides. His Religion is not an easy one: with rigorous fasts, lavations, strict complex formulas, prayers five times a day, and abstinence from wine, it did not "succeed by being an easy religion." As if indeed any religion, or cause holding of religion, could succeed by that! It is a calumny on men to say that they are roused to heroic action by ease, hope of pleasure, recompense—sugar-plums of any kind, in this world or the next! In the meanest mortal there lies something nobler. The poor swearing soldier, hired to be shot, has his "honor of a soldier," different from drill regulations and the shilling a day. It is not to taste sweet things, but to do noble and true things, and vindicate himself under God's Heaven as a god-made Man, that the poorest son of Adam dimly longs. Show him the way of doing that, the dullest daydrudge kindles into a hero. They wrong man greatly who say he is to be seduced by ease. Difficulty, abnegation, martyrdom, death are the allurements that act on the heart of man. Kindle the inner genial life of him, you have a flame that burns up all lower considerations. Not happiness, but something higher: one sees this even in the frivolous classes, with their "point of honor" and the like. Not by flattering our appetites; no, by awakening the Heroic that slumbers in every heart, can any Religion gain followers. Mahomet himself, after all that can be said about him, was not a sensual man. We shall err widely if we consider this man as a common voluptuary, intent mainly on base enjoyments—nay, on enjoyments of any kind. His household was of the frugalest; his common diet barley bread and water: sometimes for months there was not a fire once lighted on his hearth. They record with just pride that he would mend his own shoes, patch his own cloak. A poor, hard-toiling, ill-provided man; careless of what vulgar men toil for. Not a bad man, I should say; something better in him than hunger of any sort—or these wild Arab men, fighting and jostling three and twenty years at his hand, in close contact with him always, would not have reverenced him so! They were wild men, bursting ever and anon into quarrel, into all kinds of fierce sincerity; without right, worth and manhood, no man could have commanded them. They called him Prophet, you say? Why, he stood there face to face with them; bare, not enshrined in any mystery; visibly clouting his own cloak, cobbling his own shoes; fighting, counseling, ordering in the midst of them; they must have seen what kind of a man he was, let him be called what you like! No emperor with his tiaras was obeyed as this man in a cloak of his own clouting. During three and twenty years of rough, actual trial. I find something of a veritable Hero necessary for that, of itself.

His last words are a prayer; broken ejaculations of a heart struggling up, in trembling hope, towards its Maker. We cannot say that his religion made him worse; it made him better; good, not bad. Generous things are recorded of him; when he lost his daughter, the thing he answers is, in his own dialect, everyway sincere, and yet equivalent to that of Christians, " The Lord giveth, and the Lord taketh away; blessed be the name of the Lord." He answered in like manner of Seid, his emancipated, well-beloved Slave, the second of the believers. Seid had fallen in the War of Tabuc, the first of Mahomet's fightings with the Greeks. Mahomet said, It was well; Seid had done

his Master's work, Seid had now gone to his Master; it
was all well with Seid. Yet Seid's daughter found him
weeping over the body—the old gray-haired man melting
in tears! "What do I see?" said she. "You see a friend
weeping over his friend." He went out for the last time
into the mosque, two days before his death; asked, If he
had injured any man? Let his own back bear the stripes.
If he owed any man? A voice answered, "Yes, me three
drachms," borrowed on such an occasion. Mahomet ordered them to be paid: "Better be in shame now," said
he, "than at the Day of Judgment." You remember
Kadijah, and the "No, by Allah!" Traits of that kind
show us the genuine man, the brother of us all, brought
visible through twelve centuries—the veritable Son of our
common Mother.

Withal I like Mahomet for his total freedom from cant.
He is a rough self-helping son of the wilderness; does not
pretend to be what he is not. There is no ostentatious
pride in him; but neither does he go much upon humility;
he is there as he can be, in cloak and shoes of his own
clouting; speaks plainly to all manner of Persian Kings,
Greek Emperors, what it is they are bound to do; knows
well enough, about himself, "the respect due unto thee,"
In a life-and-death war with Bedouins, cruel things could
not fail; but neither are acts of mercy, of noble natural
pity and generosity, wanting. Mahomet makes no apology for the one, no boast for the other. They were each
the free dictate of his heart; each called-for, there and
then. Not a mealy-mouthed man! A candid ferocity,
if the case call for it, is in him; he does not mince matters! The War of Tabuc is a thing he often speaks of; his
men refused, many of them, to march on that occasion;
pleaded the heat of the weather, the harvest, and so forth;
he can never forget that. Your harvest? It lasts for a
day. What will become of your harvest through all Eternity? Hot weather? Yes, it was hot; "but Hell will be
hotter!" Sometimes a rough sarcasm turns up. He says
to the unbelievers: Ye shall have the just measure of your
deeds at that Great Day. They will be weighed out to
you; we shall not have short weight! Everywhere he
fixes the matter in his eye; he sees it; his heart, now and
then, is as if struck dumb by the greatness of it. "Assur-

edly," he says; that word, in the Koran, is written down
sometimes as a sentence by itself: "Assuredly."

No dilettantism in this Mahomet; it is a business of
Reprobation and Salvation with him, of Time and Eternity: he is in deadly earnest about it! Dilettantism, hypothesis, speculation, a kind of amateurish search for
Truth, toying and coquetting with Truth: this is the sorest
sin. The root of all other imaginable sins. It consists in
the heart and soul of the man never having been open to
Truth—"living in a vain show." Such a man not only utters and produces falsehoods, but is himself a falsehood.
The rational moral principle, spark of the Divinity, is sunk
deep in him, in quiet paralysis of life-death. The very
falsehoods of Mahomet are truer than the truths of such
a man. He is the insincere man: smooth-polished, respectable in some times and places; inoffensive, says nothing harsh to anybody; most cleanly—just as carbonic acid
is, which is death and poison.

We will not praise Mahomet's moral precepts as always
of the superfinest sort; yet it can be said that there is always a tendency to good in them; that they are the true
dictates of a heart aiming towards what is just and true.
The sublime forgiveness of Christianity, turning of the
other cheek when the one has been smitten, is not here:
you are to revenge yourself, but it is to be in measure, not
overmuch, or beyond justice. On the other hand, Islam,
like any great Faith, and insight into the essence of man,
is a perfect equalizer of men: the soul of one believer out-
weighs all earthly kingships; all men, according to Islam
too, are equal. Mahomet insists not on the propriety of
giving alms, but on the necessity of it: he marks down by
law how much you are to give, and it is at your peril if
you neglect. The tenth part of a man's annual income,
whatever that may be, is the property of the poor, of
those that are afflicted and need help. Good all this: the
natural voice of humanity, of pity and equity dwelling in
the heart of this wild Son of Nature speaks so.

Mahomet's Paradise is sensual, his Hell sensual: true;
in the one and the other there is enough that shocks all
spiritual feeling in us. But we are to recollect that the
Arabs already had it so; that Mahomet, in whatever he
changed of it, softened and diminished all this. The worst

sensualities, too, are the work of doctors, followers of his, not his work. In the Koran there is really very little said about the joys of Paradise; they are intimated rather than insisted on. Nor is it forgotten that the highest joys even there shall be spiritual; the pure Presence of the Highest, this shall infinitely transcend all other joys. He says, "Your salutation shall be, Peace." *Salam,* Have Peace!— the thing that all rational souls long for, and seek, vainly here below, as the one blessing. "Ye shall sit on seats, facing one another: all grudges shall be taken away out of your hearts." All grudges! Ye shall love one another freely; for each of you, in the eyes of his brothers, there will be Heaven enough!

In reference to this of the sensual Paradise and Mahomet's sensuality, the sorest chapter of all for us, there were many things to be said; which it is not convenient to enter upon here. Two remarks only I shall make, and therewith leave it to your candor. The first is furnished me by Goethe; it is a casual hint of his which seems well worth taking note of. In one of his Delineations, in "Meister's Travels" it is, the hero comes upon a Society of men with very strange ways, one of which was this: "We require," says the Master, "that each of our people shall restrict himself in one direction," shall go right against his desire in one matter, and make himself do the thing he does not wish, "should we allow him the greater latitude on all other sides." There seems to me a great justness in this. Enjoying things which are pleasant; that is not the evil: it is the reducing of our moral self to slavery by them that is. Let a man assert withal that he is king over his habitudes; that he could and would shake them off, on cause shown: this is an excellent law. The Month Ramadhan for the Moslem, much in Mahomet's Religion, much in his own Life, bears in that direction; if not by forethought, or clear purpose of moral improvement on his part, then by a certain healthy manful instinct, which is as good.

But there is another thing to be said about the Mahometan Heaven and Hell. This namely, that, however gross and material they may be, they are an emblem of an everlasting truth, not always so well remembered elsewhere. That gross sensual Paradise of his; that horrible flaming

Hell; the great enormous Day of Judgment he perpetually insists on: what is all this but a rude shadow, in the rude Bedouin imagination, of that grand spiritual Fact, and Beginning of Facts, which it is ill for us too if we do not all know and feel: the Infinite Nature of Duty? That man's actions here are of infinite moment to him, and never die or end at all; that man, with his little life, reaches upwards high as Heaven, downwards low as Hell, and in his three-score years of Time holds an Eternity fearfully and wonderfully hidden: all this had burnt itself, as in flame-characters, into the wild Arab soul. As in flame and lightning, it stands written there; awful, unspeakable, ever present to him. With bursting earnestness, with a fierce savage sincerity, halt, articulating, not able to articulate, he strives to speak it, bodies it forth in that Heaven and that Hell. Bodied forth in what way you will, it is the first of all truths. It is venerable under all embodiments. What is the chief end of man here below? Mahomet has answered this question, in a way that might put some of us to shame! He does not, like a Bentham, a Paley, take Right and Wrong, and calculate the profit and loss, ultimate pleasure of the one and of the other; and summing all up by addition and subtraction into a net result, ask you, Whether on the whole the Right does not preponderate considerably? No; it is not better to do the one than the other; the one is to the other as life is to death— as Heaven is to Hell. The one must in nowise be done, the other in nowise left undone. You shall not measure them; they are incommensurable: the one is death eternal to a man, the other is life eternal. Benthamee Utility, virtue by Profit and Loss; reducing this God's-world to a dead brute Steam-engine, the infinite celestial Soul of Man to a kind of Hay-balance for weighing hay and this-tles on, pleasures and pains on—if you ask me which gives, Mahomet or they, the beggarlier and falser view of Man and his Destinies in this Universe, I will answer, It is not Mahomet!

On the whole, he will repeat that this Religion of Ma-homet's is a kind of Christianity; has a genuine element of what is spiritually highest looking through it, not to be hidden by all its imperfections. The Scandinavian God *Wish*, the god of all rude men—this has been enlarged into a Heaven by Mahomet; but a Heaven symbolical of sacred Duty, and to be earned by faith and well-doing, by valiant action, and a divine patience which is still more valiant. It is Scandinavian Paganism, and a truly celestial element superadded to that. Call it not false; look not at the falsehood of it, look at the truth of it. For these twelve centuries, it has been the religion and life-guidance of the fifth part of the whole kindred of Mankind. Above all things, it has been a religion heartily believed. These Arabs believe their religion, and try to live by it! No Christians, since the early ages, or only perhaps the English Puritans in modern times, have ever stood by their Faith as the Moslem do by theirs,—believing it wholly, fronting Time with it, and Eternity with it. This night the watchman on the streets of Cairo when he cries, "Who goes?" will hear from the passenger, along with his answer, "There is no God but God." *Allah akbar, Islam,* sounds through the souls, and whole daily existence, of these dusky millions. Zealous missionaries preach it abroad among Malays, black Papuans, brutal Idolaters; displacing what is worse, nothing that is better or good.

To the Arab Nation it was as a birth from darkness into light; Arabia first became alive by means of it. A poor shepherd people, roaming unnoticed in its deserts since the creation of the world: a Hero-Prophet was sent down to them with a word they could believe: see, the unnoticed becomes world-notable, the small has grown world-great; within one century afterwards, Arabia is at Grenada on this hand, at Delhi on that; glancing in valor and splendor and the light of genius, Arabia shines through long ages over a great section of the world. Belief is great, life-giving. The history of a Nation becomes fruitful, soul-elevating, great, so soon as it believes. These Arabs, the man Mahomet, and that one century—is it not as if a spark had fallen, one spark, on a world of what seemed black unnoticeable sand; but lo, the sand proves explosive powder, blazes heaven-high from Delhi to Grenada! I said, the Great Man was always as lightning out of Heaven; the rest of men waited for him like fuel, and then they too would flame.

EDWIN HUBBELL CHAPIN

MODERN CHIVALRY

[Lecture by Edwin H. Chapin, pastor of the Fourth Universalist Church (afterward the "Church of the Divine Paternity"), New York, for upward of thirty years (born in Union Village, Washington County, New York, December 29, 1814; died in New York City, December 27, 1880), delivered repeatedly in the height of his career as a popular lyceum lecturer. Famous as a pulpit orator, Dr. Chapin early took rank among the foremost popular lecturers of his day, entering the lecture field in 1838 during the first years of his ministry when settled in Richmond, Va.; and he acquired the sobriquet of a "prince of the lyceum platform." "Modern Chivalry" was one of the lectures in the list upon which his reputation was established, and, his biographer states, served on nearly three hundred platforms. It was rewritten at least once, and often changed in its delivery to fit the place and occasion. It is here given as delivered in Boston, in the "Fraternity Course," December 27, 1859. It was Dr. Chapin who, in reply to an inquiry for his terms for a lecture, or "what he lectured for?" once sent this telegram (credited to several other lecturers): "For F-A-M-E," which, being interpreted, signified, "fifty, and my expenses." This, it is explained, was in the early days of the lyceum; Dr. Chapin's fees in later times reached the highest figures commanded by lyceum lecturers.]

LADIES AND GENTLEMEN :—A popular English periodical has recently entertained its readers with a story of a ghost in a railroad-car. Our first idea respecting this may very well be that of incongruity between the incident and the machine. The lawful domain of spectres is the bloody chamber and the crumbling tower—"Otranto," "Udolpho," or, "Marianna's Lonely Moated Grange." They hardly find congenial conditions in the general whirl and shake-up of forty miles an hour. At least, there is some-

thing demoniacal rather than ghostly in the breath of the
locomotive and the shriek of the steam-whistle. The feeling of incongruity, in this instance, however, is only one
indication of the conceit that our age of iron is not hospitable to the more spiritual elements; that spiritualism is
exhausted by science, imagination crushed by fact, and
the qualities of heroic devotion smothered in the mercenary processes of trade and manufacture.

We are told that the age of chivalry has passed away;
but it will be my object in the present lecture to show that
chivalry itself has not passed away: that its conditions, its
characteristics and its work are existent still, and likely
to exist. The actual argument in this case might, perhaps, be summed up in the general proposition, that each
age holds the contents of all the other ages; one era, of
course, distinguished from another by some predominat-
ing element. So there has been an age of chivalry—the
age of chivalry. It lies back there in its old realm of
romance, the very May-time of modern history; or, rather,
with its castellated grandeur, its picturesque shapes, its
flushings of splendid enthusiasm and adventure, it lingers
on the horizon from which we recede like a belt of clouds,
kindling our youthful imagination and feeding our rarer
memories and suggesting a region of beauty now inaccessible and far away. But when we bring it nearer to us
with the lens of historical investigation, we find that its
peculiarity consists in the culmination of certain forms,
not in the exclusive possession of the spirit.

Now, in this fact that the ages are vesicular, that history is organic, not fragmentary, and the boundaries of
epochs merely artificial, there is ground both for humility
and hope. In the first place, it rebukes our conceit of
progress, or, rather, it alters our estimate of progress,
which identifies "going ahead" with going up, and assumes a logic which would prove that the child must be
better than its father. It is interesting, but also somewhat humiliating, to see how, in all ages, the instincts of
men run on the same parallel lines, so that the grandest
achievements which appear from time to time are only
acts of repetition or recovery. We dig up Trojan's galley
from the depths of an Italian lake, and discover our own
practice of caulking and sheathing ships. In the lonesome

streets of Herculanaeum and Pompeii, we stumble upon types of some of our modern inventions. It startles us to find the law of gravitation taught long before Newton, and the circulation of the blood ages previous to the time of Harvey. It is as though human history ran in cycles, in which not only the general outlines of events occur, but even the specific and individual instances. In short, nothing is really gained in the way of substantial and absolute good, if the difference between one time and another is only a difference in degree—merely extension on the same plan. Our movements may be more rapid, our instruments may be more marvelous, but progress is not to be predicated merely upon an accumulation of facilities, which are only the same means to the same ends. There is no more glory in a locomotive or a steamship than in a caravan toiling through the desert, or a Phœnician boat coasting the shores of Britain, if the purposes they represent are the same. The glory of human achievement is not in its instruments; the idea of human action is according to its nature.

In these similitudes of history, then, there is this amount of repression for this most vociferous age, the Nineteenth century, which is so much inclined to play the game of brag with all its predecessors. But this tendency to exultation is fully balanced by the tendency to disparagement. It seems as if the main current were running in the latter direction. Serious complaints are lodged against the period in which we live as being utterly sordid, materialistic, and empty of any real noble life. Those old ages of trust and valor, glorified with elevated achievement, enriched with a manhood that tried to build itself up for some sublime type, are sorrowfully contrasted with the time when the sharp outlines of knowledge leave but few recesses for faith, when superstition, which was at least inspiring, seems chiefly exchanged for a barren rationalism, and the investigation of nature dissolves before the science which calculates the mechanical value of a cubic mile of sunshine. [Applause.]

And here, in opposition to this severe disparagement of the present, I take up the purpose of my lecture, to maintain that what was essentially admirable in those chivalric ages crops out even in this, and redeems it from this heavier allegation. My object is strictly practical. I believe that it is best for every man to think well of his own time. We have no more right to calumniate an age than we have to slander a man; and I think there are a good many instances in which our Nineteenth century would be fully warranted in bringing an action and suing for damages. [Applause.] At least, I believe there is more inspiration for effort in the hopeful than in the despondent conception, and, therefore, that we are justified in giving prominence to the elements upon which that hope may rest. I shall endeavor to show that we have, in our own period, first, the conditions; second, the characteristics; and, finally, the work of a genuine chivalry.

In estimating the conditions of true chivalry we ought to take into consideration the tendency which exists in the human mind to magnify the stature and the glory of the past. Distance lends the same advantages in time that it does in space. In surveying the historical landscape, we must allow for perspective. We have by no means all the bad things or all the shabby things. Ideal excellence was as far off in the "age of chivalry" as it is now. In actual life, I suspect, there was no more poetry then than there is now. A knight-errant, "hard-up" and unable to pay for mending his helmet, must have been as prosaic a person as a man "shinning" through State street. A lascivious baron, in his vulture-vest of blood and rapine, was precisely as interesting as any genteel blood-sucker you might find about town.

Macaulay has asserted that "as civilization advances, poetry almost necessarily declines. Thus, the possibility of a great epic diminishes with the development of philosophical criticism and utilitarian influences." The soundness of this doctrine depends somewhat upon our definition of poetry. If it consists merely in the power of objective description, it may be that the best, and therefore the most enduring, poetry does cluster about the earlier ages of the world, for the poet of those days had his pick; his were the heavens, the earth, and the unbounded sea; and he saw the working of those emotions and passions which constitute the ground-swell of all poetry, which are as palpable and universal as the nature of man. The fervors of love, the clash of war, the mysterious depths of religious feeling, have long since found an unsurpassable utterance. The old kings of song abide upon their thrones forever; they are few, indeed, who may go up and sit with them. But even admitting that the possibility of poetic creation does go out with advancing civilization, still, upon this ground, I would maintain that proof of poetic vitality in our own age appears in the recognition which the age gives to genuine poetry of all ages. But if we pass beyond this objective definition, and admit the subjective element, which involves the subtle intermodifications of passion, the facts that start out under a searching introspection, then the possibility of poetic creation is not diminished with the increase of culture, and our modern era can, and does, produce works that will live through all time. However, I will not in any way admit the premises that give rise to this discussion. I do not believe that the legitimate objects of poetry are thinned out by the precision of science. In other words, I cannot consent to the proposition that there is an "irrepressible conflict" between the beautiful and the true, and that the one excludes the other. Let it be granted that the impossibilities of legend, the beautiful nonsense of mythology, and all "the fair humanities of old religion," have vanished before the accumulation of useful knowledge; still, how far has our knowledge penetrated into the region of the unknown! What mysteries of life, what vast circles of truth still quiver on the outmost rim of the great wheel of nature! Every great discovery only tends to show us that the treasury of suggestion is inexhaustible, and the galleries of imagination stretch far away. The beautiful conceits and grand shadows that are incorporated with the heart and life of the poetry of our time are only transfigured and thrown upon a broader canvas. The vulgarity, the dullness, the materialism of our day are, of course, only too conspicuous, but these, alas! seem not to be for our age, or for any age, but for all time. Meanness is a crop as old as grass! But so far as the chivalric quality needs to be saturated in poetic influences, the conditions abundantly exist. [Applause.]

It is often urged that periods of public and private greatness have always been co-ordinate with periods of intellectual obscuration. This statement amounts to the assertion that as truth comes into the world, virtue goes out of it; it is one of those statements which logic might play with as a capital paradox, but which our moral nature repudiates with immutable faith. The philosopher can never convince us that our little earth is the only home of affection and intelligence, and that the systems which burn and roll around us are only sparkling Saharas of incompleteness and desolation. No more can the historical skeptic make us believe that the largest measure of knowledge is unfavorable to the noblest types of excellence, that the richest virtues wilt in the brightest civilization. Argue as we will, our moral instincts, our faith in Providence, assure us that knowledge tends to goodness. They are not identical, yet, in their highest realization, they are inseparable. Whatever else, then, may be the cause of any prevalent skepticism, of any lack of noble achievement in our time, our scientific precision, our increased knowledge, is not the cause. The cry of degeneracy is the oldest of cries. Take up any London journal of a hundred years ago, and you will find remonstrances and satires against the same follies and vices as those which are denounced to-day. Therefore, these parallel cases in our time show us, not that we are going into the swamp, but that we have not yet got out of it. "As men learn more," say the croakers, "they grow worse." It is very true that knowledge, in itself, is not a regenerating power. It may render the soul of man glorious like a star, but, like that star, it needs some profounder force to send it on in its orbit, and to curve its sweep. But it is the indispensable ally of that deeper impulse and profounder law. Knowledge does not make evil. If it reveals facilities for its action, it also shows that it is evil. If in any way it assists the giant selfishness of the human heart, it sheds all around a halo, in which the dark shadow looms up definite and unmistakable. When we cry out against the abominations of the Nineteenth century, and say, "See what ghastly problems are here!" it may be all very true, but, then, it is no slight indication of the character of the time that these things have come to be problems. It is no insignificant thing that the moral sentiment of men has raised them up from the level of indifference into bold relief, to be seen, discussed, solved. [Applause.]

After all, the conscience, the sensitive conscience, is the live conscience. Not those who see the most evil, or feel the evils the most heavily, are the worst, but those who lie with stagnant and smothered souls. Whenever an evil comes up to a human eye, dark and heavy as it may be, and is weighed, measured, scanned, be sure that it is doomed. God's challenging trumpet has blown against it, and it is sure to fall. [Loud applause.]

No, no, not less knowledge, but more knowledge, to expose the evil, to condemn the shame and abominations of the time. [Applause.] More knowledge, mated, in its essence, with God's everlasting love, exalting in its revealing splendors, the immutable law, until men shall learn the fatal incompatibility of sin with any good, until the golden scales shall be shivered from their eyes, until their hands shall be unmanacled from all mean policy, and to know and to do shall be as the arterial unity of brain-throb and heart-beat! Silent is the force which controls the material world; sure and relentless as its burning wheels. And so, flow on, flow wide, unfolding truth and knowledge of the time! Shine, genial as the sunlight, terrible as the lightning, until wrong shall shrivel, and selfishness be put to open shame! Shine into the crannies of this strange old world, into its mold and rust and rot! Shine! until indifference grows warm and prejudices burn away, and for our pity and indignation we shall see all fetters and tear-stains and sorrows! Shine straight through our brother's rags, our brother's uncouthness, our brother's nationality, until we discern the same natures, the same heart, the same red blood as our own! Shine bright and beautiful, in toleration and comprehensiveness, giving hope to the future and significance to the past, like the sunlight which, streaming through cathedral windows, kindles up the features of heroes and martyrs, and reflects their expression upon the living crowds below! Warmly shine, until liberty shall grow as every man's vine and fig-tree, and the tendrils of sympathy, running by every creek, and carried by every ship, shall be rolled around the globe! And then if, with all this, man proves worse, we shall be sure that knowledge will not make him so, but show him so! [Loud applause.]

Let us now consider the characteristics of chivalry

that appear in our time. The forms of life differ, the spirit
abides. We do not expect to see the old knightly character in our times. We do not expect Tennyson's modern
Arthur to come out with the old paraphernalia—with the
golden dragon on his breast. Stripped, then, of its chain-
armor, and its head-piece, what are the characteristics of
chivalry, and how do they appear in living men? We may
divide society into three orders—men who have bad principles; men who contrive to have principles that pay; and
men who cannot afford to have any principles. Here is a
terrible level, a monotony of mercenary elements, broken
now and then by little spurts of superserviceable meanness, as, for instance, when people publish a book, and for
fear of offense, cut out some of the author's most vital
sentences, and send out a truncated effigy of their own.
[Applause.] We admire, because we cannot help admiring, heroism, even in a wrong cause. Even in the conditions of old despotism, the better part of our nature gravi-
tates to him who preserves his courage and self-respect—
in other words, the substance of manhood. There is a
recognized chivalry about a man who is a man. Noble
souls know each other, in some degree as they will know
when we no longer see as through a glass darkly! But
when, for groats or votes, or any other consideration, the
fair spirit of manhood gets diluted—or as you call it here,
" extended "—[loud laughter; his reference being to the
action of the then Massachusetts State liquor agency with
respect to " diluted " liquors]—for the worst extension of
spirits is of human spirits, in our time—when, I say, the
pure spirit of manhood gets diluted, and runs in a thin
decoction of maple-sap, and basswood, the case has grown
alarming. Instances of this " dilution " are seen in the
person of the present Emperor of the French, and among
the politicians at home, whose patriotic devotion to their
country always happens to appear in occultation to devotion to their own interests, who always feel a fever of patriotism when they have an ague about the Union; political Micawbers, always waiting for something to " turn
up," and if it doesn't turn up, they turn it up! [Laugh-
ter.] Is not the cause to be found in the fact that men
are not chivalric enough to stand by their own souls? Is
not this the reason that they act in masses as they would

not act in units? How else can the fact be accounted for, that they would do things for their party which, outside of such associations, they would not consent to have a decent dog do for them? In how many instances does it appear that high public office is sure to spoil a man! Put him in Jonathan, he comes out Judas! He enters as a respectable merchant, or lawyer, or farmer, and comes out a politician by profession and a thimble-rigger by practice. [Laughter and applause.] If this is not the cause, then it is to be attributed to another sort of un-chivalric meanness—that which neglects public duty, consulting only private ease. The fact is, the time wants men—good men. Great men are none too plenty, but we do not want all great men, any more than we want to make up our winter's stock of exhibition apples and potatoes. We want good and true men in the field, in the market, in the counting-room, and at home, wherever they touch the deepest life of the country or the life of coming generations. We want men, not noisy and loud-mouthed, but men who are felt as electricity is felt, that lives, but makes no racket, in the summer air. [Applause.]

The whole brotherhood of "fast men" are another class of unchivalric men. Another unchivalric quality is connected with the great lack of reverence manifest among our people. A celebrated French writer has said that "America, more than anything else, wants moral sense." The lack of reverence is one of the deepest and most shameful wants of our land. We are possessed with the demon of speed. The locomotive and the telegraph are not merely the products, but the symbols of the age. We grumble at forty miles an hour, and think seriously of a balloon express. We jump from steamboats and railway cars to save time. In our eagerness to save two seconds, many a widow gets her "thirds." We have hasty banks, hasty stocks, hasty buildings, that tumble down about as fast as they go up. The good ship "Young America" is loaded too much by the head. We are impatient of the great law that one man shall sow and another reap. We are all for realizing the imagination that the Nineteenth century shall have a monopoly of the millennium.

With this charge, I think we have made out the counts against our time, and may now hear the defendant. The question is not whether the world is growing better or worse, but what is there, after all, that is generous, brave and hopeful in our time, that may inspire with its own spirit, and induce us to work for results that shall be more generous and brave and hopeful? There always is a dark side to everything, but there comes no benefit from always looking at that side. I am sure we can make a much better use of this fruitful world, and our life lease of it, than merely to pick out occasions for whining and scolding. If we are disposed to take up the profession of croaker, we had better go down into a well and do the thing appropriately. But even then we cannot shut out the serene toplight, the beneficent arch of heaven, that quiet proclamation from day to day and night to night of God's steadfast laws, of his vast plan that wraps us around and carries us along.

Without going into any detail of characteristics, I would say that in this age there is, in the first place, that which was best in the age of chivalry, and must be best in any age, or the world itself would die. Here is the spirit of generous sentiment, here is the spirit of noble performance, here is the manifestation of a love that goes out beyond self, of a faith that, looking beyond estimates, fastens on the permanent, and a heroism that bravely tries to do what should be done. God holds the world in his own hand, and keeps the springs of its vitality fresh. In every age, some men, by their faithfulness, have kept alive the core of good there was in it, and by their heroism they have conquered for it a larger good. In the paralysis of virtue, in the profligacy of crime, around their hearts its lifeblood has rallied; and when nowhere within the lives of old civilization such men could be found, see how they have started up in barren deserts and primeval forests, and among despised, unconsidered races! The Goth sweeps down, from his Northern lair, to pour his simple virtues and youthful vigor into the body that Rome had left exhausted and diseased; the Arab, carrying his one sublime truth with the sword-sweep of desolation; the Puritan, in his flight, picks up the scattered seeds of Liberty, and, standing on a bleak rock by the sea, lets

the winds winnow them over a continent. [Applause.]
If at any time we consider the spontaneous sympathies of men, we shall find that they gravitate to that
which is noblest and best. Men may be found who make
a great clatter with ferocious sentiments and inhuman
doctrines, but they cannot assimilate them to the vital
substance of their nature, any more than they can eat
lignum-vitæ. Thank God! the human heart can never be
bought! The lips, the acts, the soul, may be bought, not
the heart; and the heart beats with thunderstrokes that
cannot be repressed against the base, the cruel, the
despotic thing. [Applause.] And so, whenever genuine
chivalry flashes out, it is always recognized, and responsive sympathy proves it to be the deepest movement of
the day and time. This sympathy for that which is right
and good runs through every age. King Henry's "Follow my white plume!" Sidney's draught to the soldier,
Nelson's battle-signal at Trafalgar, Lawrence's "Don't
give up the ship!"—all such things as these jar upon
chords that will vibrate while the world lasts. The world's
heart throbs with the memory of Humboldt, while hardly
a living pulse quickens at the name of Metternich.
[Applause.]

But there are deeds which make the time chivalric, as
well as the sentiment that is called by that name. Out of
this commonplace drapery of the Nineteenth century, out
of the thick folds of our sordidness and materialism, there
break every day flashes of splendor and power, gleams of
the grand romantic fire, like that which burned on many
a field of the olden time. Think of men lighting their
cigars in the trenches of the Redan, of the sergeant at
the battle of the Alma, mortally wounded, and urged to
give up the standard, still carrying it to the end of the
action! Think of the helmsman on Lake Erie, who stood
at the rudder of the burning vessel, while his hand
cracked with the heat, held to his position by a sublime
sense of duty! Think of the boy on the sinking steamer,
touching off the sentinel gun! Think of the soldiers
standing by their guns as the ship went down, and firing
a *feu de joie* as the waves closed over them! Take the
toils and exposures and sacrifices which characterize even
the scientific enterprises of the day, that devotion to sim-

ple truth which dreads no climate and suffers every depri-
vation; that toils through the heart of Africa, and climbs
to the Peak of Teneriffe, where Southern constellations
burn. [Applause.] All these display the spirit of the
olden valor.

I find the chivalry of the time not in the nature of the
arena, or the drapery of the performer; but wherever
there has been called out that which is most generous,
most heroic in man—whether it walks the wards of Scu-
tari or treads the ice-fields of the Northern Pole. Think
at how many solitary posts of duty, under the attritions
of hard fortune, the chill of neglect, and the harshness of
scorn, the patient hand does its work, the sweet nature
distils its love, the brave soul clings to its sublime loyalty
to principle! The age that has such men and women has
the elements of chivalry, though they make no proclamation of trumpet nor charge in the clanging lists. [Ap-
plause.]

Instances like those to which I have alluded are enough
to refute the opinion that what was best in old ages has
died out of our own. We may think them slight indications; still they show the electricity that is in our atmosphere, and that needs but occasion to become a burning light. But that which was noblest in the sentiment of
old ages is the profoundest and mightiest spirit of our
time: that was the sentiment of humanity—the idea of
achievement for the weak, the dependent, the oppressed.
It was this spirit, which was nothing else than the influence of Christianity flowing into the mold of the time,
which converted the rude Teutonic soldier into a cour-
teous knight, this which rendered him a barrier against
wrong, a foe of tyranny and injustice. This was the glory
of the chivalric age, better than its processions, its poets,
or its animal courage. This is the element that justifies
it in history, and this is the element that lives and works
now, and more than anything else redeems our time from
the charge of utter meanness. The sympathies of our
time are all in this direction. Never before has there been
such a profound conviction of the essential unity of the
human race. Your ethnologies may break up mankind
into a dozen tribes, each with distinct progenitors, and
though the earth be striped all over with diversities of

color, shape, capacity, condition—the conviction only deepens, till it becomes the tritest of doctrines, that this wide banyan-tree of ranks and races has one deep root, one central stream of life, one human heart. In this fact we feel more and more the claim of every man—in the fact that he possesses this capable and mysterious heart. We ask for no other sign. We care not what limitation of intellect, what degradation of morals may be found, what analogies may be detected between something lower than man and him. Here is the only question we ask: Does he love and fear and hope and pray with the common ground-swell of humanity? Show us the poor Indian woman who lays down her child in the woods, and folds the little palms together, kisses the dumb lips that will never prattle more; show us the slave mother, hounded, fang-torn, with revolvers cracking behind her, and the rolling flood before, holding in her lacerated hands her babe close to her breast, with a grasp that only Death can loosen,—and in this spectacle there is that which climbs over all castes and bulwarks, enters radiant and perfumed homes, transmutes all distinctions, and strikes straight into humanity, with that "one touch which makes the whole world kin." [Loud applause.]

This, then, is the deepest sentiment of the age, and I thank God it is a commonplace sentiment, for, as such, it inspires and precipitates the noblest work of the age, and is the spring of the grandest events that move in the theatre of our time. No doubt its fruits are often mistaken, fanatical, absurd; but depend upon it, here open richest opportunities for human action, here is an unexhausted field, where man can most readily test the heroism, and faith, and love that is in him. The work of humanity—that is the work of modern chivalry. Not a work such as called the old chivalry to battle for the Holy Sepulchre, but yet a work for the help and uplifting of those for whom He who triumphed over the sepulchre died; not taking the shape of that sentiment which "groined cathedral aisles," but yet a work for that which is more truly God's temple, and which His spirit fills.

Let all of us labor in this work, each in his sphere, and according to the measure of his ability. To him who, in this country, stands for God's truth and man's hope, a long array of kindred spirits—kindred with the chivalry of all the past—rise up and salute: "Good knight! stout lance! Go forth and conquer! Go forth as one of the glorious succession of those who are here achieving a better future for this old earth, ripening as it rolls!" [Prolonged applause.]

JULES ARSENE CLARETIE

SHAKESPEARE AND MOLIÈRE

[Lecture by Jules Arsene Arnaud Claretie, academician, director of the Theatre Francais, since 1885 (born in Limoges, December 3, 1840; ——), delivered at the Lyceum Theatre, London, on July 13, 1899. This lecture, which the London "Times" characterized as "full of grace, acuteness, and charm," was delivered by M. Claretie at the invitation of Sir Henry Irving and Sir Comyns Carr. Sir Charles Dilke returned thanks to M. Claretie; Mr. Forbes Robertson moved a vote of thanks to Sir Henry Irving; and M. Claretie in a few concluding words made a graceful reference to Mr. Robertson's "Hamlet."]

LADIES AND GENTLEMEN:—Morning after morning, whenever I betake myself from my dwelling to the theatre of the Comédie Française, I pass by a statue which stands erect at a corner of my boulevard, and by another seated in front of the fountain that adorns the Rue de Richelieu. The first is the statue of Shakespeare on foot and, actor-like, grasping a scroll upon which, it may be assumed, one of his favorite parts has been inscribed; the second is that of Molière, thoughtful and contemplative in aspect and bearing. It seems to me that these two statues have set me the task which I undertook to fulfil when, at the instance of the organizers of this matinée, I consented to address you on the subject of the Great Tragedian and the Great Comedian.

I deem myself honored, ladies ánd gentlemen, highly honored, by the request preferred to me; but the honor thus conferred upon me is one fraught with strenuous danger, and I should almost regret its acceptance, were I not assured of your proverbial courtesy and your absolute good-will. Unquestionably it may appear somewhat audacious that a French man of letters should discourse

229

of William Shakespeare to a British audience. Even in speaking of Molière he is perhaps over-bold, for I surmise that, if, as is but natural, you know and understand Shakespeare better than I do, most of you know and understand Molière at least as well as I do. I should, therefore, scarcely venture to address you, did I not reflect that I am not only a lecturer to whom you are good enough to listen, but a guest whom you have kindly welcomed among you, and that in free and generous England the chivalric virtue of hospitality has been a national quality from time immemorial.

I am reassured, moreover, by the presence here of many personalities particularly sympathetic to me, and by the proximity of the delightful friend and truly great artist whose presidency of this meeting to-day will henceforth rank among the most gratifying memories of my life. I confess that I would only too gladly hold my peace, leaving to Sir Henry Irving the task of speaking in my stead about Shakespeare, as he has already spoken with captivating eloquence. By this substitution we should all be gainers, for your admirable tragedian knows how to furnish you with twofold explanations of Shakespeare, that of the commentator, and that of the actor. The latter, indisputably, is the most admirable of all critics. It is the comedian who makes men of the characters in the play—men who live, speak, weep, suffer, and die. Instead of listening to me, with Shakespeare for my theme, you would have done well to lend your ears to Irving, his ablest interpreter. The best lectures on Shakespeare are his leading parts, as rendered by the great artist whose friend I am proud to be; and I cherish the hope that I shall one day hear the admiring acclamations with which he will be greeted on the other side of the channel, should he consent to play Shakespeare in Shakespeare's vernacular on a Parisian stage.

For, in order that Shakespeare should be understood and admired according to his deserts,—that is, infinitely, unrestrictedly, as the universe itself may be admired,—it is essential that he be studied in his own tongue. To translate Shakespeare in all his power and grace would require a dramatic genius no less remarkable than his own. We Frenchmen possess, too, really superior translations of Shakespeare,—those of Emile Montégut and François Victor Hugo. But, frankly speaking, to render Shakespeare adequately, the French language is lacking in mystery. Moreover, as Alfred de Vigny remarked when he was translating " Othello," a translation can only be to the original what a portrait is to its living subject. The truth is, despite the admirable translations of Shakespeare's plays into German, that music alone can convey to us the especial charm, the poetry, and the terror of Shakespeare. Victor Hugo, who cared nothing for music,—and many a poet is no less indifferent than he to the Divine Art,—opined that a Rossini could doubtless effectively set to music a witty and brilliant play like " The Barber of Seville," but that the musical composer, face to face with a psychological drama such as " Hamlet," cannot but recoil, acknowledging his impotence. " I cannot," he added, " conceive Hamlet figuring as Amleto! Amleto would be perfectly ridiculous." Not so ridiculous; for, I say again, music—the divine and universal language which gives speech to the soul—has furnished the best interpretation of your incomparable Shakespeare's poetic predominance.

How should one speak of Shakespeare, of the poet who, as Dumas the elder aptly said, was the greatest of creators, except God? He who, defining Shakespeare as the incarnation of drama, and Molière as the incorporation of comedy, should claim to have put forward a new idea would only be re-treading a beaten track and re-editing that which criticism has written throughout past ages; for it may well-nigh be asserted that in that vast world of poetry, caprice, terror, love, and grief which is Shakespeare's achievement there are no unknown nooks, no *terra incognita*. All in it has been explored, discovered, studied, and few fresh flowers can be gathered nowadays upon that beaten track. Nevertheless, in works of genius, no less than in nature's landscapes, each man sees what his soul bids him behold. A forest path assumes an aspect of mystery or sadness in conformity with the hour at which one strays along it, or with the humor for the time being of the passer-by. The sun may light up the wood's recesses as brightly as he will, if the wanderer be of melancholy mood, all the golden sheen will only bring him increase of sadness; while to him whose soul is joyous an autumn landscape, gloomy and cold, as Millais has painted it, will appear almost smiling and seductive. It is from his inner self that a man derives his judgment of works and actualities, which he lauds or condemns, not always in just proportion to their true value, but in accordance with his own humor.

Similarly, successive generations, each in its turn, see in the creations of genius that which their momentary passions compel them to see; consequently, they either admire or depreciate the works of their forbears, for reasons that often differ and are sometimes diametrically opposed to one another. Genius, appraised by the fashion of the hour, serves as a convenient text for all sorts of commentaries, just as landscapes, according to the time of day, afford different "motives" to painters. Works of art have their dawn, their high noon, and their gloaming. It is Shakespeare's unique privilege to be admirable at all times. The man of the Elizabethan age is a man of all the ages.

Henri Heine discovered in him "a lunar grace," and the other day, while glancing over some of Alfred de Vigny's as yet unpublished papers, I came across this deeply thoughtful sentence, written *apropos* of Shakespeare's Brutus, and of the remorse experienced by the murderer of Cæsar: "The word remorse is nowhere pronounced, and yet remorse is everywhere. Great poets are masters of the great secret of suggestion." And De Vigny was right; to suggest a drama is to heighten its effect tenfold. Suggestion foreshadows action. The Night is a great poet, and also suggests *(laisse deviner)*. In her suggestions lies the "lunar grace" spoken of by Heine. Balzac, the author of the "Comédie Humaine," said one day of Victor Hugo: "Hugo is a great man; let us say no more about him." Of Shakespeare and Molière it might also be said: "*Ce sont des grands hommes; n'en parlons plus.*" Listen to them, admire them; that is the best way to appreciate and honor them. They were judged long ago.

Hence I would fain compare these two great geniuses as simply as one and the other of them have understood certain characters and certain vices common to humanity at large—peculiar to no race or country in particular, but of all times and nations. As Shakespeare and Molière have designed and depicted the jealous man and the miser, the misanthrope and the hypocrite, so would I essay to set forth careful studies of these admirable dramatists.

Comparison, always somewhat arbitrary, do what one may, cannot of course be sustained with respect to any two complete works of these men. There are certain general types which here and there are utilized alike by the author of " Hamlet " and the author of " Tartuffe." But many of Shakespeare's plays, to wit, his admirable historical dramas, admit of no parallel; they are purely English, personally, I may say, as well as nationally. They belong to your records, just as the exclusive satirical plays of Molière, studies of the manners of his day, criticisms of the jargon of " Les Précieuses Ridicules," or of the grimaces and costumes of fashionable fops, are chronicles of the Louis-Quatorze epoch, and appear to be purposely aimed at certain follies of the court and affectations of " polite society." Which is as much as to say, not as the discovery of a novelty, but merely as a statement of fact, that each of these geniuses seems to wear two faces,—the one essentially national, the other absolutely human. Shakespeare and Molière are of their time and race, respectively, because there is something actual in all their work. They belong to all countries and ages in virtue of I know not what, superior, indefinite, eternal, which renders certain geniuses comparable to those stars at which so many human beings of various nationalities gaze simultaneously, recognizing in them the same luminous poesy and lucidity.

M. Paul Stapfer, in his excellent work dealing with Molière and Shakespeare, tells us that, about the commencement of the present century, John Kemble the actor, your illustrious fellow-countryman, came to Paris. His comrades of the Comédie Française entertained him at a banquet. The conversation at table turned upon the tragic poets of both nations. With lively eloquence Kemble pointed out that Shakespeare was manifestly superior to Racine and Corneille. Under the influence of politeness—may be of conviction—the French comedians were gradually giving way to him, when Michot the actor suddenly exclaimed: " So be it; we are agreed; but what do you say to Molière? " Smiling, Kemble replied, " Molière? That is another question. Molière was not a Frenchman." Those present protested vehemently. " No," continued Kemble, " Molière was a man. One day it pleased the Almighty to permit mankind to taste, in all their perfection and plenitude, the joys of which Comedy is the source. Forthwith He created Molière, and said to him: ' Go, depict men, your brothers, and amuse them; if you can, make them better than they now are!' Then he cast Molière earthwards. On what part of our globe's surface would he fall, to the north or to the south—on this or that side of the channel? Chance allotted him to France; but he belongs as much to us as to yourselves. No people or age can claim him as its own; he belongs to all time and to every nation." You may be acquainted with this just and humorous judgment, pronounced by Kemble, but you are probably unaware that our celebrated historian Michelet cherished a theory of his own in relation to Shakespeare. Did he record it on any page of his published works? I doubt it. But one day he told me—and I quote this opinion of a gifted writer as a paradox—that Shakespeare, by his mother's side, was Welsh, that is to say, partly French, and that, as all children, especially of the male sex, take after their mothers, the Welshwoman's son inherited from her the French temperament and genius. I well remember the vexation of Victor Hugo when our friend Castelar, proud to recognize the Spanish inspiration in " Hernani " and " Ruy Blas," said to him: " Dear master, you are a Castilian genius!" Hugo replied: " I do not know that I am a genius; but I do know that I am a Frenchman!" In the land of Shadows, Shakespeare may have replied to Michelet: " I am an Englishman, deeply and essentially an Englishman!"

It is precisely one of the glories of his work to have placed among his studies of the human heart,—of jealousy, love, and hatred,—and among his fairy-tales, his delicious journeys in the realm of fancy and in dreamland, those admirable historical frescoes which revive, with all their tragic heroisms, the picturesque, sanguinary, and thrilling chronicles of Old England. It is his glory to have blended with the followings of his kings, barons, and knights, the Tudor Henrys, fourth, fifth, sixth, and eighth of their house, the dukes, cardinals, and lords by whom they were environed, the heterogeneous throng of burgesses, falconers, apprentices, soldiers, peasants, and people of no account, which classic French tragedy has banished from her marble palaces, that throng which is the cement of glory and the nameless backbone of battle. All these dialogued chronicles of Shakespeare teem with valiant, persistent, and noble patriotism,—patriotism that is steadfastly and exclusively English.

Had I the time, I could pause a while before these superb historical dramas, the value of which cannot be compared with that of any of our tragedies, assuredly not with any of Molière's plays. It is in certain episodes of those inimitable dramas that the true greatness of Shakespeare manifests itself to me most saliently. The love of Romeo, the jealousy of Othello, the remorse of Macbeth, the doubts of Hamlet, abound in long-admired beauties; but the familiar talk of two sentinels chatting about war; the meeting on the battle-field (Henry VI) of a son who has slain his sire and a father who has killed his son,—these, in my opinion, attain the topmost height of sublimity, and I can discover nothing comparable to them in tragic horror, save certain humorous and genial conversations which took place, in the pages of Aristophanes, between pacific citizens and bellicose Athenians. Shakespeare's war pictures teach us to hate war. Appeals for mercy seem to issue from the gaping wounds of the corpses which he piles up on the field of carnage. The old soldier who has slaughtered his son exclaims:—

> O pity, God, this miserable age!
> What stratagems, how fell, how butcherly,
> Erroneous, mutinous, and unnatural,
> This deadly quarrel daily doth beget!

Molière seems to have seen nothing of Louis XIV's battles. They are echoed in the writings of Madame de Sévigné; not in those of Molière.

Let us leave aside history, which Shakespeare's genius has verified for evermore, and turn to the consideration of man, generally speaking, and of what may be termed "The Human Comedy."

Men have two ways of looking at the incidents and accidents of life. Have you ever seen a passer-by stumble and fall down in the street? The luckless wretch runs the risk of breaking his leg or splitting his head open. Nevertheless, the spectators of his mishap are differently impressed by it, according to their respective temperaments. Some, seeing him fall, exclaim, "Poor fellow!" while others ejaculate, "Stupid fool!" The former, moved by a feeling of pity, perceive something dramatic in the trifling, commonplace, every-day occurrence; the latter only see its ridiculous side. Taking these two diverse temperaments into one account, we may sum up the totality of dramatic authors on the one hand, and of theatrical spectators on the other.

Ever since the world has existed, mankind has worn two different masks wherewith to dissimulate or express, as it may be, the feelings that move him; and the theatre, which symbolizes every kind of sentiment by one or other of these masks, the mask of tragedy and the mask of comedy, has thus in some sort materialized the two eternal forms of passion. The fundamental law, the absolute *mot d'ordre*, of the theatre is to make people laugh or cry. This is an æsthetic truism, repeated and insisted upon ever since Molière, in the "Ecole des Femmes," and Goethe, in the prologue to "Faust," the dialogue between a theatrical manager, a dramatic poet, and a casual wag, established the only immutable rule of dramatic art, viz., to please. One may give pleasure, be it remembered, by striking the spectator's soul with terror. Schiller, in his essay or dissertation "On the cause of the pleasure we derive from matters tragical," observes that "the sufferings of a scoundrel are not less replete with dramatic charm than those of a virtuous man." In Shakespeare, we find "that majestic sadness which constitutes the whole pleasure of tragedy," as Racine has admirably said; and even in Molière we experience an analogous impression, thus characterized by Châteaubriand: "Molière's humor, by its extreme profundity, and, if I may venture to say so, by its sadness, keeps touch with tragic truth." "The world," said Horace Walpole, "is at once a comedy and a tragedy,—a comedy for the man of thought, a tragedy for the man of feeling."

Let me turn to one of Molière's masterpieces,—in my opinion, his absolute masterpiece, "Le Misanthrope," which I might compare with "Timon of Athens," but that it seems to me more closely to resemble "Othello"; for Molière's Alceste was devoured by jealousy before he lapsed into misanthropy. How does Alceste reply to Célimène when she makes mock of him, asking, with a gay smile:—

> Et que me veulent dire et ces soupirs poussés
> Et ces sombres regards que sur moi vous lancez?

His answer is more tragical than comical:—

> Que toutes les horreurs dont une âme est capable
> A vos déloyautés n'ont rien de comparable:
> Que le sort, les démons, et le ciel en courroux
> N'ont jamais rien produit de si méchant que vous.

And, in cursing the coquette, this comedy-character rises, or, rather, is raised by indignation, to the lofty region of tragical morality:—

> Mais d'un aveu trompeur voir ma flamme applaudie
> C'est une trahison, c'est une perfidie
> Qui ne saurait trouver de trop grands châtiments,
> Et je puis tout permettre à mes ressentiments.
> Oui, oui, redoutez tout après un tel outrage;
> Je ne suis plus à moi, je suis tout à la rage.
> Percé du coup mortel dont vous m'assassinez,
> Mes sens par la raison ne sont plus gouvernés;
> Je cède aux mouvements d'une juste colère,
> Et je ne réponds pas de ce que je puis faire.

Do we not find in the Shakespearean tragedy the same feeling—expressed almost in the same words—of frightful jealousy which drives Alceste to despair and Othello to crime? Does not Desdemona take note of Othello's "gloomy glances," just as Célimène observes the "sombres regards" of Alceste?

> DESD. My lord, what is your will?
> OTH. Pray you, chuck, come hither.

Desdemona is not Célimène; the simple, loving girl is

not the accomplished coquette who plays with the misanthrope as she would play with her fan:—

> DESD. I understand a fury in your words,
>   But not the words.
> OTH.   Why, what art thou?
> DESD. Your wife, my lord; your true and loyal wife.
> OTH. Come, swear it, damn thyself,
>   Lest, being like one of heaven, the devils themselves
>   Should fear to seize thee: therefore be double-damned,
>   Swear—thou art honest.
> DESD.   Heaven doth truly know it.
> OTH. Heaven knows that thou art false as hell.

The two scenes are practically identical. Desdemona
and Célimène question their jealous lovers in similar
terms. "*Quel est donc le trouble où je vous vois paraître?*"
asks Célimène. It might be Desdemona. And Alceste,
the hero of comedy, replies almost as tragically as Othello,
the hero of drama. Passion and pain cause almost the
same words to spring from their burning lips. Othello
speaks of hell, Alceste of demons. Both are convulsed by
the same terrific rage. In his fury Alceste raises his hand
against the smiling coquette, exclaiming:—

> Et je ne réponds pas de ce que je puis faire!

Transform the Louis XIV salon into "a room in the
castle of Cyprus," place the damascened poniard of the
Moor of Venice in the hand of the French misanthrope,
and who knows that Alceste will not exclaim, like
Othello:—

> O, that the slave had forty thousand lives;
> One is too poor, too weak for my revenge!

The only difference between them is the courtly politeness which stays the threatening hand of Alceste and the
savage brutality which arms the Moor with a trenchant
dagger.

Now let us inquire why one and the same feeling, which
attains a highly tragical development in Othello and
Alceste, is deeply lowered in tone, becoming comical after

having been intensely painful, in Sganarelle? This tormented being is another jealous husband, incessantly racked by delusions, who, when jealousy prompts him to pick a quarrel with the gay spark whom he suspects of being his wife's lover, is suddenly balked in his fierce purpose by a singularly practical prudence, by which neither Alceste at Versailles nor Othello in Cyprus could ever have been restrained from action. Sganarelle yearns to strike his rival; but, should he do so, he will have to take to the cold steel. This contingency causes him to ponder, and nothing can be droller than his reflections:—

> Je hais de tout mon cœur les esprits colériques,
> Et porte grand amour aux hommes pacifiques.
> Je ne suis point battant, de peur d'être battu,
> Et l'humeur débonnaire est ma grande vertu.
> Mais mon honneur me dit que d'une telle offense
> Il faut absolument que je prenne vengeance.
> Ma foi, laissons-le rire autant qu'il lui plaira.
> Au diantre qui pourtant rien du tout en fera.
> Quand j'aurai fait le brave et qu'un fer pour ma peine
> M'aura d'un vilain coup transpercé la bedaine,
> Que par la ville ira le bruit de mon trépas,
> Dites-moi, mon honneur, en serez-vous plus gras?

He finds consolation in the thought that, after all, it is not such a very great misfortune to be deceived by one's wife:—

> Quel mal cela fait-il? La jambe en devient-elle
> Plus tortue, après tout, et la taille moins belle?
> Peste soit qui premier trouva l'invention
> De s'affliger l'esprit de cette vision,
> Et d'attacher l'honneur de l'homme le plus sage
> Aux choses que peut faire une femme volage!
> Puisqu'on tient, à bon droit, tout crime personnel,
> Que fait là notre honneur pour être criminel?

I have quoted these lines in order to exemplify the different views taken of jealousy by two men of genius. Let me here repeat that every human situation has two aspects, the one tragical, the other comical. Othello crumples up the kerchief which he believes Desdemona to have given to Cassio, and, recognizing it, roars with fury like a wounded lion. Sganarelle snatches from his wife's hands the portrait of Lélie, which Célie has let fall, and which he believes to have been presented to his spouse by her lover. But in the reasons for not fighting, which Sganarelle lays down to himself, do you not recognize the identical arguments put forward by fat Jack Falstaff? *"Dites-moi, mon honneur, en serez-vous plus gras?"* says Sganarelle, shaking his head; and Falstaff, declaring that "the better part of valor is discretion," takes the same view of honor as that entertained by Sganarelle:—

> Can honor set a leg? No. Or an arm? No. Or take away the grief of a wound? No. Honor hath no skill in surgery, then? No. What is honor? A word. What is that word, 'honor'? Air. . . . . . Who hath it? He that died o' Wednesday. Doth he feel it? No. Doth he hear it? No. Is it insensible, then? Yea, to the dead. But will it not live with the living? No. Why? Detraction will not suffer it: therefore, I'll none of it: honor is a mere scutcheon, and so ends my catechism.

In the case of Falstaff, as of Othello, or of Alceste, or of Sganarelle, nature claims her rights in drama and comedy alike, and it is so absolutely true that laughter and tears are close neighbors, so undeniable that drama and comedy alike influence human action, that I have heard an eminent comedian declare that such and such a Shakespearean monologue—for instance, the famous "To be or not to be" of Hamlet—may be spoken either in the tragical or comical tone and spirit, retaining in both cases its admirable dramatic and human character.

The comedian in question was a brilliant, but incomplete, man of genius. George Sand was very fond of him, and even wrote expressly for him a sort of adaptation of Shakespeare's "As You Like It," which was performed at the Comédie Francaise. His name was Rouvière, and he played the part of Hamlet in 1847, when Alexandre Dumas and Paul Meurice produced their translation of the immortal tragedy at the Théâtre Historique. Rouvière was short, slender, and fragile, but full of animation, and, as it were, consumed by an ardent inward heat. As he could not make a living as an actor, he took to painting, and his pictures were not devoid of merit.

We have one of them in the Museum of the Rue Richelieu. One evening, I remember, at a dinner-party of
friends and comrades—Léon Gambetta was one of us on
that occasion—Rouvière maintained that Hamlet's solilo-
quy could be spoken in two ways, comically and tragically.
"Always the two masks!" In compliance with Gambetta's request, he recited "To be or not to be" with
extraordinary effect, firstly, in the pensive, melancholy,
anxious manner, and, secondly, in the light and airy tone
of comedy. Rouvière, I must add, had discovered a third
way of interpreting the immortal monologue. "Would
you like," he asked Gambetta, "that I should show you
how—leaving the theatre aside, and altogether irre-
spective of the dramatic and comic points of view—I can
render the 'To be or not to be' of Shakespeare?"
"I should indeed, my dear Rouvière," replied Gambetta.

And I must confess that the actor's third recitation was
altogether incomprehensible, being surcharged with epi-
leptic gestures, exasperate exclamations, fury, and madness. "To be or not to be!" said Gambetta; "Rouvière
has changed the venue. It is the monologue itself which
ought to be, and *is not!*"

The interpretations of poets by comedians are subject
to essentially personal variations. Diderot quotes a saying
attributed to Garrick: "The actor who is capable of rendering Shakespeare to perfection has no understanding
whatever of Racine." Nothing is more incorrect than
this dictum. Within the limits of a single week I have seen
Mounet-Sully play in "Hamlet" and in "Iphigenia," as
much at his ease with the quiver and darts of Achilles as
in the pourpoint of the Danish prince. But the actor who
interprets the special methods of the creative author must
strive to render them in the spirit as well as the letter,
just as the etcher of a picture must endeavor to reproduce
with his graver the color as well as the design of the
painter.

Here arises once more the eternal question of translations and translators. Frenchmen have been accused of
an incapacity to arrive at a perfect understanding of
Shakespeare. Do you remember that exquisite page,
winged and tuneful like a singing-bird, which Henri

Heine, the German Parisian, wrote one day *apropos* of the comedies of your inimitable poet? He reproached us Frenchmen for not comprehending, "with our small ratiocinating heads," the delicious poetry of those fairy-tales which impart a special charm to Shakespeare's works—the language which sounds like a fluttering of wings: the idiom which, he says, can only be learned by dreamers. In that rare page which characterizes two races as well as their two most eminent representative men, in relation to whom I am addressing you to-day Henri Heine says: "Frenchmen understand the sun, but are incapable of understanding the moon."

The saying is not absolutely correct, but it is altogether beautiful. As a matter of fact, the moon seems to enwrap and bathe in its flood of light Shakespeare's most fanciful works, to which it imparts I know not what new charm, to which we may give the name of "mystery." Mystery is one of the greatest poets with whom I am acquainted; it is he who, with his silent and shadowy hands, opens to us the gates of the infinite. But it is not fair to assert that Frenchmen have no understanding of Shakespeare's delicious fancies. The other day I recognized the seductive grace of the personages who figure in Shakespeare's comedies while listening to the Alexandrines of Corneille's "Menteur," the rhymes of which pick up the verses much as a chiseled sword-hilt raises a fold of a velvet cloak. And in our Eighteenth century has not Marivaux, the author of so many miniature *chefs d'œuvre* of sentiment and grace, shed upon the satin coats of his marquesses and the white caps of his soubrettes some reflection of the poetic Shakespearean moonlight which so delighted Henri Heine? Paul de St. Victor justly remarked that the doors of Marivaux's boudoir opened upon Shakespeare's forest. And Musset—our Musset—the Musset of "On ne badine pas avec l'amour," of "Les Caprices de Marianne," and of "Carmosine"—has he not dreamed under Shakespeare's moon, the moon that his Lorenzaccio execrated, reviling it as "a livid face"? If the French love brightness, light, and the sun, as Heine says, are not their Nineteenth century poets votaries of Chimæra and of the moon? Have not Théophile Gautier and Théodore de Banville, for instance, the former in "Le Baiser," the latter in "Le Pierrot Posthume," asked "*l'ami Pierrot, au clair de la lune,*" to lend them a pen wherewith to write delicious verses? This love of phantasy incarnate in the Pierrot of pantomime is Shakespeare's own humor equipped in French guise.

"Nature, nature!" exclaimed Molière; and the great comedian's ejaculation is also Shakespeare's *mot d'ordre.* Even in their profession and destiny the two men may be aptly compared to one another. It is the love of nature— of that which is natural—which is common to them, and to which Shakespeare gives expression in Hamlet's admirable advice to the actors, and Molière in his no less admirable hints to the performers of "L'Impromptu de Versailles." It is this human strain of realism in Shakespeare and Molière which tempts me to consider them as comedians, before treating of them as poets. Was Shakespeare a good comedian? Was Molière an excellent actor? Their works are manifest in incomparable magnificence. Whether they rendered them ill or well only interests the curious nowadays. But the curious are excellent literary *juges d'instruction,* who insist upon knowing and understanding everything, and will not hear of leaving any branch of research to the tender mercies of posterity. They have made it their business to ascertain whether or not these two great men were meritorious comedians. In respect to Shakespeare, I have nothing positive to say; but it is certain that Molière was an excellent actor. Proof of his histrionic excellence is afforded by the attacks to which his foes subjected him. Our enemies often render us better service than our friends, even as far as the future is concerned; and Molière had plenty of them. Those who were his contemporaries, desiring to demonstrate the magnificence of his works, lit upon an argument which, though favorable to the comedian, was damaging to the author. "His plays," they said, "seem to us good because he acts in them. When he shall cease to do so, they will appear to be what they really are,—*i. e.,* mediocre." The *amour-propre* of actors is proverbial, although, as a matter of fact, they are no vainer than other people, but only somewhat more frank and expansive. I doubt, nevertheless, that, however conceited Molière may have been as an actor, he can have been agreeably flattered by compliments addressed to the comedian at the expense of the playwright. However that may be, the fact is established that he was a good comedian, and played admirable parts excellently well.

A characteristic of genius is the multiplicity of its faculties. The great Florentine artists were at once painters, sculptors, architects, and poets. Michelangelo was all these, and an engineer and soldier to boot. Shakespeare's intellect was absolutely encyclopædic.

An admiral, who was also a distinguished meteorologist, once observed that not only the most beautiful, but the most exact, description of a storm, regarded from the strictly scientific point of view, was that chronicled minute by minute, so to speak, in "Les Travailleurs de la Mer." Shakespeare's "Tempest" is in no respect less admirable or convincing. Take Shakespeare as a word-painter of landscape; the seashore in "Lear" is a masterly picture. He may confidently be classed as an eminent historian; and long ago his amazing genius, which anticipated so many modern ideas, most eloquently gave the alarm in "Othello," in relation to Cassio's drunken fit, anent "accursed wine," which transforms men into beasts. I would that Cassio's denunciation of drunkenness might serve as an epigraph for every publication of the anti-alcoholic associations which throughout the world fight the good fight against that abominable form of insensate indulgence which kills men and sows the seeds of anæmia, degeneration, and madness. Shakespeare, as honorary president of all existing total-abstinence and temperance leagues, would occupy a position, in my humble opinion, by no means to be disdained. Cassio may be qualified as the ordinary drunkard who may be usefully held up to general reprobation as a "frightful example." "Drunken savage" was one of the epithets applied to Shakespeare by Voltaire!

There is no more striking exemplification of the occasional stupidity of clever men than Voltaire's letter to the French Academy, read aloud by D'Alembert on August 25, 1776. That protest against Shakespeare to a corporation to whose judgment Cardinal de Richelieu, Pierre Corneille, and George Scudéri had submitted "Le Cid," is a monument of narrow-minded and absolutely ridiculous criticism. Voltaire, who loved, understood, and imparted to Frenchmen a knowledge of English literature at a time when, as he himself alleged, France knew nothing of England but the name of Marlborough and the doggerel song, " Marlbrook s'en va-t-en guerre "; Voltaire, who had translated Milton, Pope, and Dryden, complimented Locke, and praised Newton; analyzed in that memorable letter " Macbeth," " Othello," and " Hamlet," applying to those masterpieces the critical process which an obscure Boulevard journalist might to-day apply to a drama of the Ambigu or the Porte Saint-Martin. He went so far with his facile pleasantries, aimed at " Billy " Shakespeare, that D'Alembert advised him to suppress certain offensive sentences, and eventually did not read his friend's letter to the Academy in its entirety.

This episode goes to prove what enormous progress has been achieved by the knowledge and, I may say, the cult of Shakespeare among intelligent Frenchmen in the course of a century—say, from 1776 to 1876. Voltaire admitted that Shakespeare, " low, unruly, and absurd as he was, displayed sparks of genius." Voltaire gave himself credit for audacity when he declared that " in this obscure chaos, composed of murder and buffoonery, heroism and turpitude, vulgar chatter and great interests, there were natural and striking features." Features!

A hundred years later Victor Hugo proclaims Shakespeare " the master of drama, one of those demi-gods before whom men bow down, one of the forces and glories of nature." The proscribed poet was gazing at the sea from the Guernsey beach, and his son, François Victor, suddenly asked him how the long, slow, dull hours of exile might best be utilized?

" Translate Shakespeare," replied his father. " I will contemplate the ocean! "

Thus Victor Hugo invested Shakespeare with the grandeur, power, charm, music, storminess, infinite seduction, and infinite terror of the sea. He was, indeed, an ocean of thought, an ocean which reflected heaven itself. The Nineteenth century poet was endowed with a far more open mind, a far more vigorous understanding than the Eighteenth century philosopher. But one must do Voltaire the justice to admit that, although he criticised

Shakespeare with a silly vivacity which smacks more strongly of the dramatic author's professional jealousy than of critical justice, he also frequently sang his praises with convincing fervor. He did even better, for he imitated Shakespeare. Voltaire's " Mort de César " and " Zaïre " are timid, but genuine, Shakespearean adaptations. That admirable musician, Gounod, said to me one day, while listening to some of the " Faust " melodies, miserably droned out by a peripatetic barrel-organ: " You can hear, my dear friend, that we composers only reach popularity by the way of calumny!" I am tempted to say that Voltaire was one of the first to make Shakespeare known to us, and to popularize him in France— as the organ-grinder popularized Gounod—by calumniating him.

Let me, quite temperately, defend Voltaire, who has been accused of despising Shakespeare, whereas the only acceptable pieces of Voltairean drama were borrowed from the plays of the author of " Hamlet." The truth is that Voltaire bows down as deeply as anybody before Shakespeare's genius. While pointing out its defects, he places him side by side, in admiring appraisement, with Newton and—perhaps ironically—with Frederick II. Now, in Voltaire's opinion, Newton was " the sublime man!"

When at the production of " Zaïre " (August 13, 1732) Voltaire put forward Orosmane upon the French stage, it was Shakespeare, or, at least, the shade of Shakespeare, that made a first appearance there. Thirty-seven years later (October 30, 1769), Hamlet " came on," somewhat timidly, impersonated by Ducis. Romeo and Juliet did not make their Parisian *début* until July, 1772, and De Rozay's colorless version of " Richard III " was first staged in July, 1781. Then, between 1783 and 1792, Ducis introduced " King Lear," " Macbeth," and " Othello " to the French theatrical public. In 1828 Frederic Soulié translated " Romeo and Juliet." Alfred de Vigny's adaptation of " The Merchant of Venice " dates from the following year. It was not until 1856 that " Hamlet " was produced at the Théâtre Historique—the " Hamlet " of Alexandre Dumas and Paul Meurice, which I had the honor to add to the répertoire of the Comédie

Française in 1886. And some of Shakespeare's very
terms (employed in stage directions as well as dialogue)
only found acceptance in French acting versions by degrees and at long intervals. In 1732 and 1792 Desdemona, or, rather, Edelmone, let fall either a letter or a
diamond ornament; in 1820 Marie Stuart "dropped a tis-
sue"; in 1829 Mademoiselle Mars spoke the true word
"handkerchief" for the first time, as Desdemona, on the
French stage.

Everybody should read in the pages of Stendhal—the
literary precisian whose books simply teem with facts
and ideas—Henri Beyle's account of the first perform-
ances given in France by an English company which
came over to Paris to play Shakespeare. There was a
terrific row. Berlioz, who shortly afterwards composed a
symphony in "The Tempest," fell in love at one and the
same time with the author of "Hamlet" and with the
actress who impersonated Ophelia—Henrietta Smithson,
whom he married. Shakespeare certainly inspired the
very great musician who composed "La Damnation de
Faust." Berlioz was dazzled by Shakespeare, before he
undertook to interpret Goethe in music. He wrote in
his "Mémoires,"—"I recognized true greatness, true
beauty, absolute dramatic truth. I lived, I understood,
I felt that I was a live man." Berlioz was not alone in
feeling and acknowledging the influence of Shakespeare.
The whole new literary school—Victor Hugo, Alexandre
Dumas, Alfred de Vigny, Emile Deschamps, etc.—ac-
claimed "Hamlet" and its author unanimously. Berlioz,
however, felt assured that only Shakespeare's drama—
not his humor—could be acclimatized in France, for he
wrote: "It is more difficult for a Frenchman to gauge
the depths of Shakespeare's style than for an Englishman
to appreciate the delicacy and originality of that of
Molière or La Fontaine." If it be difficult to appreciate
a poet's originality, the actor of genius is capable of interpreting it in such sort that his or her rendering is far
more intelligible than the pallid literary translation. Miss
Smithson explained Shakespeare to a whole generation of
fascinated audiences, and I feel certain that, if Sir Henry
Irving, the illustrious tragedian of whom the British stage
is justly proud, should play Shakespearean parts in Paris,

the Parisians would greet him with acclamations as the
most admirable of living "translators."

All men of genius resemble one another in some particular respect. Molière and Shakespeare, for instance,—
two misanthropes whose disappointed love takes the form
of bitter irony. The Jaques of "As You Like It," it has
been well said, is an Alceste of the Renaissance. But he
himself has a brother—an elder brother in respect to
anger and hatred—Timon of Athens. Misanthropy incor-
porate never gave utterance to such eloquent curses as
Timon hurled against mankind.

Never did incensed prophet rain down upon social corruption more scathing invectives.

> Be abhorred
> All feasts, societies, and throngs of men;
> His semblable, yea, himself, Timon disdains:
> Destruction fang mankind!

Here Alceste is far surpassed. The two geniuses,
moreover, depict themselves in their respective works.
Molière studies a man; Shakespeare, humanity. Alceste
is a misanthrope; Timon was misanthropy itself.

Shakespeare's torrents of rage may be readily accounted
for by the fact that he lived at a time when men bore
with difficulty "the burden and heat of the day." The
pains suffered during heavy and sinister hours are reflected in the lamentations of his personages. The
gloomy story of his age underlies his work. He wrote,
so to speak, as one wading through blood; and he suffered, though not of his personal ills, for fortune had
come to him with maturity of years. The poet might
have allowed himself to lead a happy life; but could he?
The man of imagination was also a man of conscience.
It did not suffice him, as Taine will have it, to obey the
genius that inspired him with terrible drama or sparkling
comedy, manifesting to him the ghost of Banquo, or the
chariot of Queen Mab. He insisted upon raising his
voice in protest on behalf of the weak and oppressed, and
in crying out aloud for justice. The historian of English
literature, as unjust to Shakespeare as he was to Sterne,
either did not or would not see that Shakespeare was a
humanitarian. The poet's eminent commentator turned

a deaf ear to the appeals he addressed to the future,—
heart-rending ejaculations, which resounded like consola-
tory anachronisms in Elizabeth's time, when the heads-
man's axe was constantly imbrued in English blood.
Was Shakespeare a democrat? I am inclined to think
so. In "King Lear," for instance, there are outbreaks
which shed sudden light upon his inmost thoughts. The
king, destitute and straying about the country in the rain
with his fool and one faithful follower, takes refuge in an
empty hovel. His thoughts turn towards the poor
wretches whom he had erstwhile treated as beggars, and
whom, in his misery, he recognizes as his brethren :—

> Poor naked wretches, wheresoe'er you are,
> That bide the pelting of this pitiless storm,
> How shall your houseless heads and unfed sides,
> Your looped and windowed raggedness, defend you
> From seasons such as these? O, I have ta'en
> Too little care of this! Take physic, pomp;
> Expose thyself to feel what wretches feel,
> That thou may'st shake thy superflux to them
> And show the heavens more just.

Lear—that is, Shakespeare—thus recommends self-
sacrifice and preaches pity, inspired not only by heaven's
decree, but by a profound love of justice. At other times
Shakespeare, with cruel irony, shows us the dust of
Alexander stopping a beer-barrel. He goes still further,—*e. g.* :—

KING. Now, Hamlet, where's Polonius?
HAML. At supper.   .   .   .   Not where he eats, but where
he is eaten: a certain convocation of [politic] worms are e'en at him.
.   .   .   Your fat king and your lean beggar is but variable service; two dishes, but to one table: that's the end.   .   .   .   A
man may fish with the worm that hath eat of a king; and eat of the fish
that hath fed of that worm.
KING. What dost thou mean by this?
HAML. Nothing, but to show you how a king may go a progress
through the guts of a beggar.

Louis XIV would have been extremely surprised had
Molière taken the liberty of putting such realism as this
into words. Molière, however, did not indulge in these

infernal pleasantries. He was more reasonable and less formidable than Shakespeare, while every whit as human. His Tartuffe, to my mind, is a greater hypocrite than Iago, whose contrivances are somewhat clumsy. Again, I might compare, for instance, Harpagon with Shylock; or, rather, the women created by the genius of the supreme English and French dramatists. In the latter case I should venture to say that, if Shakespeare's women—the offspring of dreams and magic spells—are made to be worshipped, Molière's women, delicious in their simplicity, reasonableness, and grace, are made to be espoused. But why compare, and why prefer? Let us admire and love!

A few months ago, in the presence of its author, M. Jean Aicard, I was conducting a rehearsal of the last translation of Shakespeare produced in France, that of "Othello." While the eternally thrilling drama was being acted on the stage, while Desdemona, surrounded by captains, soldiers, and Cypriotes, was awaiting her tempest-tossed consort, another storm seemed to be brewing between two great nations made to esteem and love one another, and to strive in common throughout the world in the cause of progress and liberty. In a word, Fashoda just then cast its shadow over our Shakespearean rehearsals, and the latest translator of "Othello," admiring like myself the great poet of sempiternal passion and pain, said to me: "Is it not amazing that, far above the contingent rivalries of politics and the futile questions which arise between peoples meant by nature to think, feel, and act in union, the poet's genius should soar like the sun above the clouds? It is in vain that newspapers, eagerly read to-day, torn up and forgotten to-morrow, essay to inflame anger and foment dissension. The poet is at his post, intent upon making all nations listen to the imperishable words 'Concord and Peace.' "

And, in fact, while disquietude darkened the horizon, Shakespeare, everlasting Shakespeare, was drawing towards each other the publics of France and England by the agency of one of his master-works. The dead man, entombed centuries ago, was mobilizing troops who were the soldiers of art, and who, from Mounet-Sully down to the humblest " super " of the Venetian senate, took arms to fight for his glory. I admired that histrionic legion, stirred to action by the posthumous will of genius, those men of to-day, moved by passions of the Sixteenth century man, those artists of another race, interpreting, resuscitating, vivifying the work of a profoundly English genius which belongs to all nations; and I said to myself: "Nothing is finer, nobler, and greater than dramatic art." Just as heaven is the same for all men, art is the same for all nations. Genius is the great reservoir of human peace. And I glorified Shakespeare in my native land with the same pride that I experience here in paying homage, in the name of the great Frenchman, Molière, to the great Englishman, and to grand Old England.

It is my earnest wish that next year, at the Universal Exhibition which is to show the world the wonders of human industry, England will furnish us with ample opportunity for admiring the incomparable products of her manual labor and the superb creations of her genius; that the English men of letters whom we know, translate, and reverence, will join with us in applauding the two dramatists who link France and England together, Shakespeare and Molière; and that we may inaugurate for all time to come the fraternal era of free interchange, as far as dramatic and literary masterpieces are concerned.

SAMUEL LANGHORNE CLEMENS

("MARK TWAIN")

THE SANDWICH ISLANDS

[Lecture (in part) by Samuel L. Clemens ("Mark Twain"), humorist (born in Florida, Missouri, November 30, 1835; ———), delivered in the Academy of Music, New York City, about 1877. The manuscript was not preserved, and this fragment is reprinted from a newspaper report made at the time. "Hawaii," as it was popularly called, was one of Mr. Clemens' early lectures, and, repeated in many parts of the country, it added materially to his fame as an American humorist of high degree.]

LADIES AND GENTLEMEN:—There doesn't appear to be anybody here to introduce me, and so we shall have to let that go by default. But I am the person who is to deliver the lecture, and I shall try to get along just the same as if I had been formally introduced. I suppose I ought to apologize for the weather [the night was very stormy], but I can't hold myself altogether responsible for it, so I will let it go as it is.

The only apology which I can offer for appearing before you to talk about the Sandwich Islands is the fact that the recent political changes there have rendered it rather necessary for us to post ourselves concerning that country; to know a little something about the people; what we have forgotten, to gather up again; and as I have spent several months in the Islands, several years ago, I feel competent to shed any amount of light upon the matter. [Laughter.]

These islands are situated 2,100 miles southwest from San Francisco, California, out in the middle of the Pacific Ocean. Why they were put away out there, so far away

from any place and in such an out-of-the-way locality, is a
thing which no one can explain. [Laughter.] But it's
no matter. They are twelve in number, and their entire
area isn't greater than that of Rhode Island and Connecticut combined. They are all of volcanic origin and
volcanic construction. There is nothing there but lava
and pumice stone—except sand and coral. There isn't
a spoonful of legitimate dirt in the entire group.
Eighty or ninety years ago they had a native population
of full 400.000 souls, and they were comfortable, prosperous, and happy. But then the white people came, and
brought trade, and commerce, and education, and complicated diseases, and civilization, and other calamities,
and as a consequence the poor natives began to die
off with wonderful rapidity, so that forty or fifty years
ago the 400,000 had become reduced to 200,000. Then
the white people doubled the educational facilities, and
this doubled the death rate. The nation is doomed.
It will be extinct within fifty years, without a doubt.
Some people in this house may live to hear of the death
of the last of the "Kanakas." In color the natives are
a rich dark brown. The tropical sun and their easy-going
ways have made them rather indolent. They are not a
vicious, but a very gentle, kind-hearted, harmless race.
In the rural districts the women wear a single long loose
gown. But the men don't. [Laughter.] The men
wear,—well, as a general thing, they wear—a smile, or a
pair of spectacles,—or any little thing like that. [Laugh-
ter.] But they are not proud. They don't seem to care
for display. [Laughter.]

In the old times the King was the owner of all the
lands, and supreme head of Church and State. His voice
was superior to all law. If a common man passed by the
King's house without prostrating himself, or came near
the King with his head wet, or even allowed his shadow
to fall upon the King's person, that man had to die.
There was no hope for him. The King exercised absolute authority over the lives and property of his subjects.
He could place a "taboo" (we get that word from the
Hawaiian) upon land, or article, or person, and it was
death for any man to walk on the ground or touch the
article or speak to the person so "tabooed." And this

King, Kamehameha, who died the other day, never had ceased to chafe at the restrictions imposed upon the power of his ancestors by the laws and constitution promulgated by the American missionaries.

Next after the King, at least in authority, came the priests of the old superstition. And they regulated "church affairs"—that is, they decreed the human sacrifices, they captured the victims and butchered them. After the priests came the chiefs, who held land by feudal tenure as they do in England to-day from the King—and did him service. But both the chiefs and priests were little better than slaves to the King. After them came the plebeians, the common men, who were slaves to priests and chiefs and King, a class who were cruelly treated and often killed upon any trifling provocation. After all this—at the bottom of this hideous pyramid of brutality, and superstition, and slavery—came the women, the abject slaves of the whole combination. They did all the work; they were degraded to the level of brutes, and were considered to be no better. They were cruelly maltreated, and they had absolutely no rights nor privileges. It was death for a woman to sit at table with her own husband, and even to eat from a dish from which he had eaten; and at all times it was death for a woman to eat of certain of the rarer fruits of the Islands, at any time, or in any place. Perhaps the men remembered the difficulty between another woman and some fruit some time back and didn't feel justified in taking any more chances. [Laughter.]

But by and by the American missionaries came, and they struck off the shackles from the whole race, breaking the power of the kings and chiefs. They set the common man free, elevated his wife to a position of equality with him, and gave a piece of land to each to hold forever. They set up schools and churches, and imbued the people with the spirit of the Christian religion. If they had had the power to augment the capacities of the people, they could have made them perfect; and they would have done it, no doubt.

The missionaries taught the whole nation to read and write, with facility, in the native tongue. I don't suppose there is to-day a single uneducated person above

eight years of age in the Sandwich Islands! It is the
best educated country in the world, I believe. That has
been all done by the American missionaries. And in a
large degree it was paid for by the American Sunday-
school children with their pennies. I know that I contributed. [Laughter.] I have had nearly two dollars
invested there for thirty years. But I don't mind it. I
don't care for the money [laughter], if it has been doing
good. I don't say this in order to show off. I only
mention it as a gentle humanizing fact that may possibly
have a beneficent effect upon some members of this
audience. [Laughter.]

These natives are very hospitable people indeed—very
hospitable. If you want to stay a few days and nights in
a native's cabin, you can stay and welcome. They will
make you feel entirely at home. They will do everything
they can to make you comfortable. They will feed you
on baked dog, or poi, or raw fish, or raw salt pork,
or fricasseed cats,—all the luxuries of the season.
[Laughter.] Everything the human heart can desire
they will set before you. Perhaps now, this isn't a captivating feast at first glance, but it is offered in all sincerity, and with the best motives in the world, and that
makes any feast respectable whether it is palatable or
not. But if you want to trade, that's quite another thing
—that's business! And the Kanaka is ready for you. He
is a born trader, and he will swindle you if he can. He
will lie straight through from the first word to the last.
Not such lies as you and I tell [laughter], but gigantic
lies, lies that awe you with their grandeur, lies that stun
you with their imperial impossibility. He will sell you a
mole-hill at the market price of a mountain and will lie
it up to an altitude that will make it cheap at the money.
[Laughter.] If he is caught he slips out of it with an
easy indifference that has an unmistakable charm about
it. [Laughter.] Every one of these Kanakas has at
least a dozen mothers—not his own mothers, of course,
but adopted ones. They adhere to the ancient custom
of calling any woman " mother," without regard to her
color or politics [laughter], that they happen to take a
particular liking to. It is possible for each of them to
have one hundred and fifty mothers,—and even that num-

ber will allow of a liberal stretch. This fact has caused some queer questions among people who didn't know anything about it.

They are an odd sort of people. They can die whenever they want to. [Laughter.] They don't mind dying any more than a jilted Frenchman does. When they take a notion to die, they die, and it doesn't make any difference whether there is anything the matter with them or not, and they can't be persuaded out of it. When one of them makes up his mind to die, he just lies down and is as certain to die as though he had all the doctors in the world hold of him! [Laughter.]

This people are peculiarly fond of dogs; not great, magnificent Newfoundlands, or stately mastiffs, or graceful greyhounds, but little mean curs that a white man would condemn to death on general principles. There is nothing about them to recommend them so far as personal appearance is concerned. These people love these puppies better than they love each other, and a puppy always has plenty to eat, even if the rest of the family must go hungry. When the woman rides, the puppy sits in front; when the man rides, the puppy stands behind—he learns to ride horseback with the greatest ease. They feed him with their own hands, and fondle and pet and caress him, till he is a full-grown dog, and then they eat him. Now, I couldn't do that. [Laughter.] I'd rather go hungry two days than eat an old friend that way. [Laughter.] There's something sad about that. [Laughter.] But perhaps I ought to explain that these dogs are raised entirely for the table, and fed exclusively on a cleanly vegetable diet all their lives. Many a white citizen learns to throw aside his prejudices and eat of the dish. After all, it's only our own American sausage with the mystery removed. [Laughter.] A regular native will eat anything—anything he can bite. It is a fact that he will eat a raw fish, fresh from the water; and he begins his meal too, before the fish has breathed his last. Of course, it's annoying to the fish, but the Kanaka enjoys it.

In olden times it used to be popular to call the Sandwich Islanders cannibals. But they never were cannibals.

That is amply proven. There was one there once, but he was a foreign savage, who 'stopped there a while and did quite a business while he stayed. He was a useful citizen, but had strong political prejudices, and used to save up a good appetite for just before election, so that he could thin out the Democratic vote. [Laughter.] But he got tired of that, and undertook to eat an old whaling captain for a change. That was too much for him. He had the crime on his conscience, and the whaler on his stomach, and the two things killed him. [Laughter.] He died. I don't tell this on account of its value as an historical fact [laughter], but only on account of the moral which it conveys. I don't know that I know what moral it conveys, still I know there must be a moral in it somewhere. I have told it forty or fifty times and never got a moral out of it yet. [Laughter.] But all things come to those who wait.

With all these excellent and hospitable ways, these Kanakas have some cruel instincts. They will put a live chicken in the fire just to see it hop about. In the olden times they used to be cruel to themselves. They used to tear their hair and burn their flesh, shave their heads, and knock out an eye or a couple of front teeth, when a great person or a king died—just to testify to their sorrow; and if their grief was so sore that they couldn't possibly bear it, they would go out and scalp a neighbor or burn his house down. And they used to bury some of their children alive when their families were too large. But the missionaries have broken all that up now.

These people do nearly everything wrong end first. They buckle the saddle on the right side, which is the wrong side; they mount a horse on the wrong side; they turn out on the wrong side to let you go by; they use the same word to say "good-by" and "good-morning"; they use "yes" when they mean "no"; the women smoke more than the men do; when they beckon to you to come, they always motion in the oppositte direction; they dance at funerals, and drawl out a dismal sort of dirge when they are peculiarly happy. In their playing of the noble American game of "seven-up," the dealer deals to his right instead of to the left; and what is worse, the ten takes the ace! [Prolonged laughter.] Now, such ignorance as that is reprehensible, and for one, I am glad the missionaries have gone there. [Laughter.]

Now, you see what kind of voters you will have if you take these Islands away from these people, as we are pretty sure to do some day. They will do everything wrong end first. They will make a deal of trouble here, too. Instead of fostering and encouraging a judicious system of railway speculation, and all that sort of thing, they will elect the most incorruptible men to Congress. [Prolonged laughter and applause.] Yes, they will turn everything upside down.

There are about 3,000 white people on the Islands, and they will increase instead of diminishing. They control all the capital, and are at the head of all the enterprises in the Islands.

These white people get to be ministers—political ministers, I mean. There's a perfect raft of them there. Harris is one of them. Harris is minister of—well, he's minister of pretty much everything. [Laughter.] He's a long-legged, light-weight, average lawyer from New Hampshire. Now, if Harris had brains in proportion to his legs, he would make Solomon seem a failure. [Laughter.] If his modesty equaled his vanity, he would make a violet seem ostentatious. And if his learning equaled his ignorance, he would make Humboldt seem as unlettered as the back side of a tombstone. [Laughter.] If his ideas were as large as his words, it would take a man three months to walk around one of them. [Laughter.] Mr. Clemens them reviewed at some length the history of the late and present King of the Sandwich Islands; described the great volcanic eruption of 1840; told several funny stories, and closed his lecture as follows: The land that I have tried to tell you about lies out there in the midst of the watery wilderness, in the very heart of the limitless solitudes of the Pacific. It is a dreamy, beautiful, charming land. I wish I could make you comprehend how beautiful it is. It is a land that seems ever so vague and fairy-like when one reads about it in books. It is Sunday land, the land of indolence and dreams, where the air is drowsy and lulls the spirit to repose and peace, and to forgetfulness of the labor and turmoil and weariness and anxiety of life.

ROBERT COLLYER

Photogravure after a photograph from life

ROBERT COLLYER

CLEAR GRIT

[Lecture by Robert Collyer, pastor of the Church of the Messiah, New York, since 1879 (born in Keighly, Yorkshire, England, December 8, 1823; ——), delivered originally during his pastorate of the Unity Church, Chicago (1860-1879), and in later years repeated with variations in text many times on many platforms in various parts of the country.]

LADIES AND GENTLEMEN:—Clear Grit, as I understand it, and propose to speak of it in this lecture, may be defined as the best there is in a man, blossoming into the best he can do in a sweet and true fashion, as a rose blossoms on a bush or a bird sings in a tree.

It is that fine quality in a man or woman that can never give way except in a true fashion and for good reason; the power to walk barefoot over the flints that lie on the true line of life, rather than to go through soft and flowery ways that deflect from it.

Clear Grit is the power to say No to what may seem to be a multitude of angels when they would counsel you away from a downright loyalty to your instant duty, while if it were possible for you to feel that by following steadily the true path, for all that you can see, you will go into outer darkness and stay there. But that unspeakable felicity may crown the false way, to make no argument about one way or the other, but simply to determine once for all that any torment for being a true man or woman, is to be preferred to any bliss for failing.

Now, you will understand from this, of course, that there is a false and a true in grit, as there is in all great and good things in creation, and that we need to know the one from the other, as the prime condition of being clear grit at all. In Westall's splendid designs for " Paradise Lost," if you have ever seen them, you will remember that in one of them Satan, as he stands on the burning marl with his hand lifted and shouts to his fallen host, is still a mighty angel, erect and strong, and not to be distinguished from his unfallen peers, except for the shadow that begins to pass over his face out of his darkened soul. It is the painter's way of telling a truth we have all seen some time in our life. The truth men like Aaron Burr and Lord Byron, and others I might name, have made clear to us through their lives, that there is nothing in this world so nearly like a splendid angel as a splendid devil.

When I worked at the anvil, as a boy, we would sometimes show the boys who came in with their horses to shoe, a great wonder. We would take a nail-rod and make it white hot; but, then, instead of making a nail, we would plunge the iron, hot as it was, into a pan of brimstone, and it would turn to mere slag. It was the truth I want to teach about clear grit in a crucible. The substance out of which you can forge all sorts of noble things shall be in two men just about alike, and in both it shall be capable of growing white hot under some intense pressure of soul or circumstance. But one man shall dip this substance of his manhood into some infernal element and it will all turn to cinder, while the other man will make what will be like a nail in a sure place.

So Clear Grit, as I think of it, is never base or mean, either in its nature or tendency. Whatever it may be that you compress into this compact vernacular of two syllables, here is the point where you get at the rights of it; the scratch of the diamond that cuts into everything except a diamond. A man may have all sorts of shining qualities; he may be as handsome as Apollo, as plausible as Mercury, and as full of fight as Mars, yet this shall show you, when you scratch him, he is a bit of mere shining paste and no diamond at all; or his faults and failings may be an everlasting regret to those who love him best, as they are in a man like Robert Burns. But because there's Clear Grit in him, because there's a bit of manhood running through his life, as grand and good as ever struggled through this world of ours toward a better; a heart that could gather everything that lives within the circle of its mighty sympathy, from a mouse shivering down there in the furrow, to a saint singing up yonder in Heaven; because there's a heart like that in him, we cling to his knees, we will not let him go; sin-smitten, but mighty, manful man as he is, we gather him into our heart, every one of us, and love him with an everlasting love. [Applause.]

Then, as I am led to see how Clear Grit comes to be an intimate part of your life and mine, I have to trace the root of it, first of all, to a certain austerity and self-denial in our personal character and life. There was a story many years ago going the round of our papers, about a black man who was traveling on one of the Sound steamers from New York to Boston, and found there was no room for him in a stateroom, upstairs or down, and no such chance of his getting comfortably through the night as there would have been for a decent yellow dog. It was a wild night, and was getting dark, when one of the officers on the steamer discovered this man trying to make the best of it in as snug a corner as he could find, pitied his forlorn condition, and thought he would try to help him. He noticed he was not so very black, so he hit on a plan for giving him a stateroom. There would be no sort of trouble about an Indian if he should come and look as well, generally, as this negro did. And so he said to himself, "I will run him in as an Indian." He went up to the man, looked him in the eyes, and said: "You are an Indian, ain't you?" Well, Douglass, for it was Fred, saw in an instant what the man was after. I don't know how he felt, but I know exactly how I should have felt if I had been in his place. I should have felt like giving a little nod, and saying, "Well, yes, I guess I'm an Indian." But what this black man did was to look right back into the eyes of the officer, and say: "No, I'm a nigger," to curl himself up as the officer turned and left him, and get what comfort he could in his gusty nest. [Applause.] Now there you touch the first thing I know of in Clear Grit, and that is the power and the will to say No to every temptation toward a good time that can come between a man and his manhood.

And I think these temptations usually begin down among our passions and appetites. I suppose it is not a rule without an exception that the man who cares most of all about himself, cares very little about anybody else; or that in proportion to the fuss a man makes about his dinner, for instance, is the utter worthlessness of that man to have any decent woman cook for him. I think a very fair sort of man may sometimes make a fuss about his dinner, and my dear wife thought so, too. Isaac Walton said "that very good dishes should only be eaten by very good men," and that's the reason I have sometimes thought that when we ministers go round to one of the best houses in the parish about tea-time, as we sometimes do, and are invited to stay to tea, which we generally do, the good lady is sure to bring out her best cakes and preserves, and to broil her tenderest chicken. She knows what dear old Walton knew, that very good things should only be eaten by very good men, so the minister gets them, of course. [Laughter and applause.] And thinks, no doubt, as St. Thomas à Becket thought, when a man saw him eating the breast of a pheasant as if he liked it very much, and said to him sourly: "That is no dinner for a saint of the Church." "One man," the saint replied, "may be a glutton on horse-beans, while another man may eat the breast of a pheasant like a gentleman, and be a good man all the same."

All this is true, of course, but it is no less true that the devouring determination in a great majority of men and women nowadays to have a good time in getting every good thing they hanker after, and dirt-cheap at that, if they can, is one of the most dangerous evils we have to encounter if we want, above all things in this world, to be Clear Grit. "It is a fortunate thing for the world," a man of another race and nation said to Thomas Guthrie, the fine old Scotchman, "that you Anglo-Saxons eat and drink so much, because you have such a genius for hard work and for going ahead in everything you take hold of, that, if it were not for this, the nations round about would have no chance to compete with you. You would be the masters of the world." Well, it was true, no doubt, and only one truth of a good many that belong to this side of our character and our life.

Now, let us see how this works. I went to live in Chicago when the population numbered about a hundred thousand souls. I lived there twenty years, so that I was quite intimate with the life of that great city. In the early times I think I knew every man who had come to the front, and was wielding a real power of any sort for good. I do not remember one among them who did not begin his life as a poor man's son. They all came up, so far as I could trace them, without any good time at all, except as boys ought to have a good time in growing strong as a steel bar on plenty of wholesome work and what we should call hard fare; fighting their way to an education through a great deal of effort, and then, when they were ready, coming out West from the East with that half-dollar in their pocket, and that little lot of things done up in a valise that you will notice every young fellow is said to start with, who ends by making his mark or making a fortune. [Applause.] A great German writer says that riches are always harder on youth than poverty, and that many a man sees now he would not for much money have had much money in his youth. "When we started the 'Edinburgh Review,'" Sidney Smith says, "we thought of putting this motto on the cover: 'We cultivate literature on a little oatmeal,' but it was so literally true that we concluded not to tell." And John Bryant, of Princeton, in Illinois, told me once that when his brother, William Cullen Bryant, was a young man, he durst not have taken a five years' lease of his life; but William, he said, adopted the habits of a Spartan, omitting, of course, the stealing. He would take some brown bread and butter, with a glass of milk or water, for his breakfast, then he would do a bit of real hard work, and then go down to his office; and, with very little alteration, John thought he was keeping up that habit down to the time that we had the talk, and thought also that this had a great deal to do with both the length and the worth of his brother's most noble career. "I shall be glad if you will stay and dine with me, but when my wife is away, I just browse around," Mr. Lincoln said once to a friend when he was President of the Republic and living in the White House in Washington. "Just browse around!" How much that fine temperance in eating and drinking, and in all the habits of his life, had to do with the man's Clear Grit, we can only or hardly guess. [Applause.] And so, turn where you will, I think you are sure to touch this as one of the first things in Clear Grit: "to make much of myself, I must make sure of myself; in my power to say No to these good servants but bad masters, my passions and appetites."

We all know, however, there must be more than this to make a man Clear Grit. The power must begin there, but it cannot end there. There are hosts of men who have this quality so far as I have tried to touch it. They are hardy and temperate, they have pluck and courage, but not an atom of it is used for any other purpose than to serve some end of their own. And so they may become simply so many instances of the truth I have told already, that there is nothing in this world so like a splendid angel as a splendid devil.

And so the next thing we want to make Clear Grit is the power and the will to help others even more than you help yourself. When George Peabody died the Queen of England sorrowed with thousands more for that great, generous banker. But another man died about the same time in England for whom no tears were shed except by a few friends who knew him and loved him, but who did better still, I think, with his money than Peabody. This man was Faraday, the prince of chemists in his time. It came out after his death that as far back as 1832 Faraday's income was about £5,000 a year, and he could easily have made it ten or fifteen thousand, but from that time he gave up his whole income, except enough to keep himself and his family in good case, that he might devote his whole time to the great science in which he was such a master, and in that way enrich the whole world. He died a poor man, when, I suppose, he might have been a millionaire, but then the world was richer by untold millions for what the man had done. [Applause.] That is the second thing in Clear Grit. After the power to save yourself comes the power to give yourself. There is an old city in France where, down to the middle of the last century, the people had to depend upon the wells for their water. But one dry summer these wells gave out, and there was hardly any water to be found.

In a poor hovel at that time a child lay sick of a fever, moaning for water, and the mother had none to give him. He worried through, however, and grew to be a man. But then it was found that he was a miser, the closest and most niggardly man ever heard of in that town. He lived alone, in the most miserable fashion, and he was so unpopular with the folks that the boys would hoot him and pelt him as he went along the street. Then he died, and it was found that he had left an enormous fortune, every penny of which was to go for a grand system of water-works, and from that fountain the water pours plentifully into every home down to this day. [Applause.] There you touch the second thing in Clear Grit —the power to help others, no matter what it may cost you, when the thing faces you as a clear duty. Every ounce of the power that man had, from the day he made his resolution to the day he died, went into Clear Grit, so he was a miser and a martyr together, and I think sometimes that when the poor soul went out of him, all crippled, as it must have been, by that stern struggle to save money through all those years, it was very beautiful to those who watched him from above and knew all about it. Just as when we still see, on our streets or in their homes, the men that came back to us all broken from the war for the Republic, we feel that no perfection in form or feature can ever be robed to us in such a noble beauty as the scarred faces and shorn trunks of our boys in blue. [Applause.]

And this brings me to the last thing I want to touch in this exposition of Clear Grit. When a man has these two things in his life—first, the power to save himself, and then the power to give himself—and he sees something to be done and knows he ought to do it, he never stops to count the cost, but, as we say, he pitches right in and does it there and then. That was what our soldiers did, what the old miser did, what Faraday did, and what all men do who show their Clear Grit right through. There it stands, the thing to be done, and there is the man with the grit to do it. Something comes into him, he cannot tell you what. He wonders, very likely, after it's all done, how he did it, but then it's done once and forever. The power has possessed him as Italy possessed

Garibaldi, as Germany possessed Bismarck, as Methodism possessed Wesley, as freedom for the slave possessed Garrison, and as honesty possessed Abraham Lincoln. [Applause.] It comes and fills the heart, as the sight of the young maiden fills the heart of the young man who goes into a room at 7 o'clock this evening, with a heart as free as that of an unmated swallow, meets a girl he never saw before, and at 10 o'clock that evening comes out of that room a captive for life. [Applause.]

And once let this power take hold of such a man, then he cares nothing about what risk he has to run or how hard it is to do—he puts on the steam and goes ahead and does it. I well remember in our great fire in Chicago, a slender young man who undertook to carry a lady and her little child in a light buggy out of the burning city. He was going down Michigan avenue, the street was crowded to a jam, and he had to stop and wait for the jam to get loose. All at once there came along behind him a great fellow driving a furniture-wagon, who yelled to him, with an oath, to get out of the way or he would run into him. "I cannot stir," the man said quietly, "and this lady is sick and has a little babe with her not a week old. Now, you must be quiet and stay where you are, and we will all come out together very soon." Then the brute swore a great oath that he would come down and pull him out of that and twist the thing out of his way. He jumped out of his wagon to do it. The young man jumped too. They were both on the ground at the same instant, but before the giant had time to strike him or clutch him, the young man had sent his fist about where the brute's dinner would go if he could get any that day, and that brought him down. But as he was coming down, he caught him with the other fist right under the chin, and that brought him up. "Now," he said, "you get onto that wagon and do just as I tell you, or I will give you the greatest licking you ever had since you were born." [Applause.] The fellow swore horribly, mounted the wagon, and drove down the avenue at the back of the buggy when the jam gave way. But the best of the story is this, and I vouch for its truth, that this young man was a minister in our city, in good standing, a mighty man in preaching and prayer, as I know, a man who wouldn't hurt a mouse, and in every way a gentleman. But the Clear Grit in him at that dire moment could only show itself in the one way; and there it was. He cared nothing for himself, only for the helpless woman and the little babe; and as he told me the story in a modest fashion on the train one day after the fire, I clasped his hand and said to him: " My friend, you can preach grand sermons, and you can say noble prayers, and you can do a great many grand things, as I know very well, but let me tell you that you never did a grander or diviner thing than on that day when, for the sake of that mother and little child, you went for that great brute, left hand first and then followed it with your right, and don't you forget it." [Loud applause.] Clear Grit, then, never cares for consequences when it's evident the thing has got to be done; you can't crush it, you can't turn it, it goes right on to its purpose, and that purpose is accomplished when the man gets through.

And now it would be very pleasant for me to go right on and talk about Clear Grit as other men have shown it in a grand or good fashion, but this is not my main purpose. I want to make some simple applications of the truth I am trying to tell, that will come right home to your life and mine, and show us how we can all know of what Grit we are made, by instances and evidences like these I want to mention. And so I will divide my lecture into three parts, for the sake of simplicity, and go on to say that the first truth of Clear Grit, to me, lies in the power to do a good, honest day's work; second, in the power to make a good home and take care of it, and raise a good family of children; and, third, the power to lose no time about it, but go ahead and see to these things while the bloom and glory and strength of our life beats in our hearts.

And I put the power to do a good, honest day's work first, because eight and twenty years of hard work, first in the factory and then in the forge, as well as such light as comes to me from my present profession as a minister, convinces me, beyond all question, that this power to do a good, honest day's work lies at the root of every true life. And yet it is just what great numbers of men try not to do, as if they felt that the true thing means to get the most money possible for the least work possible, and very often for the poorest work, too; and that the best success they can attain to in this world is that which comes through what we call " good luck." I think young men begin their life in this new world bewildered by the opportunities that open before them to make a fortune at a stroke. There is no such instant need to do something solid and steady, the moment they are out of school or college, as there is in poorer countries, and so they coquette with the chances that seem as thick as blackberries to get along easily; they will try this and then that, and generally fail at everything they do try, if this is all they want to do, and then wait for something to turn up. Now, we ought never to forget that Mr. Micawber, after trusting to his luck for all those years, waiting for something to turn up, had to strip at last and turn up something for himself. He failed entirely to do anything until he began to do something in dead earnest, and every dollar he made when he did begin to succeed over there in Australia was, no doubt, a draft honestly indorsed by his brain and muscle and dug out of the solid gold of his own manhood. So waiting for something to turn up is the greatest mistake a young man can make who wants to show his Grit. You know that, of all the adventurers that ever trod the Pacific slope waiting for something to turn up, not a man found the gold that was right there under his feet. It was found at last by a man who was doing good, honest work, digging a mill-race for a mill to grind corn. Mr. Smiles, in one of his capital books tells the story of a man in the last century who undertook to make a steam-engine. He succeeded, so far as you could see, in making a very good engine indeed. The lever lifted to a charm, the piston answered exactly, the wheels turned beautifully, and nothing could be better so far. But when it came to be fairly tried there was one drawback, and it was this: " The moment you tackled anything to it, it stood stock-still. On its own hook it would work beautifully, turn its own wheels faultlessly, but the moment you wanted it to lift a pound beside, then the lever and piston and wheels struck work, and, as it was made in an age and country in which to do nothing was to be counted a gentleman, the thing was called ' Evans' Gentlemanly Engine.' " Now, who doesn't know men whose action resembles that gentlemanly engine? What little they do they do for themselves. You can find no fault with their motion, and they may be polished to perfection, especially in those parts that are brass or steel, but they would not raise a blister on their hands to save their souls. Their one motto is to take care of number one, and in doing this they usually come to one of three things—either to depend on the old man, their father, if he has anything to spare, or on their friends, if they have any left, or, as I think, the saddest of all—go down to Washington to hunt for an office they know they can't fill, and draw money they know they don't earn; the meanest thing, I think, such a man can do. [Applause.] They bury their talent in a napkin, like the man in the Gospels; and I think sometimes that by the time they're through, they'll be mean enough and selfish enough to be ready to say when they go to their account, " Lord, there's the talent thou gavest me, but that's my napkin; give me my napkin back." [Applause.]

This is the first proof a man can give that there's no Clear Grit in him—to do nothing in particular, or come as near as he can to his own idea of a gentleman by dodging everything that is not easy and light. The question, What makes a gentleman? is not an easy one to answer, but between such a man as that and a good blacksmith or carpenter or ploughman or wood-chopper, a man who throws all his manhood into his day's work, there can be no sort of comparison. A hard-handed mechanic is beyond all question the truer gentleman, as well as the better man, and in the good time coming everybody will say so that has a right to be anybody. Honest work, well done, then, is the first proof I can give of Clear Grit. This does not mean, however, merely to work hard, because to work honestly is more essential than to work hard at anything. I had a shop-mate in the forge who was just as good a blacksmith when he did his level best as any man I ever knew, but it seems to me now that he was the most ingenious fellow at getting up any sort of a lie in iron who ever stood at the anvil. Now, a man like this may work hard, but, on the whole, the harder he works, the worse it is, because he just works hard at lying, and now poor Jack stands to me for a good many working men.* It is no matter where they're found or what they do; they may not work in iron as Jack did, but they are forgers for all that, if they are only ingenious for dishonesty and make their money by make-believes. I could show you a pair of iron gates in one of the great museums in London made by a blacksmith two hundred years ago, down in Nottinghamshire, for a great nobleman's park. I had never heard of the man until I saw the gates and found his name on the Catalogue, and if he had never done that piece of work, we should never have heard of him again. He was only a smith, he did that work with his own rough hands, but he did it so honestly and so well, it was so beautiful when it was finished, that people would come from far and wide in England to look at those gates, and then they were fain to preserve them in the museum as one of the wonders it does your heart good to see, and makes good the poet's line, "A thing of beauty is a joy forever." And so I say the blacksmith who works honestly and well from Monday morning to Saturday night, doing his good, honest day's work, and being a man to match the work he is doing, is beyond all question the nobler and better man than the minister who dawdles along through the week, doing nothing in particular one way or the other, and then on the Sunday morning preaches a poor, worthless sermon. I know that, because I have done both. [Laughter.]

I said the second proof of the truth I would tell is the power to make a good home, and to raise, if it pleases God, a noble family of children; while the good home presupposes that indispensable preliminary to all good homes, a good wife and a good husband—and I say wife and husband, because I really believe there are numbers of men who marry but don't get a wife, and a good many women who marry but don't get a husband, and perhaps never find it out until the mistake is beyond all remedy, excepting that of going, let us say, to Dakota to get a divorce. And I think sometimes the way this comes about is this: That a great many young women, before they get married, are only anxious to have what

*Jack died in the workhouse.

they call all the accomplishments; but they don't mean by this how to make good, wholesome bread, or a bowl of soup, how to roast a piece of beef, how to boil a potato (a very fine art, indeed, you may say), how to darn a stocking, and make a shirt and iron it, and keep a home smelling as sweet as wild roses, and shining like a new silver dollar; but I may mention among the modern accomplishments how to do tatting and embroidery, how to draw "wonderful shepherdesses with pink eyes," how to talk impossible French, and discourse music so difficult that when you hear it you remember Johnson's grim joke, when a friend, as they listened to some music, said, "That's very fine music, Doctor"; and the old bear said, "I wish it was impossible." [Laughter.] Now, that is what no small number call an education. All the accomplishments except those that are indispensable to a good wife the young woman gets, and then she gets married. And the young man gets an education that is just about as delectable to fit him for a husband. We call it sowing his wild oats. The worst of it I dare not tell. The better side of it very often is to train him away from all that is domestic and delicate and unspeakably sacred in a good home; to teach him to play billiards instead of reading books, to prefer cards to any other sort of picture, and sometimes to be more familiar with the inside of the hells of the city than the churches. Then he goes into society, scented and curled, meets the young woman with all the accomplishments, believes her to be the exception to all her sex in angelic beauty and excellence, gives her what heart he has left, and so the match is made, and they are wedded wife and husband so long as they both shall live, if they can stand it. [Applause.] Now, such a marriage reminds me of a wedding we had once in Yorkshire, where I was raised. As the man came out of church with his bride on his arm he met an old comrade, who said: "There, lad, I wish thee much joy; thou's got to t'end of all thy trouble." Well, this was very good of the comrade, and so he said: "Thank thee, lad," and went on his way rejoicing. But in no long time he found he had got married without getting a wife. It was a bad job altogether. Going on the street about three months after, he met his comrade again, and said to him, with

a very long face: "I thought thou told me, John, when I
came out of Guiseley church that morning, that I had
got to t'end of all my trouble." "Oh, yes, I did tell thee
so," the other man replied, with a grin, "but I didn't tell
thee which end." [Laughter and applause.] Then
there's another match not quite so bad as this, but still
bad enough, and the ruin of a great many homes, where
the husband and wife are both capable, both domestic,
and seem to have everything the heart can wish for except a good, honest love. The man is clever, so is the
woman; she wants a home, he can make one; she wants a
husband, he wants a housekeeper; he will bring in the
living and foot the bills, and she will slave and save on
one gown a year and her old bonnet, done up nobody
knows how many times, and hear a good deal of growling,
then, about the extravagance of women. Now, a good
home can no more bloom out of such a life as that than
a damask rose can bloom on an iceberg; it's tyrant and
slave, or else it's two slaves. It's two strings full of nothing but harsh discords constantly under the bow of the
daily life.

But there is a wedding that's just as good as gold, and
sure to result in a good, true home, and that is when the
man and woman, understanding what a good home
means, are drawn together by the true Providence which
still makes all true matches, in spite of the maneuverings
of our prejudice and pride; when they come together in
a fair equality, not, as the poet sings, as moonlight and
the sunlight, but as perfect music unto noble words.
[Applause.]

I was once at a meeting in which a very notable
Woman's Rights advocate was speaking about the essential equality of the sexes in the wedded life, when, rather
to my astonishment, she looked right at me and said:
"Robert Collyer, I hope when thee marries a man and
woman, thee does not ask the woman to say she will
obey the man, without asking the man to say he will
obey the woman, so that it may be fair on both sides."
I thought for a moment of telling a story that illustrates
so well what a woman will say to get the man she has
made up her mind to marry—the story of the woman who
declared she would never promise to obey, would get

around it by some means, would never say the word, and the minister who was to marry them heard all about it before he came to the wedding. The word came in as the service went on, and the woman followed the service until she came to this word, and then she was seized with a very bad fit of coughing. "Take your time," the good man said, "there is no sort of hurry; we will begin again." They began again, but she broke down at this word "obey," and the cough came on worse than ever. "We will try once more," he said, for ministers are very patient; but once more the bride broke down, and then the minister, I fear, lost his temper, and said, "Madam, it is clear to me that you cannot go through this service, and so I cannot marry you," but, at this instant, as he was saying these words, she lifted up her voice and said "obey," with an emphasis that almost took his breath away. [Laughter and applause.] I thought for an instant of telling that story, but what I said was this: "Madam, I never do ask any woman to say she will obey the man, and let the man go free, because some of the best women I have ever known said they would obey the man, and never did, beyond what was fair and right, and I have found out, therefore, that this is a promise more honored, very often, in the breach than in the observance." [Applause.]

Now, I know the common idea of the relation of the man and woman is this: That the man is the volume and the woman the supplement; but this, no doubt, is the truth, that the man is, let us say, the first volume, good enough as far as it goes, and rather interesting to study, but, if there is to be no second, a good deal more of an aggravation than if there was not any; a story half told and then broken off, as they do in the magazines, just where you feel you must know the sequel, or else it is very little use knowing what you do. The man is as good when he's made, if we follow the ancient record, as a man can be without a woman. But then there seems to be nothing even for the Creator to do but to put him to sleep until he makes a woman, and when he brings her to the man and defines their relation, you will notice they are not made one and that one the man, but they're one in a perfect oneness, as it seems, of equality, and that is

the only way to live in a true wedded life so far. Let
the man say " you shall," and the woman say " I won't,"
and let them keep running on that line, and there will be
a smash as sure as fate, or, what is worse than any such
catastrophe, imperious tyranny on the one side and
craven fear on the other. But from Eastport and San
Francisco a youth and maiden shall come with this equal
reverence each for the other in their hearts. They shall
see many youths and maidens far more beautiful and
winsome to others than they are, but they shall never see
those they are looking for until they meet some day,
somewhere, and all at once it flashes on them that they
are meant for husband and wife. It is no matter then if
the one is rich and the other poor, or the woman is
beautiful and the man is homely, or that they have met
by what seems to be a mere accident, or that the world
wonders at the match. Theirs is still the greater wonder
that there could be such a man and woman in this world,
and then that they could have found each other when
there were so many chances, as it seems to them, against
it. I tell you love and troth like that abides where there
is no marrying and giving in marriage, but where men
and women are as the angels of God. [Applause.] Yet,
I feel quite free to say this is no snap judgment, but
as a rule we can trust, if my observation is worth
anything, the weddings that turn out usually the
best are those in which the young folks know each other
in a pure, sweet fashion, it may be for years, before they
take this step. If they live in the country, they go to
school together, and singing-school, and apple-bees, and
huskings; he knows all about her bread and butter and
pies and doughnuts, and other things dear to the heart of
man. I mean, of course, his stomach, by very much experience. And she knows about his faculty for holding
his own and going ahead on the farm or in the work-
shop, and what kind of temper he has, and how he can
manage a span of horses in a sleigh on a frosty night and
hold the reins with one hand. [Laughter and applause.]
And if she is in the kitchen when he calls to see her, she
doesn't rush upstairs to put on a silk dress and a simper;
she comes in just as she is to see him, and if he gives her
a kiss, as he has a perfect right to do, his breath doesn't

smell of cloves. They are clean, honest, wholesome young folk, who know they have good reason why they should love and trust each other, and then when they are made one, their life blends sweetly together, as two streams run together to make a river, and so they live on, full of content, to their golden wedding. I do not say one word to show that the man and wife will never say a sharp thing to each other, or get up a little breeze, for, if my own experience goes for anything, I think they are pretty sure to do that now and then; but then I think also that a thunderstorm can clear the atmosphere under the roof as well as it can above the roof, if it be not a cruel storm. [Applause.] So when I hear people say they have lived together five and twenty years and never had the least difference, I have wondered whether they have not had a good deal of indifference. I think a pair of clams could live as quiet and even a life as that, but I don't want to be one of the clams. The truth is that the best woman who ever lived with a man may say things to her husband now and then she will let no other woman say about him, or they will get such a piece of her mind as they never thought of getting, and the best husband may now and then make his will known to his wife in tones so imperious that if he heard another man use them to her, he would lash out and knock him down if he was a Quaker in good standing, for daring to speak in that way to the mother of his children. [Applause.]

I said just now a love and troth like that abides where there is no marrying or giving in marriage, but where men and women are like the angels of God. Chance and change make no difference, but on the golden wedding day, after fifty years of such a life together, the glory of the maiden of twenty cannot be seen by reason of the glory which excelleth in the good old wife of seventy. [Applause.]

Then I said the next thing I consider indispensable to a good home and a true man and womanhood is a fine family of children, because there is no question we can consider in our generation, in America, of a deeper moment than this of the generation to come. It is the gravest problem we can sit down to study. Figures of our births and deaths show us that the American who

has been longest on the soil seems to be losing ground,
and the newcomer from the world over is taking his
place, and the best wisdom of the country makes the citizen responsible for this sad state of things. It is said
there are multitudes of men whose fathers were willing
to die for their country in the great old time
we remember who are not willing to live for it now,
and that the daughters of good women, who
could give their husbands and sweethearts, and
work their own fingers to the bone to defend the land
then, are not willing now to give sons and daughters to
people it. Now, one of the things I recollect with most
pride about my great old mother country was her homes
full of children. Everybody, as it seems to me, had plenty
of children. Six or eight was a good family, ten to fifteen
was a large family, and if there was not over-much to give
them, they made the best of what they had, and said God
would send the meat if he sent the mouths; and then, if
it came very hard to find meat for so many mouths, my
own experience leads me to the conclusion that they did
as a man did on Nantucket I heard of one summer. He
raised a mighty brood of children, lads and lasses, on a
rather small place, and when some one said to him, " How
in the world do you manage to feed so many children on
that small farm?" "Oh, it is no trouble at all," he answered; "I find out what they don't like, and give them
plenty of that, so we get along very well." [Laughter.]
The consequence of this great income of children in the
motherland is this, that the common people, the families
at the foundation of the English life, never die out. They
hold their own through all the generations, they fill the
land full, and send out great swarms for the new hives
the Divine Husbandman has provided here, and out in
Australia, and over in Africa and India, and wherever besides they are needed. When the son of William the Conqueror was killed by a glancing arrow in the New Forest,
more than seven hundred years ago, a man named
Purkiss, as the story runs, found the body of the King
as he went through the forest with a load of charcoal, and
carried it to Winchester on his cart for burial. I don't
know how it may be now, but fifty years ago, if you had
gone to that new forest in Hampshire, the odds are that

you might meet a man named Purkiss, going down that same road with a load of charcoal. His family outlived the oaks that were acorns when William Rufus fell, for aught I know, on the same spot, and he will be there, going for a load of charcoal, when Macaulay's traveler comes from New Zealand to stand on a broken arch of London Bridge and sketch the ruins of St. Paul's. [Applause.]

In what we call the good old times—say three hundred years ago—a family lived on the border between England and Scotland, with one daughter of a marvelous homeliness. Her name was Meg. She was a capital girl, as homely girls generally are. She knew she had no beauty, so she made sure of quality and faculty. But the Scotch say that "while beauty may not make the best kail, it looks best by the side of the kail-pot." So Meg had no offer of a husband, and was likely to die in what we call "single blessedness." Everybody on the border in those days used to steal, and their best "holt," as we say, was cattle. If they wanted meat and had no money, they would go out and steal as many beef-cattle as they could lay their hands on, from somebody on the other side of the border. Well, they generally had no money, and they were always wanting beef, and they could always be hung for stealing by the man they stole from if he could catch them, and so they had what an Irishman would call a fine time entirely. [Laughter.] One day a young chief, wanting some beef as usual, went out with part of his clan, came upon a splendid herd on the lands of Meg's father, and went to work to drive them across to his own. But the old fellow was on the lookout, mustered his clan, bore down on the marauders, beat them, took the young chief prisoner, and then went home to his peel very much delighted. Meg's mother, of course, wanted to know all about it, and then she said, " Noo, laird, what are you gaun to do with the prisoner?" " I am gaun to hang him," the old man thundered, "just as soon as I have had my dinner." " But I think ye're noo wise to do that," she said. " He has got a braw place, ye ken, over the border, and he is a braw fellow. Now, I'll tell ye what I would do. I would give him his chance to be hung or marry o'or Meg." It struck the old man as a good idea, and so he went presently down into the dungeon, told the young fellow to get ready to be hung in thirty minutes, but then got round to the other alternative, and offered to spare his life if he would marry Meg, and give him the beef into the bargain. He had heard something about Meg's wonderful want of beauty, and so, with a fine Scotch prudence, he said: " Ye will let me see her, laird, before I mak' up my mind, because maybe I would rather be hung." "Aye, mon, that's fair," the old chief answered, and went in to bid the mother get Meg ready for the interview. The mother did her best, you may be sure, to make Meg look winsome, but when the poor fellow saw his unintentional intended he turned round to the chief and said: "Laird, if ye have nae objection, I think I would rather be hung."   [Laughter.] "And sae ye shall, me' lad, and welcome," the old chief replied, in a rage. So they led him out, got the rope around his neck; and then the young man changed his mind, and shouted: "Laird, I'll tak' her." So he was marched back into the castle, married before he had time to change his mind, if that was possible, and the tradition is that there never was a happier pair in Scotland, and never a better wife in the world than Meg. [Applause.] But I have told the story because it touches this point, of the way they hold their own over there when there are great families of children. They tell me that the family flourishes famously still; no sign of dying out or being lost about it. Meg's main feature was a very large mouth, and now in the direct line in almost every generation the neighbors and friends are delighted, as they say, to get Meg back. "Here's Meg again," they cry when a child is born with that wonderful mouth. Sir Walter Scott was one of the descendants of the family. He had Meg's mouth, in a measure, and was very proud of it when he would tell the story.

A good home and a good family of children—that is the great hope of your life and mine, and the life of our Republic. So I tell you that when the father was willing to die for his country in the great old time, and the son is not willing to live for it now in raising up, please God, a noble line of sons and daughters, there is something radically wrong in that home. I need not tell you what a difficulty I encounter in touching this matter in any way, and I can hardly tell you how impossible I have found it to put my meaning into words. But I speak for this which should give every man courage, when I say whatever the reason may be, if there be one, for keeping the home empty or only half full, I think it is the most fatal blow any man can strike, either at his own soul or the soul of his country. For it is not merely what we may take from the measure of life, but what we may take from its hope and joy. What would have been the result, think you, if something like this had been hidden away in a secret chamber in Stratford-on-Avon, or in the auld clay biggen, where Robert Burns was born, or in a farmhouse on the Rappahannock, where George Washington was born, or in a poor cabin in Kentucky, where a child was born and baptized by the name of Abraham Lincoln, or in many homes beside that were out of sight then, as ours are now; but now they are lifted and set on the shining summits of the world. I think sometimes I could wish no worse hell for my worst enemy, if I ever take to bad wishing, than that one should haunt him in the world to come, wherever he goes, and say, " I might have come into the great Commonwealth of America and made it rich beyond all computation by my gift from on High; but I had to come through your home, if I came at all, and you were not man enough, or woman enough, to receive me. You broke down the frail footway by which I was trying to cross over into the life down there, and then you thought you had circumvented Providence and done a clever thing." [Applause.]

I said the third condition of Clear Grit is this: that a man shall make sure, as soon as he can, all this is true as Gospel, and order his life accordingly. Because it is a great mistake in a young man to think that he can wait as long as he will before he begins to gather these conditions about him I have tried to describe—a true wife, a good home, and such a family as he can find in his heart; and, then, when he has made his fortune and can keep a wife and family in a certain social standing, with all the luxuries he wants, he thinks he has done his whole duty. If you ask him why he does this, he will tell you he cannot do any better; he cannot ask a woman to marry him

out of a mansion and go to live in what he would call a
cabin.   The woman he wants could not live in a cabin if
she would, and would not if she could.   " She is not fit to be
a poor man's wife," he says, and so he cannot ask her to
marry him until he has got a good income.   Now, by
the time a man has cut his wisdom teeth, he begins to
find out some secrets on that question, I would like to
mention.   First of all, he finds out that the woman who is
not fit to be a poor man's wife, as a general rule, is not
fit to be any man's wife, especially in a land and life
where no man knows how soon he may be poor—and
most men of this sort are poor two or three times in the
course of their lifetime.   Suppose, again, that the woman
is fit to be a poor man's wife, and, therefore, all the fitter
to be a rich man's wife, and he dare not ask her to leave
her father's mansion and live with him in a poor man's
home, but "Lets I dare not wait upon I would" until
she's thirty or more and he is thirty-five to forty, and
then proposes and starts off, as he imagines, all right at
last.   One of the first things she tells him, most probably,
is this : that she would have jumped at him ten years ago
if he had only said so ; she wanted him to say so, and was
heavy of heart because he did not see as she did, how
important it was that they should not put off the time too
long, and would have infinitely preferred a four-room
cottage and a dinner of herbs, if he was there to share it,
to all the blessings his money can bring when the bloom
of their youth is over.   So one of the greatest mistakes
a young man can make is to "shunt over," shall I say, on
a sidetrack, and wait ten or fifteen years for a train of
circumstances that will enable him to get married and
have a home.   Very sad altogether is the outlook of the
man who hears the voice say to him in his Eden when he
is, let us say, twenty-five, "Here is the woman I have
made for thee," and answers, "I cannot take her yet for
ten or fifteen years to come."   It must be a very sacred
reason that can make a man do this, because, while he is
saving money, he is wasting life—his own life and another—and all that is hidden in the secret places of life
and time.   And I speak by the Book when I say this, in
the most literal sense.   In the best statistical tables I
could find when I was thinking of these questions, those

of Scotland, made out by Dr. Starke, the register-general
of that time, it was shown that from the age of twenty to
twenty-five twice as many bachelors die as married men.
I was appalled when I read this, at the risk I had run in
staying single until I was almost twenty-five [laughter],
and thought if I had it to do over again I would take my
chance of living. From twenty-five to thirty, he says, of
every thousand men that die the proportion is eight
married, fourteen single. From thirty to thirty-five, eight
married, fifteen single; and so on to eighty and eighty-
five, when you can give it up as a bad job. But the whole
average gives the married man nineteen years more of
life than the single man. So you see we still raise
martyrs—only they die now, not for faith, but for fear.
[Laughter.] The average for single women is a little
better, and so it ought to be, because they are not so
much to blame as the men. But the whole tale of a
single life, from the time when the call comes to the man
and maiden to plight their troth and make their home, is
a tale of heavy risks, against which I know of no insurance but the minister's wedding fee. And what young
men and women lose beside in saying "It shall not be
spring until—let us say—the end of June," I can only
leave to their good sense and yours. About all the birds
that sing in the woods begin to be a little silent by the
end of June, and all the spring flowers are dead then, and
the best of the spring is over and gone for the year. So
the weddings that are almost as sad as funerals to me,
sometimes, are those that might have come, and should
have come, in the May days of our life. And so, if any
young man who hears me has been waiting like that, and
will go right away and pop the question before Sunday,
the money he paid for his ticket to this lecture will be
one of the best investments he ever made in his life.
[Laughter and applause.]

One thing more will complete this question of Clear
Grit, so far as I propose to follow it: and that is, when a
man has got things about as I have tried to describe
them, he shall feel sure he's one of the happiest men anywhere on the planet, and settle down to live his life to
this good purpose. It is the curse, and the blessing also,
of our American life that we are never quite content. We

all expect to go somewhere before we die, or do something that will give us a far better time than we can have now. We are going to have a good time in the future; just let us make our fortune and get everything as we want it, and be able to do as we wish, and then we say we are going to be as happy as the day is long. Well, I had an old neighbor once, a blacksmith, who got that notion into his head. He said, "When I get money enough to retire, me and my wife are going to have a real good time." By and by he had got all the money he wanted, sold out his forge, and began, as he thought, with his wife, to have a good time. He slept in the morning until he couldn't sleep another wink to save him. Then he began to get up at the old hour by the clock. He went round to see everybody and everything he could think of, read his paper all through, pottered in his garden until he got a crick in his back and a pain in his knees, and then he went to the man that had bought him out and said: "Any time when you want somebody to come in and lend a hand, you just ask me, and I won't charge you nothing." [Applause.] I knew an old gentleman and lady who came from England a great many years ago and went to work to make a fortune, but always said that just as soon as they had made their fortune they would go back home. They could never be happy in this country; dear old England was the place for them; if they could once get back to that blessed old home, there wouldn't be a wish left in their hearts to be satisfied. In about twenty years they found they were independent, sold out their business, and prepared to go back to England and the felicity of which they had been dreaming so long. Their old home was in Cheshire, so their port was Liverpool. They thought they would stay a few days in Liverpool to get a foretaste of the joy before they went forward to Cheshire; and so they went about Liverpool to enjoy themselves with all their might. At the end of three days, the old man said: "Wife, I don't think Liverpool is exactly what we expected, is it?" "Husband," the old wife said, "I don't think England is what we expected, either." And then he said again: "If things are no better when we get to the old place in Cheshire, I shall vote for going back to Milwaukee."

"Oh, husband," she said, "I am ready to go back this moment. Let's go *home*." They called it home at last over here. And he answered: "Well, I don't know but you're right; but as we have come to try Cheshire and the old place, we had better carry out the programme." And so they did. They went back, stayed there six weeks, took their passage on a steamer at the end of that time, made a bee-line for Milwaukee, where he went again into business. They have been dead now some years, but when I knew them they were just as happy as the day was long. They had got *home*. The bane of our life is our discontent. We say we will work so long, and then we will begin to enjoy ourselves; but we find it is very much as Thackeray said: "When I was a boy," he said, "I wanted some taffy. It was a shilling. I hadn't a shilling. And then, when I was a man, I had a shilling, but I didn't want any taffy." I say not one syllable against that splendid discontent that all the time makes a man strike for something better, while he still holds on to what he has got already. I like this idea: that every boy born in America of the good American blood dreams some time of being President of the Republic. They say in Scotland that if you aim at a gown of gold you are pretty sure to get a sleeve; and I say no man has any right to be content not to be his best or do his best, and not to do better to-morrow than he is doing to-day. [Applause.] But the truth I am after is that all this will come by keeping close to this manful and true life; and while we work steadily along to whatever fortune waits for us in the future, about the best thing we can do is to feel sure that this work we are doing, and the wife and the home and the children, these are the choicest earth-ward blessings Heaven has to give us. It is our birth-right to get the good of life as we go along, in these things that to a true man and woman are like the rain and sunshine to an apple-tree. But when we will not be-lieve this, and will still dream that the best of our life is to come when we have made our fortune and exhaust the springs of life in making the fortune, then, you see, we sell our birthright, like Esau in the old time, for a mess of pottage; but we do not get even the satisfaction Esau got out of his bargain, because the mess of pottage is apt to give us the dyspepsia; and so we lose the good of birthright and pottage together. [Applause.]

MONCURE DANIEL CONWAY

DEMONOLOGY AND ENGLISH FOLK-LORE

[Lectures by Dr. Moncure D. Conway, editor, author, clergyman, sometime minister of the South Place Ethical Society, London, England (born in Stafford County, Virginia, March 17, 1832; ———), delivered in Masonic Temple, New York City, during the lecture season of 1875. These lectures were of a series treating Demonology, Ancient Fable, and English Folk-Lore, and the origin and present condition of Oriental Religions, which Dr. Conway repeated in various places.]

LADIES AND GENTLEMEN:—An English lady said to a friend of mine, both being mothers of families, " Do you make your children bow their heads whenever they hear mentioned the name of the devil? I do. I think it is safer." It is curious to find this respect for Satan cropping up among Christian families, though devel (two e's) is the gypsy name for God. Lucifer means light-bearer, the morning-star; and many demonic names agree with our fables of devils fallen from a bright abode. In early ages this fable of rebellious spirits falling out of heaven was taken in a literal way. Jupiter was believed to have thrown Vulcan from heaven. He took nine days in falling, and was lamed by the fall. It was in that way that Mephistopheles also got his lameness.

We have to deal with deities if we would find the origin of demons. In the elaborate contrivances in nature for good and for evil, primitive man felt himself surrounded by contrarious gods, as we feel surrounded by diverse laws. We have long taken gods and goddesses out of the laws of nature; science has taught us how to unmask them, and their masks now belong to the mythology of races. Having done their part in investing each phase of nature with a sentiment, they remain now as records of our own primitive history,—what you and I did in the ages when we were sacrificing or sacrificed.

In the earliest personifications of nature, no devil was ever conceived. No malignant spirit was thought of. The forces of nature, and their personifications, were never thought of as good or evil, but simply as sometimes afflicting and sometimes benefiting men. The reason why we find no devils in primitive books is because no devils were needed, the gods being amply equal to any evil doings that had to be gotten up. [Laughter.] Even when this happy family of gods was broken up there was as yet no notion of a devil. It is of importance to bear in mind the mythological distinction between devil and demon. A devil is evil for the sake of being evil, does harm for the sake of doing harm. A demon is simply a poor, wandering being, whose harm is incidental to the satisfaction of his own pressing necessities. He is like the pitiful shark, impelled by insatiable hunger. The demons were ghosts suffering from cold, heat, hunger, thirst, and the way to deal with them was to offer them what they needed. When distinction between demons and deities began, deities represented the pure sky, sunlight, air; demons the black cloud, storm, lightning, all horrible and terrible things in nature, and the obstacles men had to encounter. And, indeed, by gathering together the chief demons, we can find, stage by stage, the main difficulties with which man had to contend in his struggle for existence.

First of all, there was hunger. In every part of the earth, the chief struggle of man was for his daily bread. He had to get his fish in the sea, animals in the forests, birds in the air, which he saw all around him living by the same avocation; and there seemed to be a spirit of hunger abroad. There seemed to be a hunger principle in the universe and at the same time the resources of nature were so rare, the animals, fishes, and birds so hard to get, that he imagined there was an invisible being similarly voracious who wanted the fishes and cattle for himself.

There is an African tribe whose representation of their

devil is a great stomach. It has two claws to hold its prey and a mouth to swallow it, but otherwise nothing but a stomach; and that is a type of half the demons. It is the ghoul that makes the Arab shudder on the desert, and it is the vampire, which in superstition takes many forms. Only last year, a man absolutely had the body of his daughter taken up and the heart burned because it was believed that she was drawing the whole family to the grave with her, whereas they were all dying of consumption as she had died.

The race has been haunted by this demon that " goeth about seeking whom it may devour." Everything in nature that seemed to swallow up something was regarded as one of the voracious demons. If a village was engulfed by an earthquake, if the sun was eclipsed, it was a demon's work. The English Government sent an expedition to India to observe the recent solar eclipse. When the officers had arranged the instruments on the morning of the eclipse, the natives gathered a large pile of brushwood, and when the eclipse began they lit the brush, and screamed at the top of their voices. They thought the sun would be devoured unless they frightened off the Swallower. The officers, as the smoke rose up, saw that the atmosphere would presently be filled with it, and that the object of the expedition might be defeated. Courageous Englishmen scattered the brush and trampled out the fire. It was a type of the courage that there should always be to disperse the smoke that obscures the vision of science. [Applause.] When the eclipse came the natives threw out all the food they had in their houses, which was to say to this demon: " Only let the sun alone and satisfy thyself with the food in our houses."

The English were astonished at such long survival of the dragon story, but it was substantially the same with one revealed in England about that time. A mine in England was flooded and 200 workmen drowned. The news came to the neighboring village and all the women went out and screamed at the top of their voices,—no lamentation, no feeling, but simply a yelling at the top of the pit. These women refused to eat, and stayed there all day and all night; this was all on the same principle that the Hindoos threw out all the food, for when asked why they did this, they said that the sons and fathers might be saved.

Many famous demons have been pictured as Shakespeare pictures Cassius, with "a lean and hungry look." Such were the demons of antiquity. The German peasant says that the devil's back is hollow, and he is too thin to cast a shadow.

Disease was a prolific source of demons. There was a special demon behind every plague. The cholera was a great stern woman, very beautiful, and snowy white. An Eastern poet says that he met this being, and asked, "Who art thou?" And the demon replied, "I am the plague; I have come from Damascus, where ten thousand are dying; I slew a thousand, terror slew the rest."

When there was a plague among the animals it was an indication that a furious being wished to devour the cattle. When I was in Moscow last, the cattle plague was raging in a suburban village, and one morning the women drove all their cattle into the village; then harnessing themselves to a plow, they plowed around the village; when they reached the point from which they had started, they buried a dog and cat alive, and cried out all day, "Cattle plague! cattle plague! Spare our cattle, and take instead this cat and dog!"

There were demons of the burning sun, and demons of extreme cold. In Iceland witches were supposed to be possessed by cold demons, it would seem as their victims, and are said to haunt the fireside, their favorite articles being those that belong to the fireside, such as the shovel.

There were demons of strong winds, such as Typhon. This idea of a spirit living at the center of a gale of wind was a universal one. In Japan, the phrase "raising the wind," is equivalent to "raising the devil." There were demons in poisonous plants; belladonna (beautiful women) is said to have got its name from the fascinating sorceress supposed to favor that plant. There were demonic animals. Cats (diminished tigers) preserve enough diabolism in tradition to make some people, even to this day, tremble when they see a black cat at night. The dog, too, was demonic. In ancient India and in Greece the dog watched at the gates of death, and still there are thousands to whom the howl of a dog at night conveys the idea of death. When it was reported that the Prince of Wales was dying at Sandringham, it was telegraphed through Europe that a dog had been heard howling near his window at night. Of all zoological demons the serpent was the most distinguished. The serpent has indeed been more widely worshiped than cursed, but it was worshiped because feared, and for the purpose of appeasing it. There is an intensely destructive personality in that reptile. Observe what a perfect movement the viper's head has for giving the heaviest blow possible for an organism of its size; and its tooth is a syringe which shoots the poison from a hidden bag behind it into its prey. Some serpents are provided with an extra set of teeth, so that if one set breaks the other will instantly start into action. The cobra is the most deadly of all snakes, and being so favored it is regarded as a Brahman of high caste.

There were demons in the rock and desert, in everything dangerous, everything hard to subdue. There are innumerable mountain wilds named after the devil— "Devil's Peak," "Devil's Gorge," and so forth, and in the Hartz there are places called for some reason " Devil's Pulpits." In California some very hot springs bear such portentous names as " Devil's Mush-Pot " and "Devil's Tea-Kettle." There is a gorge running through a little city on the Danube which is called "The Devil's Ditch." It was used as a ditch or trench for carrying off refuse, but last year the miasma made it so dangerous that the people vaulted it over. But this year a flood came, a usual July flood, and, not being able to go through this gorge, it went over the town, and swept away many houses and people. At this the people went into their churches and prayed to be delivered from the devil and his ditch. For the work of the water was taken as proof positive that the devil had a special interest in the "Devil's Ditch " and was displeased at the city's covering it over.

So much for demons. Let us now consider devils. The moral evolution of mankind furnished the material out of which devils were made. Nothing but the ascending ideal of man ever suggested so black an impersonation as pure malignancy. The contrast between man's inner ideal and his animalism, the antagonism in his growing consciousness, could not be ascribed to one and the same source, and this inward conflict was reflected in external phenomena. This however took place at an advanced stage of thought, when monotheism was being developed. It was to relieve the supreme deity from responsibility for what was ferocious and ugly in both human and external nature that the devil was evoked. Ages of physical struggle for life had absorbed the forces of man, but at last by his skill, little by little he mastered the problems of nature, and so scientific inquiry began. There is the refrain of many ages in William Blake's apostrophe to the tiger:—

> "Tiger, tiger, burning bright
> In the forests of the night,
> What immortal hand or eye
> Could frame that fearful symmetry?"

And in his terrible question: "Did He who made the lamb make thee?"

The idea of a personal devil originated in Persia. A philosopher of that country conceived the universe as a great arena of combat between the Good Mind and the Evil Mind.

The devil theory was adopted in other religions than that of Persia only partially, and not to relieve God of responsibility for evil in nature, but to relieve man by giving him a Prince of Darkness on whom to lay the blame for his own misdeeds. That was a want that had long been unmet. [Laughter.] You remember in Eden, Adam laid the blame on Eve, and Eve laid it on the snake. It went no further. Some of the ancients laid their offenses on the backs of scapegoats.

We do not find in the biblical account of Satan any stain upon his character. In the Book of Job he is the son of God and the official prosecuting-attorney of the universe. In that book there is not one sentence indicating anything immoral or wicked about him. This picture of Satan [pointing to one of the outline crayon drawings by which the lecture was illustrated] is taken from an ancient Assyrian gem. It was also engraved on armor, and sometimes on medals. It has many of the characteristics of the Greek Nemesis. The idea of swiftness, which was one of the elements in the nature of the Greek deity, is reproduced here in Satan, in his wingéd feet. He has four hands. In two of these he bears the scales by which he is to judge accurately and justly; in the other two he holds instruments of punishment. This being looks forth from the gems with a strangely beautiful expression of eye and face, but looks with the severity which is always given by the ancients to the personifications of their gods.

The Europeans paint Satan black, and the Africans with sufficient reason paint him white. [Laughter.] The Arabs explain his existence by saying he was an archangel, and that when God created the universe he called all to come and prostrate themselves before this His greatest work. Satan alone refused to bow down to Adam, saying that Adam was but clay, and he could not bring himself to do it. God said to him, "It is not fit that you should bear yourself proudly in Paradise," and drove him out of the Garden, and Satan vowed that in revenge he would always lie in wait for man.

In ancient Jewish legend Adam's first wife was not Eve, but Lilith. When Lilith was created she was told by Adam that she was to be his obedient helpmate, but this she respectfully but firmly declined. [Laughter.] She said she was just as old as he was [Gen., 1 :27], made of as good clay, and she did not see why she should be obedient to Adam any more than he to her. She was given the choice of submission or leaving Paradise; she left, and then Eve was created out of Adam in order that this difficult question might never rise again. Lilith was represented as possessing very seductive beauty. She tried to rescue Eve from her subordinate destiny, and in the form of a serpent gave her the apple of knowledge. This legend influenced ancient art, and gave the serpent a woman's head in many old pictures, as in Michelangelo's "Fall of Man," in the Sistine Chapel.

The curse on the serpent that he should crawl has puzzled theologians, and Dr. Adam Clarke concluded that originally the serpent had the shape of a monkey. [Laughter.] But I have another theory. The Hebrews had no idea of transmigration. To a Hindoo no animal must be eaten, for to him every animal form is the way-station of a transmigrating soul. The biblical story was, I believe, Oriental, and the curse on the serpent was that it should never transmigrate, but should remain forever transfixed in that prostrate form.

The ancient judicial and punitive Satan has a quaint survival in an old Teutonic deity supposed to go around and give presents to all the good children, and punishment to all the bad. The mothers got in the habit of saying to naughty children, " Old Rupert will catch you." The Christian change came, and this useful deity had to be preserved, and was made a saint. They called him St. Nicholas, which later was corrupted into Santa Claus. The mothers said, " Old Nicholas will catch you," and this was corrupted into " Old Nick"; and so a harmless saint has given the devil one of his most popular names. [Applause and laughter.]

Man made two great migrations. One was geographical. He migrated from regions of ferocious storms, from regions of intolerable heat, into temperate and fertile countries. Another and more significant migration followed—that from the stone and the bronze age to the age of iron and steel. In his migrations man became master of many things he formerly feared, and so the giant demons became small. Some diminished gradually to little fairies. Others though big, became what the Germans call " stupid devils," and when Satan came to be the head of the demons he shared in this decline, lost his majesty and was pictured as a ridiculous and insignificant figure. He was the comic figure of the " miracle plays." That was the part that Satan was playing in the Middle Ages when he was on the eve of a most extraordinary revival. This was in witchcraft,—the strange and dark mediæval spiritualism.

Some think of witchcraft as an epidemic of something like insanity, that made people believe themselves in intercourse with demons who controlled their actions; but I think there is more under the phenomena. Christianity first came into Europe holding up to those poor toiling millions of serfs the gospel of a Saviour. It came to them, saying: "Give us your hearts, hands, minds; your Saviour was a poor carpenter, poorer than any of you peasants!" Influenced by this idea of a Great Brother, whose trials were akin to their own, they abandoned their old deities and altars. But then came an alliance between despot and priest, which struck terror to the hearts of the poor and left them in despair. No Saviour at all for them, but only for their oppressors! Then they began to invoke their old gods, and had to do it by magic in remote places. These old gods having been pronounced devils by Christianity, their devotees were declared to be worshipers of Satan whom they rode through the air to meet. This was probably the basis of the witchcraft delusion. The extorted and insane confessions of alleged witches, backed by Bible authority, gave rise to the legend of Faust, to Luther's doctrine of Satan, to Bunyan's dramatic story of the battle between Christian and Apollyon. But this revival of the Devil could not survive the advance of science, and almost the only relic of that old rehabilitation is in the Punch and Judy show. And by the way there is a notable difference between the show in London and in Paris. You will recall how the reckless London Punch kills the policeman, executes the executioner, but is at last carried off by the devil. In Paris, Punch is caught by the devil, but get's the devil's head in the noose arranged for himself, and leaves him dangling by the neck. But when he is at last apprehended by a policeman, Punch gives in at once. [Laughter.]

When man had mastered his outward foes, there came the foes of his religious life. Devils reflected all that seemed to be opposed to faith and piety. For ages there was no faith or piety maintained but that of the priests, and they could make the devil a potent instrument of authority in affairs over the ignorant. But that devil, reflecting fictitious sins, guarding unreal virtues, long ago passed out of the interest of educated people. The actual evils natural and moral were combined by poetry and art in the symbol of the dragon.

"Every man has his dragon," so Thackeray used to say. This charming author always kept a picture of "St. George and the Dragon" above his bed on the wall. "Every man has his dragon," he used to say, "and mine is a dinner-party. I am always accepting invitations to dine out. It doesn't agree with me; it plays the mischief with

all my work, and yet I go on accepting invitations."
Thackeray used to fly from his dragon when he had a
very important piece of literary work on hand. He used
to go away from home and stay,—only a couple of blocks
from his family,—for a whole week, without allowing his
family to know where he was, so that invitations could
not reach him. It was curious enough to find a symbol of
the ancient conflict between light and darkness, which
anciently swayed the passions of mankind, surviving in
the half-humorous, half-serious remark of Thackeray.
But his quaint use of this symbol was in keeping with its
history. The dragon has been turned to a new purpose
for every race; it has done little service and big service
on innumerable occasions, and has represented every
variety of man's combat with evil, physical and moral, in
all history, its very body in its combination of nonde-
scripts, generalizing nearly all the ills that flesh was heir
to.

The chief impression of the dragon is, indeed, derived
from the crocodile. Here [pointing to a drawing] is the
hydra which Hercules is supposed to slay. It is a seven-
headed hydra. There is a suggestion about it of the
octopus. The octopus is an ingeniously diabolical looking thing. There was a big one in the Brighton aquarium, and a clergyman there advised his congregation
not to visit the aquarium as he thought some of the
creatures in it might promote infidelity. [Laughter.]
To get the true dragon, we must not dwell on any little
peculiarity of the crocodile or serpent related to it, but
look in the fossil beds of the human mind. The artist
Turner painted a magnificent dragon guarding the apples
of the Hesperides. Ruskin said that the conception of
that dragon in 1806, before the great fossil saurians were
exhumed, was a triumph of the scientific imagination.
Whereupon an artist wrote that Turner himself told
him he had copied that dragon from a pantomime in
Drury Lane Theatre. [Laughter.] Turner had shown
a more scientific instinct than his critic, for the right place
to go to look at the conventional monster is in the strata
of the human mind, where alone the dragon exists.
Every Christmas this dragon appears on the London
stage, a rehearsal of the folk-lore of the past. It is al-

ways the same, just as it has existed in the human mind for thousands of years. You come face to face with the picture of antiquity when you look upon the London dragon. It is green, sedulously green,—a manager will search for weeks until he finds one green enough—dark-green because it is related to the sea. Its eyes are red, its mouth is red, for it is a storm and lightning myth. It has a speared tail, and its serpent-like scales are lustrous gems. The serpent was at the same time reverenced as the guardian and owner of everything that was under-neath the sod, wherein he lived,—minerals, metals, gems, which shone on his skin. He is the relative of Pluto (whose name means wealth), who was pictured with jew-els because he reigned over the underworld. The seed in the sod belongs to Pluto. The story of Pluto and Pros-erpine is entirely a fable of the seed and flower. Pros-erpine carried away into the underworld is simply the seed buried in the earth. When she is brought from Hades, it is the seed in flower. But she can return to the upper world only on the condition of returning to Pluto for the half of each year. The seed must be planted.

Now these rich serpents under the earth, vigilantly guarding their treasures down there, were natural ene-mies of the rain which drew up the seed, and the sun which rescued the seed, and they got wings and tried to swallow up the sun and stop the clouds from raining. The earliest wingéd serpent, who founded the race of dragons, was Vritra (in India), who stole Indra's cows (clouds), so that for want of their milk (rain), the earth suffered famine. Indra slew Vritra. Indra (god of rain) also slew the "binding serpent" Ahi, who bound up the clouds and caused drouth. From the name Ahi are de-rived our words "adder," "anguish," "ugly," "quinsy," "anxiety," and all that class of words which come from the Sanskrit word for adder, *archae*. From the same word came the name "Echidna," mother of nearly all the monsters of Greek mythology. From Ahi came also the Sanskrit *amhas*, Greek *agos*, meaning sin. When, ladies and gentlemen, you look upon that familiar figure of Laocoon and his sons, bound every limb by the folds of the serpent, you will see what the ancients meant by their spiritualization of this dragon; you will see what was their conception of the power of a vice, the power of a habit, to bind and bind every faculty.

This great fable of the binding serpent has been reproduced in manifold forms, and is turned into many moral tales for children throughout the old world. There is the story, for example, of a little boy and little girl, gathering strawberries, and presently meeting an old woman who asks for some. The little girl gives her freely, but the boy says he doesn't gather strawberries for old women. After the children pass on, the old woman calls them back, and gives each a little box. The girl opens her box and finds two snow-white caterpillars, which turn to butterflies, then grow until they become angels and bear her away to Paradise. The little boy opens his box and finds two tiny black worms, which swell until they become serpents, bind all his limbs, and take him to a forest where he is wandering to this day.

In shape these monsters recall still the terrible powers of nature. They recall the terrible dangers that threatened man's early existence; they recall the rocks that threatened to waylay his early attempts at navigation, as for instance, Scylla and Charybdis. One mountain dragon painted by Turner looks like a glacier. The gods in the Grecian mythology won their spurs by killing monsters. It is the fable of civilizing nature. They just slay a dragon, or several dragons, or else they must not pretend to be gods. Perseus rivaled Apollo by slaying two monsters—the gorgon Medusa and another. But the most important was Bellerophon who slew the Chimera. The people whom Bellerophon slew were so hairy that they were supposed to be descended from wolves, and he received the name of the slayer of the hairy. The goat was the symbol of all barbarians, and the serpent was the symbol of their preternatural power; and so Bellerophon was the St. George of his pagan times. He was the god of war at Corinth. His head was stamped upon coins, and in that way he migrated with the Aryan race. Wherever our ancestors wandered in Germany and England they carried coins marked with that figure, and that started all the dragon legends of Germany, Sweden, Norway, Scandinavia, and Britain. The Bellerophon coins were distributed over the world, and the Church when it arrived, had to rival the deeds of these heroes. They pictured their saints as having conquered even greater dragons than the pagans met. St. Andrew, St. Michael, St. Margaret, and many other saints, had all killed dragons. Sometimes the title of dragon-slayer was a misfit, as in the case of St. George the Cappadocian.

Some of us may know that there sprang up a warm feeling between two forces on the two sides of the ocean because of St. George. It is a curious thing that two scholars can get at odds through St. George of Cappadocia. Mr. Ruskin got into a state of mind with Mr. Emerson because he spoke disrespectfully of England's patron Saint, whom Ruskin was using against English dragons. Mr. Emerson says that George of Cappadocia was a low parasite, who got a large contract to supply an army with bacon; who became a rogue and informer, became rich, and then had to run for his life. He saved his money, was made Bishop of Alexandria in Egypt, and in 361 was slain by the people he had defrauded. This Bishop's name became, in time, St. George of England, emblem of chivalry. Now Mr. Ruskin hearing that, made an indignant reply to Mr. Emerson and Ruskin is deeply involved. Ruskin has founded a new Arcadian society, which is to deal darts of power and death to all the many-headed dragons of our time, from venality and wickedness in high places to sooty chimneys. I believe he is almost the only man living who sees in a gold sovereign, which has on it the stamp of St. George slaying the dragon, some power which he will hurl with all his soul against some rock. He is a man full of the spirit of chivalry, full of spirit, full of enthusiasm, with a horror against every wrong, full of enthusiasm for every right, and he sees in the gold coins,—of which I am happy to say, he has plenty—so many sunbeams of history that will drive out the clouds of this time. [Applause.] Well, now, if Mr. Ruskin calls his society the Society of St. George, it is rather hard to hear that this St. George,— his patron George,—was a man who, so far from slaying the dragon, was the dragon's most particular friend and ally. [Laughter.] Now, Mr. Ruskin makes various replies to this. In the first place, he says that even if that were the case, as Mr. Emerson says, it would not be any worse than New York's canonization of St. Jim Fisk, covering his coffin with flowers—roses, lilies, and camelias. And next, Mr. Ruskin says that if Mr. Emerson's account of George is true, it was not the story told to those who made him a patron saint of England and Russia. They believed he was a true martyr in what he believed to be a just cause. And then Mr. Ruskin says there was another St. George, and it was the other St. George and not the St. George of Cappadocia. I have examined Mr. Ruskin's treatise with great care, and I am persuaded that Mr. Ruskin cannot make it out that the St. George who is said to have slain the dragon, was none other than the old Aryan scamp of Cappadocia, while Mr. Ruskin's view is perfectly sound, however, in this, that those who made him patron saint had no such conception of his character. All they heard was that a bishop had been killed by pagans, and they did not for a moment think the bishop could be wrong and the pagans could be right.

There is a story in Japan, the most ancient, I am told, by Mr. Tatui Baba, a very learned man, of all the fables in his country, and I took it down from his lips. It is that, for a long time in the world, there was no weapon that was not made of flint or stone. At last a sword was made of iron, and it was the maiden sword of this world. It fell into the hands of a young prince. This prince, feeling the greatness of such a treasure as the first iron sword, went forth to see what wrong he could right, what good he could do; went forth a sort of primitive Quixote, but in a more serious mood. He saw a cut stick on the river, and he traveled up the river, and there he found an old man and an old woman with a beautiful maiden sitting between them, and all three were weeping. The prince asked why they wept, and they said they had had eight children, and there was in the neighborhood a terrific monster with eight heads and eight tails. This monster would devastate the country unless every year one of their children was given him to devour. They had given seven daughters, and now they had brought the last. The monster was expected momentarily. The prince looked at his sword, but did not feel that it was equal to deal with eight heads. So he hit upon the device of preparing hogsheads of wine. He had a park with eight gates, and in each of these gates he placed a hogshead of wine, and when the monster came, eight heads appeared and eight heads went into these barrels of wine. They sipped the wine, and deeper and deeper went down, until the eyes were not over the barrel, and the heads were drunk. The result was, that, where their necks met in the body the prince cut off all at one blow, and saved the maiden. The moral is plain: it is an awful warning to all bibulous dragons. [Laughter.]

It is a remarkable thing that while in Japan and China a serpent is regarded as the worst of beings, the dragon is there regarded with reverence,—originally, no doubt, as a racial ensign. Something of the same sentiment is traceable in English romance. The dragon is worn by some noble families as their symbol. It was of old a good omen for the king if an astrologer reported having seen a dragon. The dragon and dragon-slayer migrated from Greece into Britain on coins and in legends. They first came to Cornwall, where we have St. Petrox and the Dragon, and in Ireland where we have St. Patrick and the snakes.

These two have a suspicious likeness to each other. The legend was that when the first Christian missionaries came to England they were thrown into a grotto of snakes. When St. Petrox came he determined to destroy them; he took bell book and candle, went to the grotto, and his exorcisms caused them to devour each other. They devoured each other two days and a night, when there were left only two, which had grown enormous by having inside of them all the other snakes. These two were each half a mile long. Then one of them swallowed the other, and he of course was then a mile long. Then St. Petrox drove that snake out to sea, and he passed over into Ireland; and there he somehow gathered to himself all the serpents of Northern Europe, from Scotland and the Hebrides; and all Ireland was filled with snakes, brought or collected there by this king serpent expelled from Cornwall. He grew much larger in Ireland, and devastated the island. St. Patrick determined to try his powers on this serpent and all his host. His exorcisms succeeded pretty well on the lesser snakes, but it took St.

Patrick two weeks, and some authorities say three, to move this monster coiled in its cavern near Dublin. At last the saintly rites prevailed. The serpent slowly put forth to sea, and when its head was going out of Cork harbor, its tail was just leaving Dublin. [Laughter.] Since that time this snake has been going about, appearing occasionally in the vicinity of Nahant, Massachusetts. [Laughter.] It is to be seen during the "dead season" of the newspapers every year. [Laughter.]

This Irish story passed into many variants. I believe that St. Columba driving the rats out of the Hebrides is one. He was a friend of St. Petrox. He determined to found a church in the island of Iona. He took twenty or thirty companions to build it, but the devil came by night and threw down all the stones built up by day. This continued until an oracle informed them they must bury some holy man alive under the wall. This I learned from the most pious person in Iona—in fact, the only person living there. [Laughter.] At last St. Columba's dearest friend said, "I will be buried alive." They buried him, and the wall went up smoothly and pleasantly. No demon cast down the stones any more. But St. Columba could not sleep for thinking of his buried friend, and must needs look on his face again. So he had the wall pulled down, and lo! when they got to the buried man he sat up cheerful and happy, and said to them that he had been in Paradise several days, and he added, "You will find when you get there that it is a very different place from what you thought. In the first place you will find that there is no hell." When they heard that heresy, they buried him in good earnest, and there he remains to this day. [Laughter.] The extermination of the rats followed that of the heretic, there and in many northern islands.

Occasionally we find in Europe a legend resembling that of Lilith. There is a family in France to-day that think they originated in one of these women. One of their ancestors married a most beautiful woman, who had consented on condition that she should have entire privacy at certain hours. He could not restrain his curiosity, and discovered that during those hours she became a serpent. She saw him, glided away and never came back. The "Laidley Worm" in Scotland was a princess, who was transformed into a worm by a stepmother envious of her beauty.

Now all these dragons of which I have been telling you, many as they may seem, are really one. They are our old friend Python, and our modern friend the Sea Serpent. Let us analyze one, the Lambton Worm, said to have been created near Lambton, near Durham castle. Many centuries ago lived the Knight of Lambton, a young fellow who spent his Sundays fishing; and when he did not catch fish enough he filled the whole wood with his profanity while the pious were going to mass. He had a reputation for impiety. One Sunday, while fishing in the river Wear, he had a rise, but on his hook found only a tiny black worm. Whereat he swore till the whole air was purple and threw the worm into a well.

After a time Lambton was converted and joined the Crusaders. In the Holy Land he distinguished himself for piety—that is, slew a great many Saracens. [Laughter.] But while he was there engaged in this evangelical occupation [laughter] the people around Durham were suffering great things. That tiny black worm had grown and grown until at length it emerged from the well in which he had thrown it and foraged over the district, breakfasting on villagers here, and dining on citizens there. Its headquarters was a small hill around which it coiled itself nine times, its head perched on the top, and its nine eyes glaring over the country. There are still the terraces made by the weight of this monster's coils. I have seen them, and am certain of the facts because I was told them by a workingman living in a neighboring village called Washington, and, of course, a man living in a village of that name could never, never tell a lie. [Laughter and applause.]

Now an oracle declared that this monster would not devour anybody provided it were given nine cows' milk, and a milkmaid was found bold enough to carry the milk to it. If a single gill were wasted, the monster would come forth and devour the carrier. There is an old statue of this heroic milkmaid at Durham castle.

Such was the situation when the young knight, Lambton, came back from the Holy Land. He resolved to engage the monster in single combat. I should have said that all the knights in England had tried to slay this dragon but in vain, because whenever they severed the body in two, it immediately grew together again. So when the knight was about to fight the Worm, he consulted the "oracle," which said that if in armor of razor-blades he encountered the Worm in the center of the river Wear, he would conquer him; but on the condition of a previous solemn vow to sacrifice the first living being that he met after leaving the water. There is at Durham castle a statue of the knight in his razor-blade armor. When he entered the water the Worm coiled round him and was cut by the blades into so many pieces that the monster could not pull himself together before the current swept some away.

Perhaps I should mention that the knight had tied a dog near by, where he could see it when he left the water and sacrifice it; but his old father Lambton came along and untied the dog; so his father was the first living being seen by the victorious knight. He could not slay his father, and the oracle told him the penalty would be that no knight of Lambton should die in his bed for nine generations. This penalty has been faithfully inflicted by the folk-lore of Durham.

The Lambton Worm legend is the most typical one in Europe. Hindu Vritra's stealing Indra's cows is in this Worm's love of milk; the Lernean Hydra's nine heads reappear as nine eyes; and the piecing together is represented in the hydra-heads growing again when cut off by Herakles. The monster's growth from a tiny worm repeats the ancient mythology of the wolf Fenris, who began as a little pet dog of the Norse gods but when full-grown broke their chains and threatened the universe.

There are other correspondences with classic and oriental myths in the Durham legend, but to a philosopher its most instructive feature is to find all those ancient monsters appearing in Britain to guard the successive developments of religious authority. While the Druidic "oracle" remained the folk-tale celebrated it; when attending mass became a new pious duty, the legend included that; when profanity began to excite objections, the Worm story bore testimony against that too; and finally when Sabbatarianism arrived with the Puritans, breaking the Sabbath also got into the list of sins punished by the dragon's devastation of the community, with exception of the noble sinner.

Well, we have reached a time when the demons, devils, dragons are all dead; cut to pieces by the blades of science they have been swept down the stream of time; nobody fears them, no passion is restrained by them. But the evils they symbolized are not dead. The physical evils are somewhat reduced by invention and art, but moral evil as well as good can utilize arts and inventions, and the vanishing away of the old fears, breaking of the old chains of superstition, has left mankind in peril of real devils, actual dragons with a moral sense little trained to recognize them and ethical science too rudimentary to deal with them. Amid all the indifference to evil arising from the guilty optimism that evil is a disguise of good, on the one hand, and on the other the zeal without knowledge, one might find in this picture by Turner, of Apollo slaying the Python, a true suggestion for the man of to-day confronting the foes of human civilization. The god of light has sent his arrow of pure light into the monster, and steadily gazes to observe the effect. On the god's beautiful face there is no trace of anger, no frown, but that perfect serenity which is the condition of all exact observation and of real strength. For the very force of blindfold zeal increases its weakness. If men would deal effectually with evil within or without it must be without fear and with a calm firmness. But above all man must be educated out of all dread of foes that do not exist, without which he can never recognize the foes that do exist. [Loud applause.]

RUSSELL HERRMAN CONWELL

ACRES OF DIAMONDS

[Lecture by Russell H. Conwell, clergyman, platform orator, pastor of the Baptist Temple, Philadelphia, since 1882, and President of Temple College (born in South Worthington, Mass., February 15, 1843; ————), the most famous of his series of popular lectures, delivered on many platforms.]

LADIES AND GENTLEMEN:—The title of this lecture originated away back in 1869. When going down the Tigris River, we hired a guide from Bagdad to show us down to the Arabian Gulf. That guide whom we employed resembled the barbers we find in America. That is, he resembled the barbers in certain mental characteristics. He thought it was not only his duty to guide us down the river, but also to entertain us with stories; curious and weird, ancient and modern, strange and familiar; many of them I have forgotten, and I am glad I have. But there was one which I recall to-night. The guide grew irritable over my lack of appreciation, and as he led my camel by the halter he introduced his story by saying: "This is a tale I reserve for my *particular friends.*" So I then gave him my close attention. He told me that there once lived near the shore of the River Indus, toward which we were then traveling, an ancient Persian by the name of Al Hafed. He said that Al Hafed owned a large farm, with orchards, grain fields and gardens; that he had money at interest, had a beautiful wife and lovely children, and was a wealthy and contented man. Contented because he was wealthy, and wealthy because he was contented.

One day there visited this old Persian farmer one of those ancient Buddhist priests, one of the wise men of the

East, who sat down by Al Hafed's fireside and told the old farmer how this world was made. He told him that this world was once a great bank of fog, and that the Almighty thrust His finger into this bank of fog, and began slowly to move his finger around, and then increased the speed of his finger until he whirled this bank of fog into a solid ball of fire; and as it went rolling through the universe, burning its way through other banks of fog, it condensed the moisture, until it fell in floods of rain upon the heated surface of the world, and cooled the outward crust; then the internal fires, bursting the cooling crust, threw up the mountains, and the hills, and the valleys of this wonderful world of ours.

"And" said the old priest, "if this internal melted mass burst forth and cooled very quickly it became granite, if it cooled more slowly, it became copper; if it cooled less quickly, silver; less quickly, gold; and after gold, diamonds were made." Said the old priest, "A diamond is a congealed drop of sunlight." That statement is literally true.

And the old priest said another very curious thing. He said that a diamond was the last and the highest of God's mineral creations, as a woman is the last and highest of God's animal creations. That is the reason, I suppose, why the two have such a liking for each other. [Applause.]

The old priest told Al Hafed if he had a diamond the size of his thumb, he could purchase a dozen farms like his. "And," said the priest, "if you had a handful of diamonds, you could purchase the county, and if you had a mine of diamonds you could purchase kingdoms, and place your children upon thrones, through the influence of your great wealth."

Al Hafed heard all about the diamonds that night, and went to bed a poor man. He wanted a whole mine of diamonds. Early in the morning he sought the priest and awoke him. Well, I know, by experience, that a priest is very cross when awakened early in the morning.

Al Hafed said: "Will you tell me where I can find diamonds?"

The priest said: "Diamonds? What do you want of diamonds?"

Said Al Hafed: "I want to be immensely rich."

"Well," said the priest, "if you want diamonds, all you have to do is to go and find them, and then you will have them."

"But," said Al Hafed, "I don't know where to go."

"If you will find a river that runs over white sands, between high mountains, in those white sands you will always find diamonds," answered the priest.

"But," asked Al Hafed, "do you believe there is such a river?"

"Plenty of them; all you have to do is just go where they are."

"Well," said Al Hafed, "I will go."

So he sold his farm; collected his money that was at interest; left his family in charge of a neighbor, and away he went in search of diamonds.

He began his search, very properly to my mind, at the Mountains of the Moon. Afterwards he came around into Palestine, and then wandered on into Europe. At last, when his money was all gone and he was in rags, poverty and wretchedness, he stood on the shore at Barcelona, in Spain, when a great tidal wave swept through the pillars of Hercules; and the poor, starving, afflicted stranger could not resist the awful temptation to cast himself into that incoming tide; and he sank beneath its foaming crest, never to rise in this life again.

When the old guide had told me that story, he stopped the camel I was riding upon and went back to arrange the baggage on another camel, and I had an opportunity to muse over his story. And I asked myself this question: "Why did this old guide reserve this story for his *particular friends?*" But when he came back and took up the camel's halter once more, I found that was the first story I ever heard wherein the hero was killed in the first chapter. For he went on into the second chapter, just as though there had been no break.

Said he: "The man who purchased Al Hafed's farm, led his camel out into the garden to drink, and as the animal put his nose into the shallow waters of the garden brook, Al Hafed's successor noticed a curious flash of light from the white sands of the stream. Reaching in he pulled out a black stone containing a strange eye of light. He took it into the house as a curious pebble and putting it on the mantel that covered the central fire went his way and forgot all about it.

"But not long after that that same old priest came to visit Al Hafed's successor. The moment he opened the door he noticed the flash of light. He rushed to the mantel and said:—

"'Here is a diamond! Here is a diamond! Has Al Hafed returned?'

"'Oh no, Al Hafed has not returned and we have not heard from him since he went away, and that is not a diamond. It is nothing but a stone we found out in our garden.'

"'But,' said the priest, 'I know a diamond when I see it. I tell you that is a diamond.'

"Then together they rushed out into the garden. They stirred up the white sands with their fingers, and there came up other more beautiful, more valuable gems than the first.

"Thus," said the guide,—and friends it is historically true,—"was discovered the diamond mines of Golconda, the most valuable diamond mines in the history of the ancient world."

Well, when the guide had added the second chapter to his story, he then took off his Turkish red cap, and swung it in the air to call my special attention to the moral; those Arab guides always have morals to their stories, though the stories are not always moral.

He said to me: "Had Al Hafed remained at home, and dug in his own cellar, or underneath his own wheat field, instead of wretchedness, starvation, poverty and death in a strange land, he would have had ACRES OF DIAMONDS."

Acres of Diamonds! For every acre of that old farm, yes, every shovelful, afterwards revealed the gems which since have decorated the crowns of monarchs.

When the guide had added the moral to this story, I saw why he reserved it for his *particular friends*. But I didn't tell him that I could see it. It was that mean, old Arab's way of going around a thing, like a lawyer, and saying indirectly what he didn't dare say directly; that in his private opinion "there was a certain young man trav-

eling down the Tigris River, who might better be at
home, in America." [Laughter.]

I told him his story reminded me of one. You all know
it. I told him that a man in California, in 1847, owned a
ranch there. He heard that they had discovered gold in
Southern California, though they had not. And he sold
his farm to Colonel Sutter, who put a mill on the little
stream below the house. One day his little girl gathered
some of the sand in her hands from the raceway, and
brought it into the house. And while she was sifting it
through her fingers, a visitor there noticed the first shining scales of real gold that were ever discovered in California. Acres and acres of gold. I was introduced, a
few years ago, while in California, to the one-third owner
of the farm, and he was then receiving one hundred and
twenty dollars in gold for every fifteen minutes of his life,
sleeping or waking. You and I would enjoy an income
like that, now that we have no income tax.

Professor Agassiz, the great geologist of Harvard University, that magnificent scholar, told us, at the Summer
School of Mineralogy, that there once lived in Pennsylvania a man who owned a farm,—and he did with his farm
just what I should do if I had a farm in Pennsylvania. He sold it. [Applause.] But, before he sold it,
he decided to secure employment, collecting coal oil. He
wrote to his cousin in Canada that he would like to go
into that business. His cousin wrote back to him: "I
cannot engage you, because you don't understand the oil
business." "Then," said he, "I will understand it," and
with commendable zeal, he set himself at the study of the
whole theory of the coal oil subject. He began away
back at the second day of God's creation. He found that
there was once another sun that shone on this world, and
that then there were immense forests of vegetation. He
found that the other sun was put out, and that this world
after a time fell into the wake of the present sun. It was
then locked in blocks of ice. Then there rose mighty
icebergs that human imagination cannot grasp, and as
those mountains of ice did ride those stormy seas, they
beat down this original vegetation, they planed down the
hills, toppled over the mountains, and everywhere buried
this original vegetation which has since been turned by

chemical action to the primitive beds of coal, and in connection with which only is found coal oil in paying quantities.

So he found out where oil originated. He studied it until he knew what it looked like, what it smelled like, how to refine it, and where to sell it.

"Now," said he to his cousin in a letter, "I know all about the oil business, from the second day of God's creation to the present time."

His cousin replied to him to "come on." So he sold his farm in Pennsylvania for $833—even money, no cents.

After he had gone from the farm, the farmer who had purchased his place, went out to arrange for watering the cattle; and he found that the previous owner had already arranged for that matter. There was a stream running down the hillside back of the barn; and across that stream from bank to bank, the previous owner had put in a plank edgewise at a slight angle, for the purpose of throwing over to one side of the brook a dreadful looking scum through which the cattle would not put their noses, although they would drink on this side below the plank. Thus that man, who had gone to Canada, and who had studied all about the oil business, had been himself damming back for twenty-three years a flood of coal oil, which the state geologist said in 1870 was worth to our state a hundred millions of dollars. A hundred millions! The city of Titusville stands bodily on that farm now. And yet, though he knew all about the theory, he sold the farm for $833—again I say "no *sense*." [Applause.]

I need another illustration. I find it in Massachusetts. The young man went down to Yale College and studied mines and mining, and became such an adept at mineralogy, that during his senior year in the Sheffield School, they paid him as a tutor fifteen dollars a week for the spare time in which he taught. When he graduated they raised his pay to forty-five dollars a week and offered him a professorship. As soon as they did that he went home to his mother! If they had raised his salary to fifteen dollars and sixty cents, then he would have stayed. But when they made it forty-five dollars a week he said: "I won't work for forty-five dollars a week! The idea of a man with a brain like mine, working for forty-five dollars a week! Let us go out to California and stake out gold and silver and copper claims, and be rich!"

Said his mother: "Now Charley, it is just as well to be happy as it is to be rich."

"Yes," said he. "It is just as well to be rich and happy too." [Applause.]

They were both right about it. And as he was the only son, and she was a widow, of course he had his way. They always do. So they sold out in Massachusetts and went, not to California, but to Wisconsin, and there he entered the employ of the Superior Copper Mining Company, at fifteen dollars a week again. But with the proviso that he should have an interest in any mines he should discover for the company. I don't believe he ever discovered a mine there. Still I have often felt when I mentioned this fact in Northern Wisconsin, that he might be in the audience and feel mad at the way I speak about it. Still here is the fact, and it seems unfortunate to be in the way of a good illustration. But I don't believe he ever found any other mine. Yet I don't know anything about that end of the line. I know that he had scarcely gone from Massachusetts, before the farmer who had purchased his farm was bringing a large basket of potatoes in through the gateway. You know in Massachusetts our farms are almost entirely stone wall. [Applause.] Hence the basket hugged very close in the gate, and he dragged it on one side and then on the other. And as he was pulling that basket through the gateway, the farmer noticed in the upper and outer corner of that stone wall next to the gate, a block of native silver eight inches square. And this professor of mines and mining and mineralogy, who would not work for forty-five dollars a week, because he knew so much about the subject, when he sold that homestead, sat on that very stone to make the bargain. He was born on that very farm, and they told me that he had gone by that piece of silver and rubbed it with his sleeve, until it reflected his countenance and seemed to say to him, "Here, take me! Here is a hundred thousand dollars right down here in the rocks just for the taking." But he wouldn't take it. This was near Newburyport, Massachusetts. He wouldn't believe

in silver at home.   He said: "There is no silver in Newburyport.   It is all away off,—well, I don't know where,"
—and he didn't.   But somewhere else.   And he was a
Professor of Mineralogy.   I don't know of anything I
would better enjoy in taking the whole time, than telling
of the blunders like this which I have heard that "Professors" have made.

I say that I would enjoy it.   But after all there is another side to the question.   For the more I think about
it, the more I would like to know what he is doing in Wisconsin to-night.   I don't believe he has found any mines,
but I can tell you what I do believe is the case.   I think
he sits out there by his fireside to-night, and his friends
are gathered around him and he is saying to them something like this:—

"Do you know that man Conwell who lives in Philadelphia?"

"Oh, yes, I have heard of him."

"Well you know that man Jones who lives in————"

"Yes, I have also heard of him," say they.

Then he begins to shake his sides with laughter, and
he says:—

"They have both done the same thing I did precisely!"
And that spoils the whole joke.

Because you and I have done it.   Yet nearly every person here will say: "Oh no, I never had any acres of
diamonds or any gold mines or any silver mines."

But I say to you that you did have silver mines, and
gold mines, and acres of diamonds, and you have them
now.

Now let me speak with the greatest care lest my eccen-
tricity of manner should mislead my listeners, and make
you think I am here to entertain more than to help.   I
want to hold your attention on this oppressive night, with
sufficient interest to leave my lesson with you.

You had an opportunity to be rich; and to some of you
it has been a hardship to purchase a ticket for this lecture.   Yet you have no right to be poor.   It is all wrong.
You have no right to be poor.   It is your duty to be rich.

Oh, I know well that there are some things higher,
sublimer than money!   Ah, yes, there are some things
sweeter, holier than gold!   Yet I also know that there is

not one of those things but is greatly enhanced by the use of money.

"Oh," you will say, "Mr. Conwell, can you, as a Christian teacher, tell the young people to spend their lives making money?"

Yes, I do. Three times I say, I do, I do, I do. You ought to make money. Money is power. Think how much good you could do if you had money now. Money is power and it ought to be in the hands of good men. It would be in the hands of good men if we comply with the Scripture teachings, where God promises prosperity to the righteous man. That means more than being goody-good—it means the all-around righteous man. You should be a righteous man, and if you were, you would be rich. [Applause.]

I need to guard myself right here. Because one of my theological students came to me once to labor with me, for heresy, inasmuch as I had said that money was power.

He said: "Mr. Conwell, I feel it my duty to tell you that the Scriptures say that money 'is the root of all evil.'"

I asked him: "Have you been spending your time making a new Bible when you should have been studying theology." He said: "That is in the old Bible."

I said "I would like to have you find it for me. I have never seen it."

He triumphantly brought a Bible, and with all the bigoted pride of a narrow sectarian, who founds his creed on some misinterpretation of Scripture, threw it down before me and said: "There it is! You can read it for yourself"!

I said to him: "Young man, you will learn before you get much older, that you can't trust another denomination to read the Bible for you. Please read it yourself, and remember that 'emphasis is exegesis.'"

So he read: "The *love* of money is the root of all evil."

Indeed it is. The *love* of money is the root of all evil. The love of the money, rather than the love of the good it secures, is a dangerous evil in the community. The desire to get hold of money, and to hold on to it, "hugging the dollar until the eagle squeals," is the root of all evil,

But it is a grand ambition for men to have the desire to gain money, that they may use it for the benefit of their fellow men. [Applause.]

Young man! you may never have the opportunity to charge at the head of your Nation's troops on some Santiago's heights; young woman, you may never be called on to go out in the seas like Grace Darling to save suffering humanity. But every one of you can earn money honestly, and with that money you can fight the battles of peace; and the victories of peace are always grander than those of war!

I say then to you, that you ought to be rich.

"Well," you say, "I would like to be rich, but I have never had an opportunity. I never had any diamonds about me"!

My friends you did have an opportunity. And let us see where your mistake was.

What business have you been in?

"Oh," some man or woman will say, "I keep a store upon one of these side streets, and I am so far from the great commercial center that I cannot make any money."

"Are you poor? How long have you kept that store"?

"Twenty years."

"Twenty years, and not worth five hundred thousand dollars now? There is something the matter with you. Nothing the matter with the side street. It is with you."

"Oh now," you will say, "any person knows that you must be in the center of trade if you are going to make money."

The man of common sense will not admit that that is necessarily true at all. If you are keeping that store and you are not making money, it would have been better for the community if they had kicked you out of that store, nineteen years ago.

No man has a right to go into business and not make money. It is a crime to go into business and lose money, because it is a curse to the rest of the community. No man has a moral right to transact business unless he makes something out of it. He has also no right to transact business unless the man he deals with has an opportunity also to make something. Unless he lives and lets live, he is not an honest man in business. There are no exceptions to this great rule. [Applause.]

You ought to have been rich. You have no right to keep a store for twenty years and still be poor. You will say to me:—

"Now Mr. Conwell, I know the mercantile business better than you do."

My friend, let us consider it a minute.

When I was young, my father kept a country store, and once in a while he left me in charge of that store. Fortunately for him it was not often. [Laughter.] When I had it in my charge a man came in the store door and said:—

"Do you keep jack-knives?"

"No we don't keep jack-knives." I went off and whistled a tune, and what did I care for that man? Then another man would come in and say:—

"Do you keep jack-knives?" "No, we don't keep jack-knives." Then I went off and whistled another tune, and what did I care for that man?

Then another man would come in the same door and say: "Do you keep jack-knives?"

"No, we don't keep jack-knives. Do you suppose we are keeping this store just for the purpose of supplying the whole neighborhood with jack-knives?"

Do you carry on your business like that? Do you ask what was the difficulty with it? The difficulty was that I had not then learned that the foundation principles of business success and the foundation principles of Christianity, itself, are both the same. It is the whole of every man's life to be doing for his fellow men. And he who can do the most to help his fellow men, is entitled to the greatest reward himself. Not only so saith God's holy book, but also saith every man's business common sense. If I had been carrying on my father's store on a Christian plan, or on a plan that leads to success, I would have had a jack-knife for the third man when he called for it."

But you say: "I don't carry on my store like that." If you have not made any money you are carrying on your business like that, and I can tell you what you will say to me to-morrow morning when I go into your store.

I come to you and inquire: "Do you know neighbor A?"

"Oh yes. He lives up in the next block. He trades here at my little store."

"Well, where did he come from when he came to _____?"

"I don't know."

"Does he own his own house?"

"I don't know."

"What business is he in?"

"I don't know."

"Do his children go to school?"

"I don't know."

"What ticket does he vote?"

"I don't know."

"What church does he go to?"

"I don't know, and I don't care."

Do you answer me like that to-morrow morning, in your store? Then you are carrying on your business just as I carried on my father's business in Worthington, Massachusetts.

You don't know where neighbor A came from and you *don't care*. You don't care whether he has a happy home or not. You don't know what church he goes to, and you don't care! If you had cared, you would have been a rich man now.

You never thought it was any part of your duty to help him make money. So you cannot succeed! It is against every law of business and every rule of political economy, and I would give five dollars myself, to see your failure in the "Ledger" to-morrow morning. What right have you to be in business taking no interest in your fellow men, and not endeavoring to supply them with what they need? You cannot succeed.

That merchant, who, in the City of Boston, made his fifteen millions of dollars, began his enterprises out in the suburbs where there were not a dozen houses on the street; although there were other stores scattered about. He became such a necessity to the neighborhood that when he wished to move into the city to start a wholesale house, they came to him with a great petition, signed by all the people, begging that he would not close that store, but keep it open for the benefit of that community. He had always looked after their interests. He had always carefully studied what they wanted and advised them rightly. He was a necessity; and they must make him wealthy; for in proportion as you are of use to your fellow men in that proportion can they afford to pay you.

Oh my friend going through this world and thinking you are unjustly dealt with! You are poor because you are not wanted. You should have made yourself a necessity to the world, and then the world would have paid you your own price. Friends learn that lesson. I would speak tenderly and kindly to the poor; but I sometimes need to speak decidedly.

Young man, remember if you are going to invest your life or talent or money, you must look around and see what people need and then invest yourself, or your money, in that which they need most. Then will your fortune be made, for they must take care of you. It is a difficult lesson to learn.

Some young man will say to me:—

"I cannot go into that mercantile business."

"Why not?"

"Because I have no capital."

Capital! Capital! Capital! Capital! is the cry of a dudish generation which cannot see over its collar. [Laughter and applause.]

Who are the rich men now? The poor boys of fifty years ago. You know it. The rich men of your town, in whatever profession or calling they are, as a rule were the poor boys of forty or fifty years ago. If they had not been poor then they wouldn't be rich now.

The statistics of Massachusetts say, and I presume it holds good in your State, that not one rich man's son in seventeen ever dies rich. I pity the rich man's son. He is not to be praised for his magnificent, palatial home, not to be congratulated on having plenty of money, or his yachts, carriages, and diamonds. Oh no, but rather to be commiserated. It is often a misfortune to be born the son of a rich man. There are many things a rich man's son cannot know, because he is not passing through the school of actual experience.

A young man in our college asked me: "What is the

happiest hour in the history of a man's life?" The definition I gave him was this: The happiest hour in the history of a man's life is when he takes his bride for the first time over the threshold of his own door, into a house which he has earned by his own hands; and as he enters the nest he has built he says to her, with an eloquence of feeling no words of mine can ever touch: "Wife, I earned this home myself!" Oh that is the grandest moment a man may ever know. "Wife, I earned this home. It is all mine, and I divide it with thee!" [Applause.] It is a magnificent moment!

But the rich man's son cannot know that. He may go into a house that is more beautiful; but as he takes his wife into his mansion he will go all through it and say to her: "My mother gave me that! My mother gave me that. My mother gave me that!"—until his wife wishes he had married his mother. [Applause.]

I pity such a young man as that.

It is said that the elder Vanderbilt, when a boy, went to his father and said:—

"Father, did you earn all your money?"

And the old Commodore said: "I did, I earned every penny of it."

And he did. It is cruel to slander the rich because they have been successful. It is a shame to "look down" upon the rich the way we do. They are not scoundrels because they have gotten money. They have blessed the world. They have gone into great enterprises that have enriched the nation and the nation has enriched them. It is all wrong for us to accuse a rich man of dishonesty simply because he secured money. Go through this city and your very best people are among your richest people. Owners of property are always the best citizens. It is all wrong to say they are not good.

The elder Vanderbilt went to his father and said: "Did you earn all your money?"

And when the Commodore said that he did, the boy said: "Then I will earn mine."

And he insisted on going to work for three dollars a week. If a rich man's son will go to work like that he will be able to take care of his father's money when the father is gone. If he has the bravery to fight the battle of poverty like the poor boy, then of course he has a double advantage. But as a rule the rich father won't allow his son to work; and the boy's mother!—oh, she would think it a social disgrace for her poor, weak, little, lily-fingered, sissy sort of a boy to earn his living with honest toil. And so I say it is not capital you want. It is not copper cents, but common sense. [Applause.]

Let me illustrate it again. A. T. Stewart had a dollar and fifty cents to begin life on. That was of course before he was a school-teacher. He lost eighty-seven and a half cents on his very first venture. How did he come to lose it? He lost it because he purchased some needles, thread, and buttons to sell, which people did not want. And he said: "I will never do that again." Then he went around first to the doors of the houses and asked the people what they did want; then when he found out what they wanted he invested his sixty-two and a half cents and supplied a "known demand."

Why does one merchant go beyond another? Why does one manufacturer outsell any other? It is simply because that one has found out what people want, and does not waste his money buying things they do not need. That is the whole of it. And A. T. Stewart said: "I am not going to buy things people do not want. I will take an interest in people and study their needs." And he pursued that until he was worth forty millions of dollars.

"But," you will say, "I cannot do that here." Yes you can. It is being done in smaller places now, and you can do it as well as others.

But a better illustration was John Jacob Astor, the elder. They say that he had a mortgage on a millinery store. I never reach this point without thinking that the ladies will say, that "Fools rush in where angels fear to tread." [Laughter.] But John Jacob Astor had a mortgage on a millinery store, and foreclosed the mortgage and went into business with the same people who had failed on his hands. After he entered into partnership, he went out and sat down on a bench in the Park. What was the successful merchant doing out there, in partnership with people who had just failed on his own hands? Ah, he had the most important, and to my mind, the pleasantest

part of that partnership. He was out there watching the
ladies as they went by:—and where is the man who would
not get rich at that business? As he sat upon that bench
if a lady passed him with her shoulders thrown back and
her head up, and looking straight to the front, as though
she didn't care if all the world did gaze on her, then John
Jacob Astor studied the bonnet she wore; and before it
was out of sight, he knew the shape of the frame, and the
curl of the lace, and crimp of the feathers, and lots of intri-
cate things that go into a bonnet which I cannot describe.
Then he went to his millinery store and said: "Now
put in the show window just such a bonnet as I describe
to you, because I have just seen a real lady who likes
just such a bonnet." Then he went and sat down again.
Another lady, with another form and complexion came,
and, of course, she wore another style of bonnet. He
then went back and described that and had that put into
the window. He didn't fill his show window full of hats
and bonnets to drive the people away, and then sit down
in the back of the store and bawl because people went
somewhere else to trade. [Applause.] He didn't have a
hat or a bonnet that some lady didn't like. That has
since been the wealthiest millinery firm on the face of the
earth. There has been taken out of the business seventeen millions of dollars and over, by partners who have
retired. Yet not a dollar of capital have they ever put
into that business, except what they turned in from their
profits,—to use as capital. Now John Jacob Astor made
the fortune of that millinery firm not by lending them
money, but by finding out what the ladies liked for bonnets, before they wasted any material in making them up.
And if a man can foresee the millinery business, he can
foresee anything under Heaven! [Laughter and applause.]

But perhaps a better illustration may strike closer
home. You ought to go into the manufacturing business. But you will say there is no room here. Great
corporations which have gotten possession of the field
make it impossible to make a success of a small manufacturing business now. I say to you, young man, that
there was never a time in your history and never will be
in your history again when the opportunity for a poor

man to make money in the manufacturing business is so clearly apparent as it is at this very hour.

"But," says some young man to me, "I have no capital."

Oh, capital, capital! Do you know of any manufacturer around here who was not born poor? Capital! you don't want capital now. I want to illustrate again, for the best way to teach is always by illustration.

There was a man in Hingham, Massachusetts, who was a carpenter and out of work. He sat around the stove until his wife told him to "go out of doors"; and he did,—what every man in Massachusetts is compelled to do by law,—he obeyed his wife. [Applause.] He went out and sat down on the shore of the bay and he whittled out an oak shingle into a wooden chain. His children that evening quarrelled over it. So he whittled another to keep peace in the family. While he was whittling the second toy a neighbor came in and said to him: "Why don't you whittle toys and sell them? You can make money." The carpenter said "I could not whittle toys, and if I could do it, I would not know what to make!" There is the whole thing. It is to know what to make. It is the secret of life everywhere. You may take it in the ministry. You may take it in law. You may take it in mechanics or in labor. You may take it in professional life, or anywhere on earth—the whole question is what to make of yourself for other people. "What to make" is the great difficulty.

He said he would "not know what to make." His neighbor said to him, with good New England common sense: "Why don't you ask your own children what to make?"

"Oh," said he, "my children are different from other people's children."

I used to see people like that when I taught school.

But he consulted his children later, and whittled toys to please them and found that other people's children wanted the same things. He called his children right around his feet and whittled out of firewood those "Hingham tops"; the wooden shovels; the wooden buckets and such things, and when his children were especially pleased, he then made copies to sell. He began to get a little capital of his own earning, and secured a footlathe, and then secured a room, then hired a factory, and then hired power; and so he went on. The last law case I ever tried in my life was in the United States Court-room at Boston, and this very Hingham man who had whittled those toys stood upon the stand. He was the last man I ever cross-examined. Then I left the law, and went into the ministry,—left practising entirely and went to preaching exclusively. But I said to this man as he stood upon the stand:—

"When did you begin to whittle those toys?"

He said: " 1870."

Said I: "In these seven years how much have those toys become worth?"

He answered: "Do you mean the taxable value or the estimated value?"

I said: "Tell his Honor the taxable value, that there may be no question about it." He answered me from the witness-stand, under oath:—

"Seventy-eight thousand dollars."

Seventy-eight thousand dollars in only seven years, and beginning with nothing but a jack-knife (and a few hun-dred dollars of debts he owed other people), and so he was worth at least $100,000. His fortune was made by consulting his own children, in his own house, and decid-ing that other people's children would like the same thing. You can do the same thing if you will. You don't need to go out of your house to find out where the dia-monds are. You don't need to go out of your own room.

But your wealth is too near. I was speaking in New Britain, Connecticut, on this very subject. There sat five or six rows from me a lady. I noticed the lady at the time, from the color of her bonnet. I said to them, what I say to you now, "Your wealth is too near to you! You are looking right over it!" She went home after the lecture and tried to take off her collar. The button stuck in the buttonhole. She twisted and tugged and pulled and finally broke it out of the buttonhole and threw it away. She said: "I wonder why they don't make decent collar buttons?"

Her husband said to her: "After what Conwell said to-night why don't you get up a collar button yourself?

Did he not say that if you need anything other people need it; so if you need a collar button there are millions of people needing it. Get up a collar button and get rich. '*Wherever there is a need there is a fortune.*'" [Applause.]

Then she made up her mind to do it; and when a woman makes up her mind, and don't say anything about it, she does it! [Applause.] And she invented this "snap button," a kind of a button that snaps together from two pieces, through the buttonhole. That very woman can now go over the sea every summer in her own yacht and take her husband with her. And if he were dead she would have enough money left to buy a foreign count or duke, or some such thing. [Laughter and applause.]

What is my lesson in it? I said to her what I say to you, "Your fortune is too near to you! So near that you are looking over it." She had to look over it. It was right under her chin. And it is just as near to you.

In East Brookfield, Massachusetts, there was a shoe-maker out of work. His wife drove him out of doors with the mopstick, because she wanted to mop around the stove. He went out and sat down on the ash barrel in the back yard. Close by that ash barrel ran a little mountain stream. I have sometimes wondered if, as he sat there on that ash barrel, he thought of Tennyson's beautiful poem :—

> "Chatter, chatter, as I flow,
>   To join the brimming river,
>   Men may come, and men may go,
>   But I go on forever."

I don't believe he thought of it, because it was not a poetical situation, on an ash barrel in the back yard. [Laughter.] But as he sat on that ash barrel he looked down into the stream, and he saw a trout go flashing up the stream and hiding under the bank. He leaped down and caught the fish in his hands and took it into the house. His wife sent it to a friend in Worcester. The friend wrote back that they would give five dollars for another such trout. And the shoemaker and his wife immediately started out to find one. They went up and down the stream, but not another trout to be found. Then they went to the preacher. But that is not half as foolish as some other things young people go to a preacher for. That preacher could not explain why they could not find another trout. But he was true to his profession; he "pointed the way." He said: "Secure Seth Green's book on the 'Culture of Trout,' and it will give you the information you need." They got the book and found that if they started with a pair of trout, a trout would lay thirty-six hundred eggs every year, and that every trout would grow an ounce the first year, and a quarter of a pound every succeeding year, so that in four years a man could secure from two trout four tons per annum to sell. They said: "Oh, we don't believe such a great story as that. But if we could raise a few and sell them for five dollars apiece, we might make money." So they purchased two little trout and put them in the stream, with a coal sifter down the stream and a window screen up-stream to keep the trout in. Afterwards, they moved to the banks of the Connecticut River, and afterwards to the Hudson, and one of them has been on the United States Fish Commission, and had a large share in the preparation for the World's Fair in 1900 at Paris. But he sat that day, on that ash barrel in the back yard, right by his acres of diamonds. But he didn't see them. He had not seen his fortune although he had lived there for twenty-three years, until his wife drove him out there with a mopstick. It may be you will not find your wealth until your wife assumes the sceptre of power! But nevertheless, your wealth is there. [Applause.]

But the people who make the greatest mistakes are the farmers. When I could not keep my father's store he set me to work on the farm, knowing that as the ground was nearly all rock I could not do much harm there. [Laughter.]

I know by experience that a very ordinary man can be a lawyer. I also know that it does not take a man with a gigantic intellect to be a preacher. It takes a greater man than either, to make a successful farmer to-day. The farmer will be more successful when he gives more attention to what people want and not so much to what will grow, though he needs them both. But now the whole time of most of our farmers is taken up with the finding out of "what will grow."

I was going up through Iowa a while ago and saw the wheat decaying in mud, and I said to a farmer:—

"Why is it that all this grain here is decaying?"

"Oh," he said, "it is the 'awful' monopoly of the railroads." He didn't use the word "awful," but he used a word that he thought was more emphatic. [Laughter.]

I got into the train and I sympathized with the poor down-trodden farmer. The conductor came along and I asked him:—

"How much dividend does this railroad pay on its stock?"

He looked at me and said: "It has not paid any for nine years and it has been in the hands of the receiver the most of the time."

Then I changed my mind. If that farmer had raised what the people wanted, not only would he have been rich, but the railroad would have paid interest on its stock. [Applause.]

I was at Evansville, Indiana, and a man drove up in his beautiful carriage and told me: "Eighteen years ago I borrowed two hundred dollars and I went into farming. I began the first year to raise wheat, rye, and hogs. But the second year I decided to raise what the people wanted, so I ploughed the ground over and put in small fruits. Now, I own this farm and a great deal more." They told me at the hotel that he owned two-thirds of the stock in the bank of which he was president. He had made his money all because he planted what people wanted.

Let me go down through the audience now, and ask you to show me the great inventors here. You will say: "That doesn't mean me." But it does mean you. Great inventors that hear me now! Oh, you will say, we don't have any inventors here. They all live away off somewhere else. But who are the great inventors? Always the men who are the simplest and plainest. They are the great inventors. The great inventor has the simple mind, and invents the simplest machine.

Did you ever think how simple the telephone and the telegraph were? Now the simplest mind is always the greatest. Did you ever see a great man? Great in every noble and true sense? If so, you could walk right up to him and say: "How are you, Jim?" Just think of the great men you have met and you find this is true.

I went out to write the biography of General Garfield and found him crowded with other people. I went to a neighbor's to wait until they were gone. But the neighbor told me that if I wanted to get a chance to see him I had better go over at once, and he offered to introduce me. He took his old hat and stuck it on the back of his head, and climbed over the fence and went to the back-door of the house, and shouted:—

"Jim! Jim! Jim!"

Very soon "Jim" came to the door; and the neighbor said: "Here is a man who wants to see you."

I went into the home of one of the grandest men that America ever raised. To his neighbors he was "Jim," a plain man, a simple man. [Applause.]

I went to see President Lincoln one time when I was an officer in the War of 1861. I had never seen him before, and his secretary sent me in to see him as one would enter a neighbor's office. Simple, plain "old Abe." [Applause.]

The simple men are the greatest always. Did you ever see a man strut proudly along, puffed up in his individual pride, not willing to notice an ordinary mechanic? Do you think he is great? Do you really think that man is great? He is nothing but a puffed-up balloon, held down by his big feet. There may be greatness in self-respect, but there is no greatness in feeling above one's fellow men. [Applause.]

I asked a class in Minnesota once, who were the great inventors, and a girl hopped up and said, "Columbus." [Laughter.] Columbus was a great inventor. Columbus married a wife who owned a farm, and he carried it on just as I carried on my father's farm. We took the hoe and went out and sat down on a rock. But as Columbus sat on that rock on the Island of Porto Santo, Spain, he was thinking. I was not. That was a great difference. Columbus as he sat on that rock held in his hand a hoe-handle. He looked out on the ocean and saw the departing ships apparently sink into the sea, and the tops of the masts went down, out of sight. Since that time some "other Spanish ships have sunk into the sea!" [Applause]. Said Columbus: "This world is like a hoe-handle, the further off the further down, the further off the further down,—just like a hoe-handle. I can sail around to the East Indies." How clear it all was. Yet how simple the mind. It is the simplest minds that observe the very simplest things, which accomplish the greatest marvels.

I went up into New Hampshire and when I came back I said I would never go to New Hampshire to lecture again. And I said to a relative of mine, who was a professor at Harvard:—

"I was cold all the time I was there and I shivered so that my teeth shook."

Said he: "Why did you shiver?"

"Because it was cold."

"No, that is not the reason you shivered."

Then I said: "I shivered because I had not bedclothes enough."

"No, that is not the reason."

"Well," said I, "Professor, you are a scientific man, I am not, I would like to have an expert, scientific opinion now, why I shivered."

He arose in his facetious way and said to me: "Young man you shivered because you did not know any better! Didn't you have in your pocket a two-cent paper?"

"Oh yes, I had a 'Herald' and a 'Journal.'"

"That is it. You had them in your pocket, and if you had spread one newspaper over your sheet when you went to bed, you would have been as warm as you lay there, as the richest man in America under all his silk coverlids. But you shivered because you didn't know enough to put a two-cent newspaper on your bed, and you had it in your pocket." [Applause.]

It is the power to appreciate the little things that brings success. How many women want divorces, and ought to have them too; but how many divorces originate like this? A man will hurry home from the factory, and his wife rushes in from the kitchen with the potatoes that have been taken out before they seem to be done, and she puts them on the table for her husband to eat. He chops them up and eats them in a hurry. They go down in hard lumps; he doesn't feel good, and he is all full of crankiness. He frets and scolds, and perhaps swears, and there is a row in the family right there. And these hearts that were almost divinely united will separate to satanic hatred. What is the difficulty? The difficulty is that that lady didn't know what all these ladies do know, that if with potatoes raised in lime soil she had put in a pinch of salt when she put them in the kettle, she could have brought them forth at the right time, and they would have been ready to laugh themselves to pieces with edible joy. He would have digested them readily, and there would have been love in that family, just for a little pinch of salt. [Applause.]

Now, I say, it is the appreciation of these things that makes the great inventors of the world. I read in a newspaper the other day that no woman ever invented anything. Of course this didn't refer to gossip; but machines and improvements. [Laughter.] If it had referred to gossip, it would have applied better to that newspaper than to women. [Renewed laughter.] Who invented the Jacquard loom? Mrs. Jacquard. Who invented the printer's roller? A woman. Who invented the cotton-gin? Mrs. Green; although a patent was taken out on an improvement in Mr. Whitney's name. Who invented the sewing-machine? A woman. Mrs. Howe, the wife of Elias Howe. If a woman can invent a sewing-machine, if a woman can invent a printing roller, if a woman can invent a cotton-gin, we men can invent anything under Heaven! [Laughter and applause.] I say that to encourage the men. Anyhow, our civilization would roll back if we should cross out the great inventions of women, though the patents were taken out often in the names of men.

The greatest inventors are those who see what the people need, and then invent something to supply that need. Let me illustrate only once more. Suppose I were to go through this house and shake hands with each of you and say: "Please introduce me to the great men and women in this hall to-night."

You would say: "Great men! We don't have any here. There are none in this audience. If you want to

find great men you must go to some other part of the
world! Great men always come from somewhere else."

How many of your men with vast power to help your
city, how many with great genius, or great social power,
who might enrich and beautify and elevate this their own
city, are now taking their money and talents and spending
them in some foreign place, instead of benefiting their
own people here? Yet here is the place for them to be
great. There are as great men here as in any other place
of its size. But it is so natural for us to say that great
men come from afar. They come from London, from
Rome, from San Francisco, from New York, from Mana-
yunk, or anywhere else. But there are just as great men
hearing me speak to-night as there are elsewhere, and
yet, who, because of their simplicity, are not now appreciated. But "the world knows nothing of its greatest
men," says the great philosopher; and it is true. Your
neighbor is a great man and it is time you appreciated it,
and if you do not appreciate it now, you never will. The
only way to be a true patriot is to be a true patriot at
home. A man who cannot benefit his own city should
never be sent to Washington. Towns and cities are
cursed because their own people talk them down. A man
who cannot bless his own community, the place in which
he lives, should not be called a patriot anywhere else.
To these young men I want to utter this cry with all my
force. Here is the place for you to be great, and here are
your great men.

But we teach our young people to believe that all the
great people are away off. I heard a professor in an Illinois college say, that "nearly all the great men are dead."
We don't want him in Philadelphia. [Laughter.] They
don't want him anywhere. The greatest men are living
now, and will only be exceeded by the generations to
come; and he who appreciates that fact will look around
him and will respect his neighbor, and will respect his environment. I have to say to-night, that the great men
of the world are those who appreciate that which is next
to them, and the danger now to our nation is that we belittle everything that is at home.

Have you heard the campaign speeches this year? I
heard a man at the Academy of Music say that our nation

is going to ruin; that the Ship of State is drifting upon the
rocks and will soon be shattered into ten thousand frag-
ments, and this Republic will be no more; that there will
be founded an empire, and upon the empire we will put a
throne, and upon the throne will be placed a tyrant, and
he with his iron heel will grind the people into dust! It is
a lie! [Applause.]   Never in the history of God's government of mankind was there a nation stepping upward
more certainly toward all that is grand and beautiful and
true than is the Nation of America to-day! Let the
politicians say what they will for personal greed, let them
declaim with all their powers, and try to burden the people, you and I know that whichever way the elections may
go, the American people are not dead, and the nation will
not be destroyed.   It is a living body, this mighty Republic, and it cannot be killed by a single election.   And they
that will belittle our nation are not patriots.   Let the
land be filled with hope.   Some young men will say:
"Oh well, the nation is having a hard time."   But it is
not.   The Bible says: "It is good for me that I was
afflicted."   We are getting down to where we can consider and take account of stock.   In the next five years
from this 1893 you will see the most flourishing institutions; all through this land will be united a prosperity
such as this nation never knew before.   Whatever the
result of the election, don't belittle your own nation.

Some young man is saying: "There is going to be a
great man here, although I don't know of any now."

"Young man when are you going to be great?"

"When I am elected to some political office, then I
will be great."

"Oh young man, learn right now, in these exciting
times, that to hold a political office under our form of
government is no evidence of greatness.   Why, my
friends, what would become of this nation if our great
men should take office?   Suppose you select the greatest
men of your city right now, and ask them to leave their
great enterprises and go into some political office.   My
friends, what a ruin would be left if the great men were to
take political offices.   The great men cannot afford to
take political office, and you and I cannot afford to put
them there.   To hold a political office is to be a servant of

the people. And the Bible says, " He that is sent cannot be greater than he who sends him," and " the servant cannot be greater than his master." The office-holder is the servant of others. He is sent by the people, he cannot be greater than the people. You think you are going to be a great man by being elected to some political office! Young man, greatness is intrinsic, it is in the personality, not in the office. If you are not great as an individual before you go into the office, you may rattle around in it after you get in, like " shot in a tin pan." There will be no greatness there. You will hold the office for a year or more and never be heard of again. There are greater things than political office. Many a young man's fortune has been made by being defeated when he was up for political office. You never saw a really great man in office who did not take the office at a sacrifice to himself.

Another young man says: " There is going to be a great man here."

" When? "

" When there comes a war! When we get into another conflict with Spain over Cuba; with England over the Monroe Doctrine, or over the Russian boundary, or with New Jersey, or some distant country of the world [laughter], then I will sweep up among the glittering bayonets, then I will tear down their flag from the staff, bear it away in triumph, and come home with stars on my shoulders, and hold every office in the gift of the nation; then I will be great!"

Young man, remember greatness does not consist in holding office, even in war. The office does not make the great man. But, alas, we mislead the young in teaching history. If you ask a scholar in school who sank the " Merrimac," he will answer " Hobson," and tell seven-eighths of a lie. For eight men sank the " Merrimac " at Santiago. Yet where are the women here to-night who have kissed the other seven men? [Laughter.]

A young man says: " I was studying the history of the War the other day and read about Generals Grant, Meade, Beauregard, Hood, and these great leaders, and they were great."

Did you read anything about their predecessors?

There is very little in history about them. If the office had made their predecessors great, you would not have heard of Grant, or Sherman, or McClellan. But they were great men intrinsically, not made so by the office. The way we teach history leads the young to think that when people get into office then they become great men. But it is terribly misleading.

Every great general of the war is credited with many victories he never knew anything about, simply because they were won by his subordinates. But it is unfair to give the credit to a general who did not know anything about it. I tell you if the lightning of heaven had struck out of existence every man who wore shoulder-straps in our wars, there would have arisen out of the ranks of our private soldiers just as great men to lead the nation on to victory.

I will give one more illustration. I don't like to give it. I don't know how I ever fell into the habit. Indeed, it was first given off-hand to a Grand Army post of which I was a member. I hesitate to give it now.

I close my eyes and I can see my own native hills once more. I can see my mountain town and plateau, the Congregational Church, and the Town Hall. They are there spread before me with increasing detail as my years fly by. I close my eyes and I can see the crowd again that was there in that war-time, 1864, dressed in red, white and blue; the flags flying, the band playing. I see a platoon of soldiers who have returned from one term of service and re-enlisted for the second, and are now to be received by the mountain town. Oh, well do I remember the day. I was captain of the company. Although in my teens, I was marching at the head of that company and puffed out with pride. A cambric needle would have burst me all to pieces! [Laughter.] I am sincerely ashamed of the whole thing now. But what august pride, then in my youth, marching at the head of my troops, being received by the country town authorities! We marched into the Town Hall. They seated my soldiers in the middle of the hall, and the crowds came in on the right and on the left. Then the town officers filed upon the stand and took up their position in a half-circle. The good old Mayor of the town, and the Chairman of the Selectmen (his family gave me permission to use this without offense to them), he sat there in his dignity, with his powerful spectacles. He had never held an office in his life before. He may have thought that if he could get into office that would give him power to do almost anything. He never held an office before, and never made a speech before. When he had taken his place he saw me on the front seat, and he came right forward and invited me up on the platform with the "Selectmen." Invited me, me! up on the stand with the town officers! Why, no town officer ever took any notice of me before I went to war; yet perhaps I ought not to say that, because one of them, I remember, did advise a teacher to "whale" me: but I mean no "honorable mention." [Laughter and applause.] Now I am invited on the stand with the Selectmen. They gave me a chair in just about this relation to the table. [Indicating the position.] I sat down, let my sword fall to the floor and waited to be received—Napoleon the Vth!—"Pride goeth before destruction," and it ought. When the Selectmen and the Mayor had taken seats the Mayor waited for quite a while, and then came forward to the table. Oh, that speech! We had supposed he would simply introduce the Congregational minister, who usually gave such public addresses. But you should have seen the surprise when this old man arose to deliver the address, on this august occasion. He had never delivered an address before. He thought the office would make him an orator. But he forgot that a man must speak his piece as a boy if he wishes to become an orator as a man. Yet he made a most common mistake. So he had written out his speech and learned it by heart. But he brought his manuscript with him, very wisely, and took it out, opened it, and spread it on the table, and then adjusted his spectacles that he might see it. Then he walked back and came forward again to deliver that address. He must have studied the idea a great deal, because he assumed an "elocutionary attitude." He "rested heavily on his left heel, slightly advanced his right foot, threw back his shoulders, and advanced his right hand at an angle of forty-five." [Laughter.] As he stood in that elocutionary attitude, this is just the way he delivered that speech. Friends often ask me if I do not

exaggerate it. You couldn't exaggerate it. I haven't
the power to exaggerate it.—

"Fellow citizens!" —— and then he paused until his
fingers and knees shook, and began to swallow, then
turned aside to look at his manuscript.

"Fellow citizens:—We are—we are—we are—we are
very happy. We are very happy—we are very happy—we
are very happy. We are very happy—to welcome back
to their native town—to their native town—these soldiers
—these soldiers—who have fought and bled, and are back
again in their native town. We are especially,—we are
especially pleased to see with us to-night this young
hero,—(that meant me)—who in imagination—(friends,
remember he said that; if he hadn't said that I wouldn't
have been egotistic enough to refer to it to-day, I assure
you)—who, in imagination,—we have seen leading his
troops on to the deadly breach. We have seen his shining—we have seen his shining—his shining sword—we
have seen his shining sword, flashing in the sunlight, as
he shouted to his troops, 'Come on!'" [Laughter and
applause.]

Oh, dear, dear, dear! He was a good old man, but how
little he knew about the War. If he had known anything
about war at all, he ought to have known that it is next
to a crime for an officer of infantry ever, in time of danger,
to go ahead of his men. I, with "my shining sword flashing in the sunlight," and calling to my troops, "Come
on!" I never did it. Do you suppose I would go in front
of my men to be shot in front by the enemy, and in the
back by my own men? It is no place for an officer. The
place for an officer in time of danger is behind the private
soldier. It is the private soldier who faces the enemy.
Often, as a staff officer, I have ridden down the line, before the battle, and as I rode I have given the general's
order, shouting, "Officers to the rear!" And then every
officer goes behind the line of private soldiers, and the
higher the officer's rank, the further behind he goes. It
is the place for him; for, if your officers and your generals
were killed on the first discharge, where would the plan
of the battle be? How ashamed I was of the whole af-

fair. In actual battle such an officer has no right to go ahead of his men. Some of those men had carried that boy across the Carolina rivers. Some of them had given him their last draught of coffee. One of them had leaped in front of him and had his cheek-bone shot away; he had leaped in front of the boy to save his life. Some were not there at all, and the tears flowing from the eyes of the widows and orphans showed that they had gone down for their country. Yet in the good man's speech he scarcely noticed those who had died; the hero of the hour was that boy. We do not know even now where many of those comrades do sleep. They went down to death. Sometimes in my dreams I call, "Answer me, ye sighing pines of the Carolinas; answer me, ye shining sands of Florida; answer me, ye crags and rocks of Kentucky and Tennessee,—where sleep my dead?" But to my call no answer comes. I know not where many of those men now sleep. But I do know this, they were brave men. I know they went down before a brave foe, fighting for a cause both believed to be right. Yet the hero of this hour was this boy. He was an officer, and they were only private soldiers.

I learned a lesson then I will never forget, until the bell of time ceases to swing for me,—that greatness consists not in holding an office. Greatness really consists in doing great deeds with little means,—in the accomplishment of vast purposes; from the private ranks of life—in benefiting one's own neighborhood, in blessing one's own city, the community in which he dwells. There, and there only, is the great test of human goodness and human ability. He who waits for an office before he does great and noble deeds must fail altogether.

I learned that lesson then, that henceforth in life I will call no man great simply because he holds an office. Greatness! It is something more than office, something more than fame, more than genius! It is the great-heartedness that encloses those in need, reaches down to those below, and lifts them up. May this thought come to every one of these young men and women who hear me speak to-night and abide through future years. [Applause.]

I close with the words of Bailey. He was not one of

our greatest writers, but, after all, in this he was one of
our best:—

> ' We live in deeds, not years,
>   In feelings, not in figures on a dial,
>   In thoughts, not breaths;
>   We should count time by heart throbs; (in the cause of right.)
>   He most lives who *thinks most*."

Oh, friends, if you forget everything else I say, don't
forget these two lines; for, if you think *two* thoughts
where I think *one*, you live twice as much as I do in the
same length of time.—

> " He most lives who thinks most,
>   Who feels the noblest,
>   And who acts the best."

[Great applause.]

FRANCIS MARION CRAWFORD

POPE LEO XIII

[Lecture by F. Marion Crawford, novelist (born in Italy, August 2, 1854; ——), delivered first before the Contemporary Club, Bridgeport, Conn., October 28, 1897, as the initial lecture of Mr. Crawford's tour in this country during the season of 1897-98. It was repeated in various cities over the United States. Protestant clergymen it has been stated listened to it as cordially as any other persons in Mr. Crawford's audience, and several of them extended invitations to him to give it in their churches. Dr. Lyman Abbott wrote to Major James B. Pond who conducted Mr. Crawford's tour, " I am glad to be quoted everywhere as saying what I said at the close of that lecture, that I am sure wherever it is delivered it will help to remove prejudice of Protestants against Romanists, and of Romanists against Protestants." Mr. Crawford had been given unusual opportunities for studying life in the Papal palace, and his portrayal of the Pope, in this lecture, has been characterized as the most intimate that any one has ever been privileged to prepare.]

LADIES AND GENTLEMEN:—In speaking to you this evening of Pope Leo XIII in the Vatican, I must in the first place give you a very brief sketch of the circumstances which preceded his elevation to the pontificate, and must touch upon the career of Pope Pius IX; for the reign of the predecessor of Leo XIII was a contrast with the reign of Leo XIII at every point. Under Pope Pius IX the political power and influence of the Vatican steadily lost strength. Under Leo XIII it has steadily gained in power and in influence. After I have given you this brief sketch, I shall try and show you Pope Leo XIII as he lives and moves, and does his hard work, in his great old age, in the Vatican. Lastly, I shall touch upon one or two questions which intimately concern him, and which in a measure concern the whole world.

We often call this age in which we live an age of civilization and enlightenment. Yet there has been more blood shed by nations calling themselves civilized during the last 120 years, than in any equal period of history. But the carnage was not uninterrupted; that long and dreadful record of death was divided in the midst by an interval of peace extending over nearly thirty years. Napoleon had harried the world from Moscow to Cairo, from Vienna to Madrid, pouring blood upon blood, exhausting the destroying power of mankind, in an uninterrupted and cruel destruction. But when he was gone Europe sank down utterly overcome. Then it was, under the rule of comparatively timid, feeble, insignificant sovereigns, that the great republican idea began to grow, deep down under the surface, like a cutting from the stricken tree of the revolution, planted in the very heart of Europe, nurtured in secret by devoted hands, but destined to destruction in the end as surely as the parent stock. About the middle of that long period, when everything was fomenting far down out of sight, there came a man whose life is marked upon the pages of history, a man whose name calls up all manner of memories of revolutions, of uprisings, and of rebellions.

That man was Mazzini, an Italian and a man of genius in his way. He founded the Society of Young Italy, in connection with all the other secret societies of Europe, and having the same object and intention which they had, namely, to produce a universal upheaval, in the hope of founding a general and lasting republic. Neither Mazzini nor Garibaldi, nor the men who stood by them and fought with them, had any intention of founding the modern Italian country which we see to-day. They were republicans to the core. They hated the idea of monarchy. The whole theory of a kingdom was repugnant to them. It was England, pouring its wealth into the country to help the house of Savoy, because she wanted an independent monarchy to subsist in the Mediterranean, that directed the whole tide of Mazzini's and Garibaldi's victories into the channel which was to cast modern Italy, as it were, under the hands of the house of Savoy.

There was little in Italy at that time to oppose any great movement. The government of the Bourbons in the South had been feeble, bad, often cruel. That of their relatives in the small principalities in the North had been little better, and in Rome a series of insignificant Popes, politically speaking, had occupied the pontifical chair, from Pius VII, Napoleon's victim, down to Gregory XVI (and Gregory XVI died in 1846).

In his place the College of Cardinals elected Pius IX, a man still young, a man full of the highest ideals, of the loftiest enthusiasm, a man of the greatest beauty of character, a man beloved by all who knew him; but a man politically weak and vacillating. One of the first things he did when he was elected Pope was to proclaim a universal pardon and amnesty for all political offenders. Then he drifted into a sort of tacit approval of the Young Italian party, not dreaming how far it might go.

While he was still hesitating and vacillating, the great movement broke out all over Europe simultaneously in the year 1848. Not only in Italy did it manifest itself, but in Austria, in Hungary, in Germany, in France; and even in England it broke out in the shape of the Chartist riots; and even in free Switzerland, free Swiss citizens shed each other's blood in civil strife at the gates of free Lucerne.

You all know the history of 1848. It was a year of riots, rebellions, new constitutions, some of which have passed away and a few of which have remained; a year in which an emperor, more than one king, and many princes, were scattering in all directions, like men escaping from a great fire when they know it is just creeping up to a central magazine of explosives.

Pope Pius IX fled like the rest, when his favorite minister had been murdered on the steps of the palace devoted to the new Parliament which Pius IX had given to his people with a constitution. It was France that brought him back to Rome, France that kept him on his throne, and until she herself, in her need and death-struggle with Germany, was obliged to summon home every man she could muster and give up fighting the battles of others, in order to fight her own.

During that long period from his return, after the year

1849 to the fall of the temporal power in 1870, Pius IX governed Rome kindly; he was much beloved by his subjects, and did a great deal for Rome. He converted the city from an old mediæval town, with dark, winding streets, and dismal open places where heaped-up rubbish half hid the monuments of ancient Rome, into a fairly creditable modern capital. Yet his government was detested, hated, one of the most unpopular governments that ever was known in history. The reason for that was this: The Pope was politically a weak man, but at his right hand there was a strong, unscrupulous individual, who had the Pope's interests at heart, but who seemed incapable of using any honest means to protect them. This man was Cardinal Antonelli. In palliation of much he did, which was far from creditable, you must remember that, although a cardinal, he was not a priest. Cardinal Antonelli lived to see his defeat and shut himself up within the Vatican as a prisoner with Pius IX, and there he went on plotting and scheming until at last he died. Then there came a great change.

When the troops of King Victor Emmanuel took Rome, there was a sort of siege during which they shelled the city a part of one day. It is sometimes said that Rome was taken without any fighting. But one of these shells fell into the library of my mother's house in the very center of Rome, and exploded, destroying almost everything in the room.

Eight years later, Victor Emmanuel, the hero of the Italians, and Pius IX, who had come to be looked upon as a martyr among Catholics, passed away within a month of each other. Old King Victor Emmanuel, who was a brave old soul, and a fine fellow at heart, had once given his word of honor that he would never seize the temporal power. Under great political pressure, urged by his ministers, and yielding to the universal uprising of the people, he took back his word and seized Rome. But he always regretted it. When they assigned the palace of the Popes upon the Quirinal for his royal residence, he refused to sleep a night under that roof. During the rest of his life he lived in a small adjoining palace communicating with the big one by a corridor. And there, when he was dying, he was very anxious to obtain the absolution and the blessing of Pius IX for what he had done.

And backwards and forwards between the Quirinal and the Vatican there were efforts looking to the arrangements of matters. Pius IX first required some sort of formal apology, some sort of verbal retraction from the king for his act of usurpation. But the king would not pronounce the words. He knew that that would be used against his memory, against Italy, and against the succession of his son. At last Pius IX, always the kindest and gentlest of men, relented, and sent his blessing freely. But when it came it was too late. The old king was dead. Within a month from that time Pius IX departed this life.

Then came a great change. The tide had reached the very lowest ebb. From that moment it began to rise again. In the place of the kind old Pius IX the cardinals elected a strong statesman, Leo XIII, the man of whom I am speaking to you this evening. [Applause.]

Joachim Vincente Pecci, who has been Pope under the title of Leo XIII, since 1878, was born in the year 1810. That wonderful old man is now nearly ninety years of age. He was born in a small mountain town called Carpinato, situated thirty or forty miles to the south of Rome, on the very border of a district which is called Saldal land—the land where the people wear sandals. There, in that town, is still the residence of the family of the present Pope, and in the old residence are portraits of the Pope's father and mother. His Holiness resembles both his parents in a striking degree. He has from his father the upper part of his head and the main features, the bony forehead, the prominent cheekbones, a very aquiline nose and firm jaw. From his mother he has the piercing black eyes that seem to hold you as you get into his presence so that you cannot get away from his look. Then he has a very strong mouth, very white, very thin lips, always set in a peculiar expression, which is firm, not unkind, something like a smile, and yet not altogether gentle.

One of the most remarkable characteristics of his appearance is his complexion, which he shares with other members of his family. When the Pope comes toward you in one of those shadowy galleries of the Vatican, or in the dimmer church below, a real radiance seems to proceed from his face. It is absolutely colorless, but yet it is luminously pale. It has often been compared to a face carved out of alabaster, with a strong light within it. This peculiarity applies to his family, but is more especially noticeable in himself.

Born up there in those southern hills, he is by nature a mountaineer. He is a very tall man, in youth was a strong man, a man of good proportions, even noble proportions, but now thin to emaciation, a mere shadow of a past man, as it were.

There is, indeed, a very strong resemblance between Pope Leo XIII, Mr. Gladstone, and Abraham Lincoln. They were all three, in their prime, long, sinewy men, of very bony constitution, with great joints, with large, bony heads, high cheekbones, prominent jaws. All three men in their youth possessed very extraordinary physical strength, far beyond that of ordinary members of the race. All three were men capable of most profound study and concentration, all eloquent men on occasion, and all three, to complete the resemblance, having in them a certain something of profound melancholy and sadness which is often found in the natures of men at once very strong, very energetic, and who are also very deep thinkers. You might almost say, that some of nature's stuff had been developed by circumstances in three different ways—in the material way, the intellectual way, and the spiritual way. Abraham Lincoln was thrown back upon the hardest, the most brutal of material facts in this work-a-day world, for his self-gotten education. Mr. Gladstone received the modern form of education in its highest development, and was an eminent and learned scholar before he was a statesman.

Leo XIII was brought up under the domination of spiritual ideas at a time when they had just survived the tremendous shock of the French revolution. Born towards the close of Napoleon's career, when a great struggle had been going on for years in men's minds between believing and not believing, he was raised to the pontificate when the next great European struggle about belief was raging at the height of what was called the

" Kulturkampf," a religious war in Prussia, to which the eyes of the world were riveted upon the struggle between the Roman Catholic Church on the one side and Prince Bismarck on the other. At that juncture came Leo XIII, the great, evenly-balanced, deep-thinking, honorable statesman.

Leo XIII is one of those characters, with their suppressed energy, that come to the front when events will not wait for little men's long phrases, when the pendulum is swinging the full stroke of history, when it is glory or death to lay hands upon the weight and hold it, or to touch it, as though there was no danger in it, and make long theories about what it will do.

Leo XIII's childhood and early youth were spent in the simple surroundings of the mountain town where he was born. Early hours, constant exercise, an outdoor life, with farm interests, made a strong man of him, with plenty of common sense. He was very athletic, a great climber, a great sportsman, fond of being out whole days among the hills with his gun. Yet at the same time he was a student and when he had finished his studies he entered the priesthood, and thenceforward his career was straight—direct as careers of most men have been who have reached the very highest destinies. He was never a parish priest. He was, from the first day of his ordination immediately attached to the offices of the Vatican. Not very long after that we find him promoted, in the due course of events, to the diplomacy, representing the Vatican abroad in Brussels as Nuncio, learning something of that great game of European politics in which he was afterwards to play so important a part. Then he is back in Italy again, consecrated an archbishop, with an archdiocese in Tuscany, in central Italy, and there he remains until he is elected Pope.

But it was while there that he showed the courage, the personal independence, which was very much remarked at that time, long before it was ever thought that he could possibly be Pope.

And it was in this way: In those days, the struggle between the Church, the Vatican and the young Italy was very bitter. Churchmen and statesmen were at swords' drawn, and churchmen shut themselves up and would have nothing to do with politics nor with persons engaged in politics. Leo XIII did just the contrary. He opened the doors of his house, he received constantly and daily and familiarly the Italian government officials, and the officers of the Italian government stationed nearby, and conversed with them upon current topics, conversed with them earnestly and freely showed them that he was not only a churchman and archbishop, but that he was an Italian and could love his country.

That required a man of courage and independence of which we have no idea now that these things are all smoothed over. And that love of conversation, that love of talking freely with the men of the time, still characterizes Leo XIII. It is a part of his nature. Few persons of distinction ever pass through Rome without being taken to his presence, and he will talk freely with them, sometimes as much as two hours without stopping. And yet, though he is one of the greatest living conversationalists, perhaps, there is something in his manner while talking which is far from pleasant, sometimes authoritative, sometimes very formal, sometimes almost harsh. You feel that he is using his words like blades, and using them like a fencer. You feel that he will let no possible opportunity escape, and you feel that, whatever he says, he wishes to be obeyed. It is a strong, dictatorial mode of conversation. But those who are near him soon become used to it, and see that he not only expresses his ideas wonderfully, but that there is also a brilliancy behind all, which is lost at the time in that something harsh that is peculiar to his manner.

His voice is just as attractive as his way of using it. You may not think it very loud; you would not call it a deep voice. But it has a certain far-reaching, carrying utility that makes it audible at an immense distance and to a vast multitude of people. To persons in various parts of St. Peter's, upon one occasion not long since, he made himself distinctly heard, and there were within St. Peter's at that time sixty thousand persons.

Pius IX always contrasted with Leo XIII, had no such power of making himself heard to the enormous multitude. But, on the other hand, he possessed one of the most beautiful, one of the sweetest and richest voices that ever fell to the lot of a singer. No one who ever heard him intone the great "Te Deum" in the chapel can forget the music of those notes. And, too, Pius IX was one of the handsomest men of his day. He had a ready wit, and always a quick retort, and above all he possessed the most serviceable of all qualities, personal charms. But he had also a superabundance of the most unserviceable of all virtues, which is political humanity.

Leo XIII has only to speak a half dozen words in that trenchant, dominant voice of his, and give one glance of his flashing eyes one gesture of his long arm, with his thin white hand, and the moral distance between him and his predecessor is apparent in a moment. There is strength in every movement. There is deliberate decision in every tone. There is personal independence in every gesture. Behind that there may be kindness, gentleness, charity, all the milder virtues, but what is most apparent is a certain trenchancy, which imposes respect rather than awakens sympathy. Of course, it is not always true that a man's outward gestures, a man's way of speaking, even a man's words, or his public actions, correspond with his inmost self. The discrepancies are often lamentably great.

The contrast between Leo XIII and his predecessor is well illustrated by this anecdote: It is the custom, when the Pope holds a semi-public reception to from five to thirty persons in one of the ante-rooms of the Vatican chambers, for those who attend to kneel in two rows, and for his holiness to pass down the center, blessing those present, and saying a few words to each. At one of the receptions held by Pius IX a young Englishman had the bad taste to stand up at the end of the line. Etiquette, not religion, demands that all should kneel. When Pius came to this young man he said: "Will you not kneel, young man, and receive an old man's blessing?" The young man was so touched by the Pope's kindly manner that he knelt at once. The same thing happened two years ago during one of Pope Leo's receptions.

As soon as he entered the ante-room he noticed the one figure standing bolt upright. He said nothing at the time, but passed along the line, blessing as he went and chatting for a moment with each. When he came to the end and saw the youth standing stiffly he turned to the chamberlain who was following him, and looking from the stranger to the court official, he said to the latter: "What is the meaning of this? Have that statue taken back to the Vatican at once."

Of his statesmanship, of his scholarship, we shall hear more while he lives; most, perhaps, hereafter, when he is gone, when a weaker and a less significant man sits in the great Pope's chair. For he is emphatically a great Pope, a great individuality. We have not seen such a man at the head of the Roman Catholic Church for centuries.

Leo XIII is a man who has accomplished a wonder in Europe in twenty years. He has turned the opinion of all Europe from a hostile one to a favorable one with regard to the Roman Catholic Church, with a unanimity of opinion which has not been seen, perhaps, for centuries. He is a great individuality. Without pretending that he is the greatest man that ever lived, I say, and those who have known and followed his life, will also say, that of all great men of his time, he possesses the most evenly balanced, the most stubbornly sane disposition, under all circumstances, of them all. And that fact alone speaks well for the men who elected him Pope at the time when Italy was crazed with grief over the loss of her hero king.

In spite of his great age, Leo XIII leads a life of constant activity and hard work. He sleeps very little, not more than four or five hours in the night. He sometimes takes a nap in the afternoon but rarely of more than twenty minutes. When his faithful old servant comes to his room every morning at 6 o'clock and not at 7 (as I have sometimes seen it stated) he more often finds the Pope up, busy writing, than asleep. Once, to my knowledge, he has been found in his chair at his writing-table sound asleep upon the sheet of paper upon which he had been working in the night, not having been to bed at all.

As soon as he is dressed, he says mass in his private chapel. Immediately afterwards, according to an old custom, he hears another mass said by one of the chaplains on duty for the week. Then he has a very light breakfast, which consists almost entirely of coffee and goat's milk—that mountain taste has clung to him since he was a boy. Then begins the work of the day, which lasts from 8 o'clock until 2 in the afternoon. He not only directs all letters connected with the Catholic Church in general, but he oversees the Vatican household. He knows everything that goes on. He receives many persons in audience and besides that, he keeps himself constantly acquainted with European politics, and constantly in communication with his own political agents, the Nuncios, in the various courts in Europe. At 2 o'clock he dines.

What is hard to understand is, that with hardly any nourishment he can maintain such unceasing efforts and such a vast expenditure of energy.

It is said of him by his physician that what Leo XIII eats in a week would not suffice him for a day. After his dinner Leo XIII goes down into the Vatican gardens, whenever the weather is fair. He is taken down from his apartments in a modern elevator, from which he steps into a Sedan chair and is carried into the gardens. When he drives his carriage waits for him at the gate, a simple brougham, such as any ordinary personage in Europe might have. One hour after dark, no matter at what time by the clock, he retires to his private apartments. After prayers he is generally left to himself, and he reads, writes, and occupies himself until 10 o'clock. Then he has a simple supper, a very light meal, and after that he goes to his own room and is not disturbed again until 6 o'clock the next morning, though he spends much of the time in reading, writing, study, and keeping himself informed upon political conditions in the world at large.

Leo XIII is more than a statesman; he is an eminent modern Italian poet. And though his reputation as a statesman will hereafter outshine his reputation as a man of letters, his verses will in the future, I think, rank high in the literature of his country. His favorite poets are Virgil and Dante, and Virgil was Dante's favorite poet. The Pope has a good verbal memory and can quote long passages from his favorite authors.

He reads a great deal of modern literature, even novels and newspapers. Nothing is ever cut and handed to him, but articles of importance are often marked to attract his attention. Like all other men whom I have ever known who have attained to anything like greatness (and it has been my good fortune to know several), he does his writing with his own hand and only dictates unimportant matters to his secretary. All of his wonderfully eloquent encyclicals are autograph letters which are afterwards printed on the Vatican press, which is a very modern place, provided with every kind of modern machinery for artistic printing. Leo XIII has opened the archives of the Vatican to scholars after they had been closed for centuries, and he has caused to be reproduced facsimiles of some of the most beautiful manuscripts in the Vatican.

The Pope is very rarely seen in public. Those solemn, gorgeous ceremonies which used to be the delight and wonder of thousands of people who flocked to Rome at Easter and Christmas, have all been discontinued since the fall of the temporal power. Now and then, on the occasion of a great pilgrimage, the Vatican displays all its ancient pomp and splendor, the like of which is not to be seen elsewhere in the civilized world, or in barbaric Asia either, where there is still much splendor surviving. Only twice a year regularly does he appear in the Sistine Chapel, and it is hard to get admittance to those functions which take place on the anniversary of his predecessor's death and his own coronation, two dates occurring close together.

All those vast sums of money which flow in to the Pope from all parts of the world are held as a kind of floating account current, in trust for the benefit of the Church. Thus the Vatican becomes a great accumulator of money, and a great distributor of it all over the world, and this leads to a curious condition of affairs. The money is invested in securities, and when cash is required, the securities are sold. Leo XIII invests all those sums of money in Italian national bonds, and the sums are so large that it is actually the Pope, the natural political adversary of the Italian Government, who makes the price of Italian Government securities in the money market—a fact perfectly well known in Italy, and it shows a good deal of faith on both sides.

The head of the Catholic Church to-day must be a modern man—a modern statesman, a modern administra-

tor. He must be able to lead men, as well as to guide,
able to deal with political difficulties as well as to cope
with heresies, and above all, he must be the Church's
wise, practical steward, as well as her consecrated head.
Leo has been an active man, not a contemplative one, all
his life, and the great acts of his pontificate have dealt
with political and social matters as well as theological.
His reign has been a long opposition to anarchy, against
which he alone in Europe has found something to oppose,
in the shape of Christianity, Christianity as a whole,
Christianity as the only possible basis for a stable society.
In the course of that long struggle he has necessarily
done things which have sometimes called upon him the
criticism of his enemies. It has been said that his direction to the French Catholics to accept the Republic, is
inconsistent with his action in Italy, where he counsels
the Catholic to take no part in elections; but those who
say that forget that the great question of the temporal
power has never been involved in France, while in Italy
it is still an unanswered question, not a question which
can ever involve a great struggle again, but an unsolved
political difficulty for which a solution must be found before the conditions of modern Italy can be considered absolutely stable and acceptable to all parties.

The question of the temporal power in the present day
resolves itself into such a small matter that it may be
considered almost ridiculous. It comes down to the possession of a small territory: the Popes hold they should
have that—a strip 500 yards wide running down to the
sea would solve the difficulty; but the large part of the
trouble lies in guaranteeing its possession to the Popes.
It would have to be guaranteed in such a way that they
might feel it would never be taken from them again. I
will read the words in which Leo XIII defines the question:—

"To recognize the sovereign rights of the Pontiff and
to replace him in a state of real and true independence,
would be to take away from the Catholics of the other
countries of the world all motive for considering Italy
as the enemy of their common Father; for it is merely
through a feeling of faith and by the dictates of their conscience that they lift up their voices in common consent

to claim liberty for the supreme Pastor of their souls."
[Letter to the Italian people, October 15, 1890.]
There you have the whole question in a nut-shell. In
Russia, the first article of belief with every orthodox
Russian, is that the emperor is the head of the Church
and State alike, and the Emperor of Russia is just as
much the consecrated arch-pontiff of the Russian Church
as the Pope of Rome is of the Catholic Church. Take
another instance: look at England. The position of
Queen Victoria is practically to a great extent a pontifical
position with regard to the established Church of England, of which she has the appointment of the bishops and
archbishops. That is distinctly a pontifical position.

Let us take one more case—that of Prussia under the
May Laws. The appointment of every Catholic bishop
and parish priest was subject to the approval of the King
of Prussia, who was also the Emperor of Germany.
These laws have been swept away, but their tendency
was to create for a Protestant king a pontifical position
with regard to certain Catholics who chanced to be his
subjects. I have brought up these cases simply to show
that in modern Europe, in monarchies, there is a sort of
feeling that it is wise and right and best for the country
that the head of the Church and State should be one person, that in some way these powers should be united in
the same individual, and these things being so, it is unfair
that the Popes should be blamed so bitterly for having
protested against the seizure of Rome. That seizure was
a usurpation, so far as they were concerned; it has been
called a great incident in the unification of a free people;
but since the "unification" the Popes have behaved with
great fairness. Instead of using their power among the
people who are a believing people, instead of using their
power to get a Parliament elected which would do harm,
they have advised Italians not to have anything to do
with politics, not to vote at all. That is a sufficient answer to those who say that Leo XIII would do anything
in an unscrupulous attempt to regain the temporal power.

To go into an account of the political acts of Leo
XIII's reign would be impossible at this late hour, but
there are two things which will interest you. One is—
the Pope's position as a prisoner in the Vatican. There

is something to be said about that which is not generally
known or understood. It is generally supposed that it
is a mere empty phrase, that if he chose he could go out
into the streets just as freely as you or I. There are two
points of view which show the contrary. Take the diplo-
matic point of view. For him to do that would be for
him to go out as the guest of the King of Italy. It would
not be un-Catholic, but it would be unpapal, it would be
unbecoming of one who claims a sovereignty to give it
up without a *quid pro quo*. But there is a much stronger
reason why he has to stay within the Vatican—his life
would not be safe in the streets of Rome at the present
day. I can hear my friends of united Italy cry out in
scorn against this statement, and they would be perfectly
right so far as they themselves are concerned, for Italians
are enlightened men, the people of Rome would treat the
Pope with the greatest respect if he would go out. The
King, who is tolerant in religious matters and is a gentleman, would treat the Pope with the highest consideration; the Queen, who is not only a Catholic, but a very
devout one, would be overjoyed if she could be presented
to Leo XIII and kneel at his feet and be blessed by him.
But unfortunately neither Rome nor Italy is peopled
solely by modern civilized Italians; it is a great center of
anarchists, and wherever there are anarchists there is a
band of desperate men who would do anything to obtain
their aims. What chance would Leo XIII or any other
Pope have in Rome? He is hated by the anarchists ten
times more bitterly than any living sovereign, for as the
Head of the Church he represents something that anarchy
has to fear more than any king or monarch. The idea
that the Pope's life would be safe in the streets of Rome
is absurd; it is a matter of constant congratulation that
the Pope does stay where he is in safety; that he does not
go out and risk his life.

There is one more question to which I shall ask your
attention for a few moments, and that is the question of
obedience to the Vatican in matters not connected with
dogma, faith, religion. There is a great misapprehension
in regard to this point. The idea has got abroad chiefly
through the enemies of the Church, largely originating
in the fact that Leo XIII is a great statesman and a great

political leader, that Catholics all over the world, whether in monarchies or free countries, must give their votes in accordance with the dictates of the Catholic Church in general, and of their bishop in particular, on pain of committing a very serious offense. There never was any such regulation and there never can be any such law. It is utterly contrary to all Catholic institutions that there should be. For Catholics to combine themselves to follow the Pope's political orders would mean that they must follow the political orders of all Popes hereafter and forever, because it would become a matter of faith, a part of religion, and therefore something which could not be taken back.

When one endeavors to speak briefly of such a man as Leo XIII, he exposes himself necessarily to an accusation of superficiality. But in these days we all have to deal with great questions, of which a full discussion would take half a lifetime. We have to judge them with such poor knowledge as we have, that we may pass on, and act, and do our duty in life and accomplish something. Humanity is too broad to be all brought under the lens of a single microscope. Humanity has grown too strong to be treated like a little child. In this day of many Cæsars all over the world, what imaginable political disaster shall tell us living men just what and just how much is to be rendered to each of these Cæsars? least of all, shall tell us such a thing here in our own country, where the power of Cæsar is delegated to a whole nation equally?

American Catholics are good Catholics; they are devout, energetic, ready to make great sacrifices for their faith. The very same words can be spoken, with the same truth, of Americans of other denominations. But beside that, beside our faith, we are all Americans alike, and any idea of political dictatorship is not only repugnant and distasteful to us, but it is so very different from all our other ideas that it cannot under any possibility take root in our thoughts, derive nourishment from our minds, nor flourish side by side with any of our convictions.

Leo XIII, as I say, is a great leader. He has been followed politically. But he is a leader on a higher plane than that of political dissension. He leads a great organization of Christian men and women spreading all over the world. He is at the head of a great body of human thought. He is the leader of a numerous conservative army, which will play a part in the coming struggle between anarchy and order. He himself will not be there to lead in the day of decisive battle, but he will leave a strong position for a successor to defend, and great weapons for him to wield, for he has done more to simplify and therefore to strengthen, the position of the Catholic Church in the last twenty years than a dozen Popes have done in the last two centuries.

Such men fight the campaigns of the future over and over in their thoughts, while all the world is at peace around them. And when the time comes at last, though they themselves be gone, the roads they planned are broad and straight for the march of other feet, the sword they forged lies ready for another hand, the spirit they called up still lives to lead, and they themselves, in their graves, in their well-earned rest, have their share in those victories that humanize mankind.

GEORGE WILLIAM CURTIS

Photogravure after a photograph from life

GEORGE WILLIAM CURTIS

SIR PHILIP SIDNEY

[Lecture by George W. Curtis, author, essayist, platform orator (born in Providence, R. I., February 24, 1824; died in Staten Island, New York, August 31, 1892), delivered originally in the Mercantile Library course in Boston, December 9, 1857, and repeatedly given in succeeding seasons on many platforms East and West. This was the third in Mr. Curtis' long list of lyceum lectures, and one of the most popular. He was early called an ideal platform orator. He entered the lecture field in 1853, upon his return from long absence abroad, stepping in among "the giants of those days" then occupying it; and, as John White Chadwick has said, "it was not long before his place among them was clearly defined and perfectly assured. . . . He was the most pleasing, the most gracious, the most serene and musical of the goodly fellowship. As time went on he became one of the most serious and impressive."]

LADIES AND GENTLEMEN:—Wearied of the world and saddened by the ruin of his fortunes, the Italian Count Maddalo turned from the street, which rang with tales of disaster and swarmed with melancholy faces, into his palace. Perplexed and anxious, he passed through the stately rooms in which hung the portraits of generations of ancestors. The day was hot; his blood was feverish, but the pictures seemed to him cool and remote in a holy calm. He looked at them earnestly; he remembered the long history of which his fathers were parts, he recalled their valor and their patience, and asked himself whether, after all, their manhood was not their patent of nobility; and stretching out his hands towards them, exclaimed: "Let me feel that I am indeed your son by sharing that manhood which made you noble."

We Americans laugh at ancestors; and if the best of

them came back again, we should be as likely to laugh at his wig as listen to his wisdom. And in our evanescent houses and uneasy life we would no more have ancient ranges of family pictures than Arabs in their tents. Yet we are constantly building and visiting the greater portrait gallery of all in the histories we write and read; and the hour is never lost which we give to it. It may teach a maid humility to know that her mother was fairer. It may make a youth more modest to know that his grandsire was braver. For if the pictures of history show us that deformity is as old as grace, and that virtue was always martyred, they also show that crime, however prosperous for a time, is at last disastrous, and that there can be no permanent peace without justice and freedom.

Those pictures teach us also that character is inherited like name and treasure, and that all of us may have famous or infamous ancestors perhaps without knowing it. The melancholy poet, eating his own heart out in a city garret, is the child of Tasso. Grinding Ralph Nickleby, the usurer, is Shylock's grandson. The unjust judge, who declares that some men have no rights which others are bound to respect, is a later Jeffries on his bloody assizes, or dooming Algernon Sidney to the block once more for loving liberty; while he whose dull heart among the new duties of another time is never quickened with public spirit, and who as a citizen aims only at his own selfish advantage, is a later Benedict Arnold whom every generous heart despises.

From this lineage of character arises this great convenience—that as it is bad manners to criticise our neighbors by name, we may hit them many a sly rap over the shoulders of their ancestors who wore turbans, or helmets, or bagwigs, and lived long ago in other countries. The Church especially finds great comfort in this resource, and the backs of the whole Hebrew race must be sore with the scorings they get for the sins of Christian congregations. The timid Peter, the foolish Virgins, the wicked Herod, are pilloried every Sunday in the pulpit, to the great satisfaction of the Peters, Virgins, and Herods dozing in the pews. But when some ardent preacher heading out of his metaphors, and jumping from Judea and the first century into the United States and the nineteenth, disturbs Peter's enjoyment of his ancestor's castigation by saying vehemently to his face with all the lightning of the law in his eye, and its thunders in his voice, " Thou art the man!" Peter recoils with decorous horror, begs his pastor to remember that he and Herod are sheep who were to be led by still waters; warns him not to bring politics into the pulpit, to talk not of living people, but of old pictures. So the poor shepherd is driven back to his pictures, and cudgels Peter once more from behind a metaphor.

But the fairest use of these old pictures is to make us feel our common humanity, and to discover that what seems to us a hopelessly romantic ideal of character is a familiar fact of every day. Heroism is always the same, however the fashion of a hero's clothes may alter. Every hero in history is as near to a man as his neighbor, and if we should tell the simple truth of some of our neighbors, it would sound like poetry. Sir Philip Sidney wore doublet and hose, and died in Flanders three hundred years ago. His name is the synonym of manly honor, of generous scholarship, of the finest nobility, of the spiritual light that most irradiates human nature. Look at his portrait closely; it is no stranger that you see; it is no far-off Englishman. It is your friend, your son, your brother, your lover. Whoever knew Wendell Phillips knew Philip Sidney. It is the same spirit in a thousand forms; a perpetual presence, a constant benediction. Look at his portrait and

> " The night shall be filled with music,
>   And the cares that infest the day
> Shall fold their tents like the Arabs,
>   And as silently steal away."

The gray walls, the red and peaked roof of the old house of Penshurst, stand in the pleasant English valley of the Medway, in soft and showery Kent. Kent is all garden, and there, in November, 1554, Philip Sidney was born. His father, Sir Henry Sidney, was a wise and honest man. Bred at court, his sturdy honor was never corrupted. King Edward died in his arms, and Queen Mary confirmed all his honors and offices three weeks before the birth of his oldest son, whom, in gratitude, he named Philip, for the queen's new Spanish husband. Philip's mother was Mary Dudley, daughter of the Duke of Northumberland, sister of the famous Earl of Leicester, sister also of Lord Guildford Dudley and sister-in-law of Lady Jane Grey. The little Philip was born into a sad household. Within fifteen months his grandfather and uncle had been beheaded for treason; and his sorrowing mother, a truly noble and tender woman, had been the victim of smallpox, and hid her grieving heart and poor scarred face in the silence and seclusion of Penshurst. On the south side of the house was the old garden or plaisance, sloping down to the Medway, where, in those English summers of three hundred years ago, when the cruel fires of Mary were busily burning at Smithfield, the lovely boy Philip, fair-featured, with a high forehead and ruddy brown hair, almost red—the same color as that of his nephew Algernon—walked with his shy mother, picking daisies and chasing butterflies, and calling to her in a soft, musical voice; while within the house the grave father, when he was not away in Wales, of which he was lord-president, mused upon great events that were stirring in Europe—the abdication of Charles V, the fall of Calais, and the accession of Queen Elizabeth to the throne of England. The lordly banqueting-hall, in which the politics of three centuries ago were discussed at Penshurst, is still standing. You may still sit upon the wooden benches where Burleigh, Spenser, Ben Jonson, James I, and his son Prince Charles have sat, and where, a little later, the victim of Prince Charles's cruel son, Algernon Sidney, dreamed of noble manhood and went forth a noble man; while in those shady avenues of beech and oak outside, smooth Edmund Waller bowed and smirked, and sighed compliments to his Sacharissa, as he called Dorothy Sidney, Algernon's sister.

At the age of eleven Master Sidney was put to school at Shrewsbury, on the borders of Wales, of which country his father was lord-president. His fond friend, Fulke Greville, who was here at school with him, and afterwards wrote his life, says that even the masters found something in him to observe and learn. Study probably cost him little effort and few tears. We may be sure he stood at the head of his class, and was a grave, good boy—not good as calves and blanc-mange are, but like wine and oak saplings. " My little Philip," as his mother tenderly calls him, was no Miss Nancy. When he was older he wrote to his brother Robert, then upon his travels, that "if there were any good wars he should go to them." So, at Shrewsbury he doubtless went to all the good wars among his schoolmates, while during the short intervals of peace he mastered his humanities, and at last, when not yet fifteen years old, he was entered at Christ Church, Oxford.

Great good fortune is the most searching test of character. If a man have fine friends, fine family, fine talents, and fine prospects, they are very likely to be the sirens in whose sweet singing he forgets everything but the pleasure of listening to it. If most of us had come of famous ancestry—if our father were vice-regal governor—if the sovereign's favorite were our uncle, who intended us for his heir—if marriage were proposed with the beautiful daughter of the prime minister, and we were ourselves young, handsome, and accomplished—and all this were three hundred years ago, before the rights of men and the dignity of labor had been much discussed, we should probably have come up to Oxford, of which our famous uncle was chancellor, in a state of what would be called at Oxford to-day extreme bumptiousness. But Philip Sidney was too true a gentleman not to be a simple-hearted man ; and although he was even then one of the most accomplished as well as fortunate youths in England, he writes to Lord Burleigh to confess with " heavy grief " that in scholarship he can neither satisfy Burleigh's expectation nor his own desire.

In the month of May, 1572, Philip Sidney left Oxford, and after staying a short time with his parents, following the fashion of young gentlemen of rank, he crossed over into France in the train of the Earl of Lincoln, who was Queen Elizabeth's extraordinary ambassador upon the subject of her marriage with the brother of Charles IX of France. The young King immediately made Sidney a gentleman of the bedchamber, and Henry of Navarre found him a fit companion for a future king. The Paris that Sidney saw had then twice as many inhabitants as Boston has to-day. Montaigne called it the most beautiful city in the world, and it had a delusive air of peace. But the witch Catherine de Medici sat in the smooth-tongued court like a spider in its web, spinning and spinning the meshes in which the hope of liberty was to be entangled. The gay city filled and glittered with the wedding guests of Henry and the King's sister Margaret—among others, the hero of St. Quentin, Admiral Coligny. Gayer and gayer grew the city—smoother and smoother the court— faster and faster spun the black Italian spider—until on the 23d of August, the Eve of St. Bartholomew, the bloodiest deed in all the red annals of that metropolis was done, and the young Sidney looked shuddering from Walsingham House upon the streets reeking with the blood of his fellow Huguenots.

That night made Philip Sidney a man. He heard the applause of the Romish party ring through Europe—he heard the commendation of Philip of Spain—he knew that the most eloquent orator of the Church, Muretus, had congratulated the Pope upon this signal victory of the truth. He knew that medals were stamped in commemoration of the brutal massacre, and he remembered that the same spirit that had struck at the gray head of Coligny had also murdered Egmont and Horne in the Netherlands; had calmly gazed in the person of Philip upon De Sezo perishing in the fire, and by the hand of Philip had denounced death against all who wrote, sold, or read Protestant books; and he knew that the same spirit, in the most thriving and intelligent country of Europe, the Netherlands, was blotting out prosperity in blood, and had driven at least a hundred thousand exiles into England.

Pondering these things, Sidney left Paris, and at Frankfort met Hubert Languet. Languet was not only a Protestant, but, at heart, a Republican. He was the friend of Melancthon and of William of Orange, in whose service he died. One of the most accomplished scholars and shrewdest statesmen in Europe, honored and trusted by all the Protestant leaders, this wise man of fifty-four was so enamored of the English youth of eighteen that they became life-long friends with the ardor of lovers, and Languet left his employment, as Fulke Greville says, "to become a nurse of knowledge to this hopeful young gentleman."

As they traveled by easy stages across Germany, where the campaign of Protestantism had begun, they knew that the decisive battle was yet to be fought. Europe was silent. The tumult of Charles V's reign was over, and that great monarch marched and countermarched no more from the Baltic to the Mediterranean. Charles had been victorious so long as he fought kings with words of steel. But the monk Martin Luther drew the sword of the spirit, and the conqueror quailed. Luther challenged the Church of Rome at its own door. The Vatican rained anathemas. It might as well have tried to blow out the stars; and all the fires of the furious popes who followed Leo were not sharp enough to consume the colossal heresy of free thought. But king and emperor and pope fed the fire. The reign of terror blasted the Netherlands, and when it had succeeded there, when Italy, Austria, and Holland surrounded the states of Germany, Philip knew it would be the smothering coil of the serpent around the cradle of religious liberty. But the young Hercules of free thought throttled the serpent, and leaped forth to win his victorious and immortal race.

We can see it now, but Sidney could not know it. To him the future was as inscrutable as our own to the eyes of thirty years ago. Yet he and Languet must have discussed the time with curious earnestness as they passed through Germany until they reached Vienna. There Sidney devoted himself to knightly games, to tennis, to music, and especially to horsemanship, which he studied with Pagliono, who, in praise of the horse, became such a poet that in the "Defense of Poesy" Sidney says that if he had not been a piece of a logician before he came to him, Pagliono would have persuaded him to wish himself a horse.

At Vienna Philip parted with Languet, and arrived in Venice in the year 1573. The great modern days of Italy were passed. The golden age of the Medici was gone. Lorenzo the Magnificent had died nearly a century before, in the same year that Columbus had discovered America. His son, Pope Leo X, had eaten his last ortolan, had flown his last falcon, had listened to his last comedy, and hummed his last tune, in the frescoed corridors of the Vatican. Upon its shining walls the fatal finger of Martin Luther, stretching out of Germany, had written "Mene, Mene." Beneath the terrible spell the walls were cracking and the earth was shaking, but the splendid pope, in his scarlet cloud of cardinals, saw only the wild beauty of Raphael's Madonnas and the pleasant pages of the recovered literature of pagan Greece. When Sidney stepped for the first time into his gondola at Venice, the famous Italian cathedrals and stately palaces were already built, and the great architects were gone. Dante, Boccaccio, Petrarch, who had created Italian literature, lived about as long before Sidney as we live after him. Cimabue and Giotto had begun; Raphael and Michelangelo had perfected that art in which they have had no rivals—and they were gone. Andrea Doria steered the galleys of Genoa no more, and since the discovery of the Cape of Good Hope and the West Indies, the spices of the Indian sea were brought by Portuguese ships into the Baltic instead of the Adriatic. The glory of the Lombards, who were the first merchants of Europe, had passed away to the descendants of their old correspondents of Bruges and Ghent, until, with its five hundred ships daily coming and going, and on market days eight and nine hundred; with its two thousand heavy wagons creaking every week through the gates from France and Germany and Lorraine, Antwerp reigned in the place of Venice, and the long twilight that has never been broken was settling upon the Italy that Sidney saw.

But the soft splendor of its decline was worthy its prime. The universities of Bologna and Padua, of Salerno and Pisa, had fallen from the days when at Bologna alone there were twenty thousand students; but they were still thronged with pupils, and taught by renowned professors. When the young Sidney came to Venice, Titian was just tottering into the grave, nearly a hundred years old, but still holding the pencil which Charles V had picked up and handed to him in his studio. Galileo was a youth of twenty, studying mathematics at Pisa. The melancholy Tasso was completing his "Jerusalem Delivered" under the cypress trees of the Villa d'Este.

Palestrina was composing the masses which reformed church music, and the Christian charity of Charles Borromeo was making him a saint before he was canonized. Clad in the silk and velvet of Genoa, the young Englishman went to study geometry at Padua, where twenty years later Galileo would have been his teacher, and Sidney writes to Languet that he was perplexed whether to sit to Paul Veronese or to Tintoretto for his portrait.

But he had a shrewd eye for the follies of travelers, and speaks of their tendency to come home " full of disguisements not only of apparel but of our countenances, as though the credit of a traveler stood all upon his outside." He then adds a curious prophecy, which Shakespeare made haste to fulfil to the very letter. Sidney says, writing in 1578, " I think, ere it be long, like the mountebanks in Italy, we travelers shall be made sport of in comedies." Twenty years afterwards, Shakespeare makes Rosalind say in " As You Like It," " Farewell, Monsieur Traveler: Look you, lisp and wear strange suits; disable all the benefits of your own country; be out of love with your nativity, and almost chide God for making you that countenance you are, or I will scarce think you have swam in a gondola."

But in all the gayeties and graces of his travel, Philip Sidney was not content to be merely an elegant lounger. He never forgot for a moment that all his gifts and accomplishments were only weapons to be kept burnished for his country's service. He was a boy of twenty, but his boy's warmth was tempered by the man's wisdom. " You are not over-cheerful by nature," Languet writes to him; and when Sidney sat to Paul Veronese, and sent his friend the portrait, Languet replies: " The painter has represented you sad and thoughtful."

He had reason to be so. He had seen the Massacre of St. Bartholomew, as many a young Sidney among ourselves saw the horrors of Kansas thirty years ago. He did not believe that a little timely patting on the back was statesmanship. If Spain were crushing the Netherlands, and hung upon the southern horizon of Europe a black and threatening cloud, he did not believe that the danger would be averted by gagging those who said the storm was coming. He did not hold the thermometer

responsible for the weather. " I cannot think," he wrote
in May, 1574, "there is any man possessed of common
understanding who does not see to what these rough
storms are driving by which all Christendom has been
agitated now these many years." He did not suppose,
as so many of us in our ignoble days, that while men
were the same, the tragical differences which had been
washed out with blood in all other ages could be drowned
in milk and water in his own.

In 1575 Sidney returned to England. Every author
who writes of this period breaks out into the most glowing praises of him. Indeed, he is the choice darling of
English history. The only discordant note in the chorus
of praise came long afterwards in the voice of the pedan-
tic dandy Horace Walpole, who called Goldsmith "an
inspired idiot." This is not surprising, for the earnestness and heroic simplicity of Sidney were as incomprehensible to the affected trifler of Strawberry Hill as the
fresh enthusiasm of his nephew Arthur to Major Pen-
dennis. The Earl of Leicester, who seemed to love his
nephew more than anything except his own ambition,
presented his brilliant young relative to the queen, who
made him her cup-bearer. Sidney was now twenty-one
years old—the finest gentleman, and one of the most
accomplished scholars in England. His learning was
mainly in the classics and in languages; yet he confesses
that he could never learn German, which was then hardly
worth learning, and in his correspondence with Languet
is very distrustful of the Latin, in which language they
wrote. But in urging him to grapple with the German,
Languet says to him, and it is a striking proof of the
exquisite finish of Sidney's accomplishment, " I have
watched you closely when speaking my own language (he
was a Burgundian), but I hardly ever detected you pro-
nouncing a single syllable wrongly."

In Sidney's time the classics had few rivals. After
reading Dante, Petrarch, Ariosto, Boccaccio, with Sanna-
zaro's "Arcadia," in Italian; Rabelais, Froissart, and
Comines, in French; Chaucer, Gower, and the "Mirror
for Magistrates," in English, what remained for an ardent
young student to devour? When Sidney came home,
Montaigne—whom he probably saw at the French Court

—was just writing his "Essays" at his château in the Gironde. The Portuguese Camoens had only just published his great poem, to which his own country would not listen, and of which no other had heard. The Italian Tasso's "Jerusalem" was still in manuscript, and the Spanish Ponce de Leon was little known to Europe. All was yet to come. In Spain, Cervantes, Lope de Vega, and Calderon; in France, Corneille and Racine and Molière, Fénelon and Bossuet, Rousseau and Voltaire; in Germany, everything except the Niebelungen and Hans Sachs's rhymes. When Philip Sidney kissed Elizabeth's hand as her cup-bearer, William Shakespeare, a boy of eleven, was grinding out his trousers on the restless seats of the free grammar-school at Stratford; young Francis Bacon, a youth of sixteen, was studying in France; a poor scholar at Cambridge, Edmund Spenser was just finishing his studies, and the younger brother of an old Devonshire family, Walter Raleigh, had just returned from campaigning in France; indeed, all the literature of modern times was subsequent to Philip Sidney. The young man shone at court, fascinating men and women, courtiers, scholars, and divines; and in a few months was made special ambassador to condole with the Austrian Emperor upon the death of his father. Upon this embassy he departed in great state. His mission was supposed to be purely complimentary; but he was really the beautiful eye with which England and Elizabeth, becoming the head of the Protestant movement, watched the disposition of the Protestant princes. On his way home, Sidney passed into the Low Countries to see William of Orange. He came, resplendent with chivalric magnificence, accompanied by the flower of English nobility, and met the grave William, who had been the richest citizen in the Netherlands, clad in an old serge cloak, and surrounded by plain Dutch burghers. But it was a meeting of men of one mind and heart in the great cause, and neither was disturbed by the tailoring of the other. The interview was the beginning of a faithful friendship, and among all the compliments Sidney received, none is so lofty and touching as that of William, the greatest man in Europe, who called him in their correspondence, "Philip, my master."

In 1577 Sidney was home again. He had a right to expect conspicuous advancement, but he got nothing. This was the more disagreeable, because living at Elizabeth's court was an expensive luxury for a poor gentleman's son who had magnificent tastes. His father, Lord Henry Sidney, was lord-deputy of Ireland, but he was also an honest man, and, like most honest men in high public office, he was not rich. He wrote to Philip, begging him to remember whose son, not whose nephew, he was; for Philip's companions, the golden youth of the court, blazed in silks and velvets and jewels, until the government had to impose laws, as the subjects had brought luxury from Venice, and Elizabeth, who died the happy owner of three thousand dresses, issued a solemn proclamation against extravagance in dress.

At such a time, the brilliant nephew of Uncle Leicester would have been a quickly ruined man if he had not been Philip Sidney. He bowed and flirted at court, but he chafed under inaction. A marriage was planned for him with Penelope Devereaux, sister of the famous Earl of Essex, one of the thousand fair and unfortunate women who flit across the page of history leaving only a name, and that written in tears. But Philip's father grew cool in the negotiation, and Philip himself was perfectly passive. Yet when a few years afterwards the lady was married to Lord Rich, who abused her, Sidney loved her, and wrote the sonnets to Stella, which are his best poetry, and which Charles Lamb so affectionately praised.

But while he loitered at court, beating all the courtiers with their own weapons in wit, in riding, in games, at tournament, the tales of American discovery shed a wondrous glamour upon the new continent. Nothing was too beautiful for belief, and the fiery feet of youth burned the English soil with eagerness to tread the unutterable Tropics. Francis Drake sailed from Plymouth to follow Magellan around the world, and he went in a manner consonant with the popular fancy of the countless riches that rewarded such adventures. His cooking vessels were of silver; his table plate of exquisite workmanship. The Queen knighted him, gave him a sword, and said, " Whoever striketh at you, Drake, striketh at us." A band of musicians accompanied the fleet, and the English sailor

went to circumnavigate the globe with the same non-
chalant magnificence with which in other days the gorgeous Alcibiades, with flutes and soft recorders blowing
under silken sails, came idling home from victory.

Philip Sidney, his heart alive to all romance, and longing to be his companion, saw him sail away. But he
turned and saw the black Italian spider, whose sting he
had seen on Bartholomew's Eve in Paris, still weaving
her stealthy web, and seeking to entangle Elizabeth into
a match with the Duke of Anjou. The Queen was forty-
six, and Mounseer, as the English called him, twenty-
three; and while she was coaxing herself to say the most
fatal yes that ever woman said—when Burleigh, Leicester, Walsingham, all the safe, sound, conservative old
gentlemen and counsellors were just ceasing to dissuade
her—Philip Sidney, a youth of twenty-five, who knew
that he had a country as well as a queen, that the hope of
that country lay in the triumph of Protestantism, and
that to marry Mounseer was to abandon that hope, and
for the time betray mankind—Philip Sidney, a youth who
did not believe that he could write gravely of sober
things because he had written gayly of ladies' eyebrows,
knowing as the true-hearted gentleman always knows
that to-day it may be a man's turn to sit at a desk in an
office, or bend over a book in college, or fashion a horse-
shoe at the forge, or toss flowers to some beauty at her
window, and to-morrow to stand firm against a cruel
church or a despotic court, a brutal snob or an ignorant
public opinion—this youth, this immortal gentleman,
wrote the letter which dissuaded her from the marriage,
and which was as noble a triumph for Protestantism and
human liberty as the defeat of the Spanish Armada.

I cannot follow this lovely life in detail, nor linger, as
I would, upon his literary retirement. The very name
of Sidney's "Arcadia" is aromatic in the imagination,
and its traditional place in our literature is unquestioned.
In our day it is very little read, nor is it a very interesting
story. But under its quaint and courtly conceit its tone
is so pure and lofty, its courtesy and appreciation of
women so hearty and honorable; it has so fine a moral
atmosphere, such noble thoughts, such stately and beautiful descriptions, that to read it is like conversing with a

hero. So there is no better reading than the "Defence of Poesy," that noble hymn of loyalty to intellectual beauty. Hallam well calls Sidney "the first good prose writer" in our language, and scarcely had he finished in his "Defence" an exquisite criticism of English poetry to that time than the full choir of Elizabethan poets burst into

> "the songs that fill
> The spacious times of great Elizabeth
> With sounds that echo still."

In 1582 Philip Sidney married the daughter of Walsingham, but in his retirement, whether steadfastly watching the great struggle upon the Continent or listening to the alluring music of far-off seas, he knew that the choice days of his life were passing, and if a career were not opened for him by the Queen, he must make one for himself. William of Orange had been murdered; Elizabeth promptly succeeded him as the active head of the Protestant world; Philip of Spain was the great enemy. Strike him at home, said Sidney; strike him at sea, but strike him everywhere; and he arranged with Drake a descent upon Spanish America. He hurried privately to Plymouth to embark, but at the last moment a peer of the realm arrived from the Queen forbidding his departure. The loyal gentleman bowed and obeyed.

But two months after his fleet sailed, on the 7th of November, 1585 (about the time that William Shakespeare first came to London), Elizabeth appointed Sidney Governor of Flushing, in the Netherlands. He went thither gladly on the 18th, with three thousand men, to strike for the cause in which he believed. He had already told the Queen that the spirit of the Netherlands was the spirit of God, and was invincible. His uncle, the Earl of Leicester, followed him as commander-in-chief. The earl was handsome at tournaments, but not fit for battle-fields, and Sidney was annoyed by his uncle's conduct; but he writes to his father-in-law, Walsingham, in a strain full of the music of a noble soul, and fitly precluding his end: "I think a wise and constant man ought never to grieve while he doth play, as a man may say, his own part truly."

For that he was always ready. In the misty dawn of the 22d of September, 1586, a force of three thousand Spaniards stole silently along to the relief of Zutphen, on the river Isel. Sidney, at the head of five hundred cavalry, rode forward to meet them. In the obscurity the battle was sharp and confused. Seeing his friend Lord Willoughby in special danger, Sidney spurred to the rescue. His horse was shot under him and fell. Springing upon another, he dashed forward again and succored his friend, but at the instant a shot struck him below the knee, glancing upward. His furious horse became unmanageable, and Sir Philip was obliged to leave the field. But as he passed slowly along to the rear of the soldiers, he felt faint with bleeding, and called for water. A cup was brought to him, but as he was lifting it to his mouth he saw a dying soldier staring at it with burning eyes. Philip Sidney paused before tasting it, leaned from the saddle, and handed it to the soldier, saying to him in the same soft, musical voice with which the boy called to his mother in the sunny garden at Penshurst, "Friend, thy necessity is yet greater than mine."

He was borne on to Araheim, and lived in suffering for twenty-six days. He conversed pleasantly and called for music, and said at last to his brother, whom he had loved as brothers seldom love: "Love my memory; cherish my friends. Their faith to me may assure you they are honest. But, above all, govern your will and affections by the will and word of your Creator, in me beholding the end of this world with all her vanities." "And so," says old Stowe, with fond particularity, "he died, the 17th day of October, between two and three of the clock in the afternoon."

> "The boast of heraldry, the pomp of power,
> And all that beauty, all that wealth e'er gave,
> Await alike the inevitable hour.
> The paths of glory lead but to the grave."

This is the story of Philip Sidney. A letter, a book, a battle. How little to justify his unique fame! How invisible his performance among the illustrious events of his prodigious age! Yet is not the instinct of the human heart true; and in the stately society of his time, if Bacon were the philosopher, Shakespeare the poet, Burleigh the counsellor, Raleigh the soldier, Drake the sailor, Hooker the theologian, Essex the courtier, and Gresham the merchant, was not Philip Sidney as distinctively the gentleman? Heroes stood beside him in clusters, poets in constellations; all the illustrious men of the age achieved more tangible results than he, yet none of them has carved his name upon history more permanently and with a more diamond point; for he had that happy harmony of mind and temper, of enthusiasm and good sense, of accomplishment and capacity, which is described by that most exquisite and most abused word, gentleman. His guitar hung by a ribbon at his side, but his sword hung upon leather beneath it. His knee bent gallantly to the Queen, but it knelt reverently also to his Maker. And it was the crown of the gentleman that he was neither ashamed of the guitar nor of the sword; neither of the loyalty nor the prayer. For a gentleman is not an idler, a trifler, a dandy; he is not a scholar only, a soldier, a mechanic, a merchant; he is the flower of men, in whom the accomplishment of the scholar, the bravery of the soldier, the skill of the mechanic, the sagacity of the merchant, all have their part and appreciation. A sense of duty is his mainspring, and like a watch crusted with precious stones, his function is not to look prettily, but to tell the time of day. Philip Sidney was not a gentleman because his grandfather was the Duke of Northumberland and his father lord-deputy of Ireland, but because he was himself generous, simple, truthful, noble, refined. He was born with a gold spoon in his mouth, but the gold is only the test. In the mouths of the base it becomes brass and iron. George IV, called with bitter irony the first gentleman in Europe, was born with the gold spoon, but his acrid humors turned it to the basest metal, betraying his mean soul. George Stephenson was born with the pewter spoon in his mouth, but the true temper of his soul turned it into pure gold. The test of a gentleman is his use, not his uselessness; whether that use be direct or indirect, whether it be actual service or only inspiring and aiding action. "To what purpose should our thoughts be directed to various kinds of knowledge," wrote Philip Sidney in 1578, "unless room be afforded for putting it into practice so that public advantage may be the result?" And Algernon Sidney said, nearly a century later: "I have ever had it in my mind that when God cast me into such a condition as that I cannot save my life but by doing an indecent thing, He shows me the time has come wherein I should resign it." And when that time came he did resign it; for every gentleman instinctively serves justice and liberty. He feels himself personally disgraced by an insult to humanity, for he, too, is only a man; and however stately his house may be and murmurous with music, however glowing with pictures and graceful with statues and reverend with books—however his horses may out-trot other horses, and his yachts outsail all yachts—the gentleman is king and master of these and not their servant; he wears them for ornament, like the ring upon his finger or the flower in his buttonhole, and if they go the gentleman remains. He knows that all their worth came from human genius and human training; and loving man more than the works of man, he instinctively shuns whatever in the shape of man is degraded, outraged, and forsaken. He does not make the poverty of others the reason for robbing them; he does not make the oppression of others the reason for oppressing them, for his gentility is his religion; and therefore with simple truth and tender audacity the old English dramatist Dekkar calls Him who gave the name to our religion, and who destroyed the plea that might makes right, "the first true gentleman that ever breathed."

But not only is Philip Sidney's story the poem of a gentleman, it is that of a young man. It was the age of young men. No man was thought flippant, whatever his years, who could say a good thing well, or do a brave thing successfully, or give the right advice at the right moment. The great men of the day were all young. At sixteen Bacon had already sketched his "Philosophy." At seventeen Walter Raleigh had gone to find some good wars. At seventeen Edmund Spenser had first published. Before he was twenty, Alexander Farnese, Prince of Parma, and the greatest general of Sidney's time, had revealed his masterly genius. At twenty-one Don John of

Austria had been commander-in-chief against the Moors.
The Prince of Condé and Henry of Navarre were leaders
while they were yet boys. At twenty Francis Drake
sailed, a captain, with John Hawkins; and at twenty-one
the Washington of European history, to whom an American has for the first time paid just homage with an enthusiasm and eloquence of Sidney describing his friend
—at twenty-one William of Orange commanded an army
of Charles V.

When England wanted leaders in those tremendous
days that shaped her destiny, it did just what America
did in those recent perilous hours that determined hers
—she sent young men with faith in their hearts and fire
in their veins—not old men with feathers in their hats;
and everywhere it is the young men who have made history. At thirty-two Alexander wept for another world
to conquer. On his thirty-seventh birthday Raphael lay
dead beneath his last picture. At thirty-six Mozart had
sung his swan-song. At twenty-five Hannibal was commander-in-chief of the Carthaginian armies. At thirty-
three Turenne was Marshal of France. At twenty-seven
Bonaparte was triumphant in Italy. At forty-five Wel-
lington had conquered Bonaparte, and at forty-eight retired from active military service. At forty-three Washington was chief of the Continental army. On his forty-
fifth birthday Sherman was piercing the heart of the
American Rebellion; and before he was forty-three Grant
had "fought it out on this line" to perfect victory.
Young men! Of course they were young men. Youth is
the mainspring of the world. The experience of age is
wise in action only when it is electrified by the enthusiasm of youth. Show me a land in which the young men
are cold and skeptical and prematurely wise; in which
polite indifference is called political wisdom, contempt
for ideas common sense, and honesty in politics Sunday-
school statesmanship—show me a land in which the young
men are more anxious about doing well than about doing
right—and I will show you a country in which public
corruption and ruin overtakes private infidelity and
cowardice, and in which, if there were originally a hope
for mankind, a faith in principle, and a conquering enthusiasm, that faith, hope, and enthusiasm are expiring

like the deserted camp-fires of a retiring army. Woe to a man when his heart grows old! Woe to a nation when its young men shuffle in the gouty shoes and limp on the untimely crutches of age, instead of leaping along the course of life with the jubilant spring of their years and the sturdy play of their own muscles! Sir Philip Sidney's was the age of young men: and wherever there are self-reliance, universal human sympathy, and confidence in God, there is the age of youth and national triumph; just as whenever Joan of Arc leads the army, or Molly Stark dares to be a widow, or Rosa Bonheur paints, or Hattie Hosmer carves, or Jenny Lind sings, or Mrs. Patten steers the wrecked ship to port, or Florence Nightingale walks the midnight hospital—these are the age and the sphere of woman. Queen Elizabeth's was the age of young men; but so it is always when there are young men who can make an age.

And ours is such an age. We live in a country which has been saved by its young men. Before us opens a future which is to be secured by the young men. I have not held up Sir Philip Sidney as a reproach, but only for his brothers to admire—only that we may scatter the glamour of the past and of history, and understand that we do not live in the lees of time and the world's decrepitude. There is no country so fair that ours is not fairer; there is no age so heroic that ours is not as noble; there is no youth in history so romantic and beloved that in a thousand American homes you may not find its peer to-day. It is the Sidneys we have known who interpret this Philip of three hundred years ago. Dear, noble gentleman! he does not move alone in our imaginations, for our own memories supply his splendid society. We too have seen, how often and how often, the bitter fight of the misty morning on the Isel—the ringing charge, the fatal fall. A thousand times we saw the same true Sidney heart that, dying, gave the cup of cold water to a fellow soldier. And we, for whom the Sidneys died, let us thank God for showing us in our own experience, as in history, that the noblest traits of human character are still spanned by the rainbow of perfect beauty; and that human love and faith and fidelity, like day and night, like seed-time and harvest, shall never, never fail.

RALPH WALDO EMERSON

Photogravure after a photograph from life

RALPH WALDO EMERSON

THE CONSERVATIVE

[Lecture by Ralph Waldo Emerson, essayist and poet (born in Boston, Mass., May 25, 1803; died in Concord, Mass., April 27, 1882), delivered first in the Masonic Temple, Boston, December 9, 1841. This was the second in the series of eight lectures composing Mr. Emerson's course under the general title, "On the Times," subsequently repeated separately on many lecture platforms.]

LADIES AND GENTLEMEN:—The two parties which divide the state, the party of Conservatism and that of Innovation, are very old, and have disputed the possession of the world ever since it was made. This quarrel is the subject of civil history. The conservative party established the reverend hierarchies and monarchies of the most ancient world. The battle of patrician and plebeian, of parent state and colony, of old usage and accommodation to new facts, of the rich and the poor, reappears in all countries and times. The war rages not only in battle-fields, in national councils, and ecclesiastical synods, but agitates every man's bosom with opposing advantages every hour. On rolls the whole world meantime, and now one, now the other gets the day, and still the fight renews itself as if for the first time, under new names and hot personalities.

Such an irreconcilable antagonism, of course, must have a corresponding depth of seat in the human constitution. It is the opposition of Past and Future, of Memory and Hope, of the Understanding and the Reason. It is the primal antagonism, the appearance in trifles of the two poles of nature.

There is a fragment of old fable which seems somehow to have been dropped from the current mythologies, which may deserve attention, as it appears to relate to this subject.   Saturn grew weary of sitting alone, or with none but the great Uranus or Heaven beholding him, and he created an oyster.   Then he would act again, but he made nothing more, but went on creating the race of oysters.   Then Uranus cried: "A new work, O Saturn! the old is not good again."   Saturn replied: "I fear. There is not only the alternative of making and not making, but also of unmaking.   Seest thou the great sea, how it ebbs and flows? so is it with me; my power ebbs; and if I put forth my hands, I shall not do, but undo.   Therefore I do what I have done; I hold what I have got; and so I resist Night and Chaos."   "O Saturn," replied Uranus, "thou canst not hold thine own but by making more.   Thy oysters are barnacles and cockles, and with the next flowing of the tide, they will be pebbles and seafoam."   "I see," rejoins Saturn, "thou art in league with Night, thou art become an evil eye; thou speakest from love: now thy words smite me with hatred.   I appeal to Fate, must there not be rest?"—"I appeal to Fate, also," said Uranus; "must there not be motion?"—But Saturn was silent, and went on making oysters for a thousand years.   After that, the word of Uranus came into his mind like a ray of the sun, and he made Jupiter; and then he feared again; and nature froze; the things that were made went backward, and, to save the world, Jupiter slew his father Saturn.

This may stand for the earliest account of a conversation on politics between a Conservative and a Radical, which has come down to us.   It is ever thus.   It is the counteraction of the centripetal and the centrifugal forces. Innovation is the salient energy: Conservatism the pause on the last movement.   "That which is was made by God," saith Conservatism.   "He is leaving that, he is entering this other," rejoins Innovation.

There is always a certain meanness in the argument of Conservatism, joined with a certain superiority in its fact. It affirms because it holds.   Its fingers clutch the fact, and it will not open its eyes to see a better fact.   The castle which Conservatism is set to defend, is the actual state of things, good and bad.   The project of Innovation is the best possible state of things.   Of course, Conservatism always has the worst of the argument, is always apologizing, pleading a necessity, pleading that to change would be to deteriorate; it must saddle itself with the mountainous load of all the violence and vice of society; must deny the possibility of good, deny ideas, and suspect and stone the prophet; whilst Innovation is always in the right, triumphant, attacking and sure of final success. Conservatism stands on man's incontestable limitations; Reform on his indisputable infinitude; Conservatism on circumstance; Liberalism on power; one goes to make an adroit member of the social frame; the other to postpone all things to the man himself; Conservatism is debonair and social; Reform is individual and imperious. We are reformers in spring and summer, in autumn and winter we stand by the old; reformers in the morning, conservers at night. Reform is affirmative, Conservatism negative; Conservatism goes for comfort, Reform for truth. Conservatism is more candid to behold another's worth; Reform more disposed to maintain and increase its own. Conservatism makes no poetry, breathes no prayer, has no invention; it is all memory. Reform has no gratitude, no prudence, no husbandry. It makes a great difference to your figure and to your thought, whether your foot is advancing or receding. Conservatism never puts the foot forward; in the hour when it does that, it is no establishment, but reform. Conservatism tends to universal seeming and treachery, believes a negative fate; believes that men's temper governs them; that for me, it avails not to trust in principles; they will fail me; I must bend a little; it distrusts nature; it thinks there is a general law without a particular application—law for all that does not include any one. Reform in its antagonism inclines to asinine resistance, to kick with hoofs; it runs to egotism and bloated self-conceit; it runs to a bodiless pretension, to unnatural refining and elevation, which ends in hypocrisy and sensual reaction.

And so whilst we do not go beyond general statements, it may be safely affirmed of these two metaphysical antagonists, that each is a good half, but an impossible whole. Each exposes the abuses of the other, but in a true society, in a true man, both must combine. Nature does not give the crown of its approbation, namely, Beauty, to any action or emblem or actor, but to one which combines both these elements; not to the rock which resists the waves from age to age, nor to the wave which lashes incessantly the rock; but the superior beauty is with the oak, which stands with its hundred arms against the storms of a century, and grows every year like a sapling; or the river which, ever flowing, yet is found in the same bed from age to age; or, greatest of all, the man who has subsisted for years amid the changes of nature, yet has distanced himself so that when you remember what he was, and see what he is, you say, What strides! What a disparity is here!

Throughout nature the past combines in every creature with the present. Each of the convolutions of the sea-shell, each of its nodes and spines marks one year of the fish's life, what was the mouth of the shell for one season, with the addition of new matter by the growth of the animal, becoming an ornamental node. The leaves and a shell of soft wood are all that the vegetation of this summer has made, but the solid columnar stem, which lifts that bank of foliage into the air, to draw the eye and to cool us with its shade, is the gift and legacy of dead and buried years.

In nature, each of these elements being always present, each theory has a natural support. As we take our stand on Necessity, or on Ethics, shall we go for the Conservative, or for the Reformer? If we read the world historically, we shall say, of all the ages, the present hour and circumstance is the cumulative result, this is the best throw of the dice of nature that has yet been, or that is yet possible. If we see it from the side of Will, or the moral Sentiment, we shall accuse the Past and the Present, and require the impossible of the Future.

But although this bifold fact lies thus united in real nature, and so united that no man can continue to exist in whom both these elements do not work, yet men are not philosophers, but are rather very foolish children, who by reason of their partiality, see everything in the most absurd manner, and who are the victims at all times of the nearest object. There is even no philosopher who is a philosopher at all times. Our experience, our perception is conditioned by the need to require in parts and in succession, that is, with every truth a certain falsehood. As this is the invariable method of our training, we must give it allowance, and suffer men to learn as they have done for six millenniums, a word at a time, to pair off into insane parties, and learn the amount of truth each knows, by the denial of an equal amount of truth. For the present, then, to come at what sum is attainable to us, we must even hear the parties plead as parties.

That which is best about Conservatism, that which, though it cannot be expressed in detail, inspires reverence in all, is the Inevitable. There is the question, not only what the Conservative says for himself, but, far deeper, why he must say it. What insurmountable fact binds him to that side? Here is the fact which men call Fate, and fate in dread degrees, fate behind fate, not to be disposed of by the consideration that the Conscience commands this or that, but necessitating the question, whether the faculties of man will play him true in resisting the facts of universal experience? For although the commands of the Conscience are essentially absolute, they are historically limitary. Wisdom does not seek a literal rectitude, but a useful, that is, a conditional one, such a one as the faculties of man and the constitution of things will warrant. The Reformer, the partisan, loses himself in driving to the utmost some specialty of right conduct, until his own nature and all nature resist him; but Wisdom attempts nothing enormous and disproportioned to its powers, nothing which it cannot perform or nearly perform. We have all a certain intellection or presentiment of reform existing in the mind, which does not yet descend into the character, and those who throw themselves blindly on this lose themselves. Whatever they attempt in that direction fails, and reacts suicidally on the actor himself. This is the penalty of having transcended nature. For the existing world is not a dream, and cannot with impunity be treated as a dream; neither is it a disease; but it is the ground on which you stand, it is the mother of whom you were born. Reform converses with possibilities, perchance with impossibilities; but here is sacred fact. This also was true, or it could not be: it had life in it, or it could not have ex-

isted; it has life in it, or it could not continue. Your
schemes may be feasible, or may not be, but this has the
indorsement of nature, and a long friendship and cohabi-
tation with the powers of nature. This will stand until a
better cast of the dice is made. The contest between the
Future and the Past is one between Divinity entering and
Divinity departing. You are welcome to try your experi-
ments, and, if you can, to displace the actual order by
that idle republic you announce, for nothing but God
will expel God. But plainly the burden of proof must lie
with the projector. We hold to this, until you can demonstrate something better.

The system of property and law goes back for its origin
to barbarous and sacred times; it is the fruit of the same
mysterious cause as the mineral or animal world. There
is a natural sentiment and prepossession in favor of age,
of ancestors, of barbarous and aboriginal usages, which
is a homage to this element of necessity and divinity
which is in them. The respect for the old names of places,
of mountains, and streams, is universal. The Indian and
barbarous name can never be supplanted without loss.
The ancients tell us that the gods loved the Ethiopians
for their stable customs; and the Egyptians and Chal-
deans, whose origin could not be explored, passed among
the junior tribes of Greece and Italy for sacred nations.

Moreover, so deep is the foundation of the existing social system, that it leaves no one out of it. We may be
partial, but Fate is not. All men have their root in it.
You who quarrel with the arrangements of society, and
are willing to embroil all, and risk the indisputable good
that exists, for the chance of better, live, move, and have
your being in this, and your deeds contradict your words
every day. For as you cannot jump from the ground
without using the resistance of the ground, nor put out
the boat to sea without shoving from the shore, nor attain liberty without rejecting obligation, so you are under
the necessity of using the actual order of things, in order
to disuse it; to live by it, whilst you wish to take away its
life. The past has baked your loaf, and in the strength
of its bread you would break up the oven. But you are
betrayed by your own nature. You also are conserva-

tive. However men please to style themselves, I see no other than a conservative party. You are not only identical with us in your needs, but also in your methods and aims. You quarrel with my conservatism, but it is to build up one of your own; it will have a new beginning, but the same course and end, the same trials, the same passions; among the lovers of the new I observe that there is a jealousy of the newest, and that the seceder from the seceder is as damnable as the Pope himself.

On these and the like grounds of general statement, Conservatism plants itself without danger of being displaced. Especially before this personal appeal, the Innovator must confess his weakness, must confess that no man is to be found good enough to be entitled to stand champion for the principle. But when this great tendency comes to practical encounters, and is challenged by young men, to whom it is no abstraction, but a fact of hunger, distress, and exclusion from opportunities, it must needs seem injurious. The youth, of course, is an Innovator by the fact of his birth. There he stands, newly born on the planet, a universal beggar, with all the reason of things, one would say, on his side. In his first consideration how to feed, clothe, and warm himself, he is met by warnings on every hand, that this thing and that thing have owners, and he must go elsewhere. Then he says: "If I am born into the earth, where is my part? Have the goodness, gentlemen of the world, to show me my wood-lot, where I may fell my wood; my field, where to plant my corn; my pleasant ground, where to build my cabin."

"Touch any wood, or field, or house-lot, on your peril," cry all the gentlemen of this world; "but you may come and work in ours, for us, and we will give you a piece of bread."

"And what is that peril?"

"Knives and muskets, if we meet you in the act; imprisonment if we find you afterward."

"And by what authority, kind gentlemen?"

"By our law."

"And your law—is it just?"

"As just for you as it was for us. We wrought for others under this law, and got our lands so."

" I repeat the question, is your law just? "

" Not quite just, but necessary. Moreover, it is juster now than it was when we were born; we have made it milder and more equal."

" I will none of your law," returns the youth. " It encumbers me. I cannot understand, or so much as spare time to read that needless library of your laws. Nature has sufficiently provided me with rewards and sharp penalties to bind me not to transgress. Like the Persian noble of old, I ask 'that I may neither command nor obey.' I do not wish to enter into your complex social system. I shall serve those whom I can, and they who can will serve me. I shall seek those whom I love, and shun those whom I love not, and what more can all your laws render me?"

With equal earnestness and good faith, replies to this plaintiff an upholder of the establishment, a man of many virtues:—

" Your opposition is feather-brained and overfine. Young man, I have no skill to talk with you, but look at me; I have risen early and sat late, and toiled honestly and painfully, for very many years. I never dreamed about methods; I laid my bones to, and drudged for the good I possess; it was not got by fraud, nor by luck, but by work, and you must show me a warrant like these stubborn facts in your own fidelity and labor, before I suffer you, on the faith of a few fine words, to ride into my estate, and claim to scatter it as your own."

" Now you touch the heart of the matter," replies the Reformer. "To that fidelity and labor, I pay homage. I am unworthy to arrange your manner of living, until I too have been tried. But I should be more unworthy if I did not tell you why I cannot walk in your steps. I find this vast network, which you call property, extends over the whole planet. I cannot occupy the bleakest crag of the White Hills or the Allegheny Range, but some man or corporation steps up to me to show me that it is his. Now, though I am very peaceable, and on my private account could well enough die, since it appears there was some mistake in my creation, and that I have been missent to this earth, where all the seats were already taken,—yet I feel called upon in behalf of rational nature, which I represent, to declare to you my opinion, that if the Earth is yours, so also is it mine. All your aggregate existences are less to me a fact than is my own; as I am born to the Earth, so the Earth is given to me, what I want of it to till and to plant; nor could I without pusillanimity omit to claim so much. I must not only have a name to live, I must live. My genius leads me to build a different manner of life from any of yours. I cannot then spare you the whole world. I love you better. I must tell you the truth practically: and take that which you call yours. It is God's world and mine; yours as much as you want, mine as much as I want. Besides, I know your ways; I know the symptoms of the disease. To the end of your power, you will serve this lie which cheats you. Your want is a gulf which the possession of the broad earth would not fill. Yonder sun in heaven you would pluck down from shining on the universe, and make him a property or privacy, if you could; and the moon and the north star you would quickly have occasion for in your closet and bed-chamber. What you do not want for use, you crave for ornament, and what your convenience could spare, your pride cannot."

On the other hand, precisely the defense which was set up for the British Constitution—namely, that with all its admitted defects, rotten boroughs and monopolies, it worked well, and substantial justice was somehow done; the wisdom and the worth did get into Parliament, and every interest did by right, or might, or sleight, get represented—the same defense is set up for the existing institutions. They are not the best; they are not just; and in respect to you, personally, O brave young man! they cannot be justified. They have, it is most true, left you no acre for your own, and no law but our law, to the ordaining of which you were no party. But they do answer the end, they are really friendly to the good: unfriendly to the bad; they second the industrious and the kind; they foster genius. They really have so much flexibility as to afford your talent and character, on the whole, the same chance of demonstration and success which they might have, if there was no law and no property.

It is trivial and merely superstitious to say that nothing

is given you, no outfit, no exhibition; for in this institution of credit, which is as universal as honesty and promise in the human countenance, always some neighbor stands ready to be bread, and land, and tools, and stock to the young adventurer. And if in any one respect they have come short, see what ample retribution of good they have made. They have lost no time and spared no expense to collect libraries and museums and galleries, colleges, palaces, hospitals, observatories, cities. The ages have not been idle, nor kings slack, nor the rich niggardly. Have we not atoned for this small offense (which we could not help) of leaving you no right in the soil, by this splendid indemnity of ancestral and national wealth? Would you have been born like a gypsy in a hedge, and preferred your freedom on a heath, and the range of a planet which had no shed or boscage to cover you from sun and wind,—to this towered and citied world? to this world of Rome, and Memphis, and Constantinople, and Vienna, and Paris, and London, and New York? For thee, Naples, Florence, and Venice—for thee, the fair Mediterranean, the sunny Adriatic—for thee both Indies smile; for thee the hospitable North opens its heated palaces under the polar circle; for thee roads have been cut in every direction across the land, and fleets of floating palaces, with every security for strength, and provision for luxury, swim by sail and by steam through all the waters of this world. Every island for thee has a town; every town a hotel. Though thou wast born landless, yet to thy industry and thrift and small condescension to the established usage,—scores of servants are swarming in every strange place with cap and knee to thy command; scores, nay hundreds and thousands, for thy wardrobe, thy table, thy chamber, thy library, thy leisure; and every whim is anticipated and served by the best ability of the whole population of each country. The king on the throne governs for thee, and the judge judges; the barrister pleads, the farmer tills, the joiner hammers, the postman rides. Is it not exaggerating a trifle to insist on a formal acknowledgment of your claims, when these substantial advantages have been secured to you? Now can your children be educated, your labor turned to their advantage, and its fruits secured to them after your death. It is frivolous to say that you have no acre because you have not a mathematically measured piece of land. Providence takes care that you shall have a place, that you are waited for and come accredited; and as soon as you put your gift to use, you shall have acre or acre's worth according to your exhibition of desert,—acre, if you need land;—acre's worth, if you prefer to draw, or carve, or make shoes, or wheels, to the tilling of the soil.

Besides, it might temper your indignation at the supposed wrong which society has done you, to keep the question before you, how society got into this predicament? Who put things on this false basis? No single man, but all men. No man voluntarily and knowingly, but it is the result of that degree of culture there is in the planet. The order of things is as good as the character of the population permits. Consider this as the work of a great and beneficent and progressive necessity, which from the first pulsation of the first animal life, up to the present high culture of the best nations, has advanced thus far. Thank the rude foster-mother that she has taught you a better wisdom than her own, and has set hopes in your heart which shall be history in the next ages. You are yourself the result of this manner of living, this foul compromise, this vituperated Sodom. It nourished you with care and love on its breast, as it had nourished many a lover of the right, and many a poet, and prophet, and teacher of men. Is it so irremediably bad? Then again, if the mitigations are considered, do not all the mischiefs virtually vanish? The form is bad, but see you not how every personal character reacts on the form, and makes it new? A strong person makes the law and custom null before his own will. Then the principle of love and truth reappears in the strictest courts of fashion and property. Under the richest robes, in the darlings of the selectest circles of European or American aristocracy, the strong heart will beat with love of mankind, with impatience of accidental distinctions, with the desire to achieve its own fate, and make every ornament that it wears authentic and real.

Moreover, as we have already shown that there is no pure Reformer, so it is to be considered that there is no pure Conservative, no man who from the beginning to

the end of his life maintains the defective institutions;
but he who sets his face like a flint against every novelty,
when approached in the confidence of conversation in
the presence of friendly and generous persons, has also
his gracious and relenting motions, and espouses for a
time the cause of man; and even if this be a short-lived
emotion, yet the remembrance of it in private hours miti-
gates his selfishness and compliance with custom.

The Friar Bernard lamented in his cell on Mount Cenis
the crimes of mankind, and rising one morning before
day from his bed of moss and dry leaves, he gnawed his
roots and berries, drank of the spring, and set forth to go
to Rome to reform the corruption of mankind. On his
way he encountered many travelers who greeted him
courteously; and the cabins of the peasants and the castles
of the lords supplied his few wants. When he came at
last to Rome, his piety and good-will easily introduced
him to many families of the rich, and on the first day he
saw and talked with gentle mothers with their babies at
their breasts, who told him how much love they bore
their children, and how they were perplexed in their daily
walk lest they should fail in their duty to them. "What!"
he said, "and this on rich embroidered carpets, on marble
floors, with cunning sculpture, and carved wood, and rich
pictures, and piles of books about you?"—"Look at our
pictures and books," they said, "and we will tell you
good Father, how we spent the last evening. These are
stories of godly children, and holy families, and romantic
sacrifices made in old or in recent times by great and not
mean persons; and last evening our family was collected,
and our husbands and brothers discoursed sadly on what
we could save and give in the hard times." Then came
in the men, and they said: "What cheer, brother?
Does the convent want gifts?" Then the Friar Bernard
went home swiftly with other thoughts than he brought,
saying: "This way of life is wrong, yet these Romans,
whom I prayed God to destroy, are lovers, they are lovers;
what can I do?"

The Reformer concedes that these mitigations exist,
and that, if he proposed comfort, he should take sides
with the establishment. "Your words are excellent, but
they do not tell the whole. Conservatism is affluent and

openhanded, but there is a cunning juggle in riches. I
observe that they take somewhat for everything they give.
I look bigger, but am less; I have more clothes, but am
not so warm; more armor, but less courage; more books,
but less wit. What you say of your planted and builded
and decorated world is true enough, and I gladly avail
myself of its convenience; yet I have remarked that what
holds in particular, holds in general: that the plant Man
does not require for his most glorious flowering this
pomp of preparation and convenience, but the thoughts
of some beggarly Homer who strolled, God knows when,
in the infancy and barbarism of the old world; the gravity
and sense of some slave Moses who leads away his fellow
slaves from their masters; the contemplation of some
Scythian Anacharsis; the erect, formidable valor of some
Dorian townsmen in the town of Sparta; the vigor of
Clovis the Frank, and Alfred the Saxon, and Alaric the
Goth, and Mahomet, Ali, and Omar the Arabian, Saladin
the Kurd, and Othman the Turk, sufficed to build what
you call society, on the spot and in the instant when the
sound mind in a sound body appeared. Rich and fine is
your dress, O Conservatism! Your horses are of the
best blood; your roads are well cut and well paved; your
pantry is full of meats and your cellar of wines, and a very
good state and condition are you for gentlemen and
ladies to live under; but every one of these goods steals
away a drop of my blood. I want the necessity of supplying my own wants. All this costly culture of yours is not
necessary. Greatness does not need it. Yonder poor
man, who sits neglected there in a corner, carries a whole
revolution of man and nature in his head, which shall be a
sacred history to some future ages. For man is the end
of nature; nothing so easily organizes itself in every part
of the universe as he; no moss, no lichen is so easily born;
and he takes along with him and puts out from himself the
whole apparatus of society and condition extempore, as
an army encamps in a desert, and where all was just now
blowing sand, creates a white city in an hour, a government, a market, a place for feasting, for conversation, and
for love."

These considerations, urged by those whose characters
and whose fortunes are yet to be formed, must needs

command the sympathy of all reasonable persons. But beside that charity which should make all adult persons interested for the youth, and engage them to see that he has a free field and fair play on his entrance into life, we are bound to see that the society, of which we compose a part, does not permit the formation or continuance of views and practices injurious to the honor and welfare of mankind. The objection to conservatism, when embodied in a party, is this—that in its love of acts, it hates principles; it lives in the senses, not in truth; that it sacrifices to despair; it goes for availableness in its candidate, not for worth; and for expediency in its measures, and not for the right. Under pretence of allowing for friction, it makes so many additions and supplements to the machine of society, that it will play smoothly, and softly, but will no longer grind any grist.

The Conservative Party in the universe concedes that the Radical would talk sufficiently to the purpose, if we were still in the Garden of Eden; he legislates for man as he ought to be; his theory is right, but he makes no allowance for friction; and this omission makes his whole doctrine false. The Idealist retorts, that the Conservative falls into a far more noxious error in the other extreme. The Conservative assumes sickness as a necessary fact, and his social frame is a hospital, his total legislation is for the present distress, a universe in slippers and flannels, with bib and pap-spoon, swallowing pills and herb-tea. Sickness gets organized as well as health, the vice as well as the virtue. Now that a vicious system of trade has existed so long, it has stereotyped itself in the human generation, and misers are born. And now that sickness has got such a foothold, leprosy has grown cunning, has got into the ballot-box; the lepers outvote the clean; society has resolved itself into a Hospital Committee, and all its laws are quarantine. If any man resist and set up a foolish hope he has entertained as good against the general despair, society frowns on him, shuts him out of all her opportunities, her granaries, her refectories, her water and bread, and will serve him a sexton's turn:—

> " Ashes to ashes, dust to dust,
> Here's the hole, and in thou must."

It takes as low a view of every part of human action and passion. Its religion is just as bad; a lozenge for the sick, a dolorous tone to beguile the distemper; mitigations of pain by pillows and anodynes; always mitigations, never remedies; pardons for sin, funeral honors,— never self-help, renovation, and virtue. Its social and political action has no better aim; to keep out wind and weather, to bring the day and year about, and make the world last our day; not to sit on the world and steer it; not to sink the memory of the past in the glory of a new and more excellent creation; a timid cobbler and patcher, it degrades whatever it touches. The cause of education is urged in this country, with the utmost earnestness,— on what ground? Why, on this, that the people have the power, and if they are not instructed to sympathize with the intelligent, reading, trading, and governing class, inspired with a taste for the same competitions and prizes, they will upset the fair pageant of Judicature, and perhaps lay a hand on the sacred muniments of wealth itself, and new distribute the land.

Religion is taught in the same spirit. The contractors who were building a road out of Baltimore, some years ago, found the Irish laborers quarrelsome and refractory to a degree that embarrassed the agents, and seriously interrupted the progress of the work. The corporation were advised to call off the police, and build a Catholic chapel; which they did; the priest presently restored order and the work went on prosperously. Such hints, be sure, are too valuable to be lost. If you do not value the Sabbath, or other religious institutions, give yourself no concern about maintaining them. They have already acquired a market value as conservators of property; and if priest and church member should fail, the Chambers of Commerce and the presidents of the banks, the very innholders and landlords of the country would muster with fury to their support.

Of course religion in such hands loses all its essence. Instead of that profound reliance, which the soul forever suggests in the eternity of truth and duty, men are misled into a reliance on rotten institutions, on institutions which, the moment they cease to be the instantaneous creations of the devout sentiment, are worthless. Religion among

the low becomes low.   As it loses its truth, it loses credit
with the sagacious.   They detect the falsehood of the
preaching, but when they say so, all good citizens cry:
" Hush; do not weaken the state, do not take off the
strait-jacket from dangerous persons."   Every honest
man must keep up the hoax the best he can; must patron-
ize providence and piety, and wherever he sees anything
that will keep men amused, schools or churches, or poetry, ˏ
or picture-galleries, or music, or what not, he must cry,
" Hist-a-boy," and urge the game on.   What a compliment we pay to the good Spirit with out superserviceable
zeal!

But not to balance reasons for and against the establishment any longer, and if it still be asked, in this necessity of partial organization, which party on the whole has
the highest claims on our sympathy, I bring it home to
the private heart, where all such questions must have
their final arbitrament.   How will every strong and generous mind choose its ground—with the defenders of the
old? or with the seekers of the new?   Which is that state
which promises to edify a great, brave, and beneficent
man; to throw him on his resources, and tax the whole
strength of his character?   On which part will each of
us find himself in the hour of strength and of aspiration?

I understand well the respect of mankind for war, because that breaks up the Chinese stagnation of society,
and demonstrates the personal merits of all men.   A state
of war or anarchy, in which law has little force, is so far
valuable, that it puts every man on trial.   The man of
principle is known as such, and even in the fury of fac-
tion is respected.   In the civil wars of France, Montaigne
alone, among all the French gentry, kept his castle-gates
unbarred, and made his personal integrity as good at least
as a regiment.   The man of courage and resources is
shown, and the effeminate and base person.   Those who
rise above war, and those who fall below it, it easily dis-
criminates, as well as those, who, accepting its rude conditions, keep their own head by their own sword.

But in peace and a commercial state we depend, not
as we ought, on our knowledge and all men's knowledge
that we are honest men, but we cowardly lean on the virtue of others.   For it is always at last the virtue of some

men in the society, which keeps the law in any reverence and power. Is there not something shameful that I should owe my peaceful occupancy of my house and field, not to the knowledge of my countrymen that I am useful, but to their respect for sundry other reputable persons, I know not whom, whose joint virtues still keep the law in good odor?

It will never make any difference to a hero what the laws are. His greatness will shine and accomplish itself unto the end, whether they second him or not. If he have earned his bread by drudgery, and in the narrow and crooked ways which were all an evil law had left him, he will make it at least honorable by his expenditure. Of the past he will take no heed; for its wrongs he will not hold himself responsible; he will say, all the meanness of my progenitors shall not bereave me of the power to make this hour and company fair and fortunate. Whatsoever streams of power and commodity flow to me, shall of me acquire healing virtue, and become fountains of safety. Cannot I too descend a Redeemer into nature? Whosoever hereafter shall name my name, shall not record a malefactor, but a benefactor in the earth. If there be power in good intention, in fidelity, and in toil, the north wind shall be purer, the stars in heaven shall glow with a kindlier beam, that I have lived. I am primarily engaged to myself to be a public servant of all the gods, to demonstrate to all men that there is intelligence and good-will at the heart of things, and ever higher and yet higher leadings. These are my engagements; how can your law further or hinder me in what I shall do to men? On the other hand, these dispositions establish their relations to me. Wherever there is worth, I shall be greeted. Wherever there are men, are the objects of my study and love. Sooner or later all men will be my friends, and will testify in all methods the energy of their regard. I cannot thank your law for my protection. I protect it. It is not in its power to protect me. It is my business to make myself revered. I depend on my honor, my labor, and my dispositions, for my place in the affections of mankind, and not on any conventions or parchments of yours. But if I allow myself in derelictions, and become idle and dissolute, I quickly come to love the protection of a strong law, because I feel no title in myself to my advantages. To the intemperate and covetous person no love flows; to him mankind would pay no rent, no dividend, if force were once relaxed; nay, if they could give their verdict, they would say, that his self-indulgence and his oppression deserved punishment from society, and not that rich board and lodging he now enjoys. The law acts then as a screen of his unworthiness, and makes him worse the longer it protects him.

In conclusion, to return from this alternation of partial views, to the high platform of universal and necessary history, it is a happiness for mankind that Innovation has got on so far, and has so free a field before it. The boldness of the hope men entertain transcends all former experience. It calms and cheers them with the picture of a simple and equal life of truth and piety. And this hope flowered on what tree? It was not imported from the stock of some celestial plant, but grew here on the wild crab of Conservatism. It is much that this old and vituperated system of things has borne so fair a child. It predicts, that amidst a planet peopled with Conservatives, one Reformer may yet be born.